THE RO

Roman philosophy developed from Greek Hellenistic philosophy, chiefly of the Academic, Stoic and Epicurean schools. In 155 BCE an embassy of Athenian philosophers so impressed its Roman audiences that Roman philosophy can be said to have developed from that event.

Mark Morford makes the huge output of the Roman philosophical authors (notably Cicero, Lucretius and Seneca) manageable for readers unfamiliar with the field, quoting extensively from original texts, in readable and accurate translations. He introduces figures such as Epictetus and Marcus Aurelius, whose names are well known but whose works can be hard to read, and others including the poets Manilius, Lucan and Persius, and the philosopher Musonius, who were significant in the tradition of Roman philosophy.

The Roman Philosophers is the ideal route to understanding this important era in the history of thought.

Mark Morford was Professor of Classics at the University of Virginia and at Ohio State University. He is the author of books on the Neostoic scholar Justus Lipsius and the Roman Stoic poets Lucan and Persius. He is also the co-author of *Classical Mythology* (1971, 7th edn 2002) and currently teaches and researches at Smith College, Northampton, Massachusetts.

THE ROMAN PHILOSOPHERS

From the time of Cato the Censor
to the death of Marcus Aurelius

Mark Morford

Routledge
Taylor & Francis Group

LONDON AND NEW YORK

First published 2002
by Routledge
2 Park Square, Milton Park, Abingdon, Oxon, OX14 4RN

Simultaneously published in the USA and Canada
by Routledge
270 Madison Ave, New York NY 10016

Routledge is an imprint of the Taylor & Francis Group

Transferred to Digital Printing 2007

© 2002 Mark Morford

Typeset in Garamond by Taylor & Francis Books Ltd

British Library Cataloguing in Publication Data
A catalogue record for this book is available from the British Library

Library of Congress Cataloging in Publication Data
A catalog record for this book has been requested

ISBN 0–415–18851–2 (hbk)
ISBN 0–415–18852–0 (pbk)

FOR JOAN

But if the while I think on thee, dear friend
All losses are restored and sorrows end.

CONTENTS

PREFACE

Since the eighteenth century the Roman philosophers have been underestimated in the English-speaking world, whose academic opinion-makers have generally included them in Swift's "Gleanings of Philosophy ... the Lumber of the Schools". The group of Oxford scholars led by Miriam Griffin and Jonathan Barnes, who published the two volumes of *Philosophia Togata* in 1989 and 1997, were in part atoning for the former indifference of the Oxford school of *Litterae Humaniores* towards philosophers of the nineteen centuries between Aristotle and Descartes. In the years after World War II, lectures were given on Plato's *Republic* and Aristotle's *Nicomachean Ethics*, but the Hellenistic schools of philosophy were ignored, as were the philosophical works of Cicero and Seneca, to say nothing of later philosophers in the Roman world. Lucretius was read as a Latin text rather than as a thinker, and from Augustine only the chapters on Time in the eleventh book of the *Confessions* were thought to be worth discussing. Things were no doubt less bleak at Cambridge and in other universities in France, the United States and Germany, where the record of Mommsen's contempt for Cicero most certainly needed to be erased.

Since I was one of "the hungry sheep who look up and are not fed" at Oxford, I have found the writing of this book both challenging and fulfilling, and I am grateful to Richard Stoneman, kindest of editors, for his invitation to undertake the task and for his patience as deadlines faded into the future. I am not a professional philosopher, and I have not attempted to discuss matters of interest primarily to professional philosophers in any detail. I have written as a classicist and historian of ideas, with the aim of providing a concise, but not superficial, survey of the writings and ideas of the principal philosophers in the Roman world from the middle of the second century BCE down to the death of Marcus

Aurelius in 180 CE. I have read or reread all the philosophical writings of the philosophers discussed, with the exception of Plutarch, the sheer mass of whose *Moralia* would discourage all but the most dedicated Plutarchians. In surveying the ideas of these authors I have included more quotations than is usual in books of this sort, and all the translations are my own. While I realize that many readers will have little Latin and less Greek, I have often included Greek or Latin terms and phrases as a corrective to their less exact English equivalents.

Past neglect has been more than compensated for in the explosion of publications in this field during the last twenty-five years. I am deeply indebted to the work of pioneers who have made Hellenistic philosophy available to a wider readership, most notably A. A. Long in his introductory book, *Hellenistic Philosophy*, first published in 1974, and, with David Sedley, in the indispensable two-volume collection of texts, *The Hellenistic Philosophers*, published in 1987. I regret that his *Epictetus: a Stoic and Socratic Guide to Life* (New York: Oxford University Press, 2001) appeared too late for me to use. Wolfgang Haase has performed a heroic feat in editing the seven volumes of *Aufstieg und Niedergang der römischen Welt* II. 36, of which volume 3, devoted to the Stoics, is especially useful for those concerned with Roman philosophers. The volume on *Stoics, Epicureans and Sceptics* by R. W. Sharples, published in this series by Routledge in 1996, will more than compensate readers for the philosophical shortcomings of my book. Yet there has been little published in English with the same scope and goals as those of the present book. Elizabeth Rawson's excellent book on *Intellectual Life in the Roman Republic* (published in 1985) has a rather different range and is limited to the period of the Roman Republic. Even the chapters on philosophy and ideas in the second edition of the *Cambridge Ancient History* are tantalizingly summary, and the second volume of the *Cambridge History of Classical Literature* is usually and distressingly dismissive of Roman thought.

Besides being indebted to earlier authors I am profoundly grateful to many teachers, colleagues and friends. Isobel Henderson, my tutor in Roman History at Oxford, opened my mind to the exciting possibilities of Roman history and culture, and John Lucas more than compensated for the thin diet of the public offerings for Oxford undergraduates by his patient exposition of Plato and other philosophers as we tramped many, many miles over the Berkshire downs. I am grateful to him also for timely encouragement when, fifty years later, I was tangled in the thickets of Cicero's epistemology. I have learned more than I can say from the students whom I have been privileged to teach in seminars on Tacitus, Lucan, and Roman Stoicism, not least David George at Ohio State University and David Mehl at the University of Virginia. At Ohio State I enjoyed two decades of friendship and discussion with Charles Babcock and David Hahm, and with Carl Schlam, whose memory will, I hope, be honoured by this book.

I owe a special debt of gratitude to Miriam Griffin, who read the whole of the first draft and offered many searching criticisms and corrections. She helped me particularly with references to works previously unknown or unavailable to me, all of which have helped me improve the book. I am more than grateful for her generosity.

Finally, I owe a deep debt of thanks to the colleagues who have so generously welcomed me into the Smith College community. Justina Gregory, Craig Felton and Martin Antonetti gave me warm encouragement in adversity. Their support and the resources of the libraries of Smith College and Amherst College have made the labour of writing the book a pleasure.

Northampton, Massachusetts
December 2001

ABBREVIATIONS

AJP	*American Journal of Philology*
ANRW	Temporini, H. and Haase, W. *Aufstieg und Niedergang der römischen Welt*, Berlin: de Gruyter, 1972–
BICS	*Bulletin of the Institute of Classical Studies*
CAH²	*Cambridge Ancient History*, 2nd edn
CHCL	*Cambridge History of Classical Literature* (I. *Greek Literature*, ed. Easterling, P. E. and Knox, B. M. W.; II. *Roman Literature*, ed. Kenney, E. J.), Cambridge: Cambridge University Press, 1982–89
CQ	*Classical Quarterly*
HRR	Peter, H., *Historicorum Romanorum Fragmenta*, Leipzig: Teubner, 1883
JRS	*Journal of Roman Studies*
LS	Long, A. A. and Sedley, D., *The Hellenistic Philosophers*, 2 vols, Cambridge: Cambridge University Press, 1987
MRR	Broughton, T. R. S., *The Magistrates of the Roman Republic*, 3 vols, Cleveland and Atlanta: American Philological Association, 1951, 1986
OCD³	Hornblower, S. and Spawforth, A., *The Oxford Classical Dictionary*, 3rd edn, Oxford: Clarendon Press, 1996
OCPhil	Honderich, T. (ed.), *The Oxford Companion to Philosophy*, Oxford: Oxford University Press, 1995
PIR²	Groag, E. and Stein, A. (eds), *Prosopographia Imperii Romani*, 2nd edn, Berlin: de Gruyter, 1933–
RE	Pauly, A., Wissowa, G. and Kroll, W., *Paulys Realencyclopädie der klassischen Altertumswissenschaft*, 1893–(repr.) Munich: Druckenmüller, 1980
REL	*Revue des Études Latines*
SVF	Von Arnim, H., *Stoicorum Veterum Fragmenta*, 4 vols, Leipzig: Teubner, 1905

1

PHILOSOPHIA TOGATA

Philosophia Togata – Greek philosophy in Roman dress – is the title of two stimulating collections of papers by Oxford scholars, the fruit of seminars over several years.[1] The editors define the focus of their enquiry as "the mutual interaction of philosophy and Roman life". The Roman philosophers, indeed, are distinguished by their interest in ethics and in physics (in so far as physics concerned the gods, since theology was a branch of metaphysics). Unlike the Greeks, they did not in general make original contributions to logic. In the early empire, Seneca (*c.*4 BCE to 65 CE) and Epictetus (*c.*50 to 130 CE) show, by their attacks on excessive attachment to logic, that it was perhaps the most popular area of philosophical study in their time, at least among students of Stoicism. Rather than reject logic, they subordinated it to ethics: it should be studied, they said, as a necessary aid to the study of ethics, whose goal is the good life.[2]

Focusing on ethics, the Roman philosophers were constantly concerned with "the interaction of philosophy and Roman life", for philosophy affected their lives as individuals and as citizens of Rome. If we are to believe Cicero, it affected the attitudes and actions of political and military leaders – Scipio Aemilianus (as portrayed by Cicero) is the philosophical ancestor of Marcus Aurelius. For others, however, the interaction was negative, as we can see from the suspicious attitude of Cato the Censor, who had doubts about the moral effect of Greek philosophy on young Romans; or from the intermittent hostility of Nero, Vespasian and Domitian towards philosophers and their doctrines, when these were considered to be politically dangerous; or from the dislike of Marcus Aurelius for the sophists, who in his view were not true philosophers.

The earliest stages of Roman philosophy can be found in the second century BCE, although some scholars find them in the poem

1

of Appius Claudius, Censor in 312 BCE.[3] The poem was perhaps a collection of moral *sententiae* (memorable sayings), and one surviving fragment says that "each man is the architect of his own fortunes" – hardly enough to allow us to call Appius a philosopher.[4] Cicero, however, surveying the development of philosophy in Rome, points out that Pythagoras was living in Italy at the time of the foundation of the Roman republic (traditionally dated to 509 BCE), and he conjectures that Pythagorean doctrines spread through Italy at that time.[5] He thought that the poem of Appius was Pythagorean, and he notes that the Stoic philosopher Panaetius, late in the second century BCE, praised it. But Cicero goes on to say that he cannot name a single Roman philosopher "before the time of Laelius and Scipio [Aemilianus]", that is, the decades after 155 BCE. He also says that the decisive event for the development of Roman philosophy was the visit of the three Athenian ambassadors to Rome in 155 BCE. This will be our starting point.

Of course, there had been constant interaction between Greeks and Romans for centuries before this, since Greek cities had been established in Campania and southern Italy as early as the eighth century BCE. Virgil symbolically describes Aeneas, when he had arrived in Italy and was looking for allies in the coming war, sending an embassy to the Greek hero, Diomedes.[6] Also in the time before the founding of Rome, Evander, exiled from Arcadia (a region of the Peloponnese), was said to have founded his city of Pallanteum on the site of the future city of Rome.[7] The second king of Rome, Numa, the legendary founder of Roman religious rituals, consulted Pythagoras, according to Livy and Cicero, again a story symbolic of the interaction between Romans and Greeks in the earliest period of Roman history.[8] In historical times, more than a century before the visit of the Athenian ambassadors, the Romans increasingly came into contact with Greek culture in Italy after the capture of the south Italian Greek city of Tarentum in 272 BCE.

Outside Italy, early contact between Greeks and Romans is again symbolically narrated by Livy in his story of Roman ambassadors being sent in 454 BCE to Athens and other Greek cities in order to study their laws, especially the laws of Solon.[9] And, as had happened in Italy, Roman military successes led to Roman control of Greek kingdoms that eventually became provinces of the Roman empire. After the first war with Carthage (264–241) most of Sicily became a Roman province, and during the second war with Carthage (218–202) its greatest Greek city, Syracuse (which had remained independent), was captured by the Romans in 211. Roman victories over the Macedonian king, Philip V, at Cynoscephalae in 197 BCE, and over his brother, Perseus, at Pydna in 168, were followed by the capture of the citadel of Corinth in 146 and the incorporation of the Greek mainland into the Roman empire under the supervision of the governor of the province of Macedonia, which was established in 147.[10] Thus, of the four major geographical areas of Greek culture, three – southern Italy, Sicily and the Greek mainland – were subject to Rome by the time of Scipio Aemilianus. The subjugation of the fourth, Asia Minor, was anticipated by the defeat of the Seleucid king, Antiochus, at Magnesia in 189, and the province of Asia was established when the kingdom of Pergamum was bequeathed to the Romans by King Attalus III in 133. The incorporation of much of the rest of Asia Minor was completed by Pompey in the 60s BCE.

It is clear even from this bald recital of military successes, that the Romans were inextricably involved with Greek culture long before the embassy of 155. The arrival in Rome of Greek prisoners of war led to the development of Roman literature based on Greek models, especially in the genres of epic and drama. Many Roman senators and intellectuals (for there were Roman intellectuals even at this early stage) learned Greek and admired Greek thought, art and literature. A senator, Fabius Pictor, the earliest Roman historian, wrote in Greek and is known to have been a member of an embassy sent to Delphi in 216. Livy believed that the return of the army of Manlius Vulso from Asia Minor in 188 BCE was the crucial stage in the advance of Greek influence on Roman society, which Polybius more accurately dated to the return of the army of Aemilius Paullus from Macedonia twenty years later. Important also is the attitude of individual leaders towards Greek culture, an aspect of the Greek influence on Rome that particularly interested Plutarch in his Roman lives.[11]

The picture of a sudden revelation of Greek culture to the uncultivated Romans in the middle of the second century BCE is false. Cicero was right to say that no Roman philosophers could be named before that time, and the significance of the embassy of the three philosophers in 155 is that it introduced Romans in Rome to Greek professional philosophers. The ambassadors, as Cato the Censor warned, were especially attractive to younger Romans, including Scipio Aemilianus and his friends, and we can date the development of specifically Roman philosophy from their maturity, that is, about ten or twenty years after the embassy of 155. This is also the period of the influence of the historian Polybius, resident in Rome from

168 to 150 and the companion of Scipio Aemilianus in Africa and Spain after that, and of the Stoic philosopher, Panaetius, who was in Rome for substantial periods between 146 and 129. Laelius, consul in 140, can perhaps be called the first Roman philosopher. The century after the embassy of 155 was essentially a period of *philosophia togata*, for it was Greeks who taught the Romans at Rome and in Greece, especially at Athens and Rhodes. Even discounting the biases of Cicero's idealized picture of Scipio and Laelius, we can say that in this period the Romans brought about adaptations in Greek philosophy that were needed to make it acceptable in Roman culture. Here the readiness of Panaetius to adjust the rigid doctrines of Stoicism is significant, and from his time there emerges a distinctively Roman philosophy with a strong focus on ethics, particularly the duty of Roman leaders towards the state and its gods, towards humankind, and towards their families and dependants. Thus Greek philosophy in the Roman world was split, for its ethics had practical effects on Roman life and culture, while its logic and physics very largely continued to be studied and discussed, but with fewer practical consequences. The leading Greek figures of middle Stoicism, Panaetius and Posidonius, were crucial in the development of Roman philosophy.

Important also were the consequences of the sack of Athens by Sulla in 86 BCE.[12] Like Aemilius Paullus after Pydna, Sulla brought back to Rome Greek cultural treasures, including the library of Apellicon, which "included most of the works of Aristotle and Theophrastus".[13] How this library was acquired, and its relationship to Aristotle's own library, is a tangled story involving insoluble problems. Jonathan Barnes, however, has shown that the standard picture in modern literary histories, of a sudden appearance of Aristotle's works in Rome after 86, is false.[14] While Plutarch (and before him, Strabo) may have been factually accurate in saying that Aristotle's works reached Rome in this way, it is pressing their evidence too far to say that Cicero's freedman and friend, Tyrannio, and the Peripatetic scholar, Andronicus of Rhodes, revolutionized Aristotelian studies. Barnes has shown that Aristotle was already known in some form to Cicero, and that he had continuously been known to the Greek Peripatetics in the period after his death (322 BCE), when, according to Strabo, his texts were unavailable. The famous edition of Aristotle by Andronicus has been shown by Barnes to be little more than "amateur tinkering", and his major contribution to Aristotelian studies at Rome was a catalogue (Greek, *Pinakes*) of Aristotle's works. As Cicero showed, the

Peripatetic school continued to be active in Athens, although the Lyceum (where Aristotle had taught) was destroyed by Sulla in 86.[15] Cicero himself makes the Academic Piso say that "with the exception of Plato, one might rightly call Aristotle the chief of philosophers",[16] which implies that Aristotle was known and read at Rome before the edition of Andronicus appeared, probably after the death of Cicero in 43 BCE and before 30 BCE.[17]

While there were Romans who fancied themselves as philosophers in the first part of the first century BCE, Cicero was the first to define and systematize *philosophia togata*. His adaptation of Greek philosophy stabilized Greek doctrines in ethics, epistemology and theology for Roman readers. Even more significantly, he transmitted these doctrines in Latin, for which he developed a philosophical vocabulary. Despised by Mommsen and largely neglected as a philosopher by English scholars, he has been in the last fifteen years (in the English-speaking world; somewhat earlier in Germany and France) justly rehabilitated as a philosopher and transmitter of Greek philosophy. It is to him that we owe the Stoic emphasis on duty and control of the passions, even though he was himself an Academic. His originality as a philosopher is debatable, and is chiefly to be found in his works on politics and law, in particular the *De Re Publica* and *De Legibus*, both surviving only in fragments. But after Cicero we can for the first time define a Roman philosopher as a Roman student of Greek philosophy, who has adapted Greek doctrines for the needs of Roman society and politics, with a prevailing focus on ethics.

While Cicero and (if this picture is not totally imaginary) the Roman leaders of the generation of Scipio Aemilianus emphasized the public duty of the aristocratic Roman philosopher, others, most notably the Epicureans, sought happiness (the Greek *eudaimonia*) through non-involvement in public life. Epicurean studies flourished particularly in Campania, in the cities around the Bay of Naples, whose origins for the most part were Greek. Many Romans studied philosophy with Philodemus (*c.*110–40 BCE) at Herculaneum. Through the patronage of the aristocratic family of the Pisones, he had many friends in the Roman upper classes, many of whose members were Epicureans despite their involvement in political life. The first truly original Roman philosopher, Lucretius, was Epicurean, and he seems to have succeeded in living as a private individual. His epic poem, *De Rerum Natura*, composed before 54 BCE, was inspired by Epicurus, whom Lucretius praises consecutively as man, father and god. Derivative as this sounds, the exposition of

Epicurean doctrine in Latin hexameter verse called for an original genius, who created a new language, appropriate for the dignity of epic verse, that expounded Epicurus' teaching with power and intensity. Yet even Lucretius was principally concerned with ethics, for the goal of his teaching was to enable Romans to live a life free of the fear of death, and his exposition of physics, celestial phenomena and the development of civilization, was directed towards this goal.

Lucretius remained outside the mainstream of Roman philosophy, admired by later poets (Virgil, pre-eminently) but apparently not widely read. In part this may have been due to the political convulsions in the twenty-five years after his death, which, ironically, gave Cicero the stimulus to produce a flood of philosophical works in the last three years of his life. When the social and political situation had been stabilized by Augustus, and the Principate had been formally established in 27 BCE, the contexts for leadership and patronage had changed permanently. The philosophical poets of the Augustan age – Virgil, Horace, Ovid and Manilius – composed their poems against a background of power and patronage concentrated in the person of the emperor or (as in the case of Maecenas, patron of Virgil and Horace) his associates. Whatever the poets' personal philosophies, the doctrines of their poems were consistent with the ideology of the emperor. Thus the Jupiter of the Epicurean Virgil was assimilated to Stoic Fate, and the hero, Aeneas, was driven by a Stoic sense of duty to the gods, to his state (present and future) and to human beings (again, present and future). So the Epicurean Horace, most notably in his six "Roman" odes (the first six odes of Book 3), advised young people to be involved in public duties. Ovid, whose attitude towards Augustus was equally complex, expounded a form of Pythagoreanism and a largely Stoic cosmology without overt reference to the regime. The Stoic Manilius was careful to avoid offending Augustus and Tiberius in his account of astrology, an exceptionally sensitive topic under the principate. Even so, the custom of maintaining a "house philosopher" continued: Augustus, for example, maintained the doxographer, Arius Didymus, in his home as friend and confidant.

The Cynics stayed outside the mainstream of Roman philosophy and society, as would be expected from a group whose doctrines disregarded political and social conventions. The Cynics never were a philosophical school like the Stoics, Academics and Epicureans, and their movement is better described as a way of life. Although the early Cynics wrote copiously, their texts have disappeared, and their doctrines survive mainly in the form of epigrammatic statements or ripostes (*chreiai*). Thus their place in the history of Roman philosophy is hard to define.[18]

Some features, however, can be clearly distinguished. The first is the traditional association of the early hero of Cynicism, Diogenes of Sinope (*c.*412–324 BCE), with Socrates.[19] Even if Plato criticized Diogenes as "Socrates gone mad",[20] Diogenes shared with Socrates the need for an urban context for his teaching, disregard of physical comfort, and a capacity for making his interlocutors uncomfortable by candour and rigorous interrogation. Second, there is a close relationship between Stoic ethics and Cynicism. Zeno, the founder of Stoicism, was a follower of the Cynic, Crates (*c.*368–288 BCE). His treatise on the ideal republic, *Politeia*, shared with the Cynics a disregard for conventional political, religious and social institutions, to such an extent that later Stoics were embarrassed by it.[21] More significant for the Roman Stoics was Cynic asceticism, that is the practice of physical hardship (Greek, *askesis*, literally "training") as a means towards attaining virtue. Stoic emphasis on the unimportance of physical comforts and discomforts, relative to reason and virtue, has its origins in Cynic practice. Finally, "living according to nature" was a fundamental doctrine of both Cynics and Stoics.

The common ground between Cynicism and Stoicism, therefore, further blurs the outlines of Cynic philosophy in the Roman world. Yet there is evidence for Cynicism in Rome in the late Republic, although this seems also to have been the period of Cynicism's lowest fortunes at Rome. Varro (116–37 BCE), as quoted by Augustine, included Cynicism in his list of 288 philosophical sects, but he distinguished between the Cynics and formal philosophical sects in that the "manner and custom of the Cynics" did not include an enquiry into the supreme good (*finis boni*).[22] His interest in Cynicism is indicated also by the title of his *Saturae Menippeae*, which derives from the Cynic writer of the third century BCE, Menippus of Gadara. Cicero was at pains to distinguish Stoic candour from the plain speaking of the Cynics, which often was obscene.[23] Further, the Roman satiric tradition owed a great deal to the popularizing Cynic diatribes of Bion of Borysthenes (*c.*335–245 BCE) and his younger contemporary, Teles of Megara. Horace, indeed, refers to "diatribes in the style of Bion",[24] and the tradition of forthright moral criticism, spiced with obscenity, is a prominent feature in the satires of the four great Roman satirists, Lucilius, Horace, Persius and Juvenal.

Cynicism seems to have flourished in the Roman world during the first two centuries CE. R. Bracht Branham defines the goal of

Cynicism as "to live well in order to be happy".[25] This is consistent with the Stoic emphasis on virtue (i.e. "living well") in a period when individuals turned to Stoicism for answers to the problems of preserving moral and intellectual independence under a monarchy. There are many Cynic expressions in Seneca's letters and dialogues, and Seneca himself was a friend and admirer of the Cynic philosopher, Demetrius. The most explicit exposition of Cynic doctrine for a Roman audience is that of Epictetus, and an important contemporary source for Cynicism is the orator, Dio Chrysostom (*c.*40–110 CE), who before his exile from Rome had been a follower of the Stoic, Musonius Rufus.[26]

Nevertheless, there were strong objections to the Cynics in Rome, and Cynicism was practised mostly in the Greek east of the empire.[27] The basic objection stemmed from Cynic contempt for social conventions. A central metaphor of Cynicism was "defacing the currency", that is, showing the hollowness of the usual rituals and conventions of civilized life. While this led to an asceticism that was admired by many Romans, especially Stoics, it was displayed in public behaviour offensive to Roman ideas of *decorum* and *gravitas*, appropriate behaviour and dignity.[28] Cynics made people uncomfortable, especially in the decorous (not to say, prudish) society described by Cicero, and their extremism in despising the comforts of life was unacceptable to those, like Seneca, who preferred to compromise between wealth and philosophical principles. Further, the Cynics' disregard of social and political conventions inevitably encouraged non-participation in politics and devaluation of public reputation. For the Cynics the central Roman aristocratic virtues of *officium* and *pietas* (i.e. duty in public and private contexts) were irrelevant. Finally, the Cynics' exclusive focus on ethics was at variance with Stoic emphasis on the unity of knowledge, which enjoined the study of logic and physics in order to be proficient in ethics.

Seneca deplores the feeble state of philosophy (he is thinking principally of Roman philosophers) in the century between Cicero's death and his own time. He records the rise and fall of the only completely Roman school of philosophy, that of the Sextii (father and son), which began probably in the 40s BCE, and he says that the established Greek schools suffered from absence of leadership.[29] Yet individual Romans pursued philosophical studies in Rome and in Greece, and the major schools of Greek philosophy continued to exist. The Stoics were the most successful survivors, and in Seneca (d. 65 CE) they produced the second great Latin prose author of Roman philosophy. Like Cicero, Seneca based his authority on a new

Latin prose style, at once rhetorical and dogmatic. But, unlike Cicero, the minister of Nero was compelled by circumstances to distinguish between his public life and his private doctrines. The great division between his political actions (his support of the murder of Nero's mother, Agrippina, in 59 CE, being perhaps the philosopher's nadir) and his doctrine of morally good involvement in public affairs, between his wealth and his doctrine of a life lived according to nature, have made Seneca, in his own time and ever since, a controversial figure. But of his importance as a Roman philosopher there can be no doubt, and, for centuries, in Europe of the Renaissance and the Enlightenment, he was the most influential of Roman philosophers, surpassing even Plato and Aristotle in northern Europe towards the end of the sixteenth and early in the seventeenth centuries. Seneca's focus was almost exclusively ethical: his *Naturales Quaestiones*, his only surviving work in physics, has never been widely read or admired.

Seneca and his contemporaries were compelled by their social and political contexts to be very different in their philosophical goals and strategies from the Roman philosophers of Cicero's time. They were still indebted to Greek philosophy and Greek teachers, but their studies were directed towards honourable survival under a regime that was intermittently immoral, led by a monarch who had the *de facto* arbitrary power of life and death over them. Roman politicians whose philosophy led them into politically dangerous utterance did not survive – the fate of Lucan, Thrasea and Seneca himself under Nero, and of both the Helvidii under the Flavians. All these men were executed on political grounds, but their philosophy provided them with the language of political dissent and the principles on which to persevere.

Even the satirists were muted. Whereas Lucilius (a friend of Scipio Aemilianus) had openly criticized his political contemporaries and Horace had criticized the morals of Roman society, Persius (d. 62 CE) adopted a more private mode of expression and was saved from being drawn into political controversy by his early death. A generation later, Juvenal, the greatest of Roman satirists, could not publish his satires until after Domitian's death in 96 CE, and he explicitly denied any philosophical allegiance.[30] His philosophical passages are not aligned with any one school, and he never supported imperial policy in the way that Horace did.[31] He preferred to continue the moralizing tradition of Roman satire by means of rhetorical brilliance and sustained indignation behind a mask of irony.

The period between the death of Seneca in 65 CE and the accession of Hadrian in 118 brought change and occasional turbulence to intellectuals and philosophers in the Roman world. Like Nero, the Flavian emperors (Vespasian, Titus and Domitian, 69–96) preferred to silence philosophers if their doctrine and speech were politically offensive, for example, by expelling them from Italy in 74 and 93. This period also saw the rise of Greek orators who made some claim to being philosophers. These are the orators of the Second Sophistic (so named early in the third century by Philostratus), few of whom deserved the title of "philosopher": among these Favorinus of Arles (*c.*85–165) is perhaps unique.[32] The Second Sophistic was symptomatic of developments in Roman philosophy. From the time of Nero onwards, Greek once more became the language of philosophy almost exclusively, and philosophers lectured in centres other than Rome and Athens. In the time of Nero and the Flavians, the Romans Cornutus and Musonius lectured in Greek, and among their pupils were Persius and Lucan (students under Cornutus) and Epictetus (the most famous student of Musonius), all Stoics.

In this book Epictetus is included as a Roman philosopher because of his Roman citizenship (he became a citizen on being freed from slavery), his years of residence in Rome, and the direct relevance of his doctrines to Roman life. He taught in Greece after the expulsion of the philosophers from Italy in 93 CE, and his importance to the Roman tradition is clear, for example, from the reverence with which the emperor Marcus Aurelius quotes him. His focus on the individual will and his distinction between "things in our control and not in our control" give a firmer tone to the doctrines of Seneca, while his experience as a slave makes his teaching about freedom more authentic than that of Seneca.

Plutarch, more or less contemporary with Epictetus, is definitely not a Roman philosopher, and he himself boasts of his loyalty to his home town (Chaeronea) and admits that he did not learn Latin thoroughly. He was a Roman citizen, highly honoured by the emperor Hadrian and the friend of many prominent Romans. His enormous output makes it impossible to leave him out of any consideration of philosophical developments in the second century CE. His views on Roman character and leadership, seen in his Roman *Lives*, and his criticisms of Stoic and Epicurean doctrines in the *Moralia*, are important in any assessment of Roman philosophy.

Other Greek philosophers have less claim to be considered in a survey of Roman philosophers. Nothing certain is known of the life of the Stoic Hierocles, beyond that he was writing in the first half of the second century CE. His surviving fragments are on the Stoic doctrine of *oikeiosis* ("affinity" or "affection") and on duty, in both confirming the doctrines of Panaetius, Cicero and Seneca. Especially interesting is his theory of expanding circles of duty, anticipated in Cicero's *De Officiis*.[33] Favorinus (mentioned above) was a Gaul who wrote exclusively in Greek and was himself a follower of Academic (as opposed to Pyrrhonian) scepticism. The titles of thirty of his essays are known, several of which were serious philosophical works, yet so little of his work remains that it is not profitable to include him in our survey.

Apuleius, the African orator, novelist and philosopher (*c.*125–180 CE), is apparently unique among second-century philosophers, in that he wrote in Latin. Many people would deny his claim to be a philosopher, in part because of his colourful character and opulent prose. This would be wrong, for he deals with philosophical subjects and his contemporaries called him *philosophicus Platonicus*. His treatise *De Deo Socratis*, with its discussion of angels (*daimones*), intermediaries between gods and mortals, is consistent with his search for the union of the human worshipper with the divine. This becomes explicit in the last book of his novel, *Metamorphoses*, where the hero is inspired by an epiphany of Isis – here a syncretistic goddess – whose enthusiastic devotee he becomes.[34]

By the middle of the second century CE this trend was irreversible. Stoics like Epictetus and Marcus Aurelius directed their search for virtue to the Stoic god through self-control and reason. Marcus Aurelius, the last of our Roman philosophers, found solace and hope in contemplating a world beyond the mundane and often depressing circumstances of his daily responsibilities. He is the unique example of a philosopher-king, but how far removed from Plato's ideal! Driven by the Stoic sense of duty, he strove to maintain Stoic virtue based on reason and a life lived according to nature. But this could not suffice, and he ended his *Meditations* with the call of the Stoic god to depart from life. He was sustained not just by his own sense of self-sufficiency, but by the awareness of his sharing with gods and mortals in the citizenship of the universe, and by his knowledge of the divine element in his soul.

Our survey of Roman philosophers ends with Marcus, but this does not mean that he was the last. His contemporary, Galen, was in his time equally eminent as philosopher and physician, and his surviving philosophical works contain valuable quotations from, and criticism of, earlier philosophers. Another contemporary, Sextus

Empiricus, is an almost unique source for the doctrines of the Pyrrhonian sceptics. These men herald a new age of philosophy in the Roman world, in which the search for union with the divine, and for individual comfort in passing through life and death, was taken to new heights by the Neoplatonism of Plotinus (c. 205–270 CE). In contrast, Diogenes of Oenoanda, late in the second century, sought to make the consolations of Epicureanism known to his contemporaries through the enormous inscription that he set up in his home town in the southern part of Asia Minor. He, too, was motivated by the desire to annul human fear of death, not by union with the divine, but by appeal to the doctrines of Epicurus.

Early in the third century Diogenes Laertius (about whose life nothing is known) composed his *Lives and Opinions of Eminent Philosophers* in ten books. The lives, extending from Thales to Epicurus, are very uneven in reliability and usefulness, but some are quite extensive and include titles of works now lost, and summaries of their doctrines. These are especially valuable for the Stoics and for Epicurus.[35]

Late in the fourth century CE the Christian bishop and orator, Augustine (354–430), developed the most extended system of philosophy in Latin prose, which was, despite the influence of Neoplatonism, independent of Greek models. Nearly a century after Augustine's death, the last of the Roman philosophers, Boethius, composed his *Consolation of Philosophy* as he lay in prison under sentence of death (carried out in 524 CE). This moving and powerful work, written in Latin prose alternating with poetry, closes nearly seven centuries of Roman philosophy.

Until the rise of Christian philosophy in the third century CE the authority of the Greek founders of the philosophical schools remained unquestioned. From Cicero to Marcus Aurelius, Socrates was revered not only by the Platonists, but by the Stoics. He is named by Marcus Aurelius more than any other philosopher, and he is twice quoted by Epictetus at the very end of his *Handbook*. The authority of Plato was always respected, and in the Neoplatonism of the third century CE it enjoyed a supremacy that continued long after. The influence of Aristotle, as we have seen, is harder to assess, but he, too, commanded respect second only to his master, Plato. The great Stoic founders, Zeno, Cleanthes and Chrysippus, never lost their authority, despite the many cogent criticisms of their more rigid doctrines and despite the changes in Stoicism brought about by Panaetius and Posidonius. Similarly, the founder of Epicureanism was revered by Lucretius and by Diogenes of

Oenoanda. Thus, the authority of the Greek philosophers from Socrates to Posidonius was maintained in the Roman world, even though philosophers quarreled among themselves and attacked their rivals' doctrines. And here, perhaps, lies the distinctive quality of the Roman philosophers, for the Romans accepted the authority of the Greeks and adapted Greek doctrines for their own needs. Those who sit in the seat of the scornful overlook the complexity of Roman attitudes to Greek thought and literature. The Roman philosophers, from Lucretius to Marcus Aurelius, built on Greek foundations their own philosophy, appropriate to the needs of their Roman world. They have been influential, and today they are still read for themselves, not because they imitated the Greeks. As in so much else in Roman culture, through emulation the Romans created their own philosophy.

2

THE ARRIVAL OF THE GREEK PHILOSOPHERS IN ROME

In 155 BCE an embassy was sent by the Athenians to appeal an unfavourable decision by Greek arbitrators in a dispute with Oropus.[1] The ambassadors were the leading Athenian philosophers of the day, heads of three of the leading Athenian schools of philosophy: Carneades, head of the Academy; Diogenes of Babylon, head of the Stoa; Critolaus, head of the Peripatetics.[2] The Epicurean school was not represented, presumably because of its doctrine of non-involvement in political affairs. It was the prerogative of the Senate to deal with foreign embassies, and the ambassadors made their case to the senators in Greek, interpreted by a senator, Gaius Acilius, who twelve years later wrote a history of Rome in Greek.[3] The presiding officer of the Senate that day was the praetor, Aulus Postumius Albinus, also author of a history written in Greek, who had taken part in the war against Perseus in Greece and later was to travel to Greece on diplomatic missions.[4] The senatorial setting for the embassy was extraordinary, with the leading roles taken by prominent Roman philhellenes and (evidently) a stage-managed favourable reception for the ambassadors. They themselves had also prepared for a friendly reception by giving public speeches "before a large crowd so as to advertise themselves".[5]

Cicero describes the oratory of the three ambassadors.[6] He says that Diogenes claimed to be able to teach "the art of good speaking and distinguishing between the true and the false, which the Greeks call *Dialectic*". As Cicero goes on to point out, this "art" gave no guidance in finding out the truth, but plenty for drawing intellectual distinctions and raising insoluble problems. Diogenes' style was "thin, dry, concise and detailed", whereas Roman rhetoric (Cicero seems now to be reverting to his own day, a century later) was copious and fluent, one that gave pleasure to a popular audience and led its hearers to weigh the arguments "not in the goldsmith's balance but in the scales of the people". Critolaus, on the other hand (in Cicero's opinion), was a more valuable speaker, because he had studied the *Rhetoric* of Aristotle, who brought to rhetoric the same intellectual breadth and mental acumen as he had shown in his research into the physical world, whereas the Stoic Diogenes studied only the method of making a judgement (*ars iudicandi*), without considering how to develop the substance of an argument (*ars inventionis*).[7] In fact, Diogenes, despite Cicero's criticism of his rhetoric, was an influential philosopher, not least because he was the teacher of Panaetius, some of whose modifications in Stoic ethics may well have been anticipated by him.[8]

Carneades, however, attracted the most attention. His rhetoric was powerful and varied, and he was always persuasive, whether he was defending or attacking a proposition.[9] Like his fellow-ambassadors, he gave display lectures that drew large audiences and were distinguished by their brilliance and novelty. Whereas Critolaus was elegant and polished, and Diogenes was sober and modest in his style, Carneades impressed his audiences by the violence and power of his speech.[10] He spoke in defence of justice on one day, and on the next spoke against it, refuting all that he had said the previous day. Cicero incorporated his speeches in the reverse order into the third book of his *De Re Publica*.[11] Carneades denied that justice had any foundation in nature (i.e. that there was no such thing as natural justice), and argued that Roman rule over other nations was based on injustice.

The embassy was a decisive event in the Roman experience of Greek philosophers, for it was the first time that their methods were publicly displayed, both before the august assembly of the Senate and in lectures to large audiences. As the philhellenism of Acilius and Albinus shows, there had been plenty of interaction between Greeks and educated Romans for decades, going back to the time when the Romans finally achieved control over the Greek cities of Italy in 272 BCE. After the end of the second Punic War (202 BCE) Rome became irreversibly involved with Greece and the Greeks. The Roman historian Livy believed that a crucial stage in the relationship was reached with the return of the Roman army from Asia Minor in 188 after its victory the previous year over the Seleucid monarch, Antiochus III. Livy, however, focuses on the huge quantities of booty exhibited in the triumphal procession of the victorious general, Cn. Manlius Vulso, and on the moral degeneration that followed. Polybius, a contemporary of these events, more accurately wrote that the victory of Aemilius Paullus at Pydna over the Macedonian monarch, Perseus, in 168 was the crucial stage – an indirect consequence of which was his own exile to Italy as one of 1,000 Achaean hostages, whose internment did not end until 150.[12]

Polybius became a friend and mentor of Scipio Aemilianus, the leading Roman political and military figure of the 140s and 130s BCE, whose military successes at Carthage (146) and Numantia (133) – witnessed by Polybius (the former certainly, the latter probably) – gave him unparalleled authority at Rome.[13] Polybius, who was about fifteen years older than Scipio (born in 185), tells how Scipio intervened to keep him in Rome (whereas the other hostages were sent off to various towns elsewhere in Italy) and offered him his friendship. Scipio was then "no more than 18 years old". Polybius replied that "since there was a great crowd of Greeks flowing to Rome" who were teachers (the Greek word for what they taught was *mathemata*, a general word for "studies"), Scipio would not lack for intellectual guidance, yet he (Polybius) could help him most "to speak and act so as to be worthy of his ancestors", and that thereafter the two men were close friends. Polybius then goes on to give an encomium of Scipio's virtuous character, which he contrasts with that of other young upper-class Romans, whose moral deterioration he dated to the time immediately after Pydna.[14]

This passage is important for the information it gives us about the intellectual and cultural changes that convulsed Roman society after the battle of Pydna. First, it shows that there was an influx of educated Greeks into Rome, although we cannot tell how many of these came as prisoners and slaves and how many were free. Second, it shows the delicate situation of Scipio as the descendant of two of the greatest senatorial families, for he was the son of the victor at Pydna, Aemilius Paullus, and the adopted son of Publius Cornelius Scipio, son of the great Scipio Africanus. The influence of ancestral tradition in training young Roman nobles was overwhelming, and in offering to help Scipio remain true to that tradition Polybius was meeting the most serious objection of conservative Romans to the influence of Greek intellectuals.[15] Scipio himself was familiar with Greeks and Greek customs. His adoptive father wrote a history in Greek, and Aemilius Paullus, his father, spoke Greek.[16] His early education, so Plutarch tells us, was both the traditional Roman one and Greek, which he studied "with more enthusiasm".[17] "Not only," says Plutarch, "were there [Greek] tutors and scholars and teachers of rhetoric, but also sculptors and painters and experts with horses and hounds and teachers of hunting". Scipio fought at Pydna when he was about sixteen years old, and he stayed behind in Greece to hunt in the Macedonian royal hunting preserves.[18] Back in Rome, he was allowed to take what books he wanted from the library of the Macedonian king, which Aemilius Paullus had brought to Rome after Pydna because he was "a lover of books".[19] Thus it is not surprising that he was amongst the young men (he then was about thirty years old) who listened enthusiastically to Carneades and his fellow-ambassadors in 155.

Scipio represented the coming generation, and later his social, political and military prestige (*auctoritas*) and rank (*dignitas*) were crucial to the success of Greek intellectual innovations at Rome. Greek intellectuals like Polybius and Panaetius enjoyed Scipio's patronage, which gave them the protection and status that allowed their ideas to take hold in a society in thrall to ancestral tradition. Others, however, were more sceptical of Greek influences, and their most prominent representative was Marcus Porcius Cato, born in 234 BCE, consul in 195, censor in 184, and active in politics until his death in 149 at the age of 85. As Alan Astin has shown, Cato's attitude towards Greeks and Greek culture was quite complex, far from the thoroughgoing anti-Hellenism with which he has traditionally been charged.[20] He could speak and write Greek, and in his old age (that is, at about the time of the Athenian embassy), he studied Greek and Latin literature, appropriate pursuits in old age for a Roman of his political and social standing. But knowledge does not imply approval, and Cato was hostile to Greek ideas for specific reasons. The main ancient source for Cato's attitudes is Plutarch, writing about 250 years after the Athenian embassy to Rome, and therefore not necessarily reliable. Nevertheless, he reveals a tradition that accepted Cato's hostility to the Greeks, which in part derives from Cato's own writings.

In the first place Cato was hostile to Greek medicine, believing even that Greek doctors "had sworn a mutual oath to kill all barbarians by [their] medicine". This surprising outburst comes in a passage written by Cato to his son:[21]

> I will speak about those Greeks in the appropriate place, telling you what I found out from my research at Athens, and I shall convince you of what is good in their literature to look at, but not to learn thoroughly (*inspicere, non perdiscere*). The Greeks are a most wicked and undisciplined people, and here I will say something that you can consider to be the words of a prophet: when that nation gives us its

literature, it will corrupt everything – and all the more if it sends its doctors here.

The book *Ad Filium* (*To My Son*) was probably written in the 170s BCE, about twenty years before the Athenian embassy, and was "a collection … of precepts, exhortations, instructions, and observations".[22] It preceded the battle of Pydna by about seven years and it is important evidence for the scepticism with which intelligent Romans viewed the already irreversible influence of Greek culture. For Cato the greatest danger was the corruption of young Romans by Greek ideas, for he saw that education was the real battlefield – hence his attack on the indiscipline of the Greeks and the power of Greek literature to weaken traditional Roman values. He knew enough of Greek literature to be convinced that it should not be studied too deeply. He thought that the Romans had enough skill to heal the sick with their traditional remedies, without recourse to greedy and expensive Greek doctors (one of whom, Archagathos, not long before had earned the sobriquet of "The Terminator", *carnifex*). Cato had many other grounds for prejudice against the Greeks – their political instability; their insulting attitude to "barbarians", especially Romans; their corruption in political life; their capacity for dishonesty and treachery; and their higher economic standing, which he believed was corrupting Roman morality. Yet it is notable that he admired three Greek leaders of an earlier age, Epaminondas, Pericles and Themistocles.[23] At the beginning of his *Origines* he said that the Aborigines of Italy were descended from Greeks, that the Italian city of Tibur was founded by Greeks, and that some customs of the Sabines were derived from Sparta.[24] His anti-Hellenism, then, was not total: rather, it was focused on the Greeks of his time and on their influence on Roman education.

In Cato's view the purpose of Roman education, as far as the senatorial class was concerned, was to prepare leaders in political and military affairs. Such men were to be active in the service of the state, and they were to exhibit the traditional Roman virtues – courage, honesty, loyalty, incorruptibility, justice. As a corollary they would avoid the vices that Roman conservatives came to associate with Greeks and eastern peoples – avarice, dishonesty, luxurious living, extravagance, sexual excess. The young Roman would learn by example from his ancestors, from senior members of his family, and from reading and hearing about great Roman leaders of the past, especially those of his own family. He would learn from association with older leaders in the senate at Rome, from living with an older leader on military service (*contubernium*), and from early experience in military campaigns. The two underlying principles were, first, recognition of tradition and experience in inculcating high moral principles, and, second, association with older men of experience, achievement and austere morality. Despite such uncompromising moral and practical principles, there was room in this system for cultivating the intellect, as the education of Scipio Aemilianus showed, and as Cato himself showed in his treatises and speeches, as well as in his training of his sons. But when non-Roman influences clashed with traditional Roman virtues, especially in training for service to the state, then Cato's hostility was aroused.

This, then, was the underlying cause of his hostility to philosophers, which was openly displayed after the appearance of the Athenian embassy.[25] He moved that all philosophers be escorted out of the city and that, specifically, an answer be given promptly to the Athenian embassy and a vote taken on their request. Plutarch reports his words:

> "Thus they could go home to their schools and lecture to Greek youths, and Roman youths could listen, as they did before, to the laws and the magistrates." This he did (says Plutarch), not because he was hostile to Carneades (as some people think), but because he was generally opposed to philosophy. He attacked all Greek culture and education in a partisan spirit, saying that Socrates was a violent [speaker], whose goal was tyranny over his country. Socrates (Cato said) corrupted the morality [of the city], dragged in views that were opposed to the laws, and changed the attitudes of the citizens.

Cato's concern, then, if we are to believe Plutarch, was the effect of philosophy on the young. The teachers of the future leaders of Rome should be "the laws and the magistrates". The Greek philosophers were diverting the young from their proper focus on the traditions, laws and leaders of the Roman state. Cato feared, in Plutarch's words, "that the young would rather win a reputation through rhetoric than through deeds and military campaigns". That a senior senator such as Acilius was so openly a philhellene added to Cato's concern about role-models for the young, and his view of the moral and political destructiveness of Socrates extended to Greek philosophy in general, which he characterized as "mere winding-sheets".[26] The Greek philosophers were, in a word, subversive, and to allow the young to study their writings or (worse) to listen to their lectures, would be to invite a weakening of moral, political and military leadership at Rome.

Cato was not alone in this view. Six years before the embassy (161 BCE) the praetor M. Pomponius, on instructions from the senate, refused permission for philosophers and teachers of rhetoric to stay in Rome, the first of three such expulsions recorded by Gellius.[27] The reason given by Gellius for the second expulsion was also valid for the first. The Greek teachers, the senators thought, were corrupting traditional Roman moral and practical principles in education, in particular by attracting young men to spend whole days slacking (the Latin word is *desidere*) in their schools instead of pursuing the traditional Roman military and political training. How the senate responded to Cato's motion to send the embassy back home in 155 is not recorded, but in 154 it did vote to expel two Epicurean philosophers, whose principle of pleasure must have been especially offensive to conservative Romans.[28]

The period after Pydna, then, was one of change and adjustment to foreign influences. But those influences could not be annulled. Plutarch's conclusion on Cato's hostility is accurate:[29]

> Cato's attacks [on Greek philosophy] were shown in the course of time to be in vain. For in that time the city grew to be very great and powerful, and it was hospitable to Greek learning and all Greek education.

Yet suspicion of Greek philosophers was a lasting feature of Roman political and cultural life. Two hundred years later, for example, Seneca was forbidden to train his pupil, the future emperor Nero, in philosophy, because "it was contrary to one who was going to be a ruler".[30] Cato was successful to this extent, that Roman intellectuals were more interested in the practical applications of philosophy than in arguments about logic and epistemology, which too often seemed (and were) esoteric and unproductive. Thus, the Greek philosophers achieved their most far-reaching influence in the field of ethics. Panaetius, a decade after the visit of Carneades, had greater influence on the Romans than Carneades, because he reconciled Stoic ethical doctrine to Roman intellectual and practical needs.

In a world where the spoken word was the dominant form of communication, the arts of rhetoric were of the highest importance. The lectures of Carneades, Diogenes and Critolaus alarmed conservatives like Cato, and their arts of persuasion were thought to be more dangerous than their doctrine. Their speeches brought the Romans face to face with the two aspects of logic in the context of the spoken word. Logic, along with physics and ethics, was one of the three divisions of philosophy accepted by the major schools, a system which Cicero ascribes to Plato:[31]

> There was already [i.e. in the early first century BCE] a triple system of philosophy originated by Plato. The first category concerned morality and how to live; the second concerned nature and [its] secrets; the third concerned speech and judging what is true and what is false, what is right in discourse and what is corrupt, and what is consistent and what is contradictory.

The three Platonic categories, then, were ethics, physics and logic (in Cicero's order), which Cicero, speaking for the Academics, further defined as "consisting of reason and discourse".[32]

The Stoics, however, divided logic into rhetoric and dialectic.[33] The former was "the science of speaking well in continuous discourse"; the latter was (as Diogenes Laertius puts it):

> the science of correct discussion conducted by question and answer, so that they [the Stoics] also define it as the science of what is true and false and neither true nor false.

Chrysippus, head of the Stoic school from 232 to 207 BCE, had established dialectic as a part of logic, that is, of rational discourse, which includes modes of thought and speech. Plato himself, 150 years before Chrysippus, had been concerned with dialectic that is based upon what is true, as distinct from persuasive discourse that is based on what is likely. The dialectic of Socrates was acceptable to Plato, because it was based on his knowledge of the truth, and the Stoics followed Plato in believing that "the wise man alone is a dialectician".[34] Thus the ethical aspect of dialectic was established by Plato and developed by the Stoics.

In contrast, Plato's student, Aristotle, begins his *Rhetoric* with these words: "Rhetoric is the answering voice to dialectic." For Aristotle, rhetoric and dialectic together were the means for achieving persuasive discourse. Thus he defines rhetoric as "the power of discovering the possible means of persuasion on each topic".[35] The Stoics did not follow this non-ethical view of rhetoric and dialectic. Instead, like Plato, they believed that the "wise man" (i.e. the virtuous person) was the only true dialectician. In the Academic view, as Aristotle implied and Carneades practised, dialectic could be used to argue both sides of a question. This view could, and did, lead to the conclusion that certainty of knowledge could not be achieved. Thus either one must accept that knowledge is not possible, or one must suspend judgement.

Now Cato also believed in the moral dimension of rhetoric, for his definition of the good citizen was "the good man skilled in speaking".[36] The purpose of such a man's speech was wise leadership in service of the state. Carneades, with his intellectual brilliance and his refusal to favor either side of an argument, represented the antithesis of Cato's ideal. It is small wonder, then, that Cato was eager to remove such a philosopher, who not only tempted the young to divert themselves from the traditional Roman training for leadership, but also presented arguments for and against the justice of Roman public policies, to show that "the defenders of justice had no firm or certain arguments".[37] Carneades showed the impossibility of consistently identifying virtue and self-interest, or, to put it another way, he showed that there must be a distinction between justice and prudence. A. A. Long comments:[38]

> Thus his argument is a challenge to any moral philosopher who seeks to show that justice and self-interest can be combined in a coherent ethical system.

But the acute logical reasoning of Carneades was too rigorous for the practical Roman politicians, represented by Cato.

A century after the embassy we hear an echo of the debate in Cicero's *De Re Publica*, the dramatic date of which is 129 BCE. In the third book, Cicero makes Lucius Furius Philus defend the arguments of Carneades. Philus was probably one of the young men who heard Carneades speak in 155, and himself was consul in 136. He deplores his task, but, he says, "those who look for gold will endure every hardship: we, who are searching for justice, a thing much more valuable than gold, indeed must not avoid any hardship". So Philus, the friend of Scipio Aemilianus and a Roman consular, is made to represent the arguments of Carneades, which he personally deplored. The actual date of the composition of the *De Re Publica* was 54–51, and Cicero is reflecting on the consequences of the moral relativism of people like Carneades in the light of the collapse in his own day of the republican constitution, which by then was clear for all to see. Like Cato in 155, he answered Greek logical rigour with Roman common sense, affirmed in Laelius' appeal to the universal "natural law" of justice, which Carneades had demolished a century earlier.[39]

Carneades had the finest mind of the three ambassadors, yet his methods were incompatible with Roman modes of thought. Cicero seems to be saying (in the *De Republica*) that his methods were destructive in the context of Roman society and politics, just as Cato had contended in 155. Of the other ambassadors, Critolaus seems to have made very little lasting impression, but Diogenes perhaps had a lasting influence, for he was the teacher of Panaetius, and he impressed Laelius, the friend of Scipio Aemilianus. Laelius (c. 190–125) was praetor in 145 and consul in 140. He was perhaps the first Roman noble who can be called a philosopher, for he was known as *Sapiens* (the Wise), a title given him by the satirist Lucilius.[40] Cicero makes him the principal speaker in his dialogue *De Amicitia* ("On Friendship", also known as *Laelius*), and he responds to the arguments of Carneades in Book 3 of the *De Republica*. Indeed, Cicero elsewhere says that he cannot name a single Roman "student of wisdom" earlier than the time of Laelius and Scipio Aemilianus.[41] He implies that Laelius was encouraged by the lectures of Diogenes to study with Panaetius, whose influence in Rome was profound and lasting.[42] Indeed, in *Pro Murena* 66 (a speech delivered during Cicero's consulship in 63) Cicero contrasts the easy manner of Laelius, which (says Cicero) he had learned from Panaetius, with the harsh manner of Cato Uticensis, the paragon of Stoicism in Cicero's time.

Panaetius of Rhodes (c. 185–109) came to Rome some time after 146, and stayed there, evidently for substantial (but separate) periods of time, until he returned to Athens in 129 as head of the Stoic school. Cicero says that he lived in the house of Scipio Aemilianus, and he accompanied Scipio on his embassy to Egypt and the eastern parts of the Roman empire that began in 140 and lasted, probably, for at least a year. Cicero also says that Panaetius was Scipio's only companion on the embassy, but Alan Astin has shown that we should not infer from this that Panaetius had any direct influence on the political activities of Scipio.[43] Neither did his doctrine of *humanitas* (i.e. the qualities and behaviour proper to a civilized person) necessarily influence Scipio's public actions, which were notorious for their frequent cruelty and vindictiveness.[44] Panaetius was significant at Rome because of the modifications that he made in Stoic theories, some of which were transmitted by Cicero.

In *Pro Murena* 60–66 Cicero mocks the austerity of the younger Cato's doctrinaire Stoicism. We should not, of course, take the banter of a brilliant defence lawyer (who was also consul at the time) at face value. Nevertheless, we can see from the climactic reference to Panaetius' living in Scipio's house (§66), that in Cicero's time Panaetius was revered for having made Stoicism less rigorous and dogmatic, and therefore more accessible to ordinary people. Cicero is careful to say, however, that for Panaetius' influence on Scipio's character he relies on the testimony of *senes*, i.e. men who in 63 BCE had talked with those who knew Scipio (who had died in 129 BCE) or even had as children themselves seen him. Scipio's *humanitas* was limited, and his cruelty was well attested. Cicero, however, could be more dogmatic about the *comitas* (humane manners) of Laelius, who, he says, was more pleasant (*iucundior*), serious (*gravior*), and wise (*sapientior*), because of his studies with Panaetius. In contrast, Cato the Younger remained true to the paradoxical doctrines of Zeno – that the wise man is unmoved by others; that only the fool shows pity; that only the wise man is a king; that the wise man never changes his considered opinion; that all moral delicts are equal, so that "he who wrings a chicken's neck ... is equal to the man who strangles his father".[45] Cicero appeals to Plato and Aristotle as authorities for flexibility in making moral and political judgements, which are the mark of moderate and restrained human beings. These qualities – moderation and restraint – are prominent in the humanism of Panaetius and of Cicero himself. Cicero the lawyer ridiculed Cato because he was out of step with the ethics of his contemporaries, both Stoics and Academics. Panaetius had returned to Plato and Aristotle, the ultimate sources of Stoic doctrine, in modifying the Stoic ethics of Zeno and Chrysippus. A. A. Long has rightly said that "human nature rather than universal nature was Panaetius' primary interest", and because of this, his ethics focused on human beings as they are, including (but not limited to) the wise man.[46]

Panaetius' most influential work was on appropriate behaviour (*Peri Kathekonton*), the source for the first two books of Cicero's work on duties (*De Officiis*). The distinction between actual human beings and the Stoic ideal of the wise man is made clear in this passage from Cicero:[47]

> Since we live not among human beings who are perfect and fully wise, but among those whose actions are exceptional if they achieve the likeness of virtue, I conclude that no one

should be overlooked in whom some evidence of virtue appears. Indeed, we should cultivate most of all that human being who is most of all endowed with these gentler virtues – moderation, restraint and ... justice itself. For often the spirit of courage and nobility is too fervent in a man who is not perfect nor wise, [while] these virtues seem rather to belong to the good person.

Panaetius, therefore, made Stoic ethics less rigorous and more practical, and thus more attractive to Roman leaders such as Scipio Aemilianus, Laelius, and Cicero himself. Elsewhere Cicero (speaking in his own voice in answer to the Stoic orthodoxy of Cato) says of Panaetius:[48]

he fled from the gloom and harshness [of the rigorous Stoics] and did not approve of their thorny arguments. In one branch of philosophy [i.e. ethics] he was more gentle, in the other [i.e. physics and logic] clearer. He was always quoting Plato, Aristotle, Xenocrates, Theophrastus, Dicaearchus, as his writings clearly show.

Panaetius, however, did not reject the Stoic ideal of the wise man, for Cicero says (*Pro Murena* 66) that the discourses and precepts of Panaetius were pleasing to Cato – which would not be the case if Panaetius had totally rejected the rigorous ideals of orthodox Stoicism. Rather, Panaetius included the morally imperfect human being in his doctrine, showing how such a person could aspire to the virtue of the ideal wise man. So Cicero emphasizes that Panaetius used popular vocabulary in discussing popular views and that his political discourse reflected the everyday usage of ordinary citizens.[49] Panaetius' practical focus on ordinary people found a sympathetic response among his Roman contemporaries.[50] It is the basis of Cicero's moderate doctrine in the *De Officiis*, and it finds an echo in Seneca's 75th and 116th letters. In the latter Seneca quotes Panaetius to show how the perfection of the wise man is separate from the efforts of ordinary people to deal with the passions.[51]

In other areas of Stoic philosophy Panaetius' modifications seem to have been less influential, if only because they did not affect the actual day-to-day life of his Roman followers. As Cicero says, he was clearer than his predecessors, and so inclined to be more sceptical of Stoic doctrine that could not be clearly justified.[52] In cosmology he believed the universe to be eternal and indestructible, and therefore he rejected the Stoic doctrine of periodic dissolution of the universe by fire (*ekpyrosis*), followed by reconstitution of its material elements.[53] He was sceptical about divination (an important feature of Roman religious practice) and, unlike many Stoics, he rejected astrology.[54] On the other hand, he did not reject the Stoic doctrine of divine providence and fate, which he reconciled with individual moral responsibility.[55] Cicero, without naming Panaetius, explains this by reference to the dual nature of the human soul:[56]

> For souls have a dual power and nature. One part resides in impulse (*appetitus*, Greek *hormē*), which drives a human being in different directions, and the other in reason (*ratio*), which teaches and explains what should be done and what should be avoided. Thus it comes about that reason leads, impulse obeys.

This is similar to Aristotle's theory of the soul, according to which the soul consists of two parts, one without reason and the other having reason.[57] It appears to modify the doctrine of Chrysippus, who taught that impulse was the result of "reason commanding action".[58] Whether Panaetius was responsible for the modification is debatable: what is significant is that he focused on the responsibility of human beings for their moral choices, a doctrine in keeping with the traditional emphasis on individual initiative among the Roman senatorial class.[59]

Finally, Panaetius was considered by Cicero to be an expert on political theory. In the *De Re Publica* he makes Laelius say to Scipio:[60]

> I remember that you very often used to discuss [political theory] with Panaetius in the presence of Polybius (the two Greeks perhaps the most expert on political matters), and that you would collect much material and argue that by far the best constitution is that which our ancestors have left us.

Scipio replies that he is like a craftsman in the practice of his profession, and that, despite his respect for the authority of his Greek sources (which certainly included the *Republic* of Plato and perhaps the *Republic* of Zeno, as well as the doctrines of Panaetius and Polybius), he will contribute to his exposition what he has learned from his own experience and from his education at Rome, which included family tradition:[61]

I am not content with these works on the subject (i.e. politics) that the most distinguished and wisest of the Greeks have left us, yet I would not dare to prefer my opinions to them. Therefore I ask you to hear me as one who is not entirely unfamiliar with Greek doctrine and as one who is not ready to prefer Greek works, in this field especially, to Roman [doctrine]. I ask you to hear me as a Roman (*unum ex togatis*), educated (thanks to my father's diligence) liberally and from my childhood on fire with eagerness for learning, yet also trained much more by experience and by the precepts that I learned at home than by books.

Thus Cicero, writing in the late 50s BCE, introduces his *Republic*, staking a claim through the persona of Scipio Aemilianus for the practical political ideas of the Romans, derived from experience, without denying the authority of the Greek philosophers. The deliberate mention of Panaetius indicates that he was one who, in Cicero's view, understood the Roman claim and joined it appropriately to Greek theory. At the same time, the Stoic emphasis on the duty of the virtuous person to take part in the political life of the city was compatible with Roman ideas of public service, which find their most eloquent expression in the *Dream of Scipio*, the final episode of Cicero's *Republic*. We may also see the doctrine of Panaetius behind Cicero's doctrine of the ideal Roman leader:[62]

It is therefore the proper duty of the magistrate to understand that he wears the mask of the state (*personam civitatis*); that his duty is to uphold the dignity and honour of the state, to preserve its laws and define its rights, and to remember that these things have been entrusted to his good faith.

We should especially note the precision of Cicero's metaphor of the mask, which is usually translated by some form of the word "represent". The ideal leader is recognized (as we recognize a person by his face) as *being* the state – his own appearance and personality are merged with those of the state which he leads and serves. Cicero was perhaps referring to the famous description of a Roman aristocrat's funeral in Polybius, in which the dead man's mask is prominent along with those of his ancestors, as an inspiration to his descendants to win glory in the service of the state.[63]

A. A. Long has said that "it is difficult to see anything specifically Roman in the philosophy of Panaetius".[64] This is true only in the narrow sense (as Long points out) that the modifications of Panaetius stemmed from "philosophical dissatisfaction with certain aspects of Stoicism". The importance of Panaetius in the development of Roman philosophy lay in his perception of specific Roman needs, which he satisfied by the modification of Greek theory, especially in the fields of ethics and politics. Thus he answered, in a way, the criticism of Cato the Censor that Greek philosophers were corrupting the young. For by introducing flexibility into the rigorous ethical doctrine of Chrysippus he made Stoicism acceptable to the Roman senatorial class; by developing a theory of public duty he made it possible for Roman leaders to accept Greek political theories compatible with their own experience and responsibilities. In the period leading up to the formation of the first triumvirate Cicero criticized the political inflexibility of Cato the Younger. "Cato", he said, "gives his political views as if he were in Plato's *Republic*, not among the 'dregs' of Romulus (i.e. the common people of Rome)".[65] The criticism reminds us of the achievement of Panaetius in reconciling Greek theory and the realities of Roman politics and society.

Posidonius, the greatest of the middle Stoic philosophers and the last original thinker of the school, studied at Athens under Panaetius. He was a Greek, born in about 135 BCE in the Syrian city of Apamea. After his education at Athens he settled in Rhodes, where he became an honoured and prominent citizen, serving in public office and as an ambassador to Rome in 87 and, probably, 51, the year of his death. Like Herodotus, he travelled to further his research, and he journeyed as far as Gadeira (Cadiz, on the Atlantic coast of Spain), where he observed the Atlantic tides and the constellations visible from the coast. He mentioned visits to the islands off North Africa, to the Lipari islands (in the Tyrrhenian Sea to the north of Sicily), to Gaul, and to Italy. In Rhodes he headed a Stoic school, which attracted students from Rome, including Cicero (during the years 79–77), and was visited by Roman politicians and generals during their journeys to the east. Thus Cicero refers to him three times as "my close friend" and as "our Posidonius".[66] In 60 Cicero sent Posidonius a copy of his *commentarii* (memoirs), in the hope that he would elaborate them into a formal history, a request that Posidonius declined with admirable tact.[67] He was twice visited by Pompey, in 66, before his campaigns against Mithradates, and in 62, on his way back from Syria to Rome, on each occasion being treated with the utmost respect. Of the older generation of Roman political leaders, he knew P. Rutilius Rufus (consul in 105), who had served under Scipio Aemilianus and had been a student of Panaetius. Rutilius is important as an example of the principled man who was ruined by his political enemies, being exiled in 92 BCE (when he was nearly seventy years old) to Smyrna, where he wrote in Greek a history of his own times, which was widely read and used by his contemporaries and later historians. Rutilius was a political enemy of Marius, the most powerful of Roman leaders in the years from 106 to 86. Posidonius visited Marius in Rome shortly before his death (13 January, 86), and he is mentioned by Plutarch as one of the sources for his description of the final days of Marius, when he was ill and alcoholic, obsessed with fears and memories.[68]

Thus Posidonius was a significant figure in Roman political and intellectual circles. His importance rests on the extraordinary range of his intellectual activities. Since none of his works survive complete, his philosophy must be reconstructed from the approximately 300 extant fragments, of which some are quite substantial. Cicero, Strabo, Seneca, Galen and many other ancient writers testify to his originality and importance. This has led many scholars to attribute to him more influence than can be proved.[69] More sober assessments of the achievement of Posidonius have been made from the evidence of securely attested fragments.[70]

Posidonius accepted the traditional division of philosophy into physics (i.e. study of the natural world), ethics and logic. He accepted the authority of the founders of Stoicism (most notably Chrysippus), but he believed in the progress of philosophy, which implies change and, where necessary, correction. Like Panaetius, he taught that physics was the area of philosophy from which others proceeded, whereas Chrysippus had put logic first.[71] Consequently he wrote on natural phenomena, with works on astronomy, mathematics and meteorology, among others, including a major work *On Ocean*, which "is one of the lost books of antiquity one would most like to recover".[72] From this comprehensive view of the world in which human beings exist he developed his simile for philosophy:[73]

> The Stoics plausibly liken philosophy to a garden with all sorts of fruit, in which physics is like the height of the plants, ethics is like the productivity of the fruit, and logic is like the strength of the walls. Other [Stoics] say it is like

an egg: they liken ethics to the yolk ... , physics to the white ... , and logic to the outer shell. But Posidonius, since the parts of philosophy are indivisible ... , thought it right to liken philosophy to a living creature, [in which] physics is like the blood and flesh, logic is like the bones and sinews, ethics is like the soul.

The change from Chrysippus' simile is fundamental for Posidonius' method and views. Plants, fruit and walls are separate from each other, entailing the separation of the branches of philosophy.[74] Thus logic was made the tool (*organon*) of philosophy, and therefore subordinate to the other parts. The simile of Posidonius makes logic an organic part of philosophy, to which it gives structure and movement. The tools of physics (natural philosophy) are particular sciences (geography, seismology, oceanography, etc.), which serve natural philosophy by explaining the causes of phenomena. Thus the philosopher observes natural phenomena (as Posidonius himself did on the Atlantic coast of Spain) and deduces their causes from his observations. By means of philosophy (especially logic), he will determine the right causes, distinguishing between various pieces of evidence, and he will relate his conclusions to the cosmos, which Posidonius saw as a living, organic and finite whole surrounded by an infinite void.[75] The importance of Posidonius' method is well expressed by Arthur Darby Nock:[76]

Posidonius did perhaps communicate to others a sense for the wonders of nature ... and let us note that whereas others shrank from rising to contemplate all things, philosophy did not fear this ... [T]his is a desire for knowledge of the secrets of the universe on the basis of human penetration and not of supernatural revelation.

To this extent, Reinhardt's notion of *Kosmos und Sympathie* has some validity, so long as it is realized that Posidonius came to his conclusions on the basis of rigorous observation and logical deduction of causes from the evidence. Indeed, he was criticized by the geographer and Stoic Strabo (*c.* 64 BCE to 25 CE) for being too much concerned with causes, in this, said Strabo, being an Aristotelian rather than a Stoic.[77] Strabo's facts are correct, as the Posidonian fragments show, except for the charge that the search for causes was not typical of the Stoics. For Chrysippus had looked for causes, but denied that the human mind could discover all causes.[78] Posidonius argued (in the context of deducing causes for the weakening of emotions with time) that from study of actual human behaviour its causes could be deduced, just as evidence from observed natural phenomena led to the deduction of underlying causes.[79] Posidonius used the methods of the scientist–philosopher to find the causes of human behaviour or historical events. Observation of physical and emotional behaviour or the evidence of history were the tools for the discovery of causes and therefore for acquiring knowledge of ethics, leading to correct moral choices.

Posidonius developed his theory of ethics in *On the Emotions* (*Peri Pathon*), which can be partly reconstructed from quotations in Galen's *On the Doctrines of Hippocrates and Plato*.[80] He saw that examination of the emotions was the essential beginning of ethical enquiry (the writer is Galen):[81]

> Posidonius says something like this (I quote his words) in the first book, near the beginning of his work *On Emotions*: "for I think that the enquiry about good and evil and about ends and about virtues starts from the correct enquiry about emotions."

Posidonius accepted the traditional Stoic definition of *pathos* as "excessive impulse".[82] He disagreed with Chrysippus about causes of the emotions, for Chrysippus had taught that they were caused by errors in judgement, which entails the possibility of reason itself being their cause.[83]

Posidonius differed from both Zeno and Chrysippus. He praises and accepts Plato's doctrine and disagrees with the followers of Chrysippus. He shows that the emotions are neither judgements nor the consequences of judgements, but that they are motions of separate irrational powers, which Plato called "desiring" and "spirited". In his work *On Emotions* he asks Chrysippus and his followers what is the cause of excessive impulse. For reason could not exceed its own functions and limits. So it is clear that some other irrational power causes the impulse to exceed the limits of reason.

Since reason cannot be subject to excess, and the evidence from observed human and animal behaviour contradicts Chrysippus, Posidonius renewed Plato's theory of the soul, according to which reason is the highest faculty, while the two other irrational faculties account for the emotions of anger and desire.[84] He then showed how *in fact* human beings and animals are naturally affected by the emotions, which can be controlled by reason. Thus his method relied on the observed facts, from which a consistent explanation of their causes could be deduced, leading to an understanding of correct moral choices. Chrysippus took the wise man as his starting point in arguing that reason led to correct moral choices, and errors in judgement to incorrect choices ruled by the emotions. Posidonius took human beings and animals *as they are* as his starting point, and his observations corresponded with the facts of human experience – that human beings and animals do show anger, fear and desire. From the observed evidence, he deduced his proof of the causes of the emotions, which is the basis for his ethical theory.

Finally, his definition of the end (*telos*) of human life modifies Zeno's definition, "to live in accordance with nature".[85] It is quoted by Clement of Alexandria (*c.*150–216 CE) in a catalogue of Stoic definitions of the *telos*:[86]

> to live contemplating the truth and order of the whole [i.e. all things together], and organizing it [namely, the truth] coherently as far as possible, not being led in any respect by the irrational part of the soul.

Thus Posidonius combined observation of nature, conclusions from evidence deduced by reason, and the achievement of the good life – corresponding, respectively, to the philosophical disciplines of physics, logic and ethics – into a coherent system.

Perhaps the most influential of Posidonius' works was his *History*, written in fifty-two books.[87] In time it began where the *History* of Polybius ended, 146 BCE, and in scope it ranged over the whole of the Mediterranean world, from Spain to Asia Minor, and from northern Gaul to Egypt. It may have been unfinished, and it certainly continued down to the mid-80s BCE, since it contains the narrative of Posidonius' interview with Marius shortly before the latter's death in January of 86.[88] Posidonius' usual method is apparent in the extant fragments: careful observation of human and natural phenomena, from which historical causes are deduced. He was especially concerned with the causes of human behaviour, both in individuals and groups, crowds and communities. This is clearly seen in the best known of the fragments, the account of the tyranny of Athenion in Athens in 88.[89] The episode itself was not particularly significant, and Athenion quickly disappeared from the scene to be succeeded by a more formidable tyrant, Aristion, who was executed in the sack of Athens by Sulla in 86. The story of Athenion demonstrated Posidonius' interest in causes, and specifically in the psychological causes of morally bad behaviour, both in the individual (Athenion) and the Athenian people. The same concern with the causes of human behaviour is apparent in the narrative of the interview with Marius.

Many fragments show Posidonius' precise observation of the customs of tribes and nations, for example of the Celts, from which again he deduced the causes of human behaviour.[90] Finally, Posidonius is quoted at length by Seneca in his 90th letter, which concerns the role in philosophy in human political, social and cultural development.[91] Posidonius, as quoted by Seneca, believed that philosophers were the rulers in the Golden Age and that they were responsible for political, social and cultural developments. Seneca, however, while agreeing with the first two of these categories, disagreed with Posidonius about the role of philosophers in developing the arts and sciences.

In another passage, Posidonius shows peoples of the Black Sea coast voluntarily submitting to others who were "more intelligent".[92] In his *History*, as in his other works, he deduced from the observed evidence that the greatest good is achieved by submitting to reason. People in the golden age submitted to wise men because they used reason and would provide the things that were necessary for a better life. The Mariandyni of the Black Sea coast submitted to the Heraclians because the latter, with their superior use of reason, could provide the necessities of life for them. In both cases the submission of one group to another was voluntary: as Seneca says of the golden age philosopher–rulers, "it was a duty to give commands, not a tyranny (*officium erat imperare, non regnum*)".

In the intellectual history of Rome, Posidonius' importance in the short term lay in his influence on Cicero (who was about thirty years younger). In the long term, however, the extraordinary range of his enquiries encouraged Romans to share in the Greek tradition of universal enquiry. Most important, however, was his method of enquiry, with its rigorous focus on deduction of causes from observation. He looked upon the universe as an organic whole, in which human beings had their place. In keeping with his simile of the body, he taught that just as the components of the universe are interdependent, so all knowledge is subsumed into one coherent system. He changed the intellectual life of all Roman students of philosophy and history.

3

CICERO AND HIS
CONTEMPORARIES

Marcus Tullius Cicero (106–43 BCE) was the most influential of the Roman philosophers. He most extensively interpreted Greek philosophy in Latin, and to do so he developed a Latin prose vocabulary that continued to be influential throughout the Middle Ages and the Renaissance. Only Seneca and Augustine matched his prolific output of Latin philosophical works, and they too each developed a new Latin style as the vehicle for their doctrines. All three were skilled orators, experienced in the arts of persuasion. It is usual to refer to "Cicero the Philosopher" (the title, for example, of a recent collection of papers on Cicero), but Cicero had as one of his ideals "the proper combination of philosophy and rhetoric", which he saw (rightly) as a particularly Roman development in the history of philosophy.[1] The canonical definition of the orator was that of Cato the Elder: "a good man skilled in speaking" (*vir bonus, dicendi peritus*), implying that the orator who sought to be a political leader must be morally good as well as skilled in rhetorical techniques.[2] Cicero announced this theme in his earliest rhetorical work, *De Inventione*, and elaborated it thirty years later in *De Oratore*.

Cicero expanded the implications of Cato's "good man", and to do so invoked Plato. Like Panaetius and Posidonius he revered Plato as the fountain-head of philosophy, while he understood the importance of Plato's *eloquentia* (style) in making philosophy attractive to his readers and hearers. In his *Orator* (whose subject is the perfect orator), Cicero says that he seeks to find not an eloquent individual, but "eloquence itself", which can only be seen with the "eyes of the mind" (§101). He is alluding to Plato's theory of forms, which he had endorsed earlier in the *Orator* (§§7–10). There he says that the orator to be described in the treatise is so perfect that he has perhaps never existed. But, Cicero says, he will search for the most excellent eloquence, whose beauty can be likened only to the ideal of oratory, which only the mind can comprehend. Even so, Phidias, in creating his statues of Zeus and Athena, copied a mental image of ideal beauty, not the beauty of an individual model. Cicero concludes (§§9–10):

> So just as there is something perfect and superior in statues and works of art, to whose appearance in the mind they are related (but itself it cannot be seen), so with our mind we see the appearance of perfect eloquence, we aim at its likeness with our ears. These forms of things Plato called *ideai*, Plato who is the most weighty authority and teacher not only of understanding but also of speaking. He says that the Forms do not come into being and are eternal, and that they always are comprehended by reason and intelligence. Other things come into being, die, dissolve and disintegrate, and they do not exist any longer in one and the same state. Therefore whatever exists and is the subject of methodical reasoning, must be referred to the Form and Idea of its class.

Thus Cicero combines rhetoric and philosophy: the former comes into being through reason, the servant and interpreter of philosophy; the latter needs rhetoric if its conclusions are to be communicated to and understood by a wide audience. Before he came on the scene (he implies) philosophy had been the special field of disputatious Greeks, criticism of whom in Rome goes back at least to Plautus in the early second century BCE.[3] Through his rhetoric, founded on philosophy, he will make the doctrines of the Greeks intelligible to Roman audiences. His claim has proved to be justified.

Cicero tells us a great deal about his rhetorical and philosophical training. In the last part of his *Brutus* (§305 onwards) he recalls his years in Rome during the troubles of the 80s BCE that culminated in the capture of the city by Sulla in 82 and the subsequent proscriptions. He says that he listened to the most prominent orators, some of whom he describes as "living on the speaker's platform" (§305). At this time (88) Philo of Larissa, the head of the Academy at Athens, fled to Rome from the imminent sack of Athens by Sulla. His arrival was important for Cicero (§306):

> Then, when the tribune P. Sulpicius was making speeches to the people every day, I gained a deep knowledge of the

whole field of rhetoric. And at the same time, when Philo, head of the Academy, fled from his home with the leading men of Athens in the [first] Mithradatic War and came to Rome, I gave myself over to him completely. For I was stimulated by an amazing enthusiasm for philosophy. While the variety and importance of the subjects of philosophy kept me involved in it, one reason especially made me more attentive – that the administration of justice through the courts seemed to have been permanently removed.

Cicero goes on to tell how he did not make any speeches in those years. Instead, he says (§§308–09):

during that period I spent all my days and nights in the study of every [philosophical] doctrine. I consorted with the Stoic Diodotus, who recently died at my house, where he had made his home and had lived with me.[4] He made me practise dialectic most vigorously.

Cicero is recalling 40 years later (46 BCE, but with a dramatic date of 49) the turbulent days of Marius and Sulla and explaining how he avoided the troubles in which many politicians and orators lost their lives. While his recollection is artfully narrated, he reveals four significant facts about his intellectual and professional development.

First, this account anticipates and confirms the close union of philosophy and rhetoric. His diligence in those years enabled him to transmit Greek philosophy to Roman audiences later in his life. He notes that Diodotus taught him dialectic, an essential rhetorical and logical tool for philosophical argument. He says also (§310) that under Diodotus he declaimed rhetorical exercises every day, more often in Greek than in Latin, partly because he could then be taught and criticized by Greek teachers, partly because Greek oratory provided him with style and modes of expression (his word is *ornamenta*) that could be transferred to Latin – significant evidence for the development of his Latin philosophical vocabulary.

Second, Cicero shows that he turned to philosophy when free speech was suppressed and he could not continue with his political and legal activity. When he was in political eclipse after the renewal of the first triumvirate in 56, he turned to the writing of political philosophy in his *De Re Publica* and *De Legibus*. In the last years of his life, during the domination of Caesar (and especially after the death of his daughter Tullia in February, 45), he devoted himself to philosophical writing, and it is in these few years that the great bulk of his philosophical work was written. Writing late in 45 he said:[5]

> when I was [politically] inactive in retirement and the condition of the state was such that it was necessary for one man to govern it with his responsibilities and policies, I thought that I should expound philosophy to my fellow-Romans principally for the sake of the state. And I thought that it would increase the honour and glory of the state if I should include subjects so weighty and important in Latin literature.

Cicero goes on to say that other Roman students of Greek philosophy had been unable to translate Greek doctrine into Latin, whereas "now" (by which Cicero means after the publication of his Latin philosophical works) the Romans have a Latin style and vocabulary equal to those of the Greek philosophers.

In the *Brutus* Cicero claimed that he had been consistently active on behalf of the state: when it was impossible to speak freely in the forum or the courts or the senate, then he withdrew from public activity into philosophical study and writing, an activity that was equally beneficial to the state and its citizens. This is Stoic doctrine: the wise man will participate in politics as far as he can. But if he is hindered – by disease or disability or by the suppression of free speech – then he will pursue his activity (*negotium*) in retirement (*otium*).

Third (to return to the passage from the *Brutus*), Cicero says that the teaching of the Academic sceptic, Philo, deeply influenced him. He became a follower of the Academic school, whose scepticism, however, led him to deduce the most probable conclusion from the evidence, even if it was one put forward by a rival school.[6]

Finally, Cicero says that the Stoic Diodotus became a lifelong friend. He taught Cicero dialectic (the importance of this for an understanding of logic has been discussed in Chapter 2) and supervised his daily rhetorical exercises. The association with Diodotus meant that, despite being an Academic, Cicero was sympathetic to Stoic ethics, with their emphasis on virtue and reason. He was always opposed to Stoic inflexibility and lack of human sympathy.[7]

In *De Natura Deorum* 6–7 Cicero reviewed his long involvement with philosophy (40 years at the time of writing):

I did not suddenly become involved with philosophy, and from my youth I gave considerable effort and trouble to it. When I seemed least to be involved, then was I most being a philosopher. You can see this from my speeches, which are stuffed with the maxims of philosophers. You can see it from my close friendships with the most learned men, who have always lent distinction to my home. Chief among these were Diodotus, Philo, Antiochus, Posidonius, who were my teachers. If all the teachings of philosophy are relevant to life, then I think that in my private life and my public career I have followed the precepts of reason and philosophy.

Two of the four philosophers named by Cicero in this passage were Stoics – Diodotus and Posidonius. The others, Philo and Antiochus, were Academics, and their influence on Cicero was, by his own account, the most significant in his philosophical development. In *Brutus* 306, quoted above, Cicero describes the effect of Philo's arrival in Rome in 88 BCE: "I gave myself over to him totally". Before this time Cicero had flirted with Epicureanism: writing in 51 BCE he tells Memmius that "when we were boys" he and his friend Patron had admired the Epicurean philosopher, Phaedrus, "before I met Philo".[8] So Philo was the catalyst for Cicero's mature philosophy, and from the time of their meeting in Rome in 88 Cicero was a follower of the Academic school.

In 80 Cicero achieved fame as an orator through his defence of Sextus Roscius, having previously improved his rhetoric by studying with the distinguished Greek orator, Molo of Rhodes, who had come to Rome in 81 as an envoy of the Rhodians. The speech *Pro Roscio* attacked the partisans of Sulla, and Cicero prudently left Rome for two years, 79–77, although he also withdrew (as he says in *Brutus* 313–14) for reasons of health. He went first to Athens and there spent six months studying with the Academic philosopher Antiochus of Ascalon, who may have visited Rome with Philo in 88:

When I reached Athens I spent six months with Antiochus, the noblest and wisest philosopher of the Old Academy. With his encouragement I renewed philosophical studies once more, which I had never interrupted and had pursued and augmented ever since my first years as a young man, with him as my supreme teacher.

After the time in Athens, Cicero toured Asia Minor to study with the leading Greek orators. Finally, he visited Rhodes, where once more he studied under Molo. Cicero returned to Rome in 77 as a complete orator, "not only better practised but almost changed".[9] Essential to his improvement was his renewed commitment to philosophy. His autobiography is fashioned to show how the two fields of endeavour were inseparable.

Philo taught rhetoric as well as philosophy, and this perhaps was one reason why he made such a deep impression on Cicero.[10] When he fled to Rome he had been head of the Academy for over twenty years, and apparently he continued to act as head even in Rome, where he probably spent the rest of his life (perhaps as much as a decade). Neither he nor his most important pupil, Antiochus of Ascalon (a native of Syria, like Posidonius), was a philosopher of the stature of Carneades or Posidonius, but their debate virtually put an end to the Academy as a functional school of philosophy.[11] Nevertheless, there were still Academic sceptics, such as C. Aurelius Cotta, consul in 75 and one of the participants in the dialogue *De Natura Deorum*, and Cicero himself. His older contemporary, Marcus Terentius Varro (116–27), followed the Old Academy of Antiochus. Other sceptics adopted Pyrrhonism (not mentioned by Cicero), which was revived by Aenesidemus some time in the first half of the first century. Although Cicero was a follower of Philo, he was sympathetic with much of Stoic doctrine. A. A. Long rightly has said:[12]

> the humane Stoicism of *De Officiis*, his most influential work, represents views of which he himself approved. It is the bearing of philosophy on human conduct which matters most to Cicero.

It is not surprising, therefore, that Cicero was more interested in ethics than in epistemology. Nevertheless, he would, as a lawyer, have found scepticism attractive, with its method of examining both sides of a question. Psychologically (as we can see from many of his letters to Atticus), he was slow to come to a firm decision, and the built-in dilemmas of scepticism suited him better than the dogmatism of the other schools.

Scepticism had been the principal mode of Socrates' teaching, that is, critical examination of both sides of a question, which would prove the fallibility of his interlocutor's views. Socrates himself laid no claim to knowledge beyond knowing that he knew nothing.[13] Plato saved Socrates' sceptical approach from total negativity through his magical mastery of Greek prose, and by developing the theory of Forms (Ideas) as his answer to the problem of knowledge.[14] But, as Aristotle, Plato's pupil, pointed out, Plato separated the forms from the world in which we actually live, and the more realistic doctrines of other schools (most notably the Stoics) proved more attractive, so that the Academy lost its vitality.[15] The school was reinvigorated as the New Academy by Arcesilaus, its head from about 268–242 BCE, who made the sceptical approach of Socrates (rather than the Platonic forms) its philosophical foundation. He taught that there could be no objective certainty about anything, and that the philosopher should, in the search for truth, suspend judgement. He argued particularly against the Stoic doctrine that a "cognitive impression" could be the basis of knowledge.[16] Nevertheless, he allowed that even without assenting to anything (i.e. without certain knowledge) one could make decisions by following what was reasonable.[17]

Arcesilaus' doctrine was presented more systematically by Carneades, whose speeches for and against justice had so alarmed Cato the Elder. In particular he preferred what was persuasive as the criterion of truth, which must be convincing and thoroughly examined by philosophers before they give their assent.[18]

Philo, who had been a student of Clitomachus, at first agreed with Carneades, but at about the time that he went to Rome he published two books in which he said that the Academy had always been one and the same from Plato to his own time.[19] Without reviving Plato's theory of forms, he seems to have agreed with Plato that we can comprehend universals intellectually, even if we cannot know particular things because of the fallibility of our impressions. His effort to combine scepticism with dogmatism angered Antiochus so much that he wrote a book titled *Sosus* (not extant) against Philo. In it he rejected scepticism and adopted the Stoic theory of knowledge, going back not merely to Zeno, the founder of Stoicism, but to the founder of the Peripatetic school, Aristotle, for his authority.[20] Antiochus also adopted much of Stoic ethics and, it seems, physics.[21] He said that the Stoics agreed with the Peripatetics in substance but differed in terminology.[22] It is hardly surprising, then, that Cicero described him as "one who was called an Academic, and was in fact (with only a few changes) an absolutely genuine Stoic".[23]

The conflict between Philo and Antiochus put an end to the unity of the Academy and to such vitality as it still had. It so upset the Academic Aenesidemus that he dismissed it as "Stoics fighting with Stoics",[24] and left the Academy to revive the sceptical doctrines of Pyrrho (c.365–275 BCE). Cicero does not mention Aenesidemus, whose exact dates are unknown. His chief work on Pyrrhonism was dedicated to L. Aelius Tubero (a younger contemporary and friend of Cicero), and is dated by Barnes as not earlier than the 70s BCE. In any case, he is not significant for our understanding of Cicero's scepticism, which is that of Philo before the publication of the two books that had so upset Antiochus.

These Academic squabbles could be seen, as "esoteric bickering, unintelligible to the layman and unprofitable to the discipline".[25] Cicero himself says that to many people Academic scepticism "appeared to be taking away light and veiling the world in night-like darkness".[26] Indeed, in Cicero's world, philosophy was a guide to life: the conclusions that you reached intellectually had practical consequences. Philo, in going back to Plato, seems to have understood this, while Antiochus, in rejecting scepticism, most certainly did, for he said:[27]

> The two greatest things in philosophy are discernment of the truth and the goal (*finem*) of things that are good. A man could not be wise who did not know that there was a beginning of coming to know and an end of searching, so as to be ignorant of his starting point and his goal.

Thus Antiochus linked epistemology and ethics, the process of knowledge and the goal of the good life. Long has justly said that "he succeeded in turning the Academy back towards a positivist philosophy".[28]

Epistemology is the most barren branch of philosophy if it is pursued as an intellectual chess game. Plato, Aristotle and Zeno had shown that the answers to the questions of "What do we know?" and "How do we know it?" must affect our moral and practical decisions. Plato's theory of forms is one such example, and his belief in its practical importance is eloquently and memorably expressed in Socrates' closing words of the *Republic*:[29]

> In this way, Glaucon, the myth [of Er] was saved and did not perish. It would save us, too, if we obey it, and we shall cross the River of Forgetfulness [Lethe] safely and our souls will not be defiled. But if we follow my words – that the soul is immortal and able to endure all things good and

evil – then we shall always stay on the upward path and practise justice with intelligence in every way. Our goal is to be dear to ourselves and to the gods, both while we remain here and when we receive her [Justice's] prizes, being rewarded like victors in the games. And here and in the one-thousand-year journey which we have passed through we shall do well.

Plato's poetic eloquence makes us forget that this is the conclusion to an epistemological enquiry, that is, into a definition of the universal, Justice. He expanded the logical problem of defining universals to its ethical and practical consequences for the individual and society. Antiochus, as Barnes has said, "was prepared to publish a plain and conservative system of philosophy – and to commend his system to the rulers of the world".[30] This explains why Cicero, the Philonian sceptic, found even in the dogmatism of Antiochus features to guide him in his search for the good life.

Cicero's discussion of the Academic theory of knowledge is in the *Academica*, of which only part of one book (out of four) survives of the revised version and one complete book (out of two) of the first version.[31] The composition of the work was exceptionally tortuous, as can be seen from Cicero's letters to Atticus in the period between March and July of 45 BCE.[32] Cicero originally composed the work in two books, respectively titled *Catulus* and *Lucullus.* In the *Catulus*, now lost, the consul of 78, Q. Lutatius Catulus, expounded the sceptical views of Carneades, which were those held by his father, consul in 102 and a victim in the Marian proscriptions of 87.[33] He was answered by Hortensius (son-in-law of the elder Catulus), who defended the dogmatism of Antiochus. The second book, *Lucullus*, is extant. In it Lucullus expounded Antiochus' views (§§11–42), to which Cicero replied with a defence of Philo's scepticism (§§64–147).

The choice of Lucullus to expound the views of Antiochus seemed at first logical, for he was a friend of Antiochus. M. Licinius Lucullus was consul in 74 and commander in the third war against Mithradates (which was brought to a successful conclusion by his successor, Pompey, in 66). He was beginning his political career at the time when Philo (and probably Antiochus) fled to Rome. In 87 Antiochus accompanied him on a visit to Alexandria and there read the two books of Philo that upset him so much. He went with Lucullus on his campaigns in Armenia and was present at the battle of Tigranocerta in 69, of which he said "the sun had never seen such a battle". He died not long after. The *Catulus* and the *Lucullus* were completed in mid-May of 45, some 11 years after the death of Lucullus, with a dramatic date between 63 and 60.

Cicero realized, however, that it was stretching the facts to make the military and political leader Lucullus into a philosopher discoursing on epistemology. In June he rewrote both books, so as to give Brutus and Cato (Uticensis) the principal parts.[34] He had already, however, been thinking of transferring these parts to Varro, and within two days of completing the second version he had done this. The third and final version of the work was in four books, with Varro and Cicero as interlocutors (Atticus was a third, but took a very small part), Varro speaking for Antiochus and Cicero for the scepticism of Philo. Only part of the first book is extant: in it Varro's speech occupies §§15–42 (with a few interruptions from the interlocutors) and Cicero's begins at §44: the extant part breaks off at §46. Cicero refers to the four books of the final version as *Academici Libri*, and the two books of the first version as *Catulus* and *Lucullus*. Modern editors, however, usually refer to the two surviving books as *Academica*, even though they come from different versions.[35] These books are the principal source for the views of Antiochus, together with Book 5 of the *De Finibus*, in which M. Pupius Piso (consul in 61) is the speaker for his ethical doctrines, with Cicero as respondent.[36]

The choice of M. Terentius Varro (116–27 BCE) for the revised *Academici Libri* was appropriate, for he was the greatest of Roman scholars, although he also had a public career, rising to the praetorship in the 70s and serving as propraetor in the east in 67 and in Spain in 50–49. His range of scholarship was vast, but, of the fifty-five works whose titles are known, only two are extant to any great extent (*De Lingua Latina* and *De Re Rustica*). He did write a work *De Philosophia*, known from Augustine's description, and, as the second part of his monumental *Antiquitates Rerum Humanarum et Divinarum*, he wrote sixteen books (dedicated to Julius Caesar) on the gods and their worship.[37] In a letter written towards the end of June, 46, Cicero expresses his admiration of Varro for his immersion in study (which included philosophy) at such a time of political instability:[38]

> I have always considered you to be a great man, especially because in these stormy times you are almost the only one to be enjoying in harbour the fruits of learning.

Varro had studied under Antiochus in Athens, and Cicero says of him, "no one is more fitting for the doctrines of Antiochus".[39]

Cicero agonized over the choice of Varro, as we know from a series of letters to Atticus.[40] He was never on close terms with him and Varro's hot temper made him nervous.[41] He was embarrassed by Varro's failure (after nine years) to publish the work that he had promised to dedicate to Cicero.[42] In the dedicatory letter of the *Academici Libri* to Varro, Cicero remarks that in fact the discussion between himself and Varro in the work had never taken place, striking evidence for the ability of Rome's two most distinguished intellectuals to work on parallel lines.[43] At any rate, the revised *Academici Libri* were sent by Atticus to Varro before mid-July of 45.[44] Cicero was anxious to know what Varro thought of the work, but Varro's letter (if he ever wrote one) is not extant. Cicero himself was proud of the revised work, as he writes in several letters to Atticus. For example, writing in May of 45, he says:[45]

> The books have turned out (unless human self-love deceives me) such that not even the Greeks have anything in this genre like them ... They are far more brilliant, more concise, better (*splendidiora, breviora, meliora*).

In his mention of the *Academici Libri* in *De Divinatione* (2. 1), Cicero focuses on the approachability of the work, for he knew how intimidating Greek epistemology would be for his Roman audience. He says:

> I set forth in the four books of the *Academici Libri* the kind of philosophy that I thought would be least arrogant and most consistent and elegant.

How seriously he took his task can be seen from the series of letters to Atticus, written during the revision of the first publication, to which we have referred earlier.[46] He took particular pride in making Greek philosophy intelligible to young Roman readers in Latin whose style, he claimed, outdid that of the Greeks.

Cicero dedicated the intermediate version of the *Academica* to Brutus, and it is appropriate to say more here about this younger friend of Cicero.[47] M. Junius Brutus (as he is usually called, although after his adoption into the family of the Servilii Caepiones he actually took his adoptive father's name) was born (probably) in

85 BCE and studied philosophy at Athens under Aristus, the brother of Antiochus and his successor as head of the Old Academy. (Although Cicero calls Brutus *Antiochius*, he almost certainly never heard Antiochus.) Brutus, therefore, was an Academic, despite the fact that he married (as his second wife) Porcia, daughter of M. Porcius Cato (Uticensis). In his public career, which began in 58 with a controversial mission to Cyprus on Cato's staff, he was efficient and (in Cyprus at least) rapacious, and he could be high-handed. After the battle of Pharsalus (48), in which he had fought on Pompey's side, he was pardoned by Caesar, no doubt in part because his mother, Servilia, had been Caesar's mistress. In 46 he was sent by Caesar to Cisalpine Gaul (i.e. northern Italy) as proconsul, and governed so well that he was elected Praetor for 44 and designated consul for 41. But when Caesar was made Dictator for life in February of 44, Brutus could not ignore the demands of family tradition (for his ancestor, Lucius Junius Brutus, had ended the tyranny of Tarquinius Superbus nearly five centuries earlier) and he became the leader of the conspiracy against Caesar which culminated in the murder on the Ides of March, 44. It is doubtful if solely philosophical principles led him to rid Rome of a tyrant (as has often been said), so much as the realization that with Caesar as Dictator free competition among Roman senators for political power would be ended. Brutus at first disapproved of the suicide of Cato, but he changed his mind before the battles of Philippi and said to Cassius:[48]

> I used to blame Cato for his suicide, because it was not virtuous (*hosion*) nor manly to yield to the god rather than to accept events without fear, and instead to run away. But now beset by fortune I have changed. If the god does not decide these events in my favour, I do not ask to make trial of other hopes ... but I shall leave with praise for Fortune, that I gave my life to my country on the Ides of March and have lived another life because of her with liberty and glory.

And so, after his defeat in the second battle of Philippi, Brutus killed himself.[49] We may doubt if his decision was entirely a philosophical one, although Plutarch makes him seem to act as a Stoic. Rather, realizing how hopeless his political position was after the victories of Antony and Octavian, he followed Cato in refusing to live under those who had destroyed the Republic. Plutarch also reports that the enemies said that he alone of the conspirators made it his goal to restore "the traditional Roman constitution" – that is, they said that his motives were political.[50]

Brutus did not invite Cicero to join in the conspiracy against Caesar, but they corresponded after the murder until July of 43, by which time Brutus had left Italy for Greece and the east. It is a sad correspondence to read, for it cannot conceal their deep political differences, especially over Octavian (the future emperor Augustus), whom Cicero underestimated and Brutus rightly distrusted. One hint of their common philosophy remains in the consolatory letter that Cicero wrote after the death of Porcia, Brutus' wife, in June of 43.[51] Brutus had been critical of Cicero's grief in his letter consoling Cicero after the death of his daughter, Tullia, in February of 45. Referring to this in his consolatory letter, Cicero reminds Brutus that his public position does not allow him to give way to his emotions. Though he has lost "one who had no equal on earth", he cannot allow himself to appear weak in the eyes of "almost the whole world".

Brutus first wrote to Cicero from Asia, where he had gone after Pharsalus. Cicero says that this letter (which is not extant) first revived him from the depression that the defeat of Pompey had caused and had brought him back to the study of philosophy.[52] It was a letter, says Cicero, full of prudent advice and friendly consolation, and it led to a period of intellectual closeness between Brutus and Cicero at the time when Cicero was most productive as a philosophical writer. Brutus himself wrote treatises (all lost) on Virtue (which was dedicated to Cicero), on Patience and on Duty. According to Quintilian he was a better philosophical writer than orator: "you would know that he felt what he said", says Quintilian.[53] Cicero naturally was sympathetic to an orator who was also a philosopher.

The first work that he dedicated to Brutus, the *Brutus*, was a survey of Roman oratory which included, as we have seen, an auto-biographical account of Cicero's own development in the 80s as an orator and philosopher. Cicero speaks warmly of Brutus' friendship in the *Brutus*: Brutus and Atticus together as friends who were "so dear and pleasing to me, that at the sight of them all my anxieties about the state were allayed".[54] This did not stop Brutus from criticizing Cicero's oratory which, so Tacitus tells us, quoting Brutus' own words, he said was "broken and dislocated", with reference, however, more to the rhythms than to the content of his rhetoric.[55]

At the end of the *Brutus* (§330), Cicero laments the road-block (Cicero is using the metaphor of a chariot) that the misfortunes of the state have thrown in the way of Brutus' career. Therefore, he urges him to devote himself to his continuing studies, that is, to philosophy. So, for a short time, Cicero saw in Brutus a serious philosopher, and, despite occasional irritation with him, he dedicated a series of works to him. After the *Brutus*, another work on oratory, the *Orator*, was dedicated in 46 at Brutus' request, to be followed in 45 by the *De Finibus*, the *Tusculan Disputations* and the *De Natura Deorum*. Cicero also (in 46) dedicated to him a much slighter work, the *Paradoxa Stoicorum*, which was really a rhetorical exercise rather than a serious philosophical examination of the Stoic paradoxes.

Of these dedications, those to Books 1, 3 and 5 of the *De Finibus* are especially interesting. Book 5 begins with the words, "When, Brutus, I had listened to Antiochus, as was my custom", a direct reference to their common allegiance to the Academy and a reminder of Cicero's account in the *Brutus* of his time in Athens in 79. Cicero begins the work with a defence of the writing of Greek philosophy in Latin and reminds Brutus of the supreme importance of an enquiry into the nature of good and evil for the living of the virtuous life.[56] The setting of Book 3 is the library in the Tusculan villa of the younger Lucullus (son of the Lucullus of the *Academica*), in which Cicero finds Cato Uticensis, the guardian of the young Lucullus, whose mother was related to Cato. Cato is the speaker in defence of Stoic ethics, and Brutus, as Cicero remarks, is already proficient "in philosophy and in its best field" (i.e. ethics).[57] While the dramatic date of Book 3 is the late 50s, the date of writing was a year after the death of Cato. There is poignancy in the dramatic presentation of Cato in a work written after his death and dedicated to Brutus, his son-in-law and nephew, himself destined to die in the same cause.

M. Porcius Cato (95–46 BCE) is the major figure in the background of Cicero's relations with Brutus. To Cicero he was *Stoicus perfectus*, who introduced weighty philosophical discourse into his speeches in the senate.[58] Cato did not travel to Athens to hear the philosophers' lectures, and Plutarch says that "he did not study with others and no one heard him speak", that is, that he did not take part in the exercises that were part of the usual training in philosophy.[59] On the other hand, he was a friend of the Stoic philosopher Antipater of Tyre, who aroused his interest in Stoicism:[60]

He made friends with Antipater of Tyre, a Stoic philosopher, and attached himself particularly to [Stoic] ethical and political doctrines. He was especially possessed, as if inspired, by every aspect of virtue. He was an enthusiastic lover of that part of the good that concerns inflexible justice, which never bends to allow leniency or special pleading. He trained himself also in rhetoric appropriate for addressing crowds, thinking that in a great city there would be controversy along with political philosophy.

In 67 Cato went to Macedonia as military tribune, and during this service he travelled to Asia Minor, in order to meet Athenodorus (Kordylion) of Tarsus, who was then head of the Library at Pergamum. Athenodorus was a Stoic, and Plutarch tells how Cato cajoled him into leaving Pergamum and returning with him to the camp in Macedonia. He eventually went to Rome, where he lived in Cato's house until his death. Plutarch comments that Cato was especially impressed by his refusal to make friends with rulers and military leaders.[61]

Cato's philosophy was, as it were, home-grown. He chose the style of Stoicism that suited his austere, craggy character, and he practised it in his own fashion, regardless of the cost to his political career. It made him a redoubtable political competitor, feared and hated by his opponents. Yet even Cato could not always put philosophical principle ahead of political expediency, as, for example, when he secured the election to the consulship for 59 of Bibulus, his son-in-law, through bribery.[62]

In his public career Cato infuriated Cicero by his inflexibility. His rigid adherence to principle led him to block Cicero's request for a *supplicatio* (a public thanksgiving, ranking below a triumph) in honor of his military achievements in Cilicia.[63] This caused Cicero to remark to Atticus that Cato "has been disgracefully malevolent towards me".[64] His rigidity led most disastrously to his refusal of any compromise with Caesar in the months leading up to the outbreak of the Civil War in January of 49. But Cicero admired and respected his devotion to the Stoic principle of service to the state, which led to an extraordinarily selfless patriotism. Indeed, in the *Pro Murena* he saluted Cato (who was then thirty-two years old) as "born not for yourself, but for your country", words that the epic poet Lucan adapted and expanded, "believing that he was born not for himself but for the whole world".[65]

After the victory of Caesar at Thapsus in April, 46, Cato did what he could to protect the people of Utica from harm, but for himself he resolved to die. He would not accept clemency from Caesar, and he decided that he could not live under the rule of one man. Better to die, he believed, than to compromise with a tyrant. Therefore he committed suicide, a scene vividly described by Plutarch.[66] Plutarch says that he had with him two philosophers, Apollonides (Stoic) and Demetrius (Peripatetic), with whom he discussed philosophical matters on the evening before his death, until the discussion reached the Stoic paradox that "Only the good man is free".[67] Demetrius argued against this, and Cato argued so violently for it, that those present realized that he had determined to die. Later, only the philosophers were left with him, and to them he reaffirmed his decision. They then left, and early in the morning he killed himself.

Cato's death was a public act based on Stoic principle. The virtuous man could not compromise with evil, neither could the man who was truly free live under a tyranny, nor could the Roman patriot live in a republic where the constitution had been rendered meaningless. While Stoic doctrine was ambiguous about suicide, it did allow for the wise man to withdraw – whether from political activity or from life itself – when circumstances made it impossible to live a virtuous life.[68] Thus Cato reasoned that he should die, and by that act he more effectively opposed Caesar than by any of his political acts, as Caesar himself saw.[69] In a later age (as we shall see in the discussion of Seneca and Lucan) his suicide was a beacon of encouragement for Stoics who faced similar political and moral dilemmas.

After Cato's death Cicero wrote a pamphlet praising him, at the request of Brutus, who followed with one of his own. These stimulated Caesar to publish as his response an *Anticato*. Thus Cato achieved more by his death on philosophical principles than he had been able to achieve in life by his politics. About ten years after his death Sallust wrote a comparison of Caesar and Cato as part of his narrative of the senatorial debate that preceded the execution of the Catilinarian conspirators in 63.[70] In his speech Cato refers to his many earlier speeches in the senate "lamenting the luxury and avarice of Roman citizens", and a little later, consistent with Stoic doctrine, he refuses to show mercy or pity towards the accused, whose execution he called for. These sentiments he supported with appeals to patriotism and to historical examples of harsh punishments in support of the best interests of Rome. In the comparison that follows, Sallust (himself a former Caesarian) says that in his time only two men were endowed with great virtue – Caesar and Cato. In the present context we may leave his estimate of Caesar on one side, while recognizing that for Sallust, as for many others, Cato had become the unique example in his time of the Roman who effectively transferred his philosophical principles into public life.

We have reviewed Cicero's early training in philosophy, and this has led us to review several of his friends who appear as philosophers in successive versions of the *Academica*. It is time now to turn to Cicero's own review of his philosophical works, which he gave in *De Divinatione*, 2. 1–7. This work was written in early 44 BCE, largely before the Ides of March (but completed later), so that it does not include the later works on Friendship, on Fate, on Topics and on Duty. Cicero's list is part of his defence of his philosophical activity as service to the state. He particularly justifies his making Greek works available in Latin on the grounds of educating the young (§4):

> What greater or better duty could I perform for the state than in teaching and training the young, especially in these times of low moral standards, for the young have so far deteriorated that everyone should do what they can to discipline them and put the brakes on [their moral decline]?

Thus Cicero answers the chief objection of Cato the Elder to the influence of Greek philosophy. He says also (§6) that he became so active in philosophy because it was the activity most worthy of him, as a senior statesman, in a time when free political activity had been suppressed under the rule of one man. At this stage he is beginning to resume his public career, and so he expects that he will not have time to devote his full attention to philosophy.

Cicero's survey begins with a lost work, the *Hortensius*, which he describes as an exhortation to study philosophy, written early in 45 BCE. More than 100 fragments survive, from which it has been deduced that the work consisted of a debate between Hortensius (speaking against philosophy) and Catulus (defending its study), thus introducing Cicero's preferred style of presenting arguments for and against a thesis.[71] It has also been suggested that the work is largely based on Aristotle's *Protrepticus*, a lost work defending the study of philosophy.[72] The *Hortensius* is best known for its influence on Augustine, who has preserved many of its fragments. In his

Confessions he tells how he was affected as he read the work as part of the regular curriculum in his rhetorical education:[73]

> That book contains Cicero's own exhortation to philosophy and it is called *Hortensius.* It was that book that changed my feelings and changed my prayers to you, Lord, and made my vows and desires different.

Augustine elsewhere quotes the *Hortensius* on living virtuously as preparation for life after death. If, says Cicero, we go from this life to the Islands of the Blessed, there will be no need there for the four cardinal virtues, courage, justice, temperance and prudence. But in this life they are necessary.[74] Again, Augustine quotes the end of the *Hortensius*, where Cicero ecstatically urges devotion to philosophy as the means to "an easier ascent and return to the heavens".[75] The passage shares with Cicero's *Dream of Scipio* a poetic vision of the rewards of virtue achieved through philosophy.

Cicero next lists the *Academica*, which we have already discussed in reviewing Academic skepticism and its background. After this he mentions the five books *De Finibus Bonorum et Malorum*, which he wrote between March and June of 45 BCE, concurrently with the revised *Academici Libri.* Their subject is ethics, literally *On the Ends of Good and Evil.* The Latin word *finis* translates the Greek term *telos*, which denotes both "end" (i.e. the extreme limit) and "target" or "goal", but Cicero preferred to use the plural *fines.* The title implies that the person who hits the target of what is good also reaches its ultimate limit (in Latin *summum bonum*), and so achieves the good life or, more specifically, "happiness", which the Greeks defined as *eudaimonia* and Cicero translated as *vita beata.* Conversely, the person who reaches the furthest limit of evil is afflicted with the worst life and the greatest unhappiness.

The *De Finibus* is really an introduction to ethics, or, as Cicero says, it is the "foundation of philosophy". Like university "basic" or "foundation" courses, it deals with a huge topic attractively and comprehensively, with the obvious drawbacks of such a presentation. Because of its approachability it has been highly praised and, especially since the Danish scholar, J. N. Madvig, published his monumental commentary in 1876, it has been more widely read than many of Cicero's philosophical works. Yet it does not reach the religious and emotional intensity of the *De Natura Deorum* or the intellectual precision of the *Academica*, or the Platonic enthusiasm of the *Hortensius*.[76] Nevertheless, it is still among the most readable of

Cicero's philosophical works and it is especially valuable for its exposition of the ethical doctrines of the three major schools of philosophy. Cicero claims that he dealt with the topic completely (his word is *expurgatus est*, literally "completely flushed through"), which he himself admitted was not so, for in his next work, the *Tusculan Disputations*, he says:[77]

> we ought to realize that when we have come to know (as far as a human being can know) the ends of good and evil, we can pray for nothing greater or more useful from philosophy than these things which we have been discussing in these four days.

The *Tusculan Disputations*, then, complemented the *De Finibus*.

Cicero makes especially clear the importance of his Latin terminology in the *De Finibus*. In the dedication to Brutus (§1) he says that he knows that critics object to his presenting Greek philosophy in Latin, on the grounds that it is wasted effort, that it is beneath the dignity of a man of Cicero's standing in public life, and that anyway they would prefer to read the original Greek. Cicero answers each criticism most passionately in §§10–11, where he defends the dignity of the Latin language and the patriotism that his translations display:

> I have often discoursed on the Latin language, that it is not poor (as is commonly thought), but that it is even richer than Greek ... . As for myself, since I have never (in my view) deserted my post in my work in the forum, in my labours [for the public good], in my dangers, I certainly owe it now [to the Roman people] to labour to make my fellow-citizens better informed through my diligence, my research and my labour ... For what in our lives – both in all of philosophy and in the discussions in these books – should we prefer in our enquiries to finding out the end, the limit, the ultimate goal, to which every precept for the good life and morally right action has to be related? Or what should we prefer in our enquiries into what nature should follow, as the most desirable object to look for, and what it should avoid, as the worst of evils?

The search for Latin terminology was especially important in the exposition of Stoic doctrine in Book 3. Cicero says that the Stoics were the greatest innovators in philosophy, and that Zeno (their founder) was "not so much a discoverer of new things as he was of new words".[78] Therefore Cicero is justified, he says, in developing a new terminology. He admits that some Greek words (for example, *philosophia*) are established in Latin usage, but he argues that Latin has a rich vocabulary of its own for the translation of Greek terms. Thus the important Stoic concepts of *proegmena* (things preferred) and *apoproegmena* (things to be rejected) he translates by *praeposita* and *reiecta*.[79] He uses *laetitia* (pleasure of body and mind), as opposed to *voluptas* (sensual pleasure), where the Greek uses the same word, *hedone*, for both, and the emotions (*pathe*) become in Latin *perturbationes*.[80] Cicero compliments Cato (the Stoic speaker) on his use of Latin:[81]

> Indeed, Cato, you are using lucid vocabulary, whose words say exactly what you mean! And, in my opinion, you are teaching philosophy in Latin and, so to speak, making it a Roman citizen.

Cicero certainly enjoyed the irony of giving Roman citizenship to a Greek term!

The *De Finibus* consists of three separate dialogues, each with its own dramatic date, and each devoted to the ethical doctrines of one of the major schools. The first dialogue (Books 1 and 2), whose dramatic date is 50 BCE, focuses on Epicurean ethics. The setting is Cicero's villa at Cumae – an appropriate choice, since there were many Epicureans living in the area round Naples. In Book 1, Epicurean doctrine is defended by L. Manlius Torquatus, to whom Cicero responds in Book 2. Torquatus (90–46) was a friend of Cicero's, although in 62 he was the prosecutor of P. Sulla, whom Cicero defended. Torquatus was also a poet, and his marriage to Junia Aurunculeia was celebrated by Catullus with an epithalamium.[82] He became Praetor in 49 (the year after the dramatic date of the dialogue) and fought on Pompey's side in the Civil War. After the defeat at Thapsus he committed suicide, as did Cato, the principal speaker in Book 3. Thus Cicero, by his choice of speakers, creates a memorial to those who perished in the Civil War. Torquatus' exposition focuses on pleasure (*voluptas*) and pain (*dolor*), which Epicurus had posited as the greatest good and the greatest evil.[83] Cicero mentions that he himself had heard the Epicurean philosophers Phaedrus and Zeno (who preceded Phaedrus as head of the Epicurean school at Athens), and he names two other Epicurean philosophers, Siro and Philodemus, as his close friends and sources for a further defence of Epicureanism.[84] These four philosophers, rather than the writings of Epicurus himself, are likely to be the sources for Torquatus' exposition of contemporary Epicurean doctrine.[85] Cicero's response in Book 2 probably derives from Antiochus.[86] His main argument is that pleasure is not by itself sufficient for the good life, for which only virtue is sufficient, while there are morally good objects of desire (courage, justice, etc.) which have nothing to do with pleasure. Similarly, the desire to avoid pain is not rational but natural, if unattainable. Cicero's arguments, despite their Academic origin, are closer to Stoic ethics, which is understandable, given Antiochus' own acceptance of much of Stoic doctrine. Cicero seems to have respected his Epicurean teachers and friends, even though he was consistently outspoken in his hostility to Epicureanism, and he admits that in Book 2 he is speaking rhetorically, rather than dialectically.[87] This would explain a number of distortions of Epicurean doctrine that appear in his speech.

Books 3 and 4 of the *De Finibus* consist of the second dialogue, an exposition of Stoicism by Cato and, in Book 4, a response by Cicero, again probably largely derived from Antiochus.[88] The setting is the library of the villa of Lucullus near Tusculum, where Cicero comes upon Cato, who is "surrounded by many Stoic books" (§7), and the dramatic date is 52 BCE. Book 3 is among the most important of all Cicero's philosophical writings, for it contains the only continuous exposition of early Stoic ethical doctrine that is extant.[89] In it Cicero takes great care with Latin terminology, and he is far more engaged with the topic than he was in the dialogue on Epicureanism.

Cato begins with the primal human instinct for self-preservation, developing the Stoic doctrine of *oikeiosis*, which Cicero translates by various forms of the verb *conciliare*, in English "affinity" or "affection". From this derives the desire for what is good (*honestum*), which is found to be the only good, for other things that people think are good are in fact *indifferentia*, that is, they are not necessary to the good life).[90] Some of them, to be sure, are to be preferred (*praeposita*) and some to be rejected, but it is virtue alone, gained through reason, that is necessary and sufficient for the good life. Cato defines the *summum bonum*:[91]

> the highest good is to live using the knowledge of the things that happen naturally, selecting those which are in accordance with nature and rejecting those which are

against nature. This is to live a life that is in harmony with and consistent with nature.

This definition is significant. It became the standard for the Roman Stoics' idea of the good life, and it happens that we can see exactly how Cicero developed it from the definitions of Chrysippus, Diogenes of Babylon (one of the ambassadors to Rome in 155), and Antipater of Tyre, Cato's friend and teacher.[92]

Cato touches on many other topics, and he ends with praise of the wise man, in terms that recall the Stoic paradoxes ("only the wise man is a king, is beautiful, is free, is unconquered"). The wise man and his philosophy become divine:[93]

> If it is true that only the good man is happy and all good men are happy, then what should we revere more than philosophy or what is more god-like than virtue?

Cicero's response in Book 4 criticizes each of Cato's arguments, mainly to show that the Stoics agree with the Peripatetics in much, but that their arguments are poorly expressed and their ethical ideals are impracticable. He agrees with the Stoic end as defined in 3. 31 (quoted above), but he objects to their arguments in support of it. Elsewhere he supported the Stoic view, justifying his inconsistency by saying that Zeno's doctrines derived from Plato, the source also for the views of the Peripatetics and Academics.[94]

Book 5 of the *De Finibus* consists of the third dialogue. It is set in Athens in 79 BCE, where Cicero is walking with his friends, M. Pupius Piso (consul in 61, active in the Pompeian cause in 49, but dead by 47), T. Pomponius Atticus, his brother Quintus, and his cousin Lucius Cicero.[95] They start from the Gymnasium of Ptolemy, where they had heard Antiochus lecture, for it continued to function as an educational centre even after it had been sacked by Sulla in 86.[96] They pass by the Stoa Poikile, where Zeno taught, to the Dipylon Gate (about 500 metres) and thence to Plato's Academy (six stades, says Cicero, or about 1,100 metres), passing by Epicurus' garden.[97] It is a wonderfully evocative scene, recalling the setting of some of Plato's dialogues (for example, the *Phaedrus*) or of Cicero's earlier work (for example, Book 2 of the *De Legibus*). It enables Cicero to recall the happy times of his youth and to remind us of his philosophical training in Athens. It also allows him to link himself with the great philosophers of the past – Plato and the Academy, Epicurus and the Garden, Zeno and the Stoa – along with their successors, of whom Aristotle, Speusippus, Xenocrates, Polemo, Carneades, Phaedrus and Antiochus are named. Cicero reminds Piso of a similarly evocative visit they had made to Metapontum (in southern Italy), where Pythagoras had lived and died. The great Athenian orators, Demosthenes and Aeschines, are mentioned, thus linking philosophy and rhetoric. In every part of Athens, says Cicero (§4), one is reminded of the great men of the past, but nowhere so much as in the Academy, where Carneades had lectured.

The continuing presence of great men of the past was a prominent feature of Roman upper-class culture of the last two centuries of the Republic. So Cicero makes Piso say (§2) that looking at the Academy reminds him of being in the senate house at Rome (he had entered the senate as Quaestor in 83), where he could "see" Scipio (Aemilianus), Cato (the Censor), Laelius, and his own grandfather (L. Calpurnius Piso Frugi, consul in 133). Thus the introduction to Book 5 links Greek philosophy with Roman intellectuals and with rhetoric. It links Cicero and his friends to the great philosophical schools of the past, and it reminds his audience in 45 of the very different world of his youth. It is one of Cicero's finest pieces of writing, for it supports his principal claims as a writer of philosophical works – that he is interpreting Greek philosophy in Roman terms, and that in so doing he is acting as a patriot and public servant no less than the great leaders of the past, such as Scipio and Cato the Censor.

The main part of Book 5 is the speech of Piso (§§9–74), skilfully linked to Brutus (to whom the work is dedicated) at the end of §8:

> pay close attention to Piso's speech, Brutus, and see if he has satisfactorily expounded the doctrines of Antiochus, which I think you approve of most of all, since you frequently attended the lectures of his brother, Aristus.

Thus the doctrine of Book 5 is that of Antiochus (as Piso says in §76), defining the *fines bonorum* of the so-called Old Academy. Piso essentially accepts the Stoic definition of 3. 31, but he examines closely what is meant by "good" and by "nature", and hence proves that the virtuous life is the life lived according to nature (§58), but that "virtue" includes many specific good things in life besides the abstract quality of virtue, which the Stoics said was the *only* thing necessary for the good life. Cicero, more Stoic than Academic here, criticizes Piso in the dialogue of §§75–96, and so the work ends.

The *De Finibus* is amongst Cicero's finest works. This certainly can be said of the opening of Book 5, and the importance of Book 3 cannot be denied, whatever shortcomings it may have in its philosophical argumentation.

Next, in the *De Divinatione* survey, Cicero mentions the five books of the *Tusculan Disputations*, probably his most approachable work and therefore amongst the most popular of his philosophical writings.[98] Cicero calls them "an old man's declamations", and both in form and style they are indeed more rhetorical than the earlier dialogues.[99] Instead of the dialogue form in which one speaker develops a point of view and is then criticized by another, Cicero's unnamed interlocutor proposes a thesis, which he then opposes in a virtually uninterrupted speech. The setting is his villa at Tusculum, and from his letters and the information given in the dedication to Brutus in 1. 7, it seems that the date of the five dialogues (one to each day) was an actual one, June 16–20, 45. Cicero summarizes the work as follows:[100]

> The same number of books [i.e. as for the *De Finibus*] of *Tusculan Disputations* followed. They explained the things most necessary for achieving the happy life. For the subject of the first is despising death; of the second, enduring pain (*dolor*); of the third, allaying mental distress (*aegritudo animi*); of the fourth, the other psychological disturbances (*perturbationes animi*). The fifth contains the subject that throws the most light on the whole field of philosophy, for it teaches that virtue by itself is sufficient for achieving the happy life.

The subject of Book 1 is the same as one of the central themes of Lucretius' Epicurean poem, and its goal is the same, that is, to rid the reader of the fear of death. It is remarkable that Cicero pays very little attention (§§18–25) to Lucretius' principal argument, that is, that the soul, being corporeal, disintegrates at death, so that there is nothing to fear thereafter, and instead he argues for the immortality of the soul along Platonic and Stoic lines. Again, it is striking that Virgil (in *Aeneid* 6) devoted some of his finest poetry to an account of the Underworld in its relationship to present and future lives and to past and future history. But Cicero, only two decades earlier, has very little to say about the Underworld and its traditional function as a place of judgement and punishment (§§48–50).

In Books 2–5 Cicero deals with matters that were particularly prominent in Stoic ethics, pain, grief and other emotions. In 2. 14 the interlocutor proposes the thesis that "Pain (*dolor*) is the greatest of all evils". Cicero responds that those (like the Epicureans) who say that pain is the ultimate evil are as wrong as those who (like the Stoics) say that it is not an evil at all (§§15–32). Instead Cicero shows that the antidote to pain, which is an undeniably bad human experience, is reason exercised through philosophy (§§42–67).

As the length of Book 2 shows (little more than half that of Book 1) Cicero was not as deeply engaged with its subject as with that of death in Book 1. Again, he is quite brief and not very profound with the subjects of Books 3 and 4. In 3. 12 the interlocutor proposes the thesis that "the wise man will suffer from mental distress". Cicero replies that such distress (of which grief is the most difficult manifestation) is incompatible with the virtues of the wise man, and that again, reason is its antidote. Therefore the wise man, being ruled by reason, will not suffer from it.[101]

In Book 4. 8 the interlocutor suggests that "the wise man cannot avoid all psychological disturbances", inviting a discussion of the emotions. Again, Cicero takes a Stoic point of view and shows that reason is the antidote, so that the wise man will not be subject to the *pathe* (§§9–84). Book 4 is remarkable for the focus on terminology in §§23–26, for precision is necessary where medical terms are being used as metaphors for emotional disturbances. Cicero's discussion of the *pathos* of love is thin, but he does consider the question of the Greek attitude towards homosexual love (§§70–72), once again proposing reason as an alternative.

With Book 5 the *Tusculan Disputations* take on new energy. In it the interlocutor proposes (§12) that "virtue cannot be sufficient for living a happy life". In the preface (§§1–11) Cicero rises to heights of passionate eloquence in praise of philosophy, whose historical development he surveys. It corrects all human faults and vices (§5), it is the harbour of refuge from the storms of life. Then Cicero utters a paean of praise, composed in the form of a Greek hymn, in which the formal address to the god is followed by a narrative of the god's deeds, a prayer and expressions of hope for future favour:

> O Philosophy, guide of life! O tracker (*indagatrix*) of virtue and expeller of vice! What could not only I, but all living human beings have done without you? You have brought

cities into being, you have brought separated human beings together into a life of community, you have linked them first by means of homes, then by marriage, then by the common sharing of language and writing, you have been the discoverer (*inventrix*) of laws, you have been the teacher of morality and orderly living. In you we take refuge, from you we pray for help, to you I give myself, as I did formerly in large part, so now completely and thoroughly. Indeed, one day spent in accordance with your precepts is better than eternity spent in doing wrong.

The punctuation of the narrative element ("You have brought …") shows the flood of emotion with which Cicero recalls the good deeds of philosophy, expressed in a flow of paratactic clauses quite unusual in the complex syntactic structure of Cicero's prose. Cicero invents the majestic titles ending in *-trix* (a suffix denoting activity), and *indagatrix* is a hunting metaphor.[102] Finally, the compressed account of human progress contrasts both with the myths of degeneration (best known from Hesiod's five ages) and with Lucretius' extended account in Book 5 of the *De Rerum Natura*.

The rest of Book 5 (§§12–121) is devoted to proof that virtue alone is sufficient for happiness. As Cicero admits (§§82–84), this is Stoic doctrine. He therefore argues also for the Academic view, that there are good things in addition to virtue that add to happiness, and in this section (§§83–120) he argues along the lines of Antiochus. Cicero does not resolve the dilemma between the doctrine of the Stoics (that virtue alone is sufficient) and that of the Academics.[103] And this is significant for our understanding of his philosophy, for in this, as in so much of his political career, he was able to see all sides of a question and unable to make a firm decision.

The *Tusculan Disputations* are a completion of the *De Finibus*. They also complete the list of Cicero's major philosophical works given in the *De Divinatione*, and it seems that Cicero looked upon these two works and the *Academica* at the time of writing as a complete programme for epistemology and ethics. Separately he mentions the *De Senectute* (*On Old Age*) and the *Cato*, written after Cato's suicide, which is not extant. Still to be written were the works on friendship (*De Amicitia*) and duty (*De Officiis*).

Cicero also mentions his *Consolatio*, a lost work which should be discussed here, since it is relevant to several parts (mostly in Books 1 and 3) of the *Tusculan Disputations*. Cicero's daughter, Tullia, died in February of 45 BCE, and he addressed a *Consolation* to himself, being, so he said, the first to do so.[104] The Consolation was a well-known literary form, going back at least to the Academic philosopher Crantor (335–275 BCE), whose own *Consolation* (not extant) was Cicero's model.[105] Unlike the Cynics and Epicureans, Crantor and his successors did not deny that the grief of bereavement was natural.[106] Instead they sought to use arguments to make it tolerable and so to "heal" the mourner and enable him or her to resume a normal life. Their purpose, then, as Cicero says of his own *Consolatio*, was to lessen grief rather than to deny it.[107] Cicero refers to his *Consolatio* so many times that its main outlines are known. He brought in arguments other than those of Crantor, such as those later used in the *Tusculan Disputations* on the nature of the soul.[108] Since, as he argued, the soul was divine and the souls of the virtuous ascended after death to join the gods (or rather, in Stoic doctrine, god) in heaven, Tullia's soul had joined the gods and she herself had become divine.[109] Lactantius observes that this was not "the ravings of one stricken with grief", but rather a conclusion reached by reason.

Cicero's *Consolatio* was widely admired, and the consolatory genre continued to be practised. Among surviving consolations, the introduction to Book 3 of Cicero's *De Oratore* (especially §§12–16), written in 55, is a consolation for the death of L. Licinius Crassus and other distinguished men. The letter of Servius Sulpicius to Cicero about Tullia's death is one of the shortest and most remarkable.[110] Seneca wrote several Consolations; Juvenal satirized the genre in his thirteenth satire, and, centuries later (524 CE), Boethius had Philosophy herself console him in prison with the *Consolation of Philosophy*, the greatest and last representative of the genre.

In *De Div.* 2.3, Cicero next (after the *Tusculan Disputations*) lists three theological works, *De Natura Deorum*, *De Divinatione*, and *De Fato*. The first of these he describes as completed by the time of writing the *De Divinatione*, that is, March 44 BCE, and we know from several letters to Atticus that he was working on it during the summer of 45. It may have been published before the end of 45, while the other two works followed in the spring of 44 (*De Divinatione*) and before November of 44 (*De Fato*). He says that the *De Natura Deorum* was a complete examination of its subject, while the other two works would extend and complete his enquiry into the whole field of religion.[111]

Wilhelm Süss confesses that for him the *De Natura Deorum* is "the crown of all Cicero's philosophical work", and there are many who would agree with him, as against the *communis opinio* that this title should be awarded to the *De Finibus* or the *De Officiis*.[112] Cicero was deeply engaged with its subject (he had been a member of the College of Augurs – high officials in Roman state religion – since 53) and here, as much as anywhere in his philosophical writings, he was most successful in transmitting his Greek sources to a Roman audience. In the *Dream of Scipio* in Book 6 of the *De Republica*, published six or seven years earlier, he had already shown how contemplation of the divine sphere, to which human souls would ascend after death, inspired him to write prose of poetic intensity as the vehicle for philosophical doctrine, religious exaltation and patriotic fervour. These are attributes also of the *De Natura Deorum*, particularly in the second book.

The work is in three books. Cicero sets the dramatic dialogue at the house of C. Aurelius Cotta, a senator who had been exiled in the political troubles of 91–90 and who returned in 82 to resume a career that brought him to the consulship in 75, the year in which Cicero himself entered the senate as a quaestor. The occasion was the religious festival of the *feriae Latinae* (the annual festival that celebrated the union of Rome with Latin tribes) in 76, the year before Cotta's consulship and after Cicero's return from his study-tour in the east. Cicero takes virtually no part in the dialogue, as befits a young man in the presence of an elder statesman. The main speakers are C. Velleius, a member of the senate and a leading Epicurean, and Q. Lucilius Balbus, who, says Cicero, was so expert a Stoic that he could compete with Greek Stoic philosophers. Little else is known of these two men. The dialogue seems to take place within one day, although it is likely (from internal evidence) that Cicero originally planned it for three days, one for each book.

In the first book Velleius sets forth the Epicurean doctrine on the gods, devoting only §§43–56 to the topic itself. He does not discuss the gods' immortality or where they are located. His speech is easily refuted by Cotta in §§57–124. As he says (§115), why should human beings worship gods who (according to Epicurean doctrine) have no concern with human affairs? He quotes Posidonius, who said that in fact Epicurus did not really believe in the gods.[113]

The second book is devoted to Balbus' exposition of Stoic doctrine about the gods. Here Cicero devotes four times as much space as he had allotted to Velleius, and the exposition is carefully structured. Balbus divides his speech into four sections:[114]

[The Stoics] divide the enquiry about the immortal gods into four parts. First, they demonstrate that the gods exist; second, they discuss their nature; third, they show that the universe is regulated by them; finally, they prove that the gods are concerned with human affairs.

In each section Balbus adduces detailed arguments, advancing cumulatively to the climax, which is the proof of the interaction between gods and human beings. This is especially appropriate for a Roman audience, for the successful conduct of public affairs depended on the proper relationship of gods and human beings. Proof, then, of the indissoluble bonds between the divine and the human, would have a special resonance for Cicero's readers. Here we may quote the first section of the fourth set of proofs as an example of the union of Stoic, religious and political fervour:[115]

First, the world itself was created for the sake of gods and human beings, and the things in it were produced and discovered for the advantage of humankind. For the world is, so to speak, the common home of gods and human beings, or it is the city-state of both, for they alone live making use of reason, justice and law. So just as we must suppose that Athens and Sparta were founded for the advantage of the Athenians and the Spartans – and everything that is in these cities is rightly said to belong to their citizens – so everything that is in the whole world must be supposed to belong to the gods and human beings.

Balbus continues with various aspects of the created world – the heavens, the earth and its products, the animal realm – to support this comprehensive statement. The doctrine of the two worlds – the ideal world of the Forms and the physical world of particular objects – is Platonic, and, as Aristotle pointed out, it is flawed because of Plato's separation of the two. The Stoics to some extent succeeded in uniting them through the doctrine quoted here, which proved to be so powerful in Roman thought. It is brilliantly presented in the *Dream of Scipio*, and it will find new expression in the works of Seneca, not least in his treatises on Tranquillity (*De Tranquillitate*) and Retirement (*De Otio*). Cicero, then, is showing that the divine is not, as the Epicureans said, separate from the human. On the contrary, it is intertwined with human experience, and the Stoic god (as Cleanthes had said in his *Hymn to Zeus*) was both the origin and the ultimate home of the human soul. In Roman life this had the practical consequence that the gods were very much a part of public activities, whose success they would further by their goodwill.

In Book 3, Cotta, the Academic, criticizes the Stoic view, using the four-part division of Balbus. Unfortunately nearly all of his third set of arguments (against the government of the world by the gods) is lost, and with it some of the validity of his counter-arguments. Nevertheless, he quotes the proofs of human mortality from Carneades, which no Stoic was ever able to refute.[116] Like Balbus, he stresses the importance of the gods to him as a Roman, as *pontifex* (priest, the title of high officials in the state religion) and as a senator. So he prefaces his speech with an appeal to Roman tradition:[117]

> As a Cotta and *pontifex* I should defend both the views about the immortal gods that I have inherited from my ancestors and the sacrifices, ceremonies and religious rituals. I will defend them always, and I have always defended them, nor will any speech of anyone – whether scholar or amateur – move me from the views about the worship of the immortal gods that I have inherited from my ancestors. I follow Coruncanius, Scipio and Scaevola, all chief priests (*Pontifices Maximi*), not Zeno or Cleanthes or Chrysippus. ... I am convinced that Romulus, by taking the auspices, and Numa, by establishing religious rituals, laid the foundations of our state, which never could have grown so great without the gaining the complete favour of the immortal gods.

This is a truly *Roman* statement and Cicero deserves credit for originality in casting his discussion of the gods in such a light. It is true that Greek sources can be identified for most of the *De Natura Deorum* (in particular Carneades, Panaetius and Posidonius), but the political grounds for the pious observance of Roman religion are Cicero's own contribution. Not surprisingly, he is less than whole-hearted in his support of the Academic doctrine. Cotta himself at the end of his speech expresses scepticism:[118]

> This is more or less what I have had to say about the nature of the gods. My purpose is not to deny its existence, but to

have you understand how obscure it is and how difficult to explain.

In the last sentence of the work Cicero says that the Epicurean, Velleius, was inclined to support Cotta's view, but that he himself believed that the views of the Stoic, Balbus, "seemed to be closer to the likeness of truth". As an Academic sceptic, Cicero could only commit himself to probability.

Theology was part of the philosophical category of physics, and so Cicero gives considerable attention to natural phenomena both on earth and in the heavens. Since he did not write a treatise on the physical aspects of the world it is worth mentioning here that he did, as a young man, translate into Latin hexameters the poem of the Stoic Aratus (*c.*315–240). Entitled *Phaenomena* (literally, "Appearances"), Aratus' poem gave an account of the constellations (lines 1–732) and of weather-signs (lines 733–1154), usually given a separate title, *Diosemeiai*. As part of the Stoic proof of divine governance of the world, Cicero quotes about eighty-five lines (out of about 575 extant) from his poem which was published perhaps six years before the dramatic date (76) of the dialogue.[119] By quoting the lines here Cicero is not showing any deep interest in astronomy or physics, and he is probably accurate when he makes Balbus say: "I will quote your *Aratea*, which so delight me, because they are Latin."[120] Cicero elsewhere makes Quintus quote twenty-three lines from the poem, which concern weather-signs.[121] Another Latin poet, Varro of Atax (born in 82 BCE), at about the time when Cicero was writing the *De Natura Deorum*, may have been composing his *Ephemeris* ("Almanac"), in which he adapted many lines from Aratus. Only two fragments are extant, and it is not known whether Cicero had any knowledge of the poem.[122]

In *De Natura Deorum* 3. 19 Balbus complains that Cotta is passing over important topics – specifically divination and fate – in silence, not giving him a chance to discuss them. Cicero had reserved them for separate works, *De Divinatione* and *De Fato*, both written in the first half of 44. In the preface to Book 2 of the *De Divinatione*, Cicero refers to the resumption of free political activity, that is, to the situation after the murder of Caesar on 15 March, while in *De Fato* 2 he makes an enquiry into the causes of the troubles after Caesar's death – the starting point for the work's discussion of causation. The extraordinary events of the time of composition made these works especially timely, for the custom of

Roman state religion demanded that the will of the gods be discovered in times of crisis, not least by means of divination. And knowledge of the divine will inevitably involved considerations of human free will, destiny and fate.

De Divinatione is in two books. In the first, Quintus Cicero (Cicero's brother) expounds the case for divination, which Marcus Cicero demolishes in the second. Quintus argues the Stoic case, which Cicero includes in his historical survey of divination that serves as the preface to Book 1.[123] Introducing his response, Cicero says to Quintus (2. 8):[124]

> You have defended Stoic doctrine in the Stoic manner and (a thing which gives me the greatest pleasure) you have used many Roman examples ... So I must reply to your discourse but in such a way that I should affirm nothing and question everything.

This is a neat summary of the problems that Cicero solved in composing the De Divinatione. For divination was indeed prominent in the Roman religious and political landscape.[125] Romulus himself had founded Rome with the aid of augury, and the Romans had early in their history adopted Etruscan methods of divination, to say nothing of the Sibylline Books, which had been consulted in Cicero's own lifetime.[126] There was considerable contemporary interest in divination and augury. For example, Cicero's friend, Aulus Caecina (from an Etruscan family), had written a work on the Disciplina Etrusca, which was used extensively by Seneca in his discussion of thunder and lightning.[127] In his correspondence with Caecina, Cicero shows great respect for him as a scholar but bases his political predictions on other grounds than divination, since Caesar had exiled Caecina from Italy and appeared to be implacable.[128]

Divination was approved by the Stoics.[129] Zeno approved of it, and both Chrysippus and Posidonius (as well as other Stoics) had written works on it, although Panaetius had had doubts. There was, then, a basis in philosophy, as well as in Roman religious and political custom, for arguments in support of divination. As a Roman statesman and augur Cicero could not dismiss them outright, but he could express doubt, that is, he could (and did) approach the topic from the point of view of Academic scepticism, relying particularly on Carneades for arguments against the Stoics.[130]

Cicero skilfully varied his methods, to produce "a multilayered work of surprising obliqueness and complexity".[131] In Book 1 Quintus indulges in what Schofield calls "the rhetoric of anecdote", that is, he supports his case with a multitude of examples, largely chosen from Roman history.[132] In Book 2, however, Cicero uses "the rhetoric of cross-examination", for example, the sharp questioning of 2. 85: "should we wait for animals to speak?", he asks, as opposed to acting on the best judgement of human reason. Or in 2. 56, where he cites the Theban seers who foretold the victory of Leuctra from the crowing of cocks: "that [i.e. the crowing] was the miracle", you say. "Well, what a surprise! As if fishes were crowing, not cocks!" Yet Cicero must respect the established place of divination and augury in Roman public life. Like the sceptical Cotta in *De Natura Deorum*, he defends them as an augur and a patriotic Roman:[133]

> In accordance with the opinion of the people and because these things are of great advantage to the state, we still maintain the customary ritual [of augury], its religious rites and discipline, the augural laws and the college of augurs.

Near the end of the work Cicero expands this by distinguishing between religion and superstition:[134]

> It will be greatly to our advantage and that of our fellow-Romans to root out superstition. But in removing superstition ... we must not remove religion. A wise man will preserve the traditional institutions by maintaining their rituals and ceremonies.

And having thus spoken as a Roman he ends as a sceptic:[135]

> The particular method of the Academy is not to interpose its own opinion but to approve those things which seem to be most like the truth. It will compare causes and expound the supporting arguments for each side. It will not bring its own authority to bear, but it will leave enquirers free to make their own judgement without prejudice.

Cicero calls this the Socratic method, and so the dialogue ends with an appeal to the iconic source of Academic scepticism.

In the third and final treatise on religion, *De Fato*, Cicero adopts quite a different method, described by Schofield:[136]

> [It] is technical, dense, intense, full of subtle dialectical twists and turns ... and devoted to an abstruse metaphysical topic. It conveys the interplay of ingenious minds arguing and putting fresh and unexpected lines of thought to each other better than any of Cicero's other philosophical writings ... It is the Ciceronian treatise philosophers most enjoy reading.

Schofield admits that works like the *De Divinatione* take "a lot of getting through for philosophers: it is too popular a read for them", which is testimony to Cicero's success in transmitting Greek philosophy to a Roman upper-class public which, by definition, was not made up of professional philosophers. The text of *De Fato* is fragmentary (perhaps one quarter of the whole is extant). Ostensibly a dialogue with Aulus Hirtius (consul designate for 43, the year in which he died) held at Cicero's villa at Puteoli shortly after Caesar's murder, it was written in May and June of 44, when the usual topics of discussion between Cicero and his friends were peace and withdrawal from public life (*pax et otium*). But the stunning events of 15 March inevitably led to consideration of their causes, and so to a discussion of fate. In *De Div.* 1. 127 Quintus says that "I will demonstrate in another place [that] everything happens by fate", a promise fulfilled by the *De Fato* (with Marcus as the speaker). In *De Fato* 4 Hirtius asks Cicero to propose a thesis and discuss it in the fashion of the *Tusculan Disputations*. The thesis (which is not given in the surviving part of the manuscript) must have been that contained in Quintus' words in *De Div.* 1. 127: "everything happens by fate" (*fato omnia fiunt*), and Cicero is the sole speaker discussing it.

Fate, providence and free will were prominent topics for the Stoics, Epicureans and Academics.[137] The Stoics believed in the supremacy of fate, and Chrysippus (whom Cicero quotes here extensively) had written a work *On Fate*. Likewise, Panaetius wrote a work on Providence, and Posidonius one on Divination and one on Fate.[138] Closely connected was the question of free will, which the Stoics allowed, for, they said, human beings still had moral choices which allowed them to choose to follow fate willingly. While (a century after Cicero) Seneca made this the principal topic of his dialogue *De Providentia* and of his 107th letter (in which he quotes lines from the *Hymn to Zeus* of Cleanthes expressing the doctrine), Cicero was more interested in the question of causation, which lies at the heart of the problems of fate and free will.[139] Cicero first denies the validity of the Stoic doctrine of "sympathy", that is that external factors (such as climate) determine human action (§§7–11). Later he turns to the so-called "lazy argument", which Chrysippus had criticized.[140] Cicero here relies on the syllogistic argument of Carneades. Finally, Cicero himself attacks the Epicurean grounds for positing free will, most notoriously by the doctrine of the "swerve" (Latin, *clinamen*) of atoms.[141]

Cicero had long been concerned with the question of free will. In a letter to Varro written in May, 46, he says that he has written a work on things possible (*Peri Dunaton*) which, he says, he had discussed with Diodotus, who did not agree with him.[142] Since Diodotus died in 59, Cicero had been thinking about the problem for at least fifteen years when he came to write the *De Fato*. As in the other theological works he takes the Academic approach, relying most particularly on Carneades' proof. This states that if we extend the chain of causality back infinitely, nothing can be left to free will: but, since we do make choices (and therefore exert free will), it cannot be said that all things happen through fate. Cicero argues the sceptical point of view with skill and exemplary logic, in a fashion quite different from the other theological works.

Cicero says in *De Div.* 2. 4 that he was eager to finish his programme of philosophical works but was interrupted by the events of the Ides of March. If he had done so, he says, "I would not have left any philosophical subject that was not open to all and illuminated by the Latin language". He believed then (shortly after the murder of Caesar) that he would immediately resume political activity and be unable to devote so much time to philosophy.[143] Since his effective political activity did not begin until September, 44, he still had time to write the short treatises on old age (which he does mention in the *De Divinatione* list), on glory (now lost), and on friendship, and his final major philosophical work, *De Officiis*, on duties, which was completed by December, 44, a year before his death. During this period he also wrote *Topica*, which, like the *Paradoxa Stoicorum* (written in 46), is more rhetorical than philosophical. We will postpone discussion of these works and turn now to other works that he names in the *De Divinatione* list.

First is the *De Republica*, published in 51 and written "when I still was steering the ship of state". This is accurate only in so far as Cicero was active in the senate and the courts, which continued to function according to the republican constitution. But in fact the constitution was inexorably and violently disintegrating and, since 60, political power rested with those who had money and military backing, that is, the members of the extra-constitutional alliance called the first triumvirate. These men (Pompey, Crassus and Caesar) renewed their alliance in 56, and soon after silenced Cicero, who had already been exiled in 58–57 with their tacit approval. For the next twelve years he was more or less impotent politically, although his oratory was occasionally useful when called for by the triumvirate, and he was proconsul of Cilicia for the year 51–50. Therefore he turned to philosophy as the way in which to continue his service to the state. Between 55 and 51 he wrote three works that linked philosophy to political leadership, perhaps his most original idea and certainly one foreshadowed in his early rhetorical work, *De Inventione*. The first of the three works was the *De Oratore*, published in 55. Since Cicero lists it after the *De Republica* as one of the *oratorii libri*, we will discuss it after the two political works, *De Republica* and *De Legibus*.

The *De Republica* is one of the fragmentary works of the ancient world whose missing parts are an inestimable loss. It was widely read in Cicero's time and into late antiquity, but by the seventh century it was so little valued that at the monastery of Bobbio a vellum manuscript, written in the fourth or early fifth century in a beautiful uncial hand (i.e. in large letters), was washed off and a manuscript of Augustine's *Commentary on the Psalms* was written over it. Thus the *De Republica* disappeared from sight, beyond fragmentary quotations in various Latin authors (including Augustine) and the *Dream of Scipio (Somnium Scipionis)* of Book 6, which survived intact in a separate tradition. In 1819 the Prefect of the Vatican Library, Cardinal Angelo Mai, discovered much of Cicero's text beneath that of Augustine, and he published it in 1822. Apart from the *Somnium* we have about two-thirds of Book 1, about half of Book 2, perhaps one-sixth of Book 3, and very little of the other three books. As for the *Somnium*, it survived with a Neoplatonist commentary by the fifth-century Christian author, Macrobius Theodosius.[144] Macrobius saw in Cicero's main speaker, Scipio Aemilianus, the union of all the virtues, and in the *Somnium* the union of all branches of philosophy.

Cicero did not have such an ambitious goal. The title of the work immediately draws attention to the model that he was emulating, Plato's *Republic*, although in the *De Divinatione* passage he mentions several other utopias by Peripatetic authors, while omitting the most notorious one, the *Republic* of the founder of Stoicism, Zeno.[145] To him the subject was "important and appropriate for philosophy",[146] precisely because it united politics and ethics, a traditional Roman attitude, implicit in Cato the Censor's definition of the orator, "the good man skilled in speaking". Now Plato had begun his *Republic* with a search for justice in the individual, which he expanded (by analogy) to justice in the state, returning finally to justice in the individual. Cicero found the unreality of Plato's ideal world unsatisfactory. In the introduction to his work he points out the contrast between the philosophers' teaching and the practical "school" of experience:[147]

> It is not enough to have virtue as if it were some sort of an art, unless you use it. It is true, I'll grant, that you can keep an art through knowledge, even if you do not use it. But virtue exists totally through its use. And its greatest use is the government of the state and the performance in real life, not in words, of those things that the philosophers lecture on in their corners. For there is nothing that the philosophers have said – at least nothing right and honourable – that has not been evolved and confirmed by those who have been lawgivers for states.

Thus Cicero's Republic will not be a utopia: his search will be for the ideal government and the ideal leadership for an actual state, Rome. His Republic is the reality of which Plato's is but the idea – an ironic reversal![148]

Cicero's first problem was to choose the dramatic time and the participants. He decided against setting the dialogue in his own time, for it would have been politically dangerous to have living statesmen as the speakers.[149] As we have already seen, he looked back to the third quarter of the second century as the period when the Roman republic began to decay politically and morally, and he saw Scipio Aemilianus as the best Roman leader, whatever flaws there actually were in his character and policies. We have seen also how external events of the mid-second century (the defeat of Perseus of Macedon, the destruction of Carthage, Corinth and Numantia), and in Rome the influx of Greek intellectuals and the tribunate of Tiberius Gracchus, caused cultural, social and political upheavals. Cicero was shrewd to set the dialogue in Rome of 129, a time, like the late 50s, of political instability and shortly before the death of Scipio himself, whom he made the principal speaker.[150] The dialogue is set in the grounds of the leader's suburban villa at the time of the *feriae Latinae*. Scipio is joined by eight friends, four senior politicians and four younger men. Of the former group, Laelius "the wise" had been consul in 140; Furius Philus had been consul in 136, and Manilius (an expert on the law), had been consul in 149, when Scipio served under him as military tribune.[151] The fourth senior, Spurius Mummius, was the brother of the Mummius who destroyed Corinth and was one of the two senators, along with Scipio (who was accompanied by Panaetius), sent by the senate on the embassy to Egypt and the east in 140–139. Of the four younger men, only Rutilius Rufus deserves mention here. He would have been 25 years old in 129, and Cicero visited him when he was in exile in Smyrna fifty years later. Cicero claims that Rutilius was the source for the conversations in Scipio's garden.[152]

The introduction to Book 1 is elaborate. Its apparent purpose is structural, to bring together the nine participants in the dialogue. But its main function is to establish the proper subjects for philosophical enquiry in Rome. The conversation is directed towards celestial events, in which, Scipio says, "our friend Panaetius used to be such a careful observer".[153] But, he adds, Socrates was wiser for turning away from such subjects. Eventually, after some discussion of astronomy, Laelius leads the conversation to affairs at Rome.[154] Those "Greek studies", he says, are valuable for sharpening the minds of the young, but they are preparatory for more important studies:

> those arts that make us useful to the state. For I think that that is the most excellent function of wisdom, and that it is the best evidence of virtue and its highest duty ... Therefore, let us ask Scipio to explain to us what he thinks is the best form of government (*optimum statum civitatis*).

Thus Cicero establishes his topic. Perhaps we can be critical of the length of the introduction, but it is intrinsically important for the contrast it draws between Greek enquiries into the physical world (it is convenient here for Cicero to overlook Greek ethical and political philosophy!), and the record of the Romans in political administration. It was a commonplace among Romans that the Greeks, for all their intellectual brilliance, never achieved political unity, and evidence for that was the conquest of Greece by Rome, only seventeen years before the dramatic date of the dialogue. Now, says Laelius, at a time when Roman political unity is threatened, no topic could be more important than "those arts that make us useful to the state". Further, the abortive discussion of astronomy is structurally connected with the dream with which the work ends. The work begins with the heavens as an object of study, and it ends with them as the proper home of the souls of the virtuous. It begins with the heavens separated from human beings, and it ends with the undivided universe, which human and divine beings share in timeless unity.

There are two subjects in the main discussion, as Cicero had explained in the letter to his brother Quintus.[155] First, "What is the best constitution of the state?", and, second, "Who is the best citizen?" The first question occupies the first two books and the second the last two. Book 5 began with a quotation of Ennius' famous line, "the Roman state stands firm by means of old-fashioned customs and men of old-fashioned character".[156] Book 6 ended with the description of the ideal leader and his place in the universe and in eternity, as opposed to the particular place and time of Rome in 129 BCE. Books 3 and 4 contained a discussion of the education and laws that would produce the ideal citizen. The dialogue took three days, two books for each day.

Scipio's accepts Laelius' invitation, once again drawing the contrast between Greek theory and his own training in traditional Roman precepts and his practical experience in public service. He will speak as "one of those who wear the [Roman] toga".[157] His main exposition begins with the brief definition of a republic: "a republic belongs to the people".[158] Then he considers the development of societies and surveys three types of government (monarchy, aristocracy and democracy), concluding that the best form is the "mixed" constitution, with elements of all three. When pressed by Laelius, Scipio admits that monarchy is the best of the three, because the sole ruler is the strongest executive.[159] In this Scipio seems to be anticipating arguments for a single "governor of state" (*rector reipublicae*) in Books 5 and 6, which, however, have been shown by Jonathan Powell to apply to more than one *rector* at the same time.[160] Here, as James Zetzel points out, "the argument in favour of monarchy ... emphasizes the problems of administration rather than the problem of rights".[161] Thus the discussion of the mixed constitution, which draws so much from Book 6 of Polybius' *Histories* and Book 8 of Plato's *Republic*, is given a Roman colouring appropriate to the problems of political rights and political power that (in Cicero's view) began with the tribunate of Tiberius Gracchus and led to the imminent collapse of the republic in the 50s BCE.

In Book 2 Scipio surveys the historical development of the Roman state. While Cicero owes much here to Polybius, the key statement is at the beginning, where Scipio acknowledges his debt to Cato the Elder:[162]

> he used to say that the reason for the superiority of our constitution was that in other states a single man had established the constitution by his laws and institutions. The Roman state had been established, not by the genius of one man, but of many. It had evolved not in the lifetime of one man, but over a period of many centuries and ages.

Whatever this passage says about Cato's theory of history,[163] it gives Scipio's basis for his view of Roman history, summed up in the line from Ennius quoted above. Scipio shows that the Roman constitution has evolved through the labours and virtues of individuals, but, as Tubero objects (2. 64), he has not discussed the education (*disciplina*), customs (*mores*) and laws (*leges*) which establish and maintain the state. These are the topics of Books 3 and 4.

Book 3 is concerned with the laws and therefore with justice in the state. As we have seen in the second chapter, Philus unwillingly undertakes to argue Carneades' view that a state cannot be successful without injustice.[164] Less is extant of Laelius' reply defending justice, which he bases on natural law.[165] His definition is eloquent:

> True law is right reason in accordance with nature. It applies to all human beings, it is unchanging and eternal. It calls one to duty by its command, and it deters one from wrongdoing by its prohibition. It never commands good people in vain, and never affects the bad by its commands or prohibitions. This law cannot be superseded, amended or repealed. Indeed, neither the senate nor the people can release us from this law, which needs neither commentary nor interpretation. Nor will there be one law in Rome, another in Athens; one now, another in the future, for one eternal and unchangeable law will apply to all peoples at all

73

times. There will be one master and commander for all – the god, who proposed, arbitrated and carried this law. He who disobeys this law is running away from himself and despising human nature.

The basis of this noble ideal is Stoic, for the Stoics taught that moral principles were laws of nature applicable to all human beings, of whatever time or place.[166] Whereas Plato had separated his world of ideas from the world of particulars, the Stoics emphasized the unity of the whole universe. Cicero goes further in applying the ideal of natural law to the Roman state, which, as Laelius says (3. 34), "ought to be so constituted as to be eternal". Thus a particular Roman statesman, Laelius, at a particular time, enunciates to an audience of Roman leaders an ideal that will be attainable in the *Roman* state. To underline this, Cicero uses Roman legal terms throughout the passage – the words for the processes of proposing and legislating, emending and annulling, are all common in the Latin technical and legal vocabulary. We may deplore the irony that the ideals of Laelius in 129, and of Cicero in 54–51, were little heeded and quite disconnected from the harsh realities of political power, but we must admire Cicero's vision of a better Roman political life.

Very little remains of Book 4, but enough to show that the discussion now turned to the training of the good citizen. Thus, Cicero prepared the way for consideration of the good citizen, the second of his major subjects, which is the topic of the third day's discussion, contained in Books 5 and 6. Book 5 (which survives only in a few fragments) begins with the oracular line from Ennius, immediately establishing a Roman context for the ideal citizen. Scipio evidently described the virtues of the ancient Roman leaders, which he applied to the ideal of the virtuous leader. This leader is called by the terms "governor", "steersman", "driver" (in Latin, respectively, *rector*, *gubernator*, *moderator*), all significant metaphors. As *rector*, the leader keeps the state and its citizens on a straight path with upright morality; as *gubernator*, he steers the ship of state (a metaphor that goes back to the poems of Alcaeus in the seventh century BCE); as *moderator* he drives the team of the chariot of state, reining in the citizens or relaxing his control in accordance with what is right. Cicero is not describing a single *rector rei publicae*, but the qualities and attributes of an ideal *rector*, who might be one of several existing at the same time or, exceptionally, a single *rector* if the times demand such a statesman.[167] It is most unlikely that Cicero had any particular contemporary leader in mind, and it is a waste of time to try to see in his *rector* a model for modern leaders, as has been attempted, most unfortunately, by too many commentators and politicians.[168] What is important is, first, that Cicero linked morality to political life; second, that he described his *rector* in a Roman context and in Roman terms.

None of Book 6 survives in the Vatican manuscript, but a few quotations by ancient authors survive, along with the *Dream of Scipio* and the commentary of Macrobius, which were combined only in five medieval manuscripts. Scipio introduces the subject of the rewards of the virtuous leader, which, in contrast to the metal statues and fading triumphal laurels of Roman leaders, are lasting and for ever fresh (6. 8). Laelius invites him then to describe them. The dream is Scipio's reply. It takes his hearers back to the heavens, where the discussion had begun on the first day. But now the heavens are in the same universe as that of the participants: the union of ideal and particular that underlies Laelius' definition of natural law (in 3. 33) finds its climax in the cosmos, the home of the divine human soul and the place to which it returns, the more quickly if its corporeal life on earth has been virtuous. And Cicero has already shown that the most virtuous person is the one who serves his country well. Such a person was Scipio (at least for the purposes of the *De Republica*).

In the introduction to Book 6 Cicero mentions the myth of Er, with which Plato's *Republic* ends, and this undoubtedly was his model. Here again he successfully transferred his myth from the realm of the impossible to the Roman world. As Zetzel has remarked, "the *Somnium* requires no suspension of disbelief".[169] A real Roman leader relates his dream, and he sets it in a real place, the palace of the Numidian king, Masinissa, in north Africa, at an actual time, 149 BCE (whether or not Scipio did visit Masinissa that year, rather than two years earlier, is irrelevant). At the dramatic date of the dream Masinissa was about ninety years old, and he provides the historical link with the Roman heroes of the second Punic war (which ended in 202 BCE), when he was the staunch ally of Scipio Africanus Maior, the grandfather (by adoption) of Scipio Aemilianus. The elder Scipio, together with the younger Scipio's natural father (Aemilius Paullus, another Roman military hero), are the principal speakers in the *Somnium* – another way in which Cicero unites the ideal world with Roman reality. Thus the divine cosmos and the actual Roman world are joined, for the virtuous leader ascends to the divine realm, to rejoin god, who is the *rector* of the universe. Raised to the heavens, Scipio (the dreamer) looks down on the earth and sees the universe in its true perspective. The earth is central, but its scale – and therefore the glory of its virtuous leaders – is insignificant in comparison with the heavens and the eternal glory which the virtuous soul will attain.

At the beginning of the dream Africanus foretells Scipio's career and death (§§11–12): he enunciates the reward for Scipio's virtuous actions (§13):

> For all who have saved, defended or increased their father-land, a special place in the heaven has been assigned, where they may enjoy an eternal life of happiness. For nothing that is done on earth is more pleasing to that supreme god, who governs the whole universe, than the councils and assemblies of men who have joined in just communities, which are called states (*civitates*). Those who govern and defend them come from this place, and to this place they return.

Thus the relationship between the virtuous leader and the eternal cosmic reward is established. Scipio's natural father, Aemilius Paullus, then appears (§§14–16) and urges Scipio to recognize the high seriousness of his duty in life, when his immortal soul is imprisoned in a mortal body, to act virtuously and not to leave the body (Aemilius is referring to suicide) until god releases it. He has been assigned a duty in life as if it were a military assignment: to leave it would be the equivalent of desertion. Paullus then succinctly describes this duty (§16):

> Imitate your grandfather, imitate me, your father, and love justice and duty (*pietas*), which is owed to parents and family, and most of all to one's fatherland. This is your way to heaven.

And then (§§16–26) Paullus and Africanus show Scipio the cosmos as it is in its true proportions, and they explain its astronomical organization: in this Cicero is to some extent imitating Plato (in the myth of Er and in the *Timaeus*), but his purpose is different, which is to show the proper relationship of the earth and its temporal events to the cosmos and eternity. Scipio on earth is encouraged to fix his gaze on the heavens and be drawn to the true and eternal rewards of virtue. Speaking of the soul, Africanus says, "Know, then, that you are a god" (§26): like god the soul is self-moving and eternal (§27) and therefore should be employed in the highest calling (§29):

> Use this [soul], then, in the noblest activity, which is the service of your country. And if the soul is trained and engaged in such deeds, it will fly more quickly to this, its dwelling-place and home.

So ends the *De Republica* (at least, as we now have it: perhaps there was a closing passage in which the participants left Scipio in his garden). More than any other of Cicero's philosophical works it shows the extent of his originality. It makes no pretence of complete originality, for Roman authors preferred to practise emulation (*aemulatio*) rather than imitation or innovation, not that the latter modes were ignored. Cicero, then, acknowledges his debt to Plato (which is clearly shown to be to the *Phaedrus* as well as to the *Republic* and the *Timaeus*), but he recasts the Platonic material – and, no doubt, much else from the Greek philosophers – in the context of Roman history, politics and society. Cicero's doctrine that there is a practical connection between the morality of citizens and their leaders and the success of the state, is quite different from Plato's analogy of the just state to the just individual. Finally, Cicero presents his republic in Latin of remarkable flexibility and range of style, which rises in Laelius' speech and Scipio's dream to a sublime level.[170]

The third of Cicero's political/philosophical treatises from the 50s BCE was the *De Legibus*, which he does not mention in the list in the *De Divinatione*.[171] He seems to have begun it in 52 and left it unfinished when he went to Cilicia in 51. There is no firm evidence that he returned to it, and it was not published during his lifetime. Surviving are most of the first three books, but we do not know how many books were planned or written, beyond a single reference by Macrobius to Book 5. In this work Cicero himself is the main speaker, and the participants are his brother Quintus and his friend Atticus. The setting is a summer day at his family property at Arpinum, lovingly described at the beginning of each of the first two books, where the dialogue is set on the banks of the River Liris and on an island in the river. In the introduction to Book 2 (2. 6) Cicero compares the setting to the famous opening of Plato's *Phaedrus*, another example of his emulation of Plato. His attention

77

to the setting is purposeful, for it establishes his personal involvement with Italy and with Rome and its historical virtues, not least among which is the rule of law. In Book 1 he shows that the *De Legibus* is essentially a continuation of the *De Republica*, for, he says (§20):

> since we must maintain and preserve that constitution which Scipio showed to be the best in those six books, and since all laws must be fitted to that sort of state, and since we must sow the seed of morality (and must not prescribe everything in writing) – since this is so, I will review the origin of law in Nature. She will be our guide for the whole of our discussion.

Cicero, then, repeats the theory of natural law expounded by Laelius in Book 3 of the *De Republica* and once again links ethical values to political institutions.

In Book 1 Cicero discusses natural law, which is the basis of justice, and therefore of relations between human beings (1. 28). Justice must be pursued for its own sake, and this principle will apply to all the virtues (1. 48). Quintus makes the objection that the discussion of ethical principles has little to do with the main subject, that is the laws (1. 57), but, as Marcus replies, the law must reform vice and commend virtue (1. 58). Therefore wisdom – the result of the search for virtue – is indeed relevant to a discussion of the law, and Cicero ends the book with a speech in praise of wisdom (1. 62). The discussion, then, reaffirms the conclusion of the *De Republica*, that moral excellence must be the foundation of the successful state.

In Book 2 Cicero discusses religious laws. Like a lawgiver (or, as Quintus points out, 2. 23, like Numa, the founder of Roman religious laws), Cicero pronounces the text of his laws and then gives a commentary.[172] Next, in Book 3, he discusses the offices, powers and functions of the magistrates, giving the text of his laws, followed by his commentary.[173] Both books are remarkable for Cicero's use of Latin legal language and for the adaptation of Greek ideas to a Roman context. He acknowledges his debt to Plato's *Laws*, but he adds:[174]

> Who could ever imitate Plato? It is, to be sure, very easy to translate his opinions, and this I would do, if I did not

clearly want to be my own person. For how much effort is it to say the same things in translation in the same words?

This is crucial to our estimate of Cicero's originality here and in the *De Republica*. He names his Greek models in 3. 13–14, including Theophrastus and others who had written on the laws. Most of the Greek works, he says, were theoretical, but he praises Demetrius of Phalerum (a student of Theophrastus and governor of Athens in the late fourth century) as the first to bring the discussion of law "out of the shadows of scholarship into the sunlight and dust" of practical politics. Cicero emphasizes that he too is one who has excelled in theoretical studies and in political leadership. Thus, he claims that he has expanded legal theory from its basis in Greek philosophy by adapting it to Roman law and custom and creating a Roman legal terminology. He claims further that his political career and his experience as an orator and jurist qualify him uniquely to propose a Roman legal code. As in the *De Republica*, Cicero seeks to construct an ideal *Roman* system, and he appeals to his knowledge of Greek philosophy and theory, on the one hand, and to his practical experience in Roman life, on the other, to support his goal of "being his own person". It has been suggested above that there is considerable originality in the *De Republica*, and we can confidently say the same of the *De Legibus*.

At the end of the *De Divinatione* list (*De Div.* 2. 4), Cicero says that he followed the example of Aristotle and Theophrastus in composing rhetorical works which united the precepts of rhetoric with philosophy. Here he names three works: *De Oratore*, *Brutus*, *Orator*. The first of these was written in 55, and therefore belongs to the period of Cicero's political impotence, during which he wrote the *De Republica* and some of the *De Legibus*. It is the most important of the three for an understanding of Cicero's philosophy. The *Brutus* (written in 46) is valuable for Cicero's account of his own philosophical development and for his criticism of the Stoic, Academic and Peripatetic schools in so far as they concern the orator.[175] The work is chiefly important as a critical review of Roman orators, while the *Orator*, also from 46), is principally a rhetorical work, although it, too, stresses the link between philosophy and rhetoric.[176]

Cicero had focused on this link in his earliest rhetorical work, *Rhetorici Libri* ("Books on Rhetoric", usually referred to as *De Inventione*), which he does not name in the *De Divinatione* list. It was written in the late 80s, that is, before Cicero made his journey to Athens and the east (probably before 84). Cicero dismisses it as being the unpolished product of a very young man, "not worthy of this age [i.e. Cicero's maturity] and of the experience that I have gained in so many important cases".[177] Yet the *De Inventione* announces Cicero's conviction that philosophy and rhetoric are interdependent.[178] He says that "wisdom is the guide (*moderatrix*) in everything", and he shows in the introduction to the work how political leaders who have eloquence without wisdom are demagogues who ruin the state.[179] These are fundamental themes in the *De Oratore* and the *De Republica*, and it is in order to boost the mature works that Cicero depreciates his early work.

The *De Oratore* is one of Cicero's most original works, although its length (three long books) has limited its popularity in modern times. It is a dialogue taking place over two days, set in the grounds of the Tusculan villa of M. Antonius (consul in 99) during the *Ludi Romani* of September 91. Five of the seven participants are Roman senior statesmen, and two are younger politicians of great promise. Except for C. Aurelius Cotta (exiled in 90 but recalled in 82: consul in 75) all died within a short time of the dramatic date of the dialogue, four of them murdered or driven to suicide by the supporters of Marius in the early 80s. The principal speakers are L. Licinius Crassus (consul in 95), the greatest orator of his day and revered by Cicero, whose opinions are closest to those of Cicero. He died ten days after the dramatic date of the dialogue, which honours his memory. The introduction to Book 3 is a deeply felt tribute to him and a lament for the fate of the other participants who died violently shortly afterwards. The second principal speaker is M. Antonius, consul in 99, and the closest rival to Crassus as an orator. He was murdered by the Marians in 87. In the dialogue he takes a pragmatic view of oratory and defines the ideal orator in narrower terms than Crassus.[180] The older generation is represented by Q. Mucius Scaevola, consul in 117 and known as "the Augur", who participates only in Book 1, the first day's conversation.[181] Two other senior statesmen participate in the second day's conversations (Books 2 and 3), Q. Lutatius Catulus (consul in 102 and father-in-law of Cicero's friend and rival, Hortensius), and C. Julius Caesar Strabo, aedile in 90, the year following the dialogue. Both of these men died in the Marian troubles – Catulus driven to suicide and Strabo murdered.[182] Closer in age to Cicero were P. Sulpicius (tribune in 88), who was murdered by the Marians, and Cotta (the only one of the seven participants to survive for any length of time), whom Cicero made the principal speaker in the *De Natura Deorum*. He is represented as the source for the conversations of the *De Oratore*.[183]

Cicero's choice of participants is significant. Writing in 55 and observing the collapse of constitutional processes, he looks back to another year, 91, when the principled statesmanship of leaders such as Crassus and Antonius was about to give way to the violence of the following decade, in which so many of the participants perished. The message is clear: only if political leaders (who are, by definition, orators) are men of principle and versed in philosophy, can constitutional government survive. On a personal level, Cicero pays homage to the leading orators of his early days, several of whom had been associates of Scipio Aemilianus and his friends.

In the introduction to Book 1, Cicero calls philosophy "the mother of all the praiseworthy arts" (§9). Later, Crassus repeats that leaders who were both philosophers and orators unified scattered communities and organized them into states with stable constitutions.[184] Crassus recalls his visit to Athens twenty years earlier, where he had associated with philosophers who had themselves been students of Panaetius or Critolaus or Carneades, all of whom segregated philosophy from public life.[185] As Crassus goes on to say, Plato himself, in pouring scorn on orators, showed himself to be a supreme orator.

Antonius replies to Crassus' description of the orator and his training. He defines the political leader "as the man who maintains and uses those things which result in the advantage and growth of the state".[186] He then gives his definition of the philosopher:[187]

> he who studies to know the power, the nature and the causes of all things divine and human, and to obtain and pursue every rational precept for the good life.

In amplifying his definitions (which extend also to the jurist and the orator) Antonius is forthright on the limits of the orator's training: he needs to be clever in discerning the expectations and psychology of the people he seeks to persuade.[188] As for philosophy:[189]

let him reserve the philosophers' books for himself for a holiday like the one we are enjoying to-day at Tusculum, when we are not being active in politics, so that if he does ever have to make a speech about justice and good faith, he will not need to borrow from Plato.

And, as Antonius continues to point out, Plato's republic had little to do with the politics and ethics of real cities.

Cicero resolves the debate between Crassus and Antonius in Book 3, where Crassus introduces a long digression on philosophy into his discussion of style.[190] He shows that the greatest leaders in Greece and Rome were also *sapientes* (§56), and he shows that even in the heroic age those who were tutors in living well were also teachers of oratory – Homer's Phoenix taught Achilles how to speak and how to act (§57). So philosophy was not segregated from rhetoric, for "she was the mistress both of right actions and right words": once again the allusion is to Cato's definition of the orator. Crassus ends his argument for the union of philosophy and rhetoric by modifying and uniting the definitions of Antonius:[191]

Now if anyone wishes to define the philosopher who provides us with a supply of subject-matter and words, as far as I am concerned he can call him an orator. And if he prefers to call the orator, who (I say) combines wisdom and eloquence, a philosopher, I won't stop him ... If I do have to choose [between a knowledgeable but incompetent speaker and one who is ignorant but loquacious], I would prefer tongue-tied wisdom to eloquent foolishness.

Crassus speaks here for Cicero. In good Academic fashion, he has examined all sides of the question (a type of argument that he refers to at 3. 107), and he has reached the most probable conclusion. It is one that is best for the state, and, for Cicero writing in 55 BCE, one that best prepares him for writing *De Republica* and *De Legibus*.

In the *De Divinatione* list Cicero mentions his work *De Senectute* ("On Old Age"). It is one of three shorter treatises that he wrote in 44 BCE and the only one that preceded the *De Divinatione*. The others were the *De Gloria* and the *De Amicitia*, both completed before the *De Officiis*. The *De Gloria* is lost, but from Cicero's letters and the *De Officiis* we know that it was in two books, and that Cicero was pleased with it.[192] From the introduction to Valerius

Maximus' chapter *De Gloria* we can guess that Cicero dealt with the origins and definition of glory, and its relationship to virtue.[193]

The *De Senectute*, also known as *Cato Maior* from the name of its principal speaker, is perhaps the most attractive of Cicero's philosophical works, and it is one of very few that has kept a regular place in school and undergraduate curricula. It appeals to the young, who have found in its atmosphere of friendship and self-fulfilment an attractive invitation to consider the inevitable experience of old age. This may be a distant prospect to the young, but to Cicero (and to Atticus, to whom the work is dedicated) it was more immediate (Cicero was sixty-two years old at the time of writing, and Atticus was sixty-six). Thus the work is not only a review of the life of the elder Cato, but also of Cicero's own life and career. He found in it comfort for his own situation in 44 BCE (§2), and he rightly chose to make a historical Roman figure (Cato) the speaker, rather than to set the discussion in a mythical context, as Ariston had done.[194]

Cato's listeners are Laelius and Scipio Aemilianus, and the setting is Cato's house in 150 BCE, a few months before his death. Cicero takes us to the world of the *De Republica* and its ideals. Just as he (in 44 BCE) is reviewing his life for the benefit of the young, so Cato is portrayed with two prominent leaders of the next generation. His speech, then, is a legacy for them. Cicero himself admits that Cato is made to argue more eruditely than he ever did in reality, but he also points out that in his old age Cato was a serious student of Greek books (§3). Cicero does not address the problem that strikes modern readers, that is, how to reconcile Cato's mellow persona in this work with his well-known austerity and frequent inhumanity.[195] Rather than try to defend Cato, it is better to admit that Cicero overlooked this unattractive side of him in the interests of portraying him as a patriot and defender of the republic.

Laelius proposes the topic (§4): "old age is a hateful burden to most old men". Cato, after some preliminary dialogue, replies with an unbroken speech (§§8–85). He identifies four reasons to support Laelius' thesis: that old age compels one to retire from activity; that it results in physical weakness; that it removes physical pleasures; that it is close to death. Each of these he refutes in turn, often with reference to his own life and with a wealth of examples from Roman history. One remarkable passage is his praise of the pleasures of farming (§§51–60), Cicero's special tribute to the author of the *De Agri Cultura*, but also a statement of the traditional prejudice of the

Roman senatorial class for income from landowning rather than business activities. Cato cites as an example of the political leader who serves his country selflessly L. Quinctius Cincinnatus, the historical icon of the leader–farmer.[196] He was called from the plough to serve as Dictator in the crisis of 458 BCE and laid down his office within sixteen days on completion of his task. At the end of his speech Cato puts his own career in a perspective that we have already met in the *De Republica*.[197] The reward of a virtuous life spent in service of the state is the fame of posterity and reunion with the souls of the virtuous after death:

> No one will ever persuade me, Scipio, that your father, Paullus, or your grandfathers, Paullus and Africanus, ... would have attempted such great deeds ... if they did not think that posterity had a direct connection with them. Or ... do you think that I would have undertaken such huge tasks night and day, in peace and in war, if I had thought my glory was to be limited to the term of my life? Would it not have been much better for me to have lived a peaceful and retired life, without any labour and competition? Yet somehow my soul was alert and always had posterity in view, as if it would then finally be alive once it had left this life. And if it were not the case that the soul is immortal, the souls of the best men would not strive most of all to win immortal glory.

The line from the *De Republica* through the *De Senectute* to the *De Officiis* is unbroken. Virtue in the service of the state is for Cicero the highest calling and brings the greatest reward.

The third of the shorter treatises is the *De Amicitia* ("On Friendship"). Here Cicero makes Q. Mucius Scaevola (the Augur) the first speaker. He had taken part in the first book of the *De Oratore* and Cicero brings him on stage here as the son-in-law of Laelius, who is the principal speaker: the dialogue is often referred to as *Laelius*. Laelius himself, as the friend of Scipio Aemilianus, was a paragon of friendship. The dramatic date of the conversation that Scaevola reports to his student, the young Cicero, is 129 BCE, a few days after the death of Scipio Aemilianus. Cicero returns, then, to the contemporaries of Scipio for his evocation of virtuous relationships in public life.

Laelius' main speech extends from §16 to §104, with interruptions from Fannius (consul in 122), the third participant, at §25 and §32. Fannius defines the subject at §16: "Tell us, Laelius, your views on the nature of friendship and give us precepts for it." Laelius gives a famous definition (§20):

> The great power of friendship can be realised from this, that from the unbounded community of the human race (ties that nature herself has established) friendship has been so concentrated that all affection is between two, or a few, persons.

Friendship was of great importance in Greek life, as Aristotle's treatment of it in Books 8 and 9 of the *Nicomachean Ethics* shows, and for the Romans it was important not only in personal relationships but also in public life. The stresses caused in friendships by political differences are vividly displayed in Cicero's exchange of letters with his friend, Matius, in August of 44.[198] Matius had been an intimate friend, confidant and adviser of Caesar. He had been loyal to Caesar's memory after the Ides of March, and Cicero had been critical of this and of Matius' closeness to Caesar when he was alive. Cicero's criticisms had reached Matius, who asked their mutual friend, Trebatius, to complain to Cicero. Cicero then wrote to Matius to answer his complaint and reassure him of his unshaken friendship, and Matius, in his turn, accepted Cicero's defence but still held to his own views of his friendship with Caesar. These letters illuminate some of the arguments made in the *De Amicitia*, notably the precepts on candour in §§44 and 65, and they show the practical side of the theoretical discussion in the dialogue.

Friendship was problematic for all the chief philosophical schools. For the Stoics it was inconsistent with the ideal of self-sufficiency, and they based their theory of friendship on virtue, saying that friendship could exist only between virtuous people.[199] Laelius, indeed, says (§18) that "friendship can only exist between good people", but he points out also that the Stoic ideal of friendship between wise men is impractical, because the Stoic *sapiens* is an impossible ideal. Therefore he gives his precepts in practical terms: his examples are drawn from Roman history, and his precepts are attainable. He ends with a glowing testimony to Scipio's friendship (§§102–04): it was the greatest of all blessings in his life, and his memory of Scipio will never perish, because their friendship was founded on virtue. So Laelius concludes with this advice for his younger hearers:

I encourage you so to value virtue (without which friendship is not possible) that you think that nothing, except
virtue, can be preferred to friendship.

The Stoics, then, were closer to the doctrines of Plato and
Aristotle. Plato saw friendship as an effort, based on reason, to
achieve an ideal relationship in this temporal life, while Aristotle
saw friendship in the context of the life of the community – a
doctrine consistent with the Stoic ideal of public service. Epicurus
took quite a different approach, for he based his theory on the
usefulness of friendship as a means towards a tranquil life of pleasure. Cicero expounds the Epicurean theory in Torquatus' speech in
Book 1 of *De Finibus*, refuting it himself in the next book.[200] The
difference between the Stoic and Ciceronian views and that of the
Epicureans has some bearing on the *De Amicitia*, in that the work
was dedicated to Atticus, who was an Epicurean.[201] It seems that
Atticus enjoyed friendship for its own sake, whatever the theory
behind it, and he would have approved of Laelius' statement at *De
Amicitia* 27 BCE:

friendship seems to me to spring from nature, not from
need; from the attachment of the soul together with a
feeling of love, more than from calculation of how useful it
will be.

Before we turn to the *De Officiis*, we should briefly mention two
other philosophical works. The first is the *Topica*, which Cicero says
he wrote for his friend, Trebatius, during the sea voyage between
Velia and Rhegium (towns on the south-western coast of Italy about
225 kilometers apart by sea), on his abortive journey to Athens in
July of 44. He wrote it without access to books, and his purpose
was to help Trebatius study Aristotle's *Topica*, which he had begun
to read in Cicero's library.[202] Cicero's *Topica*, however, is nothing
like Aristotle's *Topica*, which he probably had not read.[203] The work
is both rhetorical and philosophical. Cicero divides rhetorical theory
(*ratio disserendi*) into two parts, *inventio* (devising of arguments) and
iudicandum (evaluating their validity), and he says that Aristotle was
the major figure in discussing them. The Stoics, he says, elaborated
the latter in their dialectic, but they ignored the former (*inventio*,
Greek *topike*), which is to be his primary subject.[204] The work, then,
derives ultimately from Aristotle, although there can be no
certainty about the extent and depth of Cicero's reading of

Aristotle. In the discussion of consequences and antecedents (§§53–57), which Cicero describes as "a topic appropriate to dialectic", and the following discussion of causes (§§58–67), Cicero shows that he is master of logical argument, for example, in his use of the syllogism in §§53–55.[205] Boethius (c. 520 CE) certainly took the *Topica* seriously as a philosophical work and wrote a commentary in seven books, of which five and a part of the sixth survive, covering seventy-six of the 100 chapters.[206]

The second work still to be mentioned is Cicero's translation of part of Plato's *Timaeus*, of which only part of the preface and the translation of *Timaeus* 5–16 are extant. Cicero made the translation after the death in 45 of his friend Nigidius Figulus, said to be the most learned of Romans after Varro. Nigidius was a Pythagorean (as Cicero says in the first chapter of the *Timaeus*), who wrote works on the natural world and the cosmos, as well as on grammar. He was especially interested in divination and astrology, which we will discuss later in connection with Manilius. He was a senator (Praetor in 58) and a supporter of Pompey, and he went into exile after Caesar's victory at Pharsalus. In August of 46 Cicero wrote a moving consolation to him to comfort him in exile.[207] To Cicero he was "the most learned and the purest of men", whose friendship had been shown in his support when Cicero had been in despair.[208] The *Timaeus* is a memorial to Nigidius. In its preface Cicero describes how Nigidius had met him at Ephesus, in company with the Peripatetic philosopher, Cratippus, when he was travelling to take up his post as governor of Cilicia in 51. Nigidius would have been Cicero's interlocutor in the missing parts of the introduction to the translation. It was appropriate for Cicero to associate Plato's dialogue on cosmology with the scholar who, of all his contemporaries, was most interested in the stars and the cosmos.

Cicero's last philosophical work has also proved to be the most influential. The *De Officiis* (usually translated as *On Duties*) was written in the later part of 44, the period when Cicero had resumed political activity as the most outspoken opponent of Mark Antony. He first mentions the work in a letter to Atticus of 25 October, and less than two weeks later (5 November) he reports that he has finished the first two books.[209] The third book seems to have been completed before 9 December. Thus the work was written in a very short time indeed (even supposing that Cicero had been reflecting on it as early as July of 44), and it is both more personal and less carefully written than the dialogues. We do not know when it was published: Horace's poem on Regulus probably echoes Cicero's discussion of Regulus.[210] The poem was published in 23 BCE, giving a possible *terminus ante quem* for publication.

The work is addressed to Cicero's son, Marcus, at the time a student in Athens under the Peripatetic philosopher, Cratippus. Cicero had known Cratippus since at least 51, when he joined Nigidius Figulus at Ephesus, and Cicero had used his influence with Caesar to obtain Roman citizenship for him. Marcus (the son) was neither diligent nor disciplined, and Cicero was sufficiently anxious about him to contemplate (and begin) a voyage to Athens in July, 44. The political news from Rome, however, made him turn back, and the *De Officiis* took the place of his visit.[211] Thus the work is in the form of a letter, and each of the three books has a preface addressed to Marcus. It is more than likely that Cicero had in mind Cato the Elder, who in his old age addressed a hortatory work, *Ad Marcum*, to his son.[212] Cicero addresses Marcus 32 times directly: when he uses the formal address of "Marcus, my son" (*Marce fili*), he is speaking with full paternal authority, a powerful concept in Roman society. Thus at 1. 78, he says:

> I have the right, Marcus, my son, to boast to you, for yours is the legacy of my glory and the [duty of] imitating my deeds.

We are inescapably reminded of the Roman funeral in Polybius (6. 53–54), with its focus on the dead man's moral legacy to the next generation. Thus, the work is both an exhortation to Marcus and Cicero's testament. In tone it is personal and urgent, yet in style discursive. Cicero himself was proud of the work. Writing to Atticus, while the work was in progress, he says, "my exposition is splendid",[213] and in the final paragraph of the work, addressing Marcus, he says:[214]

> Marcus, my son, here is my gift – in my view a great one, but its value will depend on your reception of it ... Since my voice has travelled to you in these books, give them as much time as you can ... Farewell, my Cicero, and be assured that you are indeed most dear to me – much more dear, however, if you take pleasure in such advice and rules [as these].

The work is in three books: Book 1 concerns moral goodness (*honestum*); Book 2, expediency (*utile*, translated by Atkins as "beneficial"); Book 3, cases where *honestum* and *utile* are in conflict.[215] For the first two books Cicero's principal source was Panaetius, who wrote a treatise in three books *Peri tou Kathekontos*, which Cicero translated as *De Officiis*. The word *officium* is troublesome, and Atticus criticized Cicero's use of it to translate the Greek *kathekon*, which literally means "coming down" and then, in the philosophical sense, "fitting or proper". Zeno, the founder of Stoicism, used the word in an ethical sense, evidently in the sense of "an action in accordance with reason", and this seems to have been the basic sense of the term in Panaetius' title.[216] But *officium* in Latin meant (in Cicero's time) "that which ought to be done", with the specifically Roman connotation of one's duty towards others in a particular social context. As Atticus pointed out, it would be difficult to speak of a citizen's *officium* towards the state, as opposed to his *officium* towards an individual or a social group.[217] Cicero clearly wanted to extend the term to the political context, particularly the preservation of the established order, and he did not accept Atticus' criticism. "Give me a better word" (*da melius*) was his reply, and so the title remained *De Officiis*. Although Andrew Dyck persuasively argues for "appropriate action" as the closest English equivalent for *officium*, I have kept the translation, "duty", which is both more familiar and less cumbersome.[218]

Cicero compressed the three books of Panaetius' work into two.[219] But his work was not just a translation of Panaetius: we remember his insistence in the *De Legibus* that he intends to be "his own person", and he says here of Panaetius, "I have followed him to a great extent but have not translated him".[220] He gives a Roman cast to Panaetius' philosophy, and the *officia* are actions appropriate for a member of the Roman senatorial class. He uses Roman examples, most notably that of Regulus in Book 3.[221] Panaetius, however, only went so far. He did not, as Cicero complains, fulfil his promise of dealing with cases where the good (*kalon*, Latin *honestum*) and the expedient (*sympheron*, Latin, *utile*) were in conflict. Cicero did consult a version of the *Peri Kathekontos* of Posidonius, but he found its usefulness very limited. Therefore he was left largely on his own for Book 3, although he may have had some help from the Stoic Athenodorus (Sandon), who had procured at least a summary of Posidonius' work for him.[222] Cicero should be believed when he says:[223]

> I shall fill out this gap [i.e. in Panaetius' work] without any support, but, as they say, under my own auspices (*Marte nostro*).

The first book is the most varied and the most interesting. After the introduction, Cicero starts with a definition of *officia*, which he classifies as those which concern the "end of the good" and those which "consist of rules to which every part of our experience of life could conform".[224] Thus the first class is theoretical, the second practical, and it is this that is the subject of the work. Cicero then subdivides his topic into the good, the expedient, and cases where the two are in conflict. To these categories he adds two of his own, comparisons, respectively, between good actions and expedient actions.[225] Then he turns to discuss *honestum*, which he bases on four cardinal virtues: justice, wisdom, greatness of spirit (*magnitudo animi*, Greek *megalopsychia*), and moderation.[226] These are then analysed and discussed: wisdom very briefly, justice more fully, as we would expect from the social and civil context of Cicero's *officia*.[227] The second part of the discussion of justice extends to liberality, an appropriate attribute for aristocrats. Cicero's treatment of one of the most prominent of Roman social relationships, that between patron and client, is at best superficial.[228] When he turns to greatness of spirit he argues for the superiority of civil courage (*domesticae fortitudines*) over military courage, putting at the centre his own career and achievements.[229] In general, however, this section develops themes familiar from the *De Republica* and political speeches, arguing for patriotic loyalty and subordination of the ambitions of the individual to the needs of the state. Finally, Cicero discusses moderation.[230] Here the notion of what is "seemly" (*decorum*) predominates, allowing Cicero to expand on behaviour appropriate to a person of his son's rank.

Cicero ends the first book with a comparison of virtues, answering the first of the two questions that he had added to Panaetius' topics.[231] He gives the first place to wisdom, which he defines as "knowledge of things divine and human". But since *officium* is exercised in a social context, the virtue that is based on community (i.e. justice) must be the greatest. Therefore justice must be ranked ahead of "mere knowledge", so that wisdom, the "foremost virtue", is wisdom exercised for the good of the community. (Cicero's argument here is confusing and apparently inconsistent.) The best *officium*, then, is that which is based on life in a community. Cicero adds his own definition of the hierarchy of *officia*, a variation of Panaetius' definition which he had quoted earlier:[232]

> In our life as members of a community there are priorities in duties, so that it is easy to understand which duty takes precedence in each case. Thus our primary duties are owed to the immortal gods; secondly, to our country; thirdly, to our parents, and then the rest in descending order of priority.

Thus Cicero ends the book with a reaffirmation of the moral, social and political perspectives that had inspired the *Dream of Scipio*.

In Book 2 Cicero turns to *utile*, that is, what is expedient or beneficial. Here his subject is "the things that concern a civilized way of life and the means of getting those things that are useful, and that concern influence and wealth".[233] In the first book he had followed Stoic doctrine mostly, "using my own judgement", and here also he announces that he will follow the conclusions that he finds most probable.[234] He deplores the general custom of separating the good (*honestum*) from the useful, and he will show that the good (part of which is the just) and the expedient cannot be separated.[235]

Cicero's focus, however, in this book is exclusively on the things that are useful for pursuing a political career. Since the *officia* are exercised in a community, the support of other human beings is the first expedient thing, and the first goal of the *utile* is to persuade other human beings to support our own interests, which some people in public life do through immoral methods such as bribery.[236] The person who seeks support by virtuous methods will be loved rather than feared: he will acquire glory through good will and friendship, exercising the virtues of good faith and honour.[237] In the pursuit of glory, justice will be an essential virtue, and the young man ambitious for glory will always act with integrity.[238] Cicero refers to his previous works on glory (*De Gloria*) and on friendship (*De Amicitia*) to excuse the brevity of his discussion of these subjects: he does have plenty to say about friendship, however, in Book 3.[239]

Cicero then turns to liberality and beneficence, that is, doing good to others, whether by giving them money or doing good deeds on their behalf. In discussing the former he criticizes extravagance in courting public favour, for example in the games given by aediles.[240] He is more interested, however, in liberality shown through service to individuals and to the state. Here, as mentioned above, he deals very gingerly with the client–patron relationship, and Miriam Griffin rightly draws attention to "his lack of interest in relations with social inferiors".[241] The importance of the subject is shown by its extensive treatment in the *Satires* and *Epistles* of Horace, in the *Satires* of Juvenal, and in Seneca and Pliny the Younger.[242] Since legal representation was a common duty of the patron towards his client, Cicero could have spoken with authority, beyond the jejune remarks that he makes here.

He is more interested in service to the state.[243] The first principle, he says, that public officials must observe is the inviolability of property rights, and, after discussing the moral integrity needed for public service, he returns to this subject at the end:

> Guardians of the republic will avoid the type of gift-giving by which things are taken away from one group and given to another. Above all they will work to see that each person keeps what is his by means of the fairness of justice and the lawcourts.

Cicero develops this economic conservatism as a justification for increasing the Roman empire, for such imperialism will increase the wealth of the state, and the military leaders who benefit the state in this way will win great glory for themselves. The book ends with a perfunctory comparison of things that are useful and expedient and an anecdote about Cato the Elder, which Cicero tells to indicate his preference for income gained from farming rather than from money-lending.[244]

Book 2, although it is founded ostensibly on Panaetius, clearly has Cicero's stamp upon it. The examples are mostly Roman, and the social and economic values are those that Cicero himself proclaimed throughout his career, those of a conservative politician concerned with the stability of a social and economic order in which his affluence is assured. Those who have seen the *De Officiis* as the work of an *anima naturaliter Christiana* will have a hard time reconciling their view with those expressed by Cicero.

In Book 3 Cicero is left without Panaetius to fight his own battle. The subject of the book is both necessary and interesting: what precepts are to be followed when the good and the expedient are in apparent conflict? Here again Cicero's focus is largely political: the contexts of his dilemmas are mostly Roman, as are the examples.[245] His views are conditioned by the pessimism that he felt at his own political impotence, and his disgust at the corruption of political life under the military leaders who had destroyed the republic.[246] In the most political passage of the book he attacks Marius, Pompey and Caesar.[247] Although these examples are brought in to support the conclusion that "nothing can be expedient that is not good", the intensity of Cicero's hatred is the most striking feature of the passage.

The major ethical principle in Book 3 is that where there is apparent conflict, the good must prevail over the expedient. To act otherwise is contrary to nature and destroys the bonds of society and of humanity itself.[248] Cicero illustrates this from a series of historical and hypothetical examples, in which he makes it clear that the interests of the state outweigh those of the individual. Thus, as Andrew Dyck observes, "the *utilitas reipublicae* tends to become ... a criterion of conduct almost ... equal to the *honestum* itself".[249]

At 3. 96 Cicero reveals that he has been discussing moral conflicts within the framework of the four virtues established in Book 1. In fact, from 3. 40 onwards, he has been using wisdom and justice as his criteria, and now he turns to the other two virtues – greatness of spirit and temperance. For the former he cites the Stoic mythical example of Ulysses, just as he had used another favourite Stoic exemplar, Hercules, as an example of virtuous labour for the good of humankind. The mythical Ulysses soon yields to an example of virtue (not merely greatness of spirit) drawn from Roman history – M. Atilius Regulus, consul in 267 and 256, who was captured by the Carthaginians in 255.[250] In Cicero's narrative Regulus was sent back to Rome under oath to negotiate for the return of high-ranking Carthaginian prisoners in exchange for his freedom. At Rome he argued against the exchange and returned to Carthage, where he was executed slowly and horribly. The story fits the context – Regulus knew what was *utile* but chose what was *honestum*. But Cicero goes much further: it is a perversion of nature to choose expediency over the good (§101); Regulus exemplified justice in keeping his oath (§102), a topic that Cicero develops for the rest of the episode, with other supporting examples from Roman history. The conflict between *utile* and *honestum* is resolved in terms of the virtues analysed in Book 1, but Cicero adds a wholly Roman perspective to the discussion. Thus the virtue of justice is identified with the supremely Roman virtue of *fides* (good faith, including specifically the observance of one's oath); Regulus' actions at Rome were in accordance with the Roman law and constitution; his personal bearing was dignified, worthy of a Roman, a senator and an ex-consul. To have acted otherwise would have been shameful (the Latin word is *turpe*, with wider moral connotations than "shameful"). Cicero sums up Regulus' dilemma elegantly:[251]

> he was in better condition when he was being executed by being kept awake, than if he had stayed at home as an old man − but a prisoner of war, and as an ex-consul − but one who had broken his oath.

Finally Cicero turns to the fourth virtue, temperance.[252] Here he does not use historical examples, taking pleasure as the antithesis of temperance and using it as the basis for attacking the Epicureans. He repeats in summary form many of the arguments of Book 2 of the *De Finibus*, and concludes by emphasizing his basic principle, that nothing can be *utile* that is in conflict with *honestum*. Therefore, since pleasure is contrary to the good, and nothing that is truly *utile* conflicts with the good, pleasure can never be *utile*. And so the work ends (3. 121) with the personal farewell to young Marcus quoted above.

The *De Officiis* is in the view of many scholars the most influential of Cicero's philosophical works. In late antiquity it was read and admired by Christians and pagans: Ambrose, for example, used and adapted Cicero for his work (written *c.*390 CE), *De Officiis Ministrorum*. In the later Middle Ages and the Renaissance it was widely read and admired. Over 700 manuscripts were copied in the period from the twelfth to the fifteenth centuries, and it was the first work printed in Italy, at Subiaco in 1465, and the first classical book ever printed (at Mainz, also in 1465).[253] The high point of its popularity was in the eighteenth century, most notably in England and France, where Voltaire was moved to call it "the best work of moral philosophy that ever has been, or ever will be, written". Yet there have been other voices. Wilhelm Süss confesses that he has "the greatest difficulty in establishing a lively relationship with the *De Officiis*", and he quotes Montaigne:[254]

> Cicero's discussions are good for the school, the court-room and the pulpit, where we have the leisure to snooze and, a quarter of an hour later, enough time to pick up the thread.

The fact is that Cicero's work is rhetorical, and therefore political as well as ethical. It presents unambiguous political and social prejudices that will appeal to those who are conservative, comfortable and complacent, like the eighteenth-century snob, Lord Chesterfield. But Cicero, although conservative, was neither comfortable nor complacent. His work was overshadowed by the collapse of the Roman republic, and his views were coloured by the disappointment of seeing the "tyrant" (Caesar) replaced by something worse. This gives his ethical principles dignity and often nobility: each reader must decide whether these attributes outweigh the limitations of his political and social views.

This chapter began with the dogmatic statement that "Cicero is the most influential of Roman philosophers". Each reader of Cicero must decide whether this is justified. The statement was accepted as true until the middle of the nineteenth century, when Theodor Mommsen (following W. Drumann) with gleeful ferocity demolished Cicero as a politician, philosopher, orator and human being.[255] Mommsen's authority guaranteed that Cicero's philosophical writings would be undervalued for more than a century, as they were in Germany, the UK and North America (at least) until less than 20 years ago. Except for the *De Oratore* and *Topica*, the standard English series of classical texts, the *Oxford Classical Texts*, did not include a single philosophical work of Cicero until 1994, and only the works on Old Age and Friendship were regularly included in school and undergraduate reading.[256] Even as late as 1982, the authoritative *Cambridge History of Classical Literature* is at best patronizing, although the author does admit that "the *De Officiis* laid the foundations of liberal humanism for Europe and the world".[257] Writing in 1995, J. C. A. Gaskin sadly remarks that "Cicero is over-annotated by classicists and underestimated by recent philosophers".[258]

Not all of this can be laid at the door of Mommsen. We have seen that Cicero's political and social views were conservative and *laissez-faire*, and that the *De Officiis* appealed especially to readers who shared these views – hence Cicero's popularity in the eighteenth century. In times when strong leaders are admired or perceived to be desirable, milder politicians such as Cicero are out of fashion. Mommsen preferred "men of iron", and the most influential of twentieth-century ancient historians, Ronald Syme, had little use for Cicero's philosophical writing in the face of autocrats such as Caesar (in Cicero's time) and Hitler (in Syme's time – his *Roman Revolution* was published in 1939). In times when political, social and economic change is needed, there will be little sympathy for Cicero's conservatism: such times have existed in the Western world ever since the end of World War I.

Cicero himself is also to blame. Not only have his political and social views been found to be unacceptable to opinion-makers, but his style – rich, rhetorical and orotund – has fallen out of favour, when the sententious angularity of Sallust and Tacitus has been more popular. His efforts to make philosophy intelligible to non-philosophers naturally have degraded his value to professional philosophers, who find the *De Fato* and the *Academica* more enjoyable than the "easy" works. For a long time the school of *Quellenforschung* (the search for sources) dominated among scholars, so that Cicero tended to be diminished as a mere reporter or compiler of the works of Greek philosophers.

So much for the negatives. The fact remains that from his own day until the nineteenth century the philosophical works of Cicero were generally admired and at least respected. The record is clear in late antiquity, including the Church Fathers. Boethius thought him worth a commentary, and many of his works were read and copied in the Carolingian age. From the twelfth century his popularity and influence increased, as the huge number of manuscripts of several of his works attest. His readers were not concerned whether or not he was an original thinker, but rather with the worth of what he actually had to say. In a world where few could read (and fewer understand) Greek, Cicero's Latin was priceless, and continued to be so even after the Renaissance rediscovery in the West of Greek works. Even in our day, he still is an important source for our knowledge of many Hellenistic philosophers.

The antithesis between the Greeks as philosophers and the Romans as practical men of action is especially false where Cicero is concerned. He interpreted Greek philosophy for his contemporaries in a language that he himself developed and enlarged. He did this through the filter of Roman society and politics, in effect creating new works. He developed a new Latin literary form in his dialogues (based on the model of Aristotle rather than Plato), which was appropriate for his Academic scepticism, while being less negative in its methods and results than the Socratic dialogue. His philosophical doctrines were to some extent original in the political dialogues and in the Roman colouring of the *De Officiis*. The names of authors and thinkers influenced by him are impressive.[259] Other Roman philosophers – Seneca, Augustine, Boethius – may dispute the title of "most influential", but Cicero's achievement simply in terms of language and range of thought is indisputable. As for originality, the author of the *De Republica* (especially Laelius' speech in Book 3 and the *Somnium*) and the *De Oratore*, and even the more obviously derivative third book of the *De Finibus*, needs no apology. Finally – and most importantly – Cicero expressed the loftiest ideals of human moral attainment. To define the nature and express the meaning of *humanity* is a supreme achievement.

4

LUCRETIUS AND THE
EPICUREANS

The poem of Lucretius (*De Rerum Natura*: "On the Nature of
Things") is the most powerful work in all of Roman philosophy. Yet
hardly anything is known of its author beyond his name, Titus
Lucretius Carus, and the approximate dates of his life, *c.*95–54 BCE.
Only one of his contemporaries, Cicero, mentions him:[1]

> The poetry of Lucretius (as you say in your letter) is illumi-
> nated by many flashes of genius (*ingenium*), yet it also shows
> much craftsmanship (*ars*). But when you come, I shall
> think you a hero if you have read the *Empedoclea* of
> Sallustius, but hardly a human being.

Cicero, then, had read the poem – indeed, Jerome, writing about
400 CE, says that Cicero edited it (*emendavit*), which may mean no
more than that he corrected it for copying before publication. Given
Cicero's hostility to Epicurean doctrine and his own pretensions as a
poet, his recognition of Lucretius' excellence in the two essential
areas of poetry (inspiration and technique) is significant. Nothing is
known of Sallustius, but the title of his work suggests that his
Empedoclea was a translation of the poem (or poems) of Empedocles,
just as Cicero had called his translation of Aratus *Aratea*. Evidently
Sallustius' poem required superhuman endurance of its readers.

Lucretius worked alone, and no other contemporary mentions
him. He seems to have had little or no contact with other
Epicureans and their schools in Italy. Cicero tells us that two
authors, Amafinius and Rabirius, had written popular works
explaining Epicurean philosophy in non-technical terms.[2] The
speaker in this passage, Varro, says that Romans cannot study
philosophy without knowledge of Greek language and doctrines.
Amafinius, he says, had written on all three branches of Epicurean

98

philosophy (logic, physics, ethics) without using any Greek methods of argument, while in his ethics he equated human good with the good of cattle. But, as Cicero complains, Amafinius' works found a large audience: they were the best of a bad bunch, for they were easy reading, and their focus on the Epicurean ideal of pleasure was attractive. After him, says Cicero, many other authors wrote Epicurean works, so that "they filled the whole of Italy".

These works (now all lost), according to Cicero, made no intellectual demands, misleading their readers into thinking that they provided a firm foundation for the student of Epicureanism. It is clear that the Epicureans shared in the vigorous revival of philosophy in Rome and Italy which Cicero describes in the *Brutus*. Alone of the four major philosophical schools the Epicureans did not join in the Athenian embassy of 155, in accordance with the Epicurean doctrine of *lathe biosas* ("live unobtrusively"), which involved non-participation in politics, unless there were an overriding reason to participate.[3] Nevertheless, Cicero shows that Epicureanism did take root in Italy. The ideal of pleasure and the superficial intelligibility of the school's doctrines were attractive just because they were not austere and impossible to achieve (as were the ideals of the Stoics), or full of intellectual subtleties (as were those of the Academics and Peripatetics). Yet Cicero's Epicurean speaker, Torquatus, with more truth describes the school as "serious, disciplined, austere", epithets that apply to Lucretius, if not to Amafinius and his imitators.[4]

Cicero himself was at first attracted to the Epicureans by Phaedrus, but he turned to the Academic doctrines of Philo and Antiochus. His close friend and confidant, Atticus, was an Epicurean, and he kept up friendship with Caesar's murderer, Cassius, who was converted to Epicureanism in 46.[5] Writing to Cassius in January 45, Cicero jokes about the Latin terminology of Cassius' "new friends". In his reply Cassius points out that Epicurean pleasure and freedom from mental disturbance cannot be achieved without justice and virtue, but he agrees that people like Amafinius have misinterpreted the words of Epicurus himself.[6] Cicero had only contempt for the bad Latin of popularizers such as Amafinius, but with serious Epicureans like Atticus and Cassius he discussed Epicurean doctrine, for differences in philosophy did not stand in the way of friendship. Cicero is, nevertheless, almost uniformly critical of the school. He devoted the first dialogue of the *De Finibus* to an exposition and demolition of its ethics, and he did the same with its theology in the first book of the *De Natura Deorum*. The chief target of his criticism in the former was the Epicurean doctrine of pleasure, and in the latter the doctrine that the gods do not concern themselves with human affairs. He spent less effort in criticizing Epicurean epistemology and physics, both prominent in Lucretius' work.

Epicureanism flourished particularly in Campania (i.e. the area around Naples), where Philodemus (c.110–40) headed a school at Herculaneum.[7] Cicero says that Philodemus and Siro (another leading Epicurean in Campania) were his personal friends (*familiares*). Philodemus was a Syrian, born at Gadara (near the Sea of Galilee), and he came to Rome probably in the 70s, under the patronage of L. Calpurnius Piso Caesoninus, consul in 58 and censor in 50. Piso was the father of Caesar's wife, Calpurnia and in 55 the target of Cicero's speech *In Pisonem*.[8] He owned a splendid villa at Herculaneum, known best to the modern world through its replica, which used to house the Getty Museum at Malibu in California. Since 1754 a large number of Epicurean papyri have been discovered and unrolled in the villa at Herculaneum.[9] It is very likely that they were part of the library of the school of Philodemus. Philodemus himself was best known as a poet: Virgil was his friend and a pupil of Siro, although he was not an Epicurean. As a student in Athens Philodemus had studied under the Epicurean, Zeno of Sidon, whom Cicero had heard "as a very sharp old man" and whose teaching on Epicurean pleasure he reports with disapproval.[10] Zeno was Philodemus' guiding light, justly so in that he was the most creative Epicurean philosopher of his time. Philodemus wrote on music, rhetoric and poetry, and the Herculaneum papyri contain fragments of many of his prose philosophical works, among them a history of philosophy (including the lists of philosophers and their works in the *Index Stoicorum* and the *Index Academicorum*), and works on Epicurean logic, physics and ethics, and on the gods. Some of these probably post-date Lucretius' death, and they show that there were differences between Philodemus and Lucretius on topics common to both. For example, in his work on *Phenomena and Inferences* (usually known by its Latin title, *De Signis*), Philodemus reports Zeno's teaching on induction and inferences from phenomena, which differs from the deductive method of Lucretius. Again, Philodemus wrote a work on Death, part of the fourth book of which survives in the Herculaneum papyri, which is "gentle and sympathetic, free of the abrasiveness of Lucretius' account".[11] He shows sympathy and understanding for those who die young, since those who die old have been able to reach harbour after a life well lived; for the bereaved; for those who die in a foreign country.[12] He thinks it madness (*apoplexia*) to want to die a heroic death in war, since heroes and ordinary people are in the same predicament, "for we all live in a city that has no walls against death".[13] The teaching of Philodemus is, like that of Lucretius, full of poetic colour and energized by personal feeling, but he shows greater sympathy for human weakness than Lucretius.

Indeed, there is no evidence that Lucretius read the work of Philodemus or knew him, and there is strong evidence that he was not influenced by him.[14] The four heroes of early Epicureanism were known as "The Men" (*Hoi Andres*): these were Epicurus, Metrodorus, Hermarchus and Polyaenus. They were revered by Philodemus and Epicureans of his time – except for Lucretius. He alone revered Epicurus exclusively, as man, father and god.

Lucretius, then, stood apart from contemporary Epicureans. He does not seem to have been concerned with the philosophical debates of his time.[15] When he does attack other schools, his targets are the Academics and Sceptics, but in terms of debates that predated Epicurus. David Sedley (1998) has called him a "fundamentalist", that is, one who revered the texts of the founder of the school.[16]

The principal sources for Lucretius' Epicurean philosophy, therefore, are to be found in Epicurus' sayings and writings. Until very recently it has been assumed that these are the works reproduced by Diogenes Laertius in Book 10 of his *Lives of the Philosophers*. Sedley, however, has argued convincingly for the work *On Nature* (*Peri Physeos*) as Lucretius' only Epicurean source.[17] This work survives only in fragments in the Herculaneum papyri, and Sedley has brilliantly reconstructed the contents and their relationship to Lucretius' poem, which he believes was closely based on the first fifteen of the thirty-seven books of Epicurus' work. His second chart (p. 136), shows how Lucretius incorporated the doctrines of Epicurus, where he changed their order, and where he brought in arguments that do not appear in *On Nature*. The advantages of Sedley's thesis are that Lucretius' work appears to be more coherent and consistent, and that the obvious differences between *De Rerum Natura* and the texts given by Diogenes Laertius are no longer problematic.

Nevertheless, these texts are complete and available to readers of this book, and a review of them will be the most efficient procedure for understanding the relationship of Lucretius' philosophy to that of Epicurus. Epicurean doctrine was organized into three categories: *kanonike* (logic and epistemology), *physike* (observation of the world and nature), and *ethike* (morality). Diogenes Laertius transcribes three letters of Epicurus to his disciples. The *Letter to Herodotus* deals with physics, and therefore is closest in its material to Lucretius.[18] It contains doctrine on atoms and void, the subjects of the first two books of Lucretius and Books 1–2 and 5 of *On Nature*;[19] on images and sense-perception, treated in Book 4 of Lucretius and Books 3–4 of *On Nature*;[20] on the nature and mortality of the soul, dealt with in Book 3 of Lucretius and Books 6–9 of *On Nature*.[21] Lucretius does not deal with time, the subject of §§72–73a of the *Letter to Herodotus* and treated in Book 10 of *On Nature*. (Time does not seem to have been a problem for Roman philosophers except in so far as they were concerned with the immortality of the soul and its relationship to the mortal body. The first extended discussion in Latin appears to be in Book 11 of Augustine's *Confessions*.) Epicurus' doctrine on properties (colour, etc.) appears in Book 4 of Lucretius and in Book 10 of *On Nature*.[22] The doctrine on other worlds does not appear in Book 5 of Lucretius with the other teachings of Book 12 of *On Nature*, but in Book 2 (corresponding to the *Letter to Herodotus*, 45) as part of the discussion of atoms and their properties.[23] The doctrine on the origins of civilization takes up the last half of Book 5 of Lucretius and appeared in Book 12 of *On Nature*.[24] The *Letter to Herodotus* focuses on the origins of language, whereas Lucretius' discussion is far broader. Finally, the *Letter to Herodotus* discusses the correct attitude to the heavenly bodies, showing that inner peace (*ataraxia*) will be achieved if one has knowledge of their physical nature and does not think or fear that they can affect one's life.[25] The *Letter to Herodotus* closes (§83) with an exhortation to Herodotus to learn its doctrines by heart so as to attain calm of mind. This attitude underlies Lucretius' discussion of celestial phenomena in Book 6, corresponding to Book 13 of *On Nature*.

The *Letter to Herodotus*, then, contains many of the doctrines of Lucretius in summary form, and often in a different order (e.g. the discussions of other worlds in §§45 and 73–74).[26] Sedley has demonstrated (pp. 138–44) why Lucretius went back to the full text of *On Nature* rather than the summary in the *Letter to Herodotus*, which, as Epicurus himself said (§83), was to be learned by heart, an impossibility (at least for ordinary human beings) for the reader of the 37 books of *On Nature*.[27]

The second document recorded by Diogenes Laertius is Epicurus' *Letter to Pythocles*, which deals with celestial phenomena (in Greek, *ta meteora*).[28] This material appears in the first half of Book 5 and in Book 6 of Lucretius, corresponding to material in Books 11–13 of

On Nature. Notable is the doctrine on the size of the sun, that it is "as great as it appears to us". This was also the view of Democritus, and it was ridiculed by Cicero.[29] More important is Epicurus' reason for studying celestial phenomena.[30] Like Herodotus, Pythocles is urged to memorize Epicurus' doctrine, so as to achieve calm of mind. Here (§85) Epicurus refers to the *Letter to Herodotus* as "the short summary" (which Pythocles is commanded also to learn by heart), a clear indication that the full text of *On Nature* was the source of the letters' doctrines and therefore more likely to be the source for Lucretius.

The physical doctrines of the first two letters (including elements of the Epicurean theory of knowledge, which belongs properly in the category of *kanonike*) are means to the ethical goal of happiness achieved through peace of mind. This goal is implicit throughout Lucretius' poem and it is made explicit in many passages. Thus the ideal of freedom from anxiety, gained through knowledge of the physical world, is woven into the texture of the poem. It is not surprising, then, that Epicurus' *Letter to Menoeceus*, which deals with ethics, has fewer exact correspondences with *De Rerum Natura* than the first two letters, for there was no need for Lucretius to include a specific segment corresponding with the Epicurean category of ethics.[31] The letter begins with an urgent invitation to study philosophy:

> Let no one who is young put off studying philosophy, nor let one who is old be weary of it. For no one is too young or too old for the health of the soul ... Therefore both the young and the old should study philosophy ... So it is necessary to give our attention to the things that bring happiness, since when it is present we have everything, and when it is absent the goal of all our actions is to attain it.

The spirit of this statement drives Lucretius' poem.

Epicurus continues with doctrine about the gods, that they exist but that the common beliefs about them are false. This doctrine is expanded by Lucretius (perhaps from Book 13 of *On Nature*) in a beautiful passage in the introduction to Book 6. Here the gods are happy and good, and the pious human being will perceive the "likenesses" (*simulacra*) of atoms that flow from them, and so be able to share in their tranquillity. But if human beings ascribe anger and other human emotional disturbances to the gods, they will increase their own fear and hinder the attainment of peace of mind.[32]

Next, the *Letter to Menoeceus* turns to Epicurean doctrine on death, that it is nothing to us, and that fear of death diminishes the quality of life and the attainment of happiness.[33] Lucretius expands this in the last part of Book 3, starting with this resounding declaration:

> Death therefore is nothing to us and concerns us not at all,
> since the nature of the soul is held to be mortal.

The logic of the arguments of Epicurus and Lucretius is consistent with their ethical doctrine, for fear of death will lessen pleasure and therefore be an obstacle to happiness. Yet some Epicureans found this doctrine too austere, and Philodemus is more sensitive in his recognition of the human emotions involved in death and bereavement.

The *Letter to Menoeceus* then discusses the Epicurean doctrine of desire and pleasure.[34] Epicurus says bluntly:

> We recognize pleasure as our primary and innate good, and
> it is the beginning of every choice and aversion that we
> make. To it we return, judging every good with feeling as
> our criterion.

But Epicurus goes on to set limits to pleasure, which is truly the balance between extremes of pain and excess of pleasure, achieved through reason (*phronesis*), which he calls "more valuable even than philosophy" (§132). Thus the truly pleasurable life is one of moderation and virtue. And so the letter concludes with the picture of the virtuous man, who honours the gods, does not fear death, and achieves happiness through reason and virtue, while avoiding pain and mental disturbance.[35] If Menoeceus learns these precepts and practises them, he too will be such a man, for, Epicurus concludes:

> you will live as a god among men. For the man who lives
> among immortal good things is nothing like a mortal
> being.

Lucretius expresses this doctrine in his praises of Epicurus, who ascends from man in Book 1 to god in Book 5.

The three Epicurean letters were summaries of Epicurus' doctrine, for Epicurus wanted his students to learn his precepts by heart. More summary yet are the 40 principles, known as the

Principal Doctrines (in Greek, *Kyriai Doxai* and abbreviated here as *KD*), which Diogenes Laertius quotes as the "colophon" (literally, "the finishing touch") of his book on Epicurus.[36] The first four of the *KD* are:

1 that which is blessed and eternal has no troubles and brings no trouble upon others: it is free from anger and favour;
2 death is nothing to us;
3 pleasure reaches its full limit in the removal of pain;
4 pain in the flesh does not last long, and the time when it exceeds pleasure is limited.

These four doctrines were summarized in the famous "fourfold remedy" (*tetrapharmakos*), quoted by Philodemus:[37]

God is not to be feared, death is free from anxiety. The good is easy to attain, the terrible is easy to endure.

The *tetrapharmakos* is the basic formula for Epicurean ethics. While Lucretius does not quote it explicitly, the first pair of maxims is the basis of his poem: he explains "the nature of things" in order to prove that the gods should not be feared and that death is nothing to us. Knowledge of the physical world will make attainable the good life, that is, a life free from mental disturbance. Lucretius does not develop an argument based on the fourth maxim, but Book 6, which is incomplete, ends with the terrors of the plague at Athens. He could well have ended by showing that even such a great evil could have been endured by those who knew Epicurean doctrine, whereas in fact the people of Athens, not being Epicureans, were subject to the fear, terror, panic and divisiveness that he describes.[38]

Epicurus next focuses on the individual's relations with society: he says that one cannot live a pleasant life without being just and virtuous.[39] Yet justice is part of the social compact, not an absolute principle.[40] Again, if one can achieve personal security, then the best life is one that is peaceful and withdrawn from the multitude.[41] The most important means to individual security is friendship.[42]

These principles are based on the doctrine of "living unobtrusively" (in Greek, *lathe biosas*, a phrase known from the title of an anti-Epicurean treatise of Plutarch), which obviously conflicts with the Stoic ideal of participation in public life and with the Roman ideal of duty to the state (as expressed in Cicero's *Dream of Scipio* and *De Senectute*). In his account of the development of civilization Lucretius says:[43]

> But [i.e. in contrast to the simple life] men wished to be famous and powerful, so that their good fortune might rest on a firm foundation and that they might be wealthy and lead a peaceful life. In vain! For in the competition to reach the heights of success they made their journey dangerous, and envy cast them down from the top ... So that it is much better to live in peace and obey orders than to wish to control affairs by giving orders and holding supreme power.

Lucretius looks more unsparingly at Roman politics of his own time:[44]

> How sweet it is, when the winds stir up the sea, to look from the land upon another's struggles! Not because it is a pleasure that another should be in distress, but because it is pleasant to observe from what evils you are free. Sweet it is also to watch the mighty battles of war, armies drawn up on the battlefields, without yourself sharing in the danger. But nothing is sweeter than to live in calm and lofty precincts protected by the teachings of wise men. From them you can look down on others and see how they wander here and there, aimlessly trying to find a path through life. They compete with their abilities, they contend in noble birth, and night and day they struggle to climb to the heights of wealth and power. O unhappy minds of men! O blind hearts! How great the darkness of life and how great the danger in which you spend your span of life, whatever it is! Do you not see how nature proclaims that she demands no more than this – that pain be kept separate from the body, and that the mind, free from fear and anxiety, enjoy the sensation of pleasure?

This attitude is not irresponsible hedonism, but rather a reasoned reaction to the inhumanities of political life, both at Rome and (in Epicurus' case) in the Greek city-state. Even the Stoic Zeno, in his *Republic*, had proposed the abolition of the basic institutions of the Greek city and the establishment of a community of virtuous men

106

and women, who alone were capable of friendship, political association and freedom.[45] Epicurus suggested that instead of political competition and the envy, resentment and failure that it involves, society should adopt different customs – friendship, justice and mutual support. Lucretius recognizes that the Romans of the senatorial class will not withdraw from existing political institutions (such as elections, magistracies and other public offices), and so he falls back on the ethical doctrines of Epicurus, particularly the principle of pleasure (and its corollary, the avoidance of pain). To participate in political life is to invite disturbance of the mind: power is an illusory goal, for it is followed by envy and (often) failure. Much better, then, to seek to attain calm of mind through the avoidance of pain, and to seek a place in society through friendship.[46]

The doctrine of *lathe biosas* undercuts the very foundations of the Greek city-state and of Roman political life. Yet, in Rome, Epicureans such as Cicero's friend, Atticus, took a prominent and productive part in the life of the community without seeking political office. Some, like Cassius, reasoned that it was necessary to participate in the political struggle, because refusal to participate would be a greater evil for the community and would bring greater mental pain to the individual than involvement.[47] L. Calpurnius Piso Caesoninus was obligated by family tradition and noble ancestry to take a prominent part in public life, without abandoning Epicurean principles.[48] Moreover, friendship, in both the Greek and Roman worlds, had political connotations. Here, for example, is part of the introduction to Aristotle's discussion of friendship:[49]

> Friendship seems also to keep cities together, and lawgivers are more concerned about it than about justice. For harmony (*homonoia*) appears to be like friendship in some way, and the lawgivers make it their chief goal and most of all they drive out discord, as bringing enmity. And those who are friends do not need justice, while those who are just need friendship.

Friendship (*amicitia*) was a feature of Roman political life and, through the institution of clientship, it was an important element in ameliorating the inequalities of class distinctions. Lucretius, then, for all the potency of his satire, is following Epicurus (who himself might have known Aristotle's *Nicomachean Ethics*) in suggesting not merely individual quietism, but rather an alternative way of interacting with society.

The *Kyriai Doxai* focus also on celestial phenomena (Greek, *meteora*, the subject of the *Letter to Pythocles*). These are listed as objects of fear (along with death and pain), which can be removed by the study of the physical world.[50] If one knows the nature of the universe, then one can be rid of fear and enjoy pleasure; similarly, individual security is unattainable if one is afraid because of "things that exist above our heads and under the earth and in the whole infinite [universe]".[51] These doctrines are especially prominent in Books 3 and 6 of Lucretius, and the principle of "knowing the nature of the universe" is the foundation of his poem.

Epicurus lays down criteria for pleasure and desire and their opposites, pain and aversion.[52] These principles were expressed more fully in the *Letter to Menoeceus* (127b-32), where *phronesis* (reason) is given a higher place than philosophy in establishing the equilibrium between pleasure and pain. Epicurus shows in both the *Kyriai Doxai* and the *Letter to Menoeceus* that the greatest pleasure is achieved through reason and by living a simple life. In technical terms, such pleasure is "static", whereas physical experiences that stimulate pleasure (eating, sexual activity and other sensual experiences) involve movement.[53] Epicurus says that some desires are physical and necessary (for example, for food and clothing); some are physical and unnecessary (for example, for luxury or sexual pleasure); some neither physical nor necessary.[54] The third category should be suppressed; the first, being necessary, must be satisfied, but simply, and the second requires the exercise of reason. Epicurus clearly subordinates "kinetic" to "static" pleasure, following the lead of Plato's satirical discussion of pleasure in the *Gorgias.* There Socrates likens a life in which pleasures have to be continuously renewed to filling a jar that is full of holes.[55] So Lucretius uses the myth of the Danaids as a parable for those "who can never be filled with the joys of life".[56] Elsewhere he says that Epicurus "understood that the container [i.e. the human body] was leaky and full of holes, so that it never could be filled", and so "he set a limit to desire".[57] Lucretius expounds this doctrine in several other passages, for example:[58]

> But if anyone would guide his life by true reason, [he would learn that] it is great riches for a man to live sparingly and with mind untroubled, for never can one be poor for lack of a little.

Thus the principle of pleasure (the most controversial element of Epicurean philosophy) is found rather to involve reason and moderation, the same qualities as those taught by other philosophies.

Our survey of Epicurean doctrines has been a long but necessary preparation for discussion of the text of Lucretius' poem. The poem is a little over 7,400 lines long and its six books are arranged in three pairs. The first two books deal with atoms and void; the next pair deal with the soul and death (Book 3) and thought and sense-perception, ending with a diatribe on sexual passion (Book 4). Books 5 and 6 deal with the universe, first the mortality of the world, then the origins of the world and celestial bodies, followed by the origins of civilization and its progress (Book 5). Book 6 is concerned with celestial and meteorological phenomena and ends with a description of the plague of 431–429 BCE in Athens, which is based on Thucydides.[59] The poem may be complete as it stands, but it is probable that Lucretius would have drawn the moral from the human despair caused by the plague.[60] He would have needed to add a few lines saying that if the Athenians had been able to follow the doctrines of Epicurus (praised at the beginning of Book 6 as the greatest gift of Athens to human beings), they would not have been troubled and would not have behaved as they did. But the plague struck nearly a century before the birth of Epicurus, and so the Athenians then were trapped in the moral and mental darkness that Epicurus dispelled by his philosophy.[61]

If we suppose that the poem as we have it is complete, it ends with funerals, just as the *Iliad* had ended with the funeral of Hector. In addition, the abrupt ending, with disease, death and cremation, is a powerful contrast with the opening hymn to Venus. These arguments are, however, literary, and the thesis that the poem is incomplete is more consistent with the focus on Epicurus and his doctrine.

There are two other places where there is evidence of lack of revision or incompleteness. The proem to Book 4 contains two versions of the programmatic introduction to the discussion of "images of things" (*rerum simulacra*), that is the effluences of atoms that stream off the surface of objects and are perceived by us. In the first version (4. 45–53) Lucretius is trying to find the right Latin term for the Greek word *eidola*: he uses *simulacra* (likenesses), *membranae* and *cortex* (bark). In the second passage (4. 26–44) he keeps *simulacra*, and the effluences are now "like membranes", which then are developed into a simile. He no longer uses "bark" as an equivalent of *eidolon*, instead keeping it as the outer surface of an object from which the effluences flow.[62] Thus we can see him refining his language from the first version, which would have been removed in the final revision.

The second piece of evidence for incompleteness is at 5. 155, where Lucretius promises that he will discuss the homes and bodies of the gods "at great length", a promise that he did not fulfil. Here, as in the proem to Book 4, the inconsistency is hardly important in considering the poem as a whole.

The structure of the poem proceeds from the microcosm, through the human experience, to the macrocosm, although the ending returns to the human experience, appropriately, given the underlying purpose of the poem, which is to remove the fear of death. Within each pair of books there is a movement from the general (atoms and void in Book 1; the soul and mortality in Book 3; the world in Book 5) to particular phenomena (properties of atoms in Book 2; perception and sensation in Book 4; celestial phenomena and the plague in Book 6). If we divide the poem into two halves of three books each, then death is the climactic subject of each half: a resounding denial of its power over the followers of Epicurus in Book 3, and in Book 6 a dramatic portrayal of citizens rendered divided and dysfunctional by death in the absence of the doctrines of Epicurus.

To have organized the teachings of Epicurus into a coherent epic poem (for the epithet "didactic" totally fails to do justice to the loftiness and power of the poem) was in itself a great achievement. Lucretius, however, changed the traditional Epicurean method simply by returning to poetry, the medium of several of the pre-Socratic Greek philosophers. This meant that he had to take material written in Greek prose (that was more often than not difficult) and present it in the hexameter, a medium more appropriate for the Greek epic language of Homer and Apollonius or the philosophical poems of Empedocles and Parmenides, than for the less flexible Latin language. This he had to do with a vocabulary that was at best limited and more often non-existent. We have just seen how he set about finding the right word for the Greek *eidola*, and he is as inventive as Cicero in developing a vocabulary, as he does, for example, with the Greek *atoma* ("things which cannot be cut"). Five Latin equivalents occur in an early passage:[63]

> I shall begin to teach you about the highest system of the heavens and the gods, and I shall explain beginnings of things (*rerum primordia*) ... which in giving our account we

call matter (*materies*) and creative bodies for things (*genitalia corpora*), and we usually call them the seeds of things (*semina rerum*), and we use the term "first bodies" (*corpora prima*), because from them as the first things all things are constituted.

Lucretius did not underestimate the problem of vocabulary. In the introduction to the first book he says:[64]

I know full well how hard'it is to bring into light in Latin poetry the dark discoveries of the Greeks, especially when I must explain many things in new words, because of the poverty of the language and the novelty of the subject.

But by the beginning of the second half of the poem he exults in his pioneering achievement:[65]

I journey through the trackless regions of the Muses, never before trodden by human feet. I delight in approaching untouched springs and drinking from them. I delight in picking new flowers and gathering for my head a glorious wreath from flowers that the Muses have never before used to garland [a poet's] head. First, because I teach about great matters and my journey's goal is to untie the tight knots of superstition. Second, because my poem, bathed in light, illuminates so dark a theme, and I touch everything with the Muses' charm.

The joy and confidence of the passage is largely expressed through its poetic metaphors (eight in nine lines), and it leads to an extended simile (lines 11–25) likening his poetry to the honey that parents smear on the cup to help their children drink nasty-tasting medicine, while it is implied that Memmius will be healed (another metaphor) once he learns the nature of things.

Vocabulary and metaphor were not simply literary matters. In the *Letter to Herodotus* 38, Epicurus says that Herodotus must primarily "understand the underlying meaning of words", so as to have a criterion by which to test opinions and impressions. For, he says, he must consider the first meaning (Greek, *ennoema*) of each word, which must be clear and need no proof. This doctrine is closely connected with the doctrine of sense-perceptions (explained in the next lines of §38), which for the Epicureans are true.[66]

Lucretius says, "therefore what is perceived by the senses at any time is true".[67] Just as we perceive the effluences of atoms flowing from the surface of an object, so the effluences of atoms of words (spoken or written) give the reader or hearer the true meaning.[68] Therefore precise vocabulary and accurate metaphorical writing are essential for the teacher. If we apply this doctrine to Lucretius, we can see that his vocabulary, and, still more, his marvellously vivid metaphors and similes, are essential elements both in his poetry and in his philosophy. Don Fowler has explained the matter admirably:[69]

> Poet and philosopher must make the reader *see* ... The effect is a recontextualization of both the traditional devices of poetry and the basic elements of Epicurean epistemology, particularly the "first image" (*prolepsis*) associated with each word, the basis for live metaphor. The complexity and precision of Lucretius' imagery ... is thus also an aspect of his role as philosopher and scientist.

Sedley points out that "[Lucretius] floods his poem with Greek words, but avoids them in the course of doctrinal exposition".[70] This, too, is another facet of the importance of the first impression of a word. If the doctrines of Epicurus are to be rightly understood by a Roman audience, then the vocabulary must be precise and Roman. Lucretius uses Greek words to refer to Greek ideas that he rejects. Thus at 1. 884 (a singularly unpoetic line) he says: "now let us examine the *homoeomeria* of Anaxagoras". Anaxagoras' theory that "parts are similar to the whole" is left with its Greek term, because it and the theory that it denotes are inconsistent with both Latin language and Epicurean doctrine. Often Lucretius deliberately uses a Greek word precisely because of its difference from Latin. In the description of the Trojan War there are five Greek names, one non-Latin portmanteau-word for "sons of the Greeks" (*Graiugenarum*), and one Greek epithet for the wooden horse, *durateus*. Although there is a Latin word for "wooden" (*ligneus*), Lucretius chose to transliterate the Greek word, precisely because it was Greek and was part of a Greek myth.[71] Again, in arguing for the universality of innate powers in animals, he uses the phrase *catuli pantherarum scymnique leonum* ("panther kittens and lion cubs").[72] The word *catuli* is Latin, but the Greek word *pantherarum* refers to animals from distant parts of the world, strange to Italy. He could have used the regular word for lion-cubs (*catuli*) but instead he deliber-ately uses the Greek word *skymnoi* (Latinized as *scymni*). The bilingual vocabulary confirms his point, that the phenomenon of innate powers is universal. Finally, in comparing himself to Epicurus, he says:[73]

> Why should the swallow (*hirundo*) compete with swans (*cycnis*), or what power would kids (*haedi*) have with their trembling limbs in running compared with the mighty strength of the horse (*fortis equi vis*)?

He himself in these similes is signified by Latin words (*hirundo*, *haedi*), but Epicurus by a Greek word (*cycnus*: the Latin word for a swan is *olor*) and a Greek epic expression ("strength of a horse" for "horse"). So the point is made, that Lucretius, the Latin poet, is bringing Greek doctrine into Latin poetry.

We return now to the structure of the poem. Each book is preceded by an introductory passage. The first proem is both the longest and the most complex. It begins with an epic invocation, addressing Venus as *Aeneadum genetrix hominum divumque voluptas* ("Mother of the sons of Aeneas, the pleasure of men and gods"). The vocabulary is Greek (*Aeneadum*) and Latin; the content is political (Venus, through her son Aeneas, as origin of the Roman race) and philosophical (*voluptas*, an allusion to Epicurean *hedone*) and allusive (invocation of a divine figure, as in the first lines of the Homeric epics and the *Annales* of Ennius). This leads to a hymn and prayer to Venus as the origin of life and of the variety of the universe and its powers of procreation; Venus, too, as the bringer of peace, the lover and tamer of Mars, god of war. Venus, therefore, is the appropriate source for Lucretius' poem on "the beginnings of things, from which nature creates all things".[74] The proem then continues with praise of Epicurus; an attack on the evils of religion and superstition; and warnings to Memmius (Lucretius' patron and dedicatee) against trusting in religious stories; finally, the poet's complaint about the difficulty of expressing himself in Latin poetry.[75]

This splendid introduction is problematic. Why should a poet who will demolish traditional myths and beliefs about the gods begin with a hymn to one of those very gods? How can he ask for the intervention of a god in human affairs, when Epicurean theology expressly denied this possibility? The most persuasive answer is that of Sedley, that "the proem ... is, and is meant to be recognized as, an imitation of the proem to Empedocles' physical poem".[76] Just as Empedocles had been the great Greek poet–philosopher of Nature (his major – or only – poem was titled

On Nature), so Lucretius will be the Roman philosopher–poet of Nature. Just as Empedocles had appealed to Aphrodite (comparable to the Roman Venus), so Lucretius will appeal to Venus. Empedocles had based his theory of cosmic cycles on the conflict between Love and Strife, so Lucretius will bring about a resolution of the conflicts caused by mental and psychological distress through the philosophy of Epicurus. Not that Lucretius follows Empedocles uncritically. He says that Sicily produced no one more distinguished, and that his poetry came from a "god-like heart" and made him seem to be "hardly born of human stock", yet Lucretius attacks him for his pluralism.[77]

Whatever solutions scholars have proposed for the problems raised by the proem, the power of this opening has struck its readers in all ages.[78] As the proem to an epic poem on philosophy, it announces Lucretius' philosophical and literary allegiances: Epicurus is the source of his philosophy; Empedocles is his guide for a poem on the nature of things.

Four of Lucretius' six proems sing the praises of Epicurus, and those for Books 1, 3 and 5 each preface a two-book segment. In the first (1. 62–79) Epicurus is "a Man of Greece", whose intellect passed beyond the bounds of the universe and, through knowledge, gave men the power to crush religion and make them equal to the gods. Poetry and philosophy are wonderfully interwoven in this passage:[79]

> When human life lay on the ground in full view, a nasty sight, crushed by the weight of Religion, which showed her face from heaven, fearsome to see, threatening mortals – then first a Man of Greece dared to raise mortal eyes in defiance and to resist her. Him neither tales of the gods nor lightning nor the sky with threatening thunder could keep down. Instead, all the more did they stimulate the keen courage of his spirit to be eager to burst through the confining bars of the gates of nature. Therefore the lively power of his mind triumphed, and he passed far beyond the fiery walls of the universe (*flammantia moenia mundi*) and travelled through the whole of boundless space in mind and intellect. Thence as victor he brings us report of what can come into being and what cannot, what are the limits to the power of each thing and where is its deep-fixed boundary marker. Thus Religion in its turn is crushed beneath our feet, and his victory makes us equal to heaven.

Lucretius later shows how the tranquillity of the gods can be shared by the human being who correctly perceives their nature.[80] Epicurus was said to have been exceptionally pious and not at all an atheist, and Lucretius directs his criticism at false impressions of the gods, spread by the traditional tales of mythology and perpetuated by human fear and superstition. As an example of this he tells the story of Iphigenia, a central myth of the human dilemma between personal obligations and ambitions, between personal preferences and the demands of society and religion. The daughter, "sinfully butchered by her father – all for the happy and auspicious departure of the fleet", is the tragic example of the evils of religion. Lucretius concludes (1. 101): "such were the evils which religion had the power to suggest".[81]

Lucretius then turns to address Memmius, for he, too, may feel "terror and darkness of the mind", which Lucretius will dispel by "a survey and reasoned discussion of nature".[82] And this leads into his epic (a suitable term for *this* didactic poem), which he places in the tradition of the great epic teachers of Greece and Rome, Homer and Ennius.[83] The poet's first lesson will be about the first beginnings, and the first principle is "nothing can ever come into being from nothing by the gods' agency". Second, that nothing can dissipate into nothing, and nothing can be destroyed. Third, the nature of things consists of atoms and void.[84]

These three lessons are basic to Lucretius' doctrine, which derives from Epicurus and ultimately from the fifth-century BCE Greek atomists, Leucippus and Democritus. He presents each lesson briefly and dogmatically, and then supports the argument with examples, from which he deduces the inevitability of his conclusions. An understanding of the structure of the physical world will lead to an understanding of the true nature of the fears, superstitions and psychological disturbances that make life unnecessarily difficult for those who are ignorant of the teachings of Epicurus. Lucretius punctuates his discussion with the proem to Book 2 (quoted above). Acting on the principle of "smearing honey on the cup" (4. 10–13), he keeps before Memmius the ethical purpose of his teaching, which he relates to the political and social world of Memmius. He then returns to atomic doctrine. First he teaches about the forming of material objects from atoms and their dissolution, about their motion, their shapes and compounds, their lack of colour and other secondary qualities.[85] A famous variation from Epicurus' extant teaching on the movements of atoms is the passage on the "swerve" (*clinamen*) of atoms in their downward progress, which may have been part (now lost) of Epicurus' *On Nature*. It is a third cause for the movement of atoms, the first two being "blows" (i.e. impact of other atoms) and the second "weight" (i.e. gravity). The "swerve" is needed to account for the conjunction of atoms to form objects:

> for if they did not usually swerve, all things would fall downwards through the deep void, like drops of rain. No collision would be brought into being and no blow would come into being for atoms. Thus Nature would never have created anything.

Lucretius extends this to the freedom of the human will. If there were no "swerve", then the chain of causation would extend inexorably without variation. But the *clinamen* allows the human will to go where pleasure leads it, and allows human beings to proceed "where our mind carries us". This is possible in Epicurean doctrine, because of the materialist explanation of all things, including motions of the mind. Lucretius concludes:

> But that the mind in itself may not have some interior compulsion in all actions, that it may not be compelled, like something that has been conquered, to bear and to suffer – this is achieved by the tiny swerve of first things in no pre-ordained place at no pre-ordained time.

After the discussion of motion and properties of atoms, Lucretius completes Book 2 by considering the infinite possibilities of unions of atoms when their present formations are dissipated, since matter cannot be destroyed.[86] For there is no limit to the void, and therefore there need be no limit to the creation of worlds other than our own. Lucretius ends his two books on physics with the old farmer, worn out by a lifetime's labour, facing death and grumbling, "for he does not remember that all things gradually waste away and go to the grave (*ad capulum*) wearied by old age's long extent of life". Thus the way is prepared for Book 3 and its climactic discussion of death.

Noticeable also is the way in which Lucretius introduces the discussion on the infinity of worlds by returning to the ideas of creative Nature that so brightly coloured the Hymn to Venus at the beginning of the poem.[87] The component atoms in nature go through their cycle of creation and decay: so, too, human beings, and the world of nature and other worlds, must expect that the constitution of their material atoms must in time be dissipated to form new individuals and new worlds.

The proem to Book 3 begins with praise of Epicurus, expressed with gratitude, reverence and awe, in sublime poetry.[88] The theme of the book is darkness and light – the darkness of ignorance and superstition, the light of knowledge and freedom from fear. So Epicurus is the first to bring such light: he is "the glory of the Greek race", and Lucretius will follow him, being as a swallow to a swan, or a kid to a horse. Epicurus, who in Book 1 was "a Man of Greece", is now "father, the discoverer of things, the giver of a father's precepts", and Lucretius will feed on his "golden sayings" as bees feed on flowers. Lucretius' lines on the effect of Epicurus' teaching are central to an understanding of the nature of his poem and his own inspiration:

> For as soon as your philosophy, springing from your godlike mind, began to proclaim the nature of things, the terrors of the mind disperse, the walls of the universe are parted, I see the workings of the world throughout the void. I see the majesty of the gods in their tranquil homes … Nature, indeed, supplies [them] with everything, nor does anything diminish their peace of mind at any time. On the other hand, the regions of Acheron [the Underworld] cannot be seen … At these things [i.e. the teachings of Epicurus] a godlike pleasure and a shudder of awe takes hold of me, because through your power nature is revealed so clearly and unveiled in every part.

This is the heart of the matter. Not only does Lucretius revere Epicurus as a father, but he experiences a religious transformation, which reveals to him the truth about the nature of the universe and of human life and death, and leads him to follow with an enthusiasm that is like the "holy rapture" (the phrase is E. J. Kenney's) of a devotee of the gods. But the Epicurean gods are tranquil and their peace of mind is complete. Lucretius' readers, too, will experience such tranquillity if they understand his teachings.

The primary purpose of the poet's teaching is to remove the fear of death from the minds of human beings. Such fear is the opposite of the inner and outer peace that the doctrines of Epicurus have revealed. The rest of the proem (31–93), therefore, turns directly to the fear of death. Lucretius shows how this fear motivates men's attitudes to life, in particular their superstitions, their ambitions, crimes and envy, which lead them to disregard morality in their relations with other human beings. They are like children in the dark (87–88), and Lucretius concludes with a return to the opening theme of darkness and light (91–93):

> Therefore this terror of the mind and darkness must be dispelled, not by the rays of the sun nor by the bright shafts of daylight, but by observing nature and by reason.

This elaborate proem encompasses and anticipates the themes of Book 3. Lucretius will show why death should not be feared. He has already explained the atomic composition of the exterior world; now he will explain the composition of the human mind (*animus*) and soul, or more accurately "spirit" (*anima*), which are material, consisting of atoms.[89] The distinction between *animus* and *anima* (Greek *nous* and *psyche* respectively), which is clear in Greek, was blurred by Democritus and Epicurus. Democritus, according to Aristotle, said that "they are the same", referring (so later authors show) to their atomic composition. Both he and Epicurus said that the soul consisted of two parts, respectively reasoning and unreasoning, which were structurally identical. At any rate, it is the union of mind and spirit with the body that makes human life possible. Since they came into being with the body, they will dissipate when the body dies: they, therefore, are mortal.[90] If they die, then our existence comes to an end with their dissolution. Death, therefore, is nothing to fear; the myths of the Underworld and its torments hold no terrors for us, and we can achieve happiness by accepting our mortality.[91]

This bald summary does not do justice to the impassioned rhetoric of the poet. After giving twenty-nine proofs of the mortality of the soul, he begins his conclusion, that death is not to be feared, by quoting Epicurus: "Death therefore is nothing to us." He continues:[92]

> [Death] does not concern us at all, since the nature of the mind (*animus*) is considered to be mortal. And just as in times past we perceived no ill when the Carthaginians came from all sides to fight, when all things, shuddering in the trembling tumult of war, shook beneath the lofty realms of the upper air, and it was doubtful under which of the two [namely, Carthaginians or Romans] all things would be subjected on land and sea – so, when we no longer exist, when the dissolution of body and soul (from

whose union we are brought into existence), nothing, I say, will be able to happen to us at all, for we will not then exist, nothing will be able to affect our senses – not even if earth were mixed with sea and sea with sky.

I quote this splendid passage without changing Lucretius' punctuation, remembering how the "first impression" of the spoken or written word is important in Epicurean theory. The enormous period builds up to overwhelm the hearer with the certainty that no mass of historical or cosmic calamities can affect us after our death. The recall of the crisis of the second Punic war – the most traumatic historical event in the Roman people's collective psyche in Lucretius' time – gives the passage an immediacy for Roman hearers that would have been lacking had Lucretius followed Epicurus in every word. The rest of the book is hardly necessary after this ringing affirmation. Nevertheless, in the remaining lines Lucretius proves the foolishness of clinging to life out of fear of death, and the folly of believing the myths of the Underworld and its punishments.

Yet we must ask if his rigorously logical demonstration is adequate to parry the reality of untimely death and bereavement. We remember the humane sympathy of Philodemus, which we contrast with Lucretius' satirical mockery of those who mourn the dead:[93]

No more, no more will your happy home welcome you, nor your excellent wife, nor your lovely children running to get your kiss first and touching your heart with silent pleasure. You will not be able to prosper by your deeds and protect your family. "Miserable man", they say, "one hateful day has taken from you miserably all the rewards of life".

Lucretius drily points out that none of this matters to the dead man, who can feel nothing. Yet even Epicurus said that "the wise man will grieve".[94] We all must die: Epicurus himself died. How then can we hesitate to face death?

In a way Lucretius has completed his task by proving that knowledge of the "nature of things" will rid people of the fear of death. Nevertheless, he still has not expounded Epicurean doctrine on sensation and thought, or on cosmic and meteorological matters. While they are not now essential for dispelling the fear of death – for Lucretius has already completed this task – they are a necessary part of a complete exposition of the nature of things. So in Book 4 Lucretius turns from the universal human experience of death to the particular experiences of sensation: vision (26–521), the other senses (522–721), thought and dreams (722–822). Before starting on this part of the book he pauses to proclaim his poetic mission in the service of philosophy.[95] The poet leads his hearers through trackless places and his poetry will grip their minds, enabling them "to perceive the whole nature of things and be aware of its usefulness".

With this reminder he returns to the human mind (*animus*), whose composition and mortality had been such a large part of the doctrine of the third book. In the later preface (4. 26–44), which replaced the original one, he says:[96]

> now I will begin to discuss for you a subject that strongly concerns these matters [i.e. the nature of the *animus*], that there exist things that we call the "likenesses" of things (*rerum simulacra*).

The *simulacra* are the underlying concept of the first part of the book.[97] We have seen how in the original preface Lucretius tried different equivalents for the Greek word *eidola*, finally settling on *simulacra* (likenesses) as the best Latin equivalent. The discussion is in part about physics, that is, the physical nature of the atoms that form *simulacra*, but it even more concerns the processes of knowledge, belonging to the Epicurean category of *kanonike*. The *simulacra* are films or effluences of very fine atoms flowing from the surface of objects and resulting in the perceiver's sense-perception. Although Lucretius devotes most space to the sense of sight (26–521), the doctrine is equally valid for the other senses (522–721). Thus the atomic physics of the first two books are proved to be valid also for individual human experience, and sense-perception is shown to have a material basis.

Lucretius then turns to processes of thought (722–822), for which he gives the same materialist explanation. Like Gilbert Ryle in the twentieth century, he dismisses the notion of "the mind in the machine". Thought is caused by exceedingly fine *simulacra*, whether of things perceived that become the objects of thought, or of things imagined (for example, centaurs). Even dreams can be explained in this way, a passage where Lucretius' doctrine of the "latent image" uncannily anticipates Freud's theories of the unconscious.[98]

Lucretius next turns to the effect of the *simulacra* on the perceiver, thinker or dreamer. First, he refutes teleological explanations of functions of parts of the human body (i.e. that they were created for a purpose), since to suppose, for example, that the eyes were created for the purpose of seeing, is to suppose an intelligent creator (823–57). Then he shows how desire and will are motivated by sense-impressions, including those perceived in sleep (877–1036). The final example, erotic dreams (1030–36), leads into the last topic of the book, the stimulation of love and sexual desire by *simulacra* (1037–1287). In this extraordinary diatribe Lucretius moves beyond his primary task of expounding Epicurean doctrine, for his descriptions of lust, love and the physical aspect of sexual activity are as satirical as they are philosophical. Nevertheless, their purpose is consistent with Epicurus' doctrine that pleasure is best experienced in moderation.[99] Lucretius returns to this theme in Book 5 and in his praise of Epicurus at 6. 25, where Epicurus "set a limit to desire".[100]

It is left now for Lucretius to turn to the world, the origins and development of life and human civilization, and cosmic phenomena, which occupy the rest of the poem as far as 6. 1089. Like Books 1 and 3, Book 5 opens with praise of Epicurus, now honoured as a god:[101]

> For if we must speak as the majesty of the subject … requires, he was a god, Memmius, a god, who first discovered the philosophy of life, which now we call wisdom, and who through his skill raised life from such great waves and such deep darkness, and set it in so tranquil and so bright a light.

Epicurus is a greater benefactor of human beings than the gods who taught them skills of agriculture, greater then Hercules, who rid the world of so many terrifying monsters. Monsters, says Lucretius, still are numerous in the forests and mountains, and we are able to avoid them. But how can we avoid the equally terrifying monsters of our inner disturbances? Only the doctrines of Epicurus can conquer desires, anxieties, fears and the other things that prevent a tranquil life. That is why he should be numbered with the gods.

This extraordinary proem looks back to the mental disturbances of lust and love exposed in Book 4, and forward to discussion of the Epicurean gods, promised (but not realized) at 5. 155. Lucretius, however, now will turn to the world and prove its mortality, for that which is born must perish (5. 64–66). He shows that it is composed of atoms and not created by the gods (91–508), and then he turns to the heavenly bodies, the motions of the stars and the planets and their relationship to the earth (509–770). As Bailey observes, "the astronomical section is difficult to understand and to follow", and it interrupts the sequence of discussion of the world and of life on earth. Sedley has plausibly suggested that Lucretius was following the order of topics in Epicurus' *On Nature* and that he would in a final revision have transferred this section to the end of Book 5, where it would lead naturally to the discussion of celestial phenomena in Book 6. Certainly the gods are more prominent in the programmatic lines of Book 5, and Sedley again is plausible in suggesting that "the final pair [of books] was destined to have ... the function of dispelling the fear of god".[102]

At any rate, the astronomical section is followed by the history of life on earth: first, the origin of life and evolution and survival or extinction of species of animals.[103] The doctrine of the survival of species (855–77) is again a remarkable anticipation of modern theories, and the joyously poetical account of the origin of life (783–820) recalls the hymn to Venus in the proem to Book 1. Lucretius, even if he says that Earth is rightly called "Mother Earth" (821–22), is still following Epicurean doctrine in denying any role to a creator or to the figures of traditional mythology.

The rest of the book is taken up with a history of human society, which Kenney has called "Lucretius' greatest intellectual and imaginative achievement".[104] Epicurus spends very little time on this subject in the *Letter to Herodotus* (§§75–76), and it is likely that Lucretius' source was book 12 of *On Nature*. He proceeds methodically from the life of primitive human beings (925–1010), to the development of civilization (the origins of family and community life and law, 1011–27; of language, 1028–90; of fire, 1091–1104; the rise of kings and the desire for wealth, 1105–60; the rise of religion and superstition, 1161–1240; warfare, 1241–1349; the arts of peace – clothing, agriculture, music, 1350–1411; finally, the progress of civilization, 1412–57).

This is an extraordinary passage. Its broad yet detailed treatment of history recalls Posidonius, but in its poetic intensity it is unique. Lucretius keeps before us the purpose of his poem, to bring tranquillity of mind through knowledge. Thus he comments on the futility of political ambition;[105] and he attacks wrong religion and superstition:[106]

> O unhappy race of human beings! To assign such deeds to the gods and add to them their bitter anger! What groans did those [early mortals] bring to birth for themselves then, what wounds for us, what tears for our descendants! It is not piety at all to be seen often turning with veiled

> head to a stone, or to approach every altar, or to lie pros-
> trate on the ground and stretch out one's hands before the
> shrines of the gods, or to shower the altars with the blood
> of four-footed animals, or to make a linked chain of prayers.
> No! [Piety is] rather to be able to look on everything with
> a mind at peace.

Or again, on the death of primitive human beings, Lucretius shows that the pain and horror were real enough for beings who were ignorant of the consolations of philosophy:[107]

> For one by one they would be caught and become living
> food for wild beasts to chew. Each [victim] would fill the
> forests and mountains and woods with his groans, as he saw
> his living entrails buried in a living tomb [i.e. the wild
> beast]. But those who escaped with mutilated body would
> later hold their trembling hands over the cruel wounds and
> call on Death with frightening shrieks, until the savage
> agony robbed them of life, helpless and not knowing what
> their wounds needed.

The horrifying description of primitive death has its counterpart in the deaths by plague that end the sixth book.

Book 6 begins with praise of Athens and its greatest gift to humankind, Epicurus.[108] The proem is linked to the history of the rise of civilization at the end of Book 5, for Lucretius says that Epicurus saw that, even after civilization had advanced to its highest level in Athens, human beings were still afflicted with anxiety. And so his doctrine purified their minds, put an end to their mental disturbances, and showed the way to the highest good.

Lucretius then turns to the first main theme of the book, celestial and meteorological phenomena, followed by the second theme, terrestrial phenomena.[109] In the preliminary sketch of his subject (43–95) he especially warns his readers against attributing celestial phenomena to the gods. Thunder, lightning and storms can be explained rationally, without recourse to the gods. Here the poet takes aim not only at superstition in general but specifically at Roman religious practice, in which the rituals for divining or exor-cizing violent meteorological events were precisely prescribed:[110]

> I must come to grips with the system in the heavens and on
> earth, and I must tell in my poetry of storms and bright

> lightning. I must tell how they act and what cause brings them into being, lest you hurry in fear mindlessly to quarter the sky and ask from which quarter flying came the lightning flash, or to which quarter it turned as it left, or how it passed through walled enclosures and how it passed from them after taking possession.

Lucretius uses the technical vocabulary of augury. The Roman ritual was inherited from the Etruscans, who divided the sky into sixteen parts (a number obtained by twice doubling the four original quarters) so as to have a factual basis on which to make their divination. Lucretius develops his argument later in the book.[111] It is similar to Cicero's attack on the Stoics' support for divination from lightning, where Cicero explicitly approves of Epicurean doctrine.[112] The matter was not just theoretical, for it had practical political consequences: political processes (e.g. elections or legislation) could be postponed or cancelled if lightning was observed. In a celebrated abuse of religious ritual, Bibulus, Julius Caesar's opponent and colleague in the consulship of 59, perpetually "observed the heavens" to obstruct Caesar's legislation. Lucretius exploits the ironies: experts on divination are considered to be knowledgeable, but their knowledge is based on the false premises that the gods exist and that the lightning is an expression of their will, which must be divined by the experts. Of course, only Epicurus had true knowledge, which Lucretius expounds so as to rid his Roman hearers of their fear of the power of the gods:[113]

> This is how to understand the real nature of fiery lightning and to see with what energy it acts, and not, by reading in vain the rolls of Etruscan formulae, [attempt to] learn the will of the gods.

The second major section of Book 6, on terrestrial phenomena, consists of a series of disconnected subjects (including earthquakes, the Nile's annual flood, magnets, epidemics), linked solely by Lucretius' goal of proclaiming true knowledge. The subject of epidemics does not occur in the extant Epicurean letters or fragments, and even Sedley is hesitant in assigning it to Book 13 of *On Nature*.[114] Others have suggested that Lucretius may be drawing on Hippocratic writings, for example, the treatise *On Airs, Waters and Places*, which was written in the later part of the fifth century BCE.[115] Lucretius teaches that there are healthful atoms in the air, and others that cause disease and death (6. 1093–97).[116] The latter fly about so that "the air becomes full of disease". The air, then, is the source of disease, and it was the source of the great plague at Athens, an account of which forms the last part of the book.[117]

Lucretius is following the famous description of the plague in Thucydides, which he emulates in descriptive horror. Most important, however, is the effect of the disease on the minds and emotions of the survivors, for no longer did religious beliefs count for anything (1276–77), neither were the traditional funeral customs observed (1278–79). And so *De Rerum Natura* ends with the distressed Athenians cremating their dead in a disorderly fashion and fighting among themselves to claim the corpses of their relatives (1283–86).

The ending is abrupt. We have suggested earlier that the poem is almost complete, except for lines drawing the lesson that if the Athenians had known the doctrines of Epicurus they would have been able to understand the cause of the disaster and treat it with equanimity. Certainly, the focus on death at the end contrasts with that on life in the proem to Book 1. The mental and physical distress of the Athenians contrasts with the calm doctrines of Epicurus praised in the proem to Book 6. The wildly emotional funeral scenes recall the ending of the *Iliad*, with Hector's funeral and the passionate utterances of his widow, his mother, and his sister-in-law. Finally, the focus on death at the end of the poem reinforces the focus on death at the end of its first half. There, Lucretius proclaimed the triumph of Epicurean doctrine over death; here, the victory of death over the Athenians who lived and died many years before the coming of Epicurus. Lucretius is true to his overriding principle: those who have knowledge of "the nature of things" can achieve calm of mind and freedom from fear of death.

Lucretius' poem does not seem to have had the influence that it deserved. Within a decade of its composition the Roman republic had collapsed, Julius Caesar was dead, and fresh violence overwhelmed the quiet practice of philosophy. Cicero's murder in December of 43 BCE was symptomatic. Yet some Epicureans survived the civil wars successfully, for example, Cicero's friend, Atticus, at the price of friendship with people whose political acts were the opposite of Epicurean.[118]

More significant is the fact that Lucretius was read and admired by the leading Augustan poets, Horace and Virgil, both of whom began to publish about fifteen years after his death. Horace (an Epicurean) quotes him at *Satires* 1. 5. 101, and alludes to the opening of Book 2 of the *De Rerum Natura* in *Epistles* 1. 11. 10. The last part of the same letter (lines 22–30) is Lucretian in tone. Virgil explicitly admired Lucretius, whom he does not name. In the second *Georgic*, completed before 29 BCE, he contrasts his pastoral poetry with that of Lucretius:[119]

> Happy is he who could discover the causes of things and trample underfoot all fears and inexorable fate and the sound of greedy Acheron. Blessed also is he who knows the gods of the countryside ...

This passage follows lines in which Virgil was clearly alluding to the meteorological and cosmological themes of Lucretius. A few years earlier he had echoed Lucretius in his sixth *Eclogue*, where the song of Silenus alludes to the cosmogony of Lucretius. Later, in the *Aeneid* (written in the 20s BCE), the song of the Punic bard, Iopas, at the banquet of Dido echoes the meteorological themes both of the sixth *Eclogue* and of Book 6 of Lucretius' poem.[120] Yet one of the most original and powerful parts of the *Aeneid* is the sixth book, where Aeneas visits the Underworld and sees for himself Acheron and the fate of the dead – things that Lucretius says Epicurus had "trampled underfoot".

In the first and second centuries CE, several authors show that Lucretius was still being read. Statius, in a poem celebrating the birthday of the dead poetic genius, Lucan (d. 65 CE), refers to "the austere madness of learned Lucretius", and his contemporary, Quintilian, includes Lucretius rather grudgingly in his reading list for students of oratory.[121]

The Stoic satirist Persius (d. 62 CE), agrees with Quintilian that *De Rerum Natura* was too difficult for the ordinary reader, but he is more sympathetic. He imagines a "hairy centurion" poking fun at philosophers, with their mannerisms and their doctrines that are intelligible only to other philosophers. He paraphrases Lucretius: "nothing can come from nothing, nothing can return to nothing".[122] The target of this witty passage is the self-satisfied and ignorant "common man", not the philosophical poet.

Seneca's attitude is more complex. Although a Stoic, he often quotes Epicurus (particularly in the first thirty of his letters), and occasionally Lucretius. In letter 95, in which he debates the ability of philosophy to bring about the good life, he quotes Lucretius to illustrate the scope of philosophical enquiry, extending to cosmology and the creation of the world.[123] He quotes Lucretius again in letter 106 to show that the study of philosophical doctrine is "mere child's play", for it will make a student learned, but will not help live the good life: "our learning is for school, not for life".[124] In letter 110 he quotes Lucretius on groundless fears and improves on him: Lucretius said that we are afraid in daylight, but, says Seneca, "we make everything darkness".[125] Finally, in *De Tranquillitate* Seneca quotes Lucretius in support of the commonplace doctrine that "a human being cannot run from himself", which is found in writers from Aristotle to Juvenal.[126]

About a century after Seneca, Aulus Gellius (b. 125 CE) quotes Lucretius on a literary, rather than philosophical, matter.[127] The poem, then, was still being read two centuries after Lucretius' death, but, it seems, only by a few readers and apparently without any widespread influence. While this is regrettable, it is hardly surprising. Lucretius was too austere and his Latin too difficult for the kind of reader for whom Cicero or Seneca was writing. He was read by the Christian fathers, and Lactantius (c. 240–320 CE) quotes him frequently, both to criticize him and to use him to support his own arguments. Augustine also alludes to him in several passages, although he prefers Cicero as a source for attacks on Epicureanism.

Epicureanism continued to have a vigorous existence in the 150 years after the death of Lucretius, for which the criticisms of Plutarch (c. 50–120 CE), who was himself a Platonist, are good evidence.[128] The titles are known of nine works by Plutarch in which he criticizes Epicurus and his followers. Three of these are extant: *That Epicurus Makes a Pleasant Life Impossible* (usually referred to by the first two words of its Latin title, *Non Posse*); *Against Colotes*; *Whether Lathe Biosas Is Rightly Said* (Latin, *An Recte Dictum*). The second of these is paradoxical, since it attacks a book (no longer extant) written by Colotes, a disciple of Epicurus at Lampsacus, where Epicurus taught from 310 to 306 BCE. Colotes had criticized other philosophers (including Democritus and Plato), and perhaps Plutarch attacks him because of his hostility to Plato. On the other hand *An Recte Dictum* attacks Epicurean quietism, which, as we have seen, directly opposed the Roman ethos of public service and desire for fame. Plutarch says (*An Recte Dictum* 6):[129]

> I think that to be alive and generally to be born and become a human being are a gift from god to make a person known ... But he who hurls himself into obscurity is cloaked in darkness and buries his life in an empty tomb.

In *Non Posse* Plutarch (through participants in the dialogue, Theon and Aristodemus) attacks Epicurean doctrines, first, on pleasure and "living unobtrusively", and then on the gods and the absence of an afterlife. Plutarch was a pious man, and for the last decades of his life he held a priesthood at Delphi (which was comparatively close to his home town of Chaeronea), an honour which he prized. His attack on Epicurean theology is therefore coloured by his own experience.

Towards the end of the second century Epicureanism continued to be strong, in part because of its opposition to superstition and false prophets, as Lucian (born *c.*120) shows in his essay on *Alexander or the False Prophet*. There he says (§61) that people turned to Epicurus because he was:

> truly a holy man with a divine nature, who alone knew
> truly what was good. He passed his knowledge on and was
> a liberator of those who associated with him.

But during the third century CE Epicureanism declined noticeably, although it was still vigorous enough to attract the hostility of Christian authors. By the middle of the next century it was dying, and it was dead by the time that Justinian closed the schools of philosophy at Athens in 529.[130]

Early in the third century Diogenes Laertius compiled (in Greek) his *Lives of Eminent Philosophers*. Book 10 of this work is devoted solely to Epicurus, and it is exceptionally valuable for its preservation of the principal texts of Epicurean doctrine (which have been summarized above, pp. 101–105, as well as a catalogue of Epicurus' works.[131]

The last extensive evidence for vigorous devotion to Epicureanism comes from the city of Oenoanda, high on a mountain in northern Lycia (modern south-western Turkey). There, some time probably late in the second century CE, Diogenes, a prominent citizen, in his old age set up a huge inscription on a wall of a stoa (a colonnade for public use) recording his own Epicureanism and various Epicurean texts. The height of the inscription is 2.37 metres, and its length was more than 50m, perhaps even close to 100m. It was discovered in 1884 by Georges Cousin, who published sixty-four fragments in 1892. Since then more fragments have been published, most notably by Martin Smith, in a series of articles beginning in 1969, bringing the total number discovered to 212 as of 1990, perhaps a quarter of the whole.[132] We have seen how greatly our knowledge of Hellenistic philosophy depends on fragmentary texts, and in the inscription of Diogenes we are sadly reminded of the vagaries of destruction and survival in a remote place, subject to the damage wrought by earthquakes and builders (who used stones from the inscription) and to the ravages of neglect.

Diogenes published his inscription because he was moved, like Lucretius, by the miserable spiritual state of his fellow human beings, whose inner disturbances he likened to a plague (frag. 1.2 and 2.4). In "the sunset of life" he wished to help humankind by telling them the true nature of things and healing their pains by "cutting them down to something small and making their intensity very small indeed" (frag. 2.6). Thirteen (or more) of the *Kyriai Doxai* were inscribed along the lowest course of the wall; above them, in a parallel course, Diogenes inscribed a treatise on ethics; above that was a treatise on physics. In the top course was a treatise on old age. To the right of the treatise on ethics were three letters of Diogenes to his friends, and various philosophical maxims. To the right of the treatise on old age was a letter of Epicurus to his mother, on the subject of dreams, and two other letters of Epicurus.

Diogenes is the author of the three treatises. Most interesting is the part of the treatise on physics, which (like Epicurus' letter to his mother) dealt with dreams and has many parallels in Lucretius.[133] The treatise on ethics was given additional authority by the *Kyriai Doxai* of Epicurus, inscribed immediately below. Diogenes focused on the question, "How can our life give us pleasure?", which he answered by the doctrine that if the passions are removed then pleasure will replace them. The passions he categorized as fear of the gods, of death, and of pain: these he discussed before dealing with desires, pleasures and actions. The treatise on old age is addressed to young readers. From what little remains, it appears to have been a defence of old age against the jibes and comments of the young. Probably this, too, goes back to texts of Epicurus, whose views on old age were harshly criticized by Plutarch.[134]

Diskin Clay has shown the extent to which Diogenes follows, imitates and emulates Epicurus.[135] The Epicurean community in southern Asia Minor, late in Roman imperial times, still followed the custom of the early Epicureans, revering the founder and learning his doctrines by heart. Like Epicurus, Diogenes wished to help human beings, whether those who read his inscription, or those in the wider world, including posterity. In his treatise on old age he says that he will leave life with a joyful hymn (Greek, *paean*), having enjoyed a good life. He is referring to words of Epicurus' close friend Metrodorus, or possibly even of Epicurus himself, and they are a fitting ending to this chapter:[136]

> I have beaten you first, O Fortune, and I have blocked every one of your approaches. Never will we give ourselves up to you or to any other circumstance. But when necessity drives us out, we, greatly despising life and those who vainly cling to it, will depart from it with a beautiful hymn of victory, singing that our life has been well lived.

5

PHILOSOPHERS AND POETS IN THE AUGUSTAN AGE

Lucretius and Cicero represent the zenith of intellectual activity in the Roman republic. The murder of Cicero in December, 43 BCE, and the defeat of Brutus and Cassius at the battles of Philippi in October, 42 BCE, introduced a new political and intellectual age. For Cicero, philosophy was closely bound up with public life. Its study had practical consequences in the political activity of free men competing with each other in the public arena and mindful of their duty of service to the state. Lucretius explicitly advised against public service, yet it is the constant and contrasting background to his Epicurean system. In the military and political turmoil of the decade after Philippi the Roman world was deaf to the voices of Cicero and Lucretius. When peace and stability were restored, after the victory of Octavian at Actium in 31 BCE and the death of Mark Antony in Alexandria the following year, the Republic was dead, alive only in the brilliant use of the term *res publica* by Octavian, whose restoration of constitutional government in January, 27 BCE, inaugurated his tenure of power as the leading citizen (*princeps*), but *de facto* the first emperor, of Rome.[1] He took the title of *Augustus*, the Latin equivalent of the Greek term *sebastos* (reverend), an honorific title frequently bestowed on Roman grandees in the Greek east in republican times. As Tacitus rightly observed, the titles of public officials were the same as before, but the free republic had perished, never to be revived.[2]

The consequences for intellectual life and freedom of expression were predictable and profound. Tacitus (putting the words in the mouth of the poet, Maternus, who had written a drama on the theme of the younger Cato) asked:[3]

> What greater evidence [for the curbing of oratory] could be found than that ... peace, the prolonged passivity of the

131

people, and, above all, the discipline imposed by the *princeps*, had pacified eloquence itself just as much as everything else?

These words were published in 102 CE, but they accurately describe a process begun after Cicero's death, irreversibly advanced by the triumph of Augustus, and perpetually confirmed by the accident of his long life, for he died in 14 CE, 41 years after the transfer of power to the senate and people. Tacitus began his history of the period from 14 to 68 CE, with the death of Augustus, for that was the first (and, as events showed, the only) time that the republican constitution could possibly have been restored.[4] With the transfer of power to Tiberius the principate was confirmed, the monarchy assured. The world of Seneca (born in 4 BCE) was totally different from that of Cicero.

In this world, true freedom of speech was rare and dangerous, for outspoken criticism of those who held political and military power could bring exile or even death. And if free speech is curbed, then the process of limiting freedom of thought will begin, however insidiously. Thus, philosophical doctrines came to focus on private concerns, above all, ethical problems. The bearing of philosophy on public life became restricted to problems of coexistence with a political system in which the ruler held the power of life and death, while his fellow-citizens had the choice of cooperation, acquiescence, or retirement (often through death or exile) from the public arena. Not surprisingly, one of the most prominent problems discussed by Roman philosophers in the early empire was that of *otium*, retirement from public activity.

The period of the second Triumvirate (43–31 BCE) and the reign of Augustus (27 BCE to 14 CE) was transitional between a manifestly dysfunctional political system and a new system based on military power, in which the monarch needed the support of many people, who themselves had considerable powers, subsumed under the power and prestige of the monarch. It was a period of political ambiguities: a monarchy was dressed in the forms and words of the Republic; politicians and military men wielded great power, yet were at the mercy of the monarch if they encroached on his power and prestige; people of ability owed their political or social advancement to the monarch and his close friends; finally, a citizenry courted by the monarch (who dated his tenure of power by the annual renewal of the powers of the Tribune of the People, *tribunicia potestas*) was powerless to vote him out of office.

The goal of philosophers was still the good life, and the traditional goals of the Stoics and Epicureans were outwardly unchanged – the achievement of tranquillity and freedom from mental disturbance through reason and virtue. But the political and social context was so changed that the philosophers focused almost exclusively on problems that concerned individuals.

Even in the triumviral period, philosophy continued to be practised, and a Roman school of philosophy came into existence, led by Quintus Sextius, the details of whose life have to be gleaned mostly from references in Seneca's letters.[5] He probably died early in the first century CE (Jerome says that he flourished around 1 CE), and Seneca, writing in 62–64 CE, lists his school among those which had become defunct by his time. Indeed, the last chapter of Seneca's *Naturales Quaestiones* laments the distressing state of philosophy in his time:[6]

Who enters on the path to wisdom? Who thinks it worthy [of study] except in so far as he has a passing acquaintance with it? Who pays any attention to a philosopher or to any liberal study except when the games are suspended, or there is a rainy day which can be wasted? And so many schools of philosophy have come to an end without a new leader. Both the Old and New Academies have left us without a Principal; who is there to teach the doctrines of Pyrrho [the Sceptic]? The Pythagorean school (unpopular with the common people) has no Professor; the new school of the Sextii, which showed Roman strength in its early stages, began with great energy and now is dead.

Sextius (who was succeeded as head of the school by his son) refused the invitation of Julius Caesar to enter on an active political career in the senate. He studied in Athens, and, back in Rome, wrote philosophical works "in Greek words but with Roman character". Seneca calls him a *de facto* Stoic and quotes his use of the military metaphor for the wise man, who must advance like an army prepared for battle and on guard against the enemy. The wise man will deploy his virtues to protect himself from fear, grief, poverty, disgrace and any other adversity.[7] Seneca describes a reading with his friends of "the fifth book of Quintus Sextius the father", which he found vigorous and courageous, not anaemic and pedantic. "When you read Sextius," says Seneca, "you will say, 'this man is alive, he is vigorous, he is free, he is superhuman, he sends me away full of immense confidence'."[8] Sextius, it seems, had no use for the subtleties of Greek dialectic: his ethical doctrines were appropriate for hard times, when courage and constancy were needed, but their virile independence was dangerous under an established principate.

Sextius also taught the Pythagorean doctrine of vegetarianism, which Seneca practiced for about a year, early in the reign of Tiberius. He seems also to have taught that the soul was incorporeal.[9] But more important was his influence on the Alexandrian philosopher, Sotion, and the Roman rhetorician, Papirius Fabianus, both teachers of Seneca, who said that the latter "wrote more books of philosophy than Cicero".[10] Among the followers of Sextius also was Cornelius Celsus, who wrote an encyclopedic work on the *Artes*, of which eight books *De Medicina* survive.[11] Sextius' son may have been the Sextius Niger who wrote a book in Greek on *materia medica* that the elder Pliny used in his *Natural History*.

The most durable survivor among the intellectuals of Cicero's time was Varro, to whom Cicero dedicated the second version of his *Academica*. Varro (d. 27 BCE), seems to have kept up his scholarly activity despite proscription by Mark Antony and the destruction of his library at Casinum. His late work, *Disciplinae*, was a survey of the intellectual disciplines necessary for an educated person, and he used as a principal source the Greek work of Aëtius, known by its Latin title, *Placita*. This was a collection of the doctrines of Greek philosophers (known from fragments in later compilers), which has been variously dated as late as the first century CE or as early as the third century BCE.[12] Jaap Mansfeld has shown that the earliest version of the work was compiled before the time of Chrysippus (*c.*280–207 BCE), and that Varro used a version updated in the first century BCE. From this we learn that compilations of philosophers' doctrines, for which the technical term is *doxographies*, were being made and used in the period after the death of Cicero – significant evidence for continuing study of philosophy in the turbulent times of the second triumvirate.

Less shadowy, but still controversial, was the doxographer Arius Didymus, whose ethical compilation is largely preserved in the Greek anthology (*Eclogae*) of Johannes Stobaeus (John of Stobi, the modern Skopje).[13] Stobaeus made his anthology (much of which is extant) for his son, Septimius, early in the fifth century CE. Divided into four books of extracts from a host of authors, it is "a textbook ... aiming primarily at moral improvement and instruction in practical living".[14] Chapter 2. 7 is the first chapter to be focused on ethics, Stobaeus' primary interest for the rest of the work.[15] The chapter consists of three doxographies, which anthologize respectively the doctrines of various philosophers, Zeno and the Stoics, and Aristotle and the Peripatetics. David Hahm has shown that Arius Didymus is the author of all three parts of the chapter, and that he is the same person as the Arius (or Areus) mentioned by Plutarch and Suetonius as a friend and adviser of Augustus.[16] Suetonius (who had access to the imperial archives) says that Areus [*sic.*] and his sons "filled Augustus with varied erudition by living with him". Plutarch describes Augustus entering Alexandria in 30 BCE, "conversing with the philosopher Arius and giving him his right hand". Augustus (says Plutarch) then made a public speech in the Gymnasium from a specially prepared dais, in which he announced that he would spare Alexandria for three reasons, one of which was his wish to gratify "his friend", Arius. The historian Cassius Dio (died *c.*230 CE) says that Augustus and Arius enjoyed many philosophical conversations. Consistent with this, Seneca calls Arius "[Augustus'] philosopher", and Marcus Aurelius names him, with Maecenas, as a member of the court.[17] In 9 BCE Arius addressed a *Consolatio* to Augustus' wife, Livia, on the death of her son, Drusus, which is quoted extensively by Seneca.[18] Besides showing that, 20 years after the entry into Alexandria, Arius was still a trusted member of Augustus' inner circle, the Consolation is Stoic in tenor, for example in its advice to Livia to remain outwardly calm and inwardly self-controlled in the face of bereavement:

> Remember that it is not a great thing to behave courageously in prosperity, when the course of life is favourable. A calm sea and a following wind do not call for a show of the helmsman's skill. But when they are contrary, he must prove his courage. Then do not submit: on the contrary, walk firmly ... Nothing is more hostile to Fortune than a calm mind.

Opposition to Fortune is one of the most prominent elements in Stoic ethics of the early Roman empire. Moreover, Arius emphasizes the prominent public position of Livia, in this continuing the Ciceronian emphasis on the duty of the public leader. Seneca's Consolation for Marcia was probably written in 39–40 CE, nearly half a century after Arius' Consolation, yet Seneca can still say to Marcia (6. 1), "Arius is sitting beside you".

135

Arius was not an out-and-out Stoic, however. The doxography of Stobaeus 2. 7 shows him to be concerned with the history of philosophy, organized in such a way as to bring harmony to the dissonance of competing schools and of different voices within single schools. In particular he seems to have attempted to reconcile dogmatists (who believed that knowledge was possible) with Pyrrhonian Sceptics, who had been reinvigorated by Aenesidemus, probably in the decades after 50 BCE.[19] Aenesidemus had left the Academic school, dismayed by the quarrel between Antiochus and Philo, returning to the thoroughgoing scepticism of Pyrrho, to which his original contribution was the ten modes of suspension of judgement (recorded by Sextus Empiricus in the late second century CE). Arius, a dogmatist, sought to show that harmony between Sceptics and dogmatists was possible, in that both were seeking the truth: the sceptics potentially could find it in the future, whereas the dogmatists had already found it.

For our purpose, however, what is important is that Augustus favoured a philosopher who took a positive view of the power of reason. Given Augustus' policy of preserving the past in order to build his revolutionary political system, a philosophy that suspended judgement in all matters was unacceptable. In giving Arius a place in his entourage, Augustus was continuing the custom among the republican senatorial class of maintaining a house philosopher, as, for example, Cicero did with Diodotus. Augustus in principle maintained the fiction of being *princeps*, chief among peers. Arius was valuable as an adviser where Greek matters (political or philosophical) were concerned, as Suetonius and Plutarch made clear. His presence in the inner circle of Augustus meant that the study of philosophy was still possible, indeed encouraged, under the new regime, so long as it was not politically subversive.

The ambiguities faced by the philosophers are especially obvious in the works of the great Augustan poets. Two of them, Horace and Virgil, were themselves close to Augustus through the patronage of his principal adviser, Maecenas. A third, Ovid, was exiled in 8 CE for unspecified literary and political indiscretions, and died in exile three years after the death of Augustus. A fourth, Manilius, outlived Augustus and steered a safe course through the politically dangerous subject of astrology by advocating the continuation of the principate.

Horace (65–8 BCE) is both the most philosophical and the most ambiguous of these poets. His father, a freedman (i.e. ex-slave), was sufficiently prosperous to be able to take Horace to Rome for his education, and to send him to Athens to study philosophy, the traditional final stage of a Roman upper-class education in the Republic.[20] Horace tells us that he studied in the Academy – "Athens added something to my education, that is, that I would be disposed to distinguish the crooked from the straight, and to seek the truth in the groves of the Academy".[21] But he soon was attracted to the cause of Brutus, also an Academic, and so he fought as an officer (*tribunus militum*) at Philippi. After the defeat he returned to Italy to find his family property confiscated. He turned to poetry as his sole way of making a living, although he soon received a salaried position in the imperial civil service as a treasury official. Through his early poems he came to the notice of Virgil and his friend, Varius Rufus, who introduced him to their patron, Maecenas, in 38 BCE. Maecenas provided Horace with the patronage and economic independence (most notably through the gift of a villa in the Sabine hills) which allowed him to spend his time writing poetry and to be independent socially. Through Maecenas he came to the attention of Augustus, whose invitation to be his secretary for his private correspondence he declined, apparently without giving offence.

Horace's position was indeed ambiguous. Socially, he was an outsider, even if his father (as is likely) was an Italian, enslaved after the Social War of the 90s BCE. Politically, he had supported the losing side, and he was fortunate even to be able to return to Italy, let alone be accepted as a friend of Maecenas and Augustus. Economically, he would have been destitute if it had not been for his poetry, and it was the excellence of his early poems that guaranteed his friendship with Virgil and the circle of Maecenas. Nearly all these poems were written before Actium:[22] after the triumph of Augustus, Horace had no choice but to support the new regime, and to respond to Augustus' requests for a poem on an occasion of state, as he did in 17 BCE with the *Carmen Saeculare* celebrating the Secular Games that inaugurated a new age.

Eduard Fraenkel rightly reminds us that "in approaching a real poet it should be our main concern to try to understand his poetry".[23] An important part of Horace's poetic technique is self-irony: like any good satirist he wears a mask (Latin, *persona*), even in his non-satirical poems, and the mask is most concealing when he speaks of himself. Thus in his letter to the poet Albius Tibullus, published in 20 BCE, he describes himself as "a pig from the herd of Epicurus", saying, "when you want a good laugh, you will see me, fat, sleek and with skin well groomed" – physical results one would expect from one who makes pleasure his primary principle.[24] The self-irony does not invalidate the previous lines (12–14), with their advice to keep a calm mind in the midst of hope and anxiety, fear and anger, and to live each day as if it were one's last.

The Epicurean *lathe biosas*, "live unobtrusively", is the most significant element in Horace's philosophy of life, which we can best examine by studying his later poems, when he had achieved the tranquillity that earlier he had had to share with obligations in the city. In the first epistle to Maecenas, Horace replies to Maecenas' invitation that he continue writing poetry, three years after the publication of the first three books of his *Odes* in 23.[25] He complains that he has given up poetry to concentrate entirely on philosophy, building up philosophical capital, as it were, with which to meet the problems of old age:

> And so now I have given up poetry and other amusements. I am concerned with what is true and fitting. This is my enquiry, which occupies me totally. I am storing [philosophical precepts] and arranging them to draw from my store in the future. And, to anticipate your question about who is my leader and household god, I have sworn allegiance to no master.

As an instance of his lack of rigidity, he says that sometimes he is as austere "as any servant of true virtue", at other times he relapses into the attitude of Socrates' associate, the elder Aristippus of Cyrene (early fourth century BCE), who justified material and sensual enjoyment and defended his life with a female companion in this way:[26]

> I possess Laïs, but she does not possess me. For to be the master of pleasures is best, rather than never to enjoy them.

The middle way between Stoic rigidity and Epicurean pleasure has a long history. Long before Zeno and Epicurus, Socrates was said to have quoted Prodicus' parable of the Choice of Heracles for the benefit of Aristippus, and long after Horace's time Seneca used Aristippus' argument in defence of his own enjoyment of material possessions.[27] Horace himself, later in the letter to Maecenas, says that "virtue is the avoidance of vice", and he concludes with an ironic parody of the Stoic paradoxes:[28]

> In sum: the wise man is less only than Jupiter. He is wealthy, free, honoured, beautiful, king, finally, of kings, exceptionally healthy [sanus, punning on the double meaning of the word, "healthy" and "sane"] – unless he is suffering from a cold.

With the last phrase he undercuts the extreme position of the Stoics and affirms his own philosophy of life, that he will take life as it comes, with its pleasures and pains – in other words, his way is the middle way.

Closely related to this letter is the next, addressed to a young friend, Lollius Maximus, who, like Maecenas, is the recipient of a second letter in this book. Horace begins with Homer and the Trojan War. Homer, he says, speaks more clearly and better than Chrysippus and Crantor on ethical questions, "what is beautiful or disgraceful; what is advantageous and what is not".[29] These are the same questions as those that concerned Horace in the previous letter, and he advises Lollius to heed their lessons well, for "if a jar is not clean, whatever you pour into it turns sour".

In the second letter to Lollius (written perhaps two years later), Horace both amplifies his earlier advice and distils his own philosophy of life.[30] Since this is his most important statement it should be quoted at length:

> In the midst of everything you will read, and you will ask your teachers by what system you may pass your life gently. Ask whether desire (that always needs more) should trouble and disturb you; whether fear and hope for things that are not advantageous; whether philosophy or nature will give you virtue; what will lessen anxiety, what will make you a friend to yourself, what will bring you simple tranquillity – whether it is public honours or the pleasure of profits or the secret way and the path of a life hidden from others. As for me, when I am refreshed by the cold stream of Digentia, which Mandela drinks, a village furrowed with cold, what do you think is my opinion, my friend, what do you believe is my prayer? "Let me keep what I have now, or even less, so that I can live out the rest of my life (if the gods wish me to live longer) for myself. Let me have a good

supply of books and a year's supply of food, and may I not float hanging on the hopes of an uncertain hour." Well, it is enough to ask Jupiter for what he gives and takes away. He may grant me life, he may grant me wealth: I myself will provide a mind free from anxiety (*aequum animum*).

These beautiful and famous lines are the final expression of Horace's ethics. Although they are only indirectly concerned with pleasure and although they suggest that prayer to the gods is efficacious, they are fundamentally Epicurean. They are based on the maxim, "live unobtrusively", and they suggest the moderate enjoyment of moderate pleasures. Their goal is a life free from mental disturbance, the achievement of *ataraxia* that is as much Stoic as Epicurean. Finally, they suggest that happiness is ours to achieve through control of our will, whatever the gods may give, good or ill. Here Horace agrees with the Stoics, and this doctrine will prove to be the foundation of the ethics of Epictetus.

The first Book of Horace's *Epistles* was the first collection ever of poetic letters reflecting on problems in philosophy and, as Fraenkel has remarked, it is "the most harmonious of Horace's books".[31] The harmony is not only literary and poetic: it is also the harmony of one who has synthesized successfully the many facets of his search for happiness. Although there is much wisdom in his later poems, the lines that we have just quoted should stand as his final statement of a philosophy of life.

Horace was consistent throughout his search in maintaining the Epicurean doctrine of *lathe biosas*. It was a necessity in the fragile period after Philippi, when Octavian and his party could have destroyed him. When he became prominent through his poetry and his friendship with Maecenas and, later, Augustus, it became even more of a necessity. Thanks to his double life, as a friend of the great and a busy man at Rome, and as the owner of a villa deep in the Sabine Hills (referred to in the passage from *Epistle* 18 by its river and neighbouring village), he was able to achieve the synthesis without compromising Epicurean principles.

At the beginning of his literary career Horace's attitude to ethical questions was one of simple morality: his father trained him as a boy to tell right from wrong, in keeping with archaic Roman morality: "I will be satisfied if I can preserve the traditional morality of the ancient [Romans]".[32] Thus his ethical philosophy, however much it owes to the Greeks, is that of the conservative Roman, without the harsh austerity of the elder and younger Cato.

Indeed, Horace satirizes the Stoics for their extremism and their insistence that only the *sapiens* of the Stoic paradoxes can achieve happiness. Thus at *Satire* 1. 3. 96–98 he says that the Stoic insistence that all delicts are equal flies in the face of common sense and the facts.[33] He ridicules the Stoic paradox that "only the wise man can be a skilled craftsman or a king". The Stoic "king" is teased by a crowd of boys, and has hardly any friends, while Horace is truly happy, his peccadilloes forgiven by his friends and theirs in turn forgiven by him.

Horace returns to the Stoic paradoxes in Book 2 of the *Satires*. The third satire expounds and implicitly criticizes the Stoic paradox that "only the wise man is sane" (lines 43–46). In the second satire a Roman peasant, Ofellus (a simple Roman with archaic values), lectures Horace on the virtues of living simply and not being attached to one's possessions. In the seventh satire a slave, Davus, begins by criticizing Horace for moral inconsistency (it is the time of the Saturnalia, when slaves can speak freely), and he shows that Horace is a slave to his passions, which jerk him around like a puppet (lines 81–82). The wise man alone is truly free (lines 83–88):

> Who then is free? The wise man, who gives commands to himself; whom neither poverty nor death nor imprisonment can frighten; who has the courage to challenge his desires, to despise honours. He is complete in himself, smooth and round (*teres atque rotundus*), so that nothing external can stick on his smooth surface. Fortune always is hobbled when she rushes at him.

This satire expounds the Stoic paradox more successfully than *Satire* 2. 3, and it appears to give a positive definition of the wise man in the lines just quoted. Horace is his counterfoil, so it seems, but then we must pause and consider: is not Horace implicitly criticizing the spherical perfection of the Stoic wise man? Such perfection is still unattainable, and Horace, with his failings, emerges as the real human being. The "black companion" of desire may constantly thwart his efforts to escape his slavery (7. 115), but in the end, it is Horace who is real, and the Stoic wise man who is an unattainable ideal.

Horace expounds his ideal most memorably in the sixth satire of this book, published a few years after he had taken possession of his Sabine villa. The poem celebrates and contrasts the two sides of his life, the busy friend of Maecenas in Rome and the independent poet in the country. He begins (lines 1–23a), with a prayer fulfilled: he is at his villa, with its nearby spring of water and woods. The focus is on moderation and limits, and he asks for no more, beyond the security of continued ownership – this is his prayer to Mercury. Suddenly he is back in Rome. He prays to Janus (god of beginnings), who sends him off early for the long day's grind. The tone is still Epicurean despite the prayers to the gods, for Epicurus, too, was a pious man. Horace's prayers return with longing to the Sabine villa in line 59, as he endures the time-consuming busyness of life in the city. At the centre of his prayers is philosophy: he prays for a life that is "the pleasure of forgetting the harried life" (line 62), a memorable summary of Epicurean freedom from mental disturbance, and for the enjoyment with his friends of a simple meal, with as little or as much wine as each person wishes. An evening spent in this way is "a night of the gods" (line 65), for had not Epicurus himself said that the man who followed his precepts "would live as a god among men"?[34] Above all, the conversation of Horace and his friends is about things that matter – not gossip about games or other people's possessions, but about the good life (lines 72–76):

> we discuss subjects that concern us directly, ignorance of which is harmful: is it wealth or virtue than makes men happy? Is it virtuous character or self-interest that draws us into friendship? What is the nature of the good and what is the highest good?

These subjects, of course, were not exclusive to the Epicureans: Aristotle had discussed the importance of self-interest for friendship in Books 8 and 9 of the *Nicomachean Ethics*; Cicero sought out the *summum bonum* in the *De Finibus*, and the basic problem for Plato and the Academy was the relationship of the universal, virtue, to the particulars of daily life. By setting the discussion in the context of friendship and moderate pleasures, Horace gives all these things an Epicurean perspective. Like Plato, he illustrates his philosophy with a myth, here the fable of the two mice (lines 77–117).

The animal fable was a device of popular moralizing, the tradition in which Horace worked as a satirist. He called his satires *Sermones*, that is, "Talks", and *Sermones Bionaei*, a reference to Bion of Borysthenes, a Greek popular philosopher of the third century BCE.[35] Bion's informal talks were lectures couched in terms intelligible to ordinary hearers.[36] Works in this tradition required a light touch – a fable about two mice rather than a lecture comparing luxury to simplicity, self-irony rather than self-importance, generalities rather than precise definition, the easy conversation of friends rather than a formal lecture or the contrived setting of Platonic or Ciceronian dialogue. Horace himself instructed with a smile, "telling the truth with a laugh", and he included his hearer in his ironic self-criticism – "*you* are the subject of my story".[37] Horace shares with the Cynic philosophers the attributes of wit, irony and candour, but he did not approve of the Cynics' shamelessness and personal squalor.[38]

An ironic persona suited the poet of the *Satires*, but a different one was needed for the poet of the *Odes*. The eighty-eight poems that comprise Books 1–3 of the *Odes* (the Latin title is *Carmina*, "Poems") were published in 23 BCE. In them Horace is the bard (*vates*), the teacher of the community, that is, of Augustan Rome. The first four odes are addressed to public figures, respectively Maecenas, Augustus, Virgil, and Sestius, consul in 23 CE. In the last ode (3. 30) Horace associates his achievement in lyric poetry with the greatest of Roman public occasions, the celebration of a triumph by a victorious general. Horace, therefore, steps forth as the teacher of society, expressing the political and moral ideals of the renewed Republic. No longer does he write for Maecenas alone, or just for his friends, but for Augustus and the Roman public.[39] The Epicurean principle of *lathe biosas* was inappropriate for the *vates*, and so Horace's philosophy in the *Odes* is more complex. Horace, the private individual, is still Epicurean, but the horizons of his public doctrine are as wide as those of the policies of Augustus and the responsibilities of the renewed republic and its citizens. There are Stoic elements as well as Epicurean, the gods of Roman public religion (vigorously promoted by Augustus) appear frequently, and traditional Roman virtues are proclaimed as if the philosophical developments of the previous 150 years had not taken place.[40]

The *Odes* needed a new technique for conveying moral doctrine. In the *Satires* Horace's method had been "to tell the truth with a smile", well described by Alexander Pope:[41]

> Horace still charms with graceful negligence,
> And without method talks us into sense,
> Will, like a friend, familiarly convey
> The truest notions in the easiest way.

The *vates*, in contrast, spoke with authority appropriate to the dignity of the institutions of the state, especially the temples and gods of the state religion. Yet the private individual, Horace, speaks as an Epicurean, sometimes in poems of great complexity. In *Odes* 3. 1, Horace, as a priest (*sacerdos*) of the Muses, solemnly announces to boys and girls a new doctrine (lines 1–4). He recognizes that wealth, political power and luxurious living are a necessary part of Roman life, but also with them come fear, anxiety, danger, failure and death – "behind the horseman sits black Care" (line 40). He ends with a question: "Why should I exchange my Sabine valley for wealth that brings more trouble?" (lines 45–46). Privately he will live in the poet's world, which we have seen described in *Satire* 2. 6, but he must also teach the future statesmen, fathers and mothers of Rome, that their duty may be to leave such a world for public responsibility, and that they must be prepared to pay the price. The implication, however, is that they can do so, if (as he shows in the subsequent odes) they control the emotions and temptations that he has described. In the next ode (3. 2), his doctrine is consistent with the archaic Roman virtues of the elder Cato – a life poor in material things, rich in virtues, above all military courage, and, in private life, discretion and integrity. Here the notion of pleasure, signalled by the word *dulce* (line 13), is transferred to dying for one's country: "it is pleasurable and proper to die for one's country" (*dulce et decorum est pro patria mori*). Again, in the third ode, Horace praises the man who is "just and holds fast to his principles", which will make him equal to the gods. Here again, as in 3. 1, Horace ends by contrasting his position as a lyric poet with those who are concerned with high policies of state. In the fifth ode he uses the story of Regulus (as Cicero had done in *De Officiis*) to focus on the citizen's duty to the state, at whatever cost. Finally, in the sixth and last of these Roman Odes Horace calls for the rebuilding of temples, because neglect of the state's gods results in moral degeneration.

These odes display the complex relationship between the philosophy of the individual poet and public policy and morality. Their doctrine is proclaimed in general terms. In the so-called Maecenas Ode (3. 29) Horace narrows the focus to two persons, the poet and Maecenas. He invites Maecenas to leave the "smoke and wealth and noise of Rome" and enjoy the pleasure of dinner with him in his villa (1–16). He imagines the cares of state and the anxieties involved in conducting foreign policy (25–28), and this leads to reflections on knowledge of the future, which the god has concealed (29–30). The prudent course is to be sure of the present and to let the river of events flow as it will (it is compared to the Tiber in flood, 33–41). Thus the prudent person can say at the end of each day, *vixi*, "I have lived", untroubled by the vagaries of Fortune. For Fortune "plays her insolent play" – and now Horace directs attention to himself – and, whatever she does, he cloaks himself in virtue and takes poverty as his wife (41–56). In the final allegory, he compares a merchant-captain anxious for his cargo on the storm-tossed sea, and himself, safe in mid-ocean, bobbing along in a dinghy under the protection of Castor and Pollux (57–64).

This complex poem defies brief analysis, and it is, perhaps, the best place in which to study the poet's philosophy in the *Odes*. The contrast between the city and the Sabine villa continues the themes of *Satire* 2. 6, as does the contrast between personal interactions in the city and the conversation of friends in the country. The Epicurean principle of pleasure is implied by the doctrine (equally Epicurean) of living for the present (stated in *Odes* 1. 11, as *carpe diem*, "seize the day"). The contrast (familiar from *Satire* 1. 6) between the senior minister of state, described by the historian Velleius Paterculus as "virtually sleepless, when affairs demanded it", and the poet is elaborated by the simile of the river, and especially by the reference to Fortune.[42] This allows Horace to end the poem, as he had begun, with the contrast between Maecenas' circumstances in Rome and his own in the villa, ironically pictured by the allegory of the two boats, the laden merchant vessel and the carefree dinghy. Thus the proper distance between Horace and his patron is maintained, and he avoids the appearance of lecturing Maecenas. Horace's Epicurean philosophy, to be sure, is unchanged as far as his way of life is concerned. But he takes from the Stoics the notion of defying Fortune, and, from popular moralizing, the idea of the wise man married to poverty and wearing virtue as his cloak.[43]

Horace appropriates Stoic doctrine in his defiance of Fortune. He also appears to deviate from Epicurean orthodoxy in some of his attitudes towards the gods. The gods of the state have their place when he speaks as *vates*, but his piety towards the gods in a public context does not contradict his Epicurean views on the gods. The validity of this statement is best tested by *Odes* 1. 34, where he begins as a "niggardly worshipper of the gods", confident in his stability as an "expert in philosophy". But lightning appears in a clear sky, and he appears to go through a conversion –"now I am forced to sail backwards". In fact, nothing of the sort occurs. Lucretius had shown that the phenomenon could not and did not occur, and Horace is not here contradicting him.[44] He gives an ironic and comic picture of himself in a moment of superstitious weakness, followed (lines 12–16) by an entirely serious statement about the divine power that *can* affect human lives. This "god" is Fortune, to whom the next poem (1. 35) is addressed. The acknowledgement of the power of the abstract concept, Fortune, does not contradict Epicurean doctrine.[45]

More difficult to evaluate is Horace's attitude to death, a topic that occurs frequently in lyric poetry. Two poems especially focus on it, linking it with the renewal of springtime. In *Odes* 1. 4 Horace invokes the inevitability of death to encourage Sestius to enjoy the present and not to hope that his pleasures will last for long. While the notion of "seizing the day" is Epicurean, Horace's picture of regrets for the pleasures ended by death recalls the satirical lines in Lucretius arguing against precisely such regrets.[46] In the second poem (4. 7) the attitude of resignation to death is more consistent. It is springtime, and we know that spring has its place in the cycle of the seasons, each of which must give way to its successor. So with human beings, for even the best of us is no more than "dust and shadow".[47] In this poem, Horace is consistently Epicurean – death is inevitable but not to be feared.

Our survey of the *Odes* has necessarily been selective, for many other poems illustrate Horace's philosophy of life. Yet we can now include the *Odes* with the (earlier) *Satires* and (later) *Epistles* to attempt a synthesis. Horace is Epicurean, and there is no ground for saying that he "moved away from Epicureanism".[48] His philosophy is almost entirely ethical, extended to politics and theology in the more public contexts of the *Odes*. He does not announce pleasure as the basic principle, but he makes clear that a life free from pain and anxiety is his ideal. He addresses the gods formally (as did Lucretius at the beginning of his poem),[49] and he accepts their importance in the religion and morality of the state. As a public figure, and as a friend of Augustus and Maecenas, he accepts the religious, social, political and moral principles of their policies. In his private life he was guided by the Epicurean doctrine of "living unobtrusively", and by the principle of the middle way, memorably epitomized in the "golden mean".[50] The Epicurean principles of moderate enjoyment of pleasures, privacy, friendship and the avoidance of pain, were essential to his life as a poet. But poetry involved obligations to Maecenas and Augustus and to Rome, which could only be fulfilled at the cost of some compromise with non-Epicurean principles. The individualism of Horace's philosophy is hardly surprising – after all, he himself said that he belonged to no particular school – and it suits well this most ironic and complex of Roman poets.[51]

Virgil (70–19 BCE), like Horace, saw the world into which he was born collapse into civil war and political chaos; he probably lost his family property in the land redistributions after Philippi, regaining it through the intervention of the historian and politician, Asinius Pollio. Soon after 40 BCE he gained the friendship and patronage of Maecenas, and through him he became close to Augustus, to whom he read the *Georgics* and part of the *Aeneid*. Unlike Horace, he did not take part in the civil war after the death of Julius Caesar, and his social status as the son of free-born Italians was higher than that of Horace. Ancient sources say that he studied in Campania under the Epicurean, Siro, and that he had intended to devote his life to the study of philosophy after the completion of the *Aeneid* (he died before he could finish his final revision of the poem).[52]

Like Horace, Virgil is too complex a thinker to be identified with any one school of thought. Certainly he sought to "live unobtrusively" as far as possible, whether in Rome or in Campania, where he seems to have spent most of his time. His *Eclogues* (ten "bucolic" poems published soon after 40 BCE) are ostensibly in the tradition of the Greek pastoral poetry of Theocritus (c. 270 BCE), but their subject matter is more complex and includes philosophy. In the sixth *Eclogue*, Silenus, captured by two shepherds, sings a song so enchanting that all nature listens, for Silenus was even more bewitching than Orpheus, whose song in the epic *Argonautica* of Apollonius Rhodius (mid-third century BCE) was one of his models.[53] Like Orpheus, Silenus begins with a cosmogony (lines 31–40), the creation of the four elements, of earth's globe and of all the natural and meteorological features of the world. While these lines are full of Lucretian vocabulary, they are not especially Epicurean. Silenus then turns to the history of humankind, told through the myths of Deucalion and Pyrrha and Prometheus (lines 41–42), and myths of metamorphosis and love (lines 43–63), ending with praise of Virgil's friend, the poet Gallus (lines 64–73). The song ends at line 73, and, for the remainder of the poem, Virgil reports other tales of love and metamorphosis (lines 74–86). Clearly the song is as much about poetry as it is about philosophy, and the literary allusions are as prominent as the philosophical allusions to Empedocles and Lucretius. Virgil returned to the theme of cosmogony with the song of Iopas at the end of Book 1 of the *Aeneid*, but by then his poetry was the vehicle for a different philosophy.[54]

Nevertheless, his admiration for Lucretius was still apparent in his next poem, the *Georgics* (completed in 29 BCE). In the second book Virgil expresses his hopes for his poetic career with two alternatives.[55] In the first he prays that the Muses will teach him:

> May they show me the paths of heaven and the stars, the eclipses of the sun and the labours [i.e. phases] of the moon; may they teach me the source of earthquakes, the force that makes the seas burst their bonds and swell high and fall back again into themselves; may they teach me why the winter sun hurries to plunge himself into Ocean or why the slow [winter] nights delay.

These are to some extent themes that Lucretius dealt with in Books 5 and 6 of his poem, but, as the Song of Silenus has shown, Virgil's allusions extend beyond Lucretius. For the second alternative he prays that if cosmology and meteorology are beyond his poetic capacity, then may he live in and write poetry about the countryside.[56] Such a life, indeed, brings no fame, yet the poet who "knows the rustic gods" is blessed no less than the poet who "knew the causes of things" and rid human kind of the fear of death.[57] Here again the reference is certainly to Lucretius, as well as to Aristotle. There follow lines that again allude to Lucretius but go beyond him, as Virgil contrasts the toil of the farmer's life with the stress and anxiety of the life of the politician, statesman, merchant or warrior.[58] Virgil applies the farmer's life to the ideals of archaic Rome – a society based on the family, whose farmers worked hard and celebrated their holidays with athletic contests. Thus the tough early Romans built their society and their city, a golden age before the coming of warfare.[59]

Virgil chose bucolic poetry for himself, admitting that he could not equal the high achievement of Lucretius. But he saw that the Epicurean ideals of pleasure and "living unobtrusively" were inappropriate for Roman society. He was feeling his way towards a philosophy that combined Epicurean quietism with the duty of involvement in the leadership of the state that Cicero and the Stoics had advocated. He knew already that he could not limit himself to pastoral poetry, and in the very next passage (the opening of Book 3 of the *Georgics*) he debated his choice of epic themes, turning from the worn-out themes of mythology.[60] He knew that he would compose an epic in which Augustus would be a constant (if not explicit) presence, and that this would call for a different philosophical position. His view already extended beyond the horizon of the *Georgics*.

In the fourth *Georgic* Virgil quotes the view (not necessarily his own) that the bees, whose altruism and social coherence he has just described, share in a kind of divine world-soul:[61]

> Some people, on this evidence and following these examples, have said that the bees share in the divine mind and have drunk deeply from ethereal sources. For (they say) god proceeds through all lands and all areas of the sea and of the lofty heavens. They say that from this source [i.e. god] sheep, cattle, human beings, every type of wild animal — each for itself summons its fragile life at birth. They say, evidently, that to it everything returns and is brought back at the dissolution [of the body], and that there is no place for death, but that everything flies in number as the stars and ascends to the heavens.

Virgil is careful to report these views as those of "some people". They are largely those of the Stoics (the reunion of the soul's divine spark with the divine fire) and the Pythagoreans (the immortality of the soul and its rebirth). Virgil himself returns to the subject in Book 6 of the *Aeneid*, where Anchises is the speaker (probably expressing Virgil's own views) and where the theory is combined with patriotic and Roman themes.

The *Georgics*, of course, contain many other philosophical doctrines, but in our present context we must consider the poem as a stage in Virgil's development, that reaches its maturity in the *Aeneid*. At the end of the *Georgics* he added a *sphragis* (poetic epilogue), taking his leave of the world of bucolic poetry and contrasting his life at Naples with the military successes of Octavian.[62] He says, "at that time pleasant Parthenope [Naples] nurtured me, Virgil, as I flourished studying in inglorious retirement". This seems to be a description of the Epicurean life, for the epithet for Naples (*dulcis*) implies pleasure, and "inglorious retirement" is consistent with the doctrine of living unobtrusively.

Virgil emerged from this Epicurean life, at least in the literary sense, in composing his epic. Its crucial scenes are in Book 6, which marks both the end of the wanderings of Aeneas prior to his warfare in Italy, and the passing of authority from Anchises, representing the past, to Aeneas, the leader of the future. Virgil chose to revive the Underworld mythology of Homer and Plato as the symbolic setting for the transition, whose climax is the meeting of father and son in the Elysian fields. Anchises explains who are the souls that Aeneas sees crowding the fields and woods along the banks of Lethe,

the river of forgetfulness.[63] They are souls waiting to enter new bodies and a new life on earth, like the souls in Plato's myth of Er. Anchises explains that all living creatures share in the world soul that is immanent in the universe. This is the source of their vitality and their emotions, and, when their bodies die, the corruption that has infected their souls in their corporeal life must be purified in the Underworld. Some then are allowed to enter Elysium, but the rest must undergo another cycle of corporeal existence.

Thus Anchises uses the Pythagorean doctrine of rebirth, adapting Plato's myth. But Virgil now takes the doctrine further in a bold and original invention. He relates the cycle of death and rebirth to Roman history, for Aeneas next sees his descendants, the leaders who will make Rome great.[64] When Anchises comes to Augustus, he describes the extent of his empire, likening his rule to a renewed golden age, and calling his achievements greater than those of Hercules himself. Then he asks (lines 806–07): "and do we still hesitate to extend our virtue (*virtus*) by our deeds?" Thus Virgil takes the traditional furniture of the Underworld, where mythological heroes had symbolically conquered death, and unites it with Pythagorean and Platonic doctrine to support a philosophy of dying and renewal that is completely subsumed into Roman history and Augustan imperial ideals. And these are stated in the final and famous lines (851–53) stating Rome's political, military and moral mission:

> You, O Roman, remember to rule peoples with your power (this will be your skill), to unite justice with peace, to spare those who have submitted and to fight the arrogant to the end.

Cicero had looked to the past to develop his philosophy of the just Roman state, and he had based it on the virtuous character of its leaders, seen especially in their sense of duty. Virgil looked to the future (Aeneas stands at the threshold of history, so that we, who look back to the past, may with him see the future), and he identifies (from his standpoint in time) the Roman future with the virtues of Augustus. Thus, like Cicero, he identifies moral and political doctrines with the greatness of Rome and its leaders.

Ancient epic was defined by Aristotle's successor, Theophrastus, as "the comprehensive narrative of the deeds of gods, heroes, and mortals". Thus the philosophy of the *Aeneid* includes the gods, as well as the heroic leader, Aeneas, and the countless people (born and

unborn) whose lives depend on his leadership. His story is intertwined with the actions and passions of the gods. Except for Jupiter,
Virgil's gods are partial and passionate, and the opposition of Juno
to Aeneas and his destiny is one of the sources of the poem's
energy.[65] Jupiter, however, is both the supreme cosmic power and
the high god of the Roman state. In his former capacity he
embodies the Stoic idea of Fate, an inexorable power, to whose will
human beings must willingly conform, yet also a power that leaves
human beings with the freedom to choose. Aeneas can choose to
refuse the destiny that is revealed to him through the course of the
first half of the poem, and in Book 4 he very nearly does choose to
let love for Dido overwhelm his mission to found a new state. Only
the repeated visions of Mercury, Jupiter's divine messenger, compel
him to renounce his choice and leave Carthage. In repeated prophecies Jupiter tells us (Virgil's audience) of the destiny that awaits
Aeneas and his descendants – the founding of Rome and the deeds
of Romans that will not be limited by time or place, for "I have
given [them] rule without limits".[66] To end a bitter debate between
Venus and Juno, favouring respectively Aeneas or his enemies,
Jupiter reaffirms, "the fates will find [their] way".[67] Thus the poem
is teleological, working towards a destined goal, the success of
Aeneas and the greatness of his descendants.

Yet Fate cannot be fulfilled without the moral excellence of
human leaders. Aeneas, who first appears ocean-tossed and wishing
that he had died at Troy, comes to realize fully, after the revelations
of Book 6, what is his duty. He is distinguished by the virtue of
pietas. We have seen how Cicero had extolled *pietas* as the mark of
the Roman leader (especially in Scipio's dream), and we remember
his treatise on duty, *De Officiis*. Virgil takes the virtue of dutifulness
(*pietas*) and makes it a moral imperative: Aeneas knows that he must
choose the course of duty, at whatever cost to his private wishes and
to those people, like Dido, who will be hurt by his choice.

The first word in Greek epic is "anger",[68] and the final action of
the *Aeneid* is the killing of Turnus by Aeneas, who, Virgil emphasizes, is motivated by anger, "set on fire by furies and terrible with
anger".[69] Our view of Virgil's philosophy must be affected by our
interpretation of the end of the poem. On one view, Aeneas is overcome by the madness of anger (*furor*), the very passion that
distinguished his enemy, Turnus. On this view Aeneas fails to
observe Anchises' injunction "to spare those who have submitted"
and Virgil, by presenting his hero as morally flawed in this supreme
moment, is himself despairing of the human condition.[70]

Opponents of this view point out that Turnus himself had repeatedly displayed *furor* and extreme cruelty, not least in killing Pallas and spoiling his corpse; he had broken a treaty, and he therefore deserved no mercy. It was a historical necessity that he should be killed so that the will of Jupiter could be fulfilled. Finally, on this view, Aeneas' anger was justified: it was the anger of the just man punishing a crime (the breaking of a treaty), of the man whose friend and protégé (Pallas) had been killed and despoiled against the norms of heroic warfare.

The most vigorous proponent of this view is Karl Galinsky, who in two astringent articles has argued that the killing of Turnus was just and consistent with the expectations of Virgil's hearers.[71] He reviews the philosophical debate about anger in Virgil's time, and it is worth our while here to consider these conflicting doctrines. At one extreme is the Stoic view of the passions, according to which anger is against nature and should be suppressed by reason.[72] Against this is the Epicurean view, that anger is natural and is of two kinds, "empty" (which the wise person will suppress) and "natural", which the wise person will try to suppress as far as possible by means of reason.[73] In the Peripatetic view, anger is natural and is just if moderated by reason, whereas excessive anger or passivity (where anger would be justified) are both bad.[74] Elsewhere Aristotle defines anger as "a painful appetition towards punishment, because of a perceived slight against oneself or something concerning oneself, when the slight was not appropriate".[75] While Aeneas' action could be seen to be consistent with the Peripatetic definition, Virgil did not propose such a simple use of a Peripatetic template, for Philodemus had argued against the Peripatetic position.[76] He said that anger of both sorts (empty and natural) was painful and therefore to be avoided. Nevertheless, if a person's disposition (*diathesis*) was such that his [natural] anger resulted from a correct estimate of the circumstances, then to that extent it could be called good. Now, we must ask, what was the disposition of Aeneas at the moment when he saw Pallas' sword-belt? Virgil quite clearly says he was "set on fire by furies", reminding us in that phrase of others (Dido and Amata) who had acted from *furor*: no one can deny that *furor* was Aeneas' motivation at this moment. Horace defines anger as "a brief madness", and I have no doubt but that Virgil agreed.[77] But he is careful not to reveal what his view is: he leaves us, as a great poet should, to ponder the meaning of Aeneas' action and to resolve (if we can!) its ambiguity. Philip Hardie's warning is well taken:[78]

those who seek a philosophical solution run the risk of interpreting the end of the *Aeneid* into an unresolved dispute between ancient philosophical schools.

Virgil, it seems, like Horace, as a private individual preferred the Epicurean unobtrusive life. His philosophical interests to begin with were cosmological and physical, as well as ethical. But in the *Aeneid* he developed his own complex philosophy, in which Stoic and other doctrines were interwoven with the ideology of Augustus and the ideals of Roman leadership, extended to the hopes and failures, and the ideals and passions, of human beings in all ages.

The third of the great Augustan poets was Ovid (43 BCE to 17 CE), the only one of the three not to have experienced the free Republic (for in the twelve years of his life before Actium the Republic was at the mercy of military and political leaders competing for extra-constitutional power). In his autobiography, he tells us that from his earliest years poetry was his vocation.[79] In dealing with his exile in 8 CE to the Black Sea city of Tomis, he says:

> my mind thought it unworthy to give way to misfortune,
> and it used its own resources to stand unconquered.

This is certainly Stoic doctrine. Elsewhere in this poem Ovid refers to a life spent in retirement (*otium*) from public activity, in this being similar to Horace.[80] In fact, Ovid does not reveal a consistent philosophy, yet his most important poem, the *Metamorphoses* (completed in 8 BCE, the year of his exile), is framed by two philosophical disquisitions which clearly engage with the doctrines of Lucretius.[81] Ovid, then, after his fashion, claims a place in the philosophical debates of the time.

The *Metamorphoses* is an epic poem, which Ovid composed with explicit reference to his predecessors in Latin epic, Ennius, Lucretius and Virgil, for *aemulatio* (recognition of and competition with one's predecessors in a literary genre) was a recognized element in Roman poetry. Of these three, Lucretius is especially relevant to a discussion of Ovid's philosophy. The poem begins with a prayer to the gods:

> I am moved to tell of bodies changed into new forms. Gods (for you also changed those forms), inspire what I have begun and extend my continuous poem from the first beginning of the universe to my own times!

Ovid's poem, then, is epic ("continuous") and historical (extending from the beginning of the world to the present day), and its subject is change. Lucretius' poem was epic and dealt with change, that is, the change from unconnected atoms to the shapes of things formed by their union. It was also historical in its account of the development of human society in Book 5 and the plague in Book 6. While there are other poems to which Ovid is referring (notably the *Theogony* of Hesiod and the sixth *Eclogue* of Virgil), Lucretius is the most important canon against which he measures himself. After the brief introductory prayer Ovid moves immediately into a cosmogony, an account of the creation of the world and its physical and meteorological features (lines 5–68). Next, the stars are created in the heavens, the fishes in the seas, wild animals on the earth, and birds in the air (lines 69–75) – Ovid's way of pointing to the four elements of fire (the substance of the stars), water, earth and air. The climax to the process of creation is the creation of humankind (lines 76–89), for which Ovid gives alternative explanations: either humans were created by a divine creator from "divine seed", or they were created from earth, which retained elements of air and "heavenly seed" (i.e. fire). This Prometheus mixed with water to form humankind, the first great metamorphosis of the poem.

Ovid goes on to describe the progression of the four ages of humankind, from gold to iron (in this differing from the progress of civilization described by Lucretius), ending with the flood. The two human survivors, Deucalion and Pyrrha, create a new human race from "the bones of their mother" (i.e. stones, lines 398–415), while a new animal creation is formed from the heat and water in the earth (lines 430–33).

There are Stoic elements in Ovid's cosmogony (e.g. the five zones of the earth in lines 45–51) and features that go back at least to Empedocles' system of creative strife (e.g. the *concordia discors* of line 433). But most obvious is the response to Lucretius. While Ovid uses some Lucretian terminology (e.g. *semina*, seeds, for the constituent particles of matter), his creation is controlled by an intelligent creator (whether an unnamed god or Prometheus) and the precise account of the formation of objects from atoms is avoided. Ovid retains the traditional notion of the empty void (*Chaos*) out of which the universe was created, and he retains the creation myths of Prometheus and Deucalion. His cosmogony, then, although it has philosophical features and allusions to earlier philosophers, affirms the supremacy of myth, and his philosophical exposition is more narrative than dogmatic.

This conclusion is supported by the quasi-scientific exposition of the power of the wind spoken by Boreas, the north wind.[82] With suitable vigour, Boreas indignantly describes his violent functions in the heavens, on earth and in the sea, and under the earth. His speech explains the origin of thunder, lightning and earthquakes, all within five lines (lines 695–99). Ovid does not conceal his knowledge of Epicurean theory about these natural phenomena, but his purpose is to characterize Boreas, frustrated in his efforts to win Orithyia, as he determines to take her by force.[83]

The second philosophical exposition in the *Metamorphoses* is the speech of Pythagoras addressed to Numa, the second king of Rome, who has gone to visit him at Croton in southern Italy.[84] Numa was traditionally the founder of Roman religious ritual, but Ovid says that his intellectual goals were greater than this, for he enquired into the nature of things.[85] This was the reason for his visit to Pythagoras. The reference to the *De Rerum Natura* of Lucretius is confirmed by the introduction of Pythagoras (who is never named) as "a man of Samos", similar to Lucretius', "a man of Greece" for Epicurus.[86] Ovid's summary of Pythagoras' philosophical speculation again recalls Lucretius' Epicurus:[87]

> He approached the gods with his mind, far apart in the distant parts of heaven though they be. Things that nature denied to human sight he looked deeply into with the eyes of his intellect.

Ovid then surveys the range of his speculations in physics, theology, cosmology, meteorology and astronomy:[88]

> When he had thoroughly surveyed everything in his mind with watchful care, he gave it out for all to learn. He taught crowds of silent admirers of his words the origins of the mighty world and the causes of things. He taught what nature and the gods are, what is the source of snow and the origin of lightning; whether Jupiter or the winds cause thunder by shattering the clouds; what causes earthquakes, what is the law governing the movement of the planets, and whatever is hidden.

These are not the contents of his speech, but they do refer to the doctrines of Book 6 of Lucretius, in preparation for an exposition that is quite different in content and purpose. In this way, Ovid once again displays his knowledge of Lucretius, only to expound a different way of looking at the world.

The speech begins and ends with the doctrine of vegetarianism, which (as we have seen) was taught in Ovid's time by the school of Sextius.[89] The central doctrines of the speech are introduced by Pythagoras' claim to divine inspiration and oracular authority, attributes which Lucretius had specifically said were incompatible with philosophical truth.[90] The first doctrine starts out in a Lucretian manner:[91]

> O humankind, stunned by the fear of cold death! Why do you fear the dead and empty names – a subject for poets (*vates*) – and the dangers of an imaginary world? You should think that bodies – whether the flames of the pyre or the decay of time destroys them – cannot suffer any evils.

But the reason not to fear death is the opposite of that given by Lucretius, for, in Pythagorean doctrine, the soul (*anima*) cannot die and continues its life in a new body (lines 158–64). The idea of change of body leads to the central theme of the speech – and, indeed, of the whole of the *Metamorphoses* – the mutability of everything. "Everything changes," says Pythagoras, "and nothing perishes" (line 165), and therefore in eating animal flesh one risks eating the flesh of a former human being (lines 173–75). He returns next to the theme of change: *cuncta fluunt*, "everything is in a state of flux" (line 178), which he illustrates with many examples from the natural world, in which nature herself, "the renewer of things", brings about change. Like Ovid, he begins his narrative of change with the flood, and he continues with a catalogue of natural wonders, including many metamorphoses narrated earlier by Ovid. He ends the list with historical changes, the rise and fall of cities and peoples, among which the story of Aeneas and the founding and growth of Rome again refer to Ovid's narrative.[92]

Ovid introduces Pythagoras as a kind of proto-Epicurus, a fearless researcher into the secrets of nature, a teacher of humankind, whose doctrine sought to remove the fear of death and join humankind with animals in the harmony of nature. Yet the doctrine of Pythagoras conflicts repeatedly with Lucretius, even while recalling him in theme and terminology. At the same time Pythagoras recalls many of Ovid's themes and narratives, seen now from the philosopher's point of view, which he defines in Lucretian terms:[93]

> I delight in travelling among the lofty stars, to leave
> behind the earth and its unmoving places and be borne on
> the clouds and stand upon the shoulders of Atlas, to look
> down from afar on humankind wandering without direc-
> tion, lacking reason and fearing death – thus to encourage
> them and unwind the scroll of fate.

But the philosopher looking down on the purposeless lives of
human beings is not the sole source of authority for those who wish
"to enquire into the nature of things". Ovid's whole poem, and
much of Pythagoras' speech, has focused on the wonders of change
in nature, recorded in mythical narrative. Myth, therefore, also has
authority in explaining the workings of nature. Ovid recognizes the
doctrines of philosophy (in particular those of Lucretius), but beside
them he sets the myths, which, he suggests, are equally valid for the
enquirer into the nature of things. The speech of Pythagoras, then,
as Sara Myers has rightly said, "mirror[s] Ovid's own practice ... of
juxtaposing, but not thereby necessarily opposing, science and
myth".[94] The philosopher and the mythographer unite in the poet,
who alone at the end of the poem ascends beyond the stars,
immortal and imperishable.[95]

Virtually nothing is known of the life of Marcus Manilius, the
fourth Augustan philosopher–poet. He dedicates his poem,
Astronomica, to Augustus and mentions events late in the reign.
Later he implies that Tiberius is emperor.[96] The poem, then, was
begun under Augustus and completed under Tiberius, who became
emperor in 14 CE. It is in five books (about 4,250 hexameter lines),
and is the earliest Latin treatise on astrology and the first in any
language in verse, as Manilius boasts.[97] As a didactic poet Manilius
emulates Virgil (in the *Georgics*) and Lucretius, whose philosophy he
often criticizes, most notably where he argues for a divine governor
of the universe and its constellations.[98] He was influenced also by
the *Phaenomena* of Aratus, which at this very time was being translated into Latin by Germanicus Caesar, who died in 19 CE.

Astrology, which seeks to relate astronomical observations to
human affairs and so to predict human fortunes, is said by Cicero to
have been the particular skill of the Babylonians, who were the
mathematicians and astronomers *par excellence* of the ancient
world.[99] Divination (the art of discovering the will of the gods) was
an important feature of Roman religion, inherited from the
Etruscans. The philosophical basis of astrology is the doctrine of the
harmony of the universe, in which human lives and the constella-

tions are, to use Milton's phrase, "in perfect diapason". The doctrine of the celestial origin of the soul made astrology, which linked celestial and human events, acceptable, especially to the Stoics. Cicero argued strenuously against astrology in the *De Divinatione*, and he mentions the fundamental arguments of Carneades against divination.[100] He also mentions that the only Stoic philosopher not to accept the efficacy of astrology was Panaetius. Manilius is a Stoic, and it is the Stoic doctrines in his poem, rather than the technical exposition of astrology, that are relevant to our discussion.

Manilius' Stoicism rests on two foundations – reason and the divine nature of the human soul. In Book 1 he surveys the development of human intellect, with obvious reference to Lucretius' survey of human progress.[101] He describes humankind as at first lacking reason but in time developing the powers of reason to achieve progress in civilization. Human beings then used reason to study celestial phenomena:

> Nor did reason set a limit and boundary to things before it had climbed the heavens and understood the deepest nature of things from their causes, and had seen whatever exists anywhere.

In Book 4 Manilius argues that human reason can penetrate the utmost secrets of the skies and "rise to the stars, from whom we are born".[102] His conclusion is that through reason human beings share in the nature of god, who is their origin and exemplar:

> Can we doubt that god dwells in our breasts, that our souls come from heaven and return there? Can we doubt that, just as the universe, made up of every element of air and fire that rises and earth and water, is the home of an immanent intelligence that governs it, so in our bodies of earthly flesh and our life-giving blood there dwells a mind that governs everything and controls human life? Can we be surprised if human beings can understand the universe, when the universe is within us and each human being is an example of god writ small? Or is it right to believe that human beings have their origin in anything other than heaven?

Manilius proceeds to his triumphant conclusion: "Reason conquers all."[103]

Manilius and Lucretius draw opposite conclusions from the same evidence. For Lucretius, the liberating force of the intellect of Epicurus proves that human beings, through knowledge of the physical world, can understand the finality of death and the irrelevance of the gods. For Manilius this same knowledge proves the identity of the human soul with god, and proves therefore that the soul is immortal, reunited with the divine at death. God, therefore, pervades the universe, which is "governed by the divine power of the soul".[104]

Manilius introduces each of the first four books of his poem with a passage of literary and philosophical interest. Those to Books 2 and 4 rise to heights of passion and even beauty. In Book 2. 1–136 he puts himself in the tradition of Homer and Hesiod, which, he says, has become degraded (lines 51–52). He claims that he is renewing the purity of the tradition and that his work is original (lines 57–59), precisely because his theme is "god immanent in sky, earth and sea" (line 61). In lines of great power, he describes the divine government of the universe and its creatures as proof of the interaction of celestial and human activity. Therefore, he concludes:[105]

> Who could understand the heavens except by the gift of heaven? Who could find god, unless he were himself part of the gods?

And it is reason that gives human beings this licence, reason that "cannot be deceived nor ever be deceiving" (line 131). Thus, he argues, reason, because of the link between the human and celestial spheres, can gain knowledge of Fate and human fortune (lines 132–35).

Manilius appeals again to Stoic Fate in the preface to Book 4. Like Lucretius, he argues that human beings should not fear the future, but he draws a different conclusion. For Lucretius, knowledge of the dissolution of body and soul at death leads to freedom from fear. For Manilius, knowledge of Fate gives human beings the power to rid themselves of fear, for (as the Stoics taught) the wise person will be reconciled to fate and so achieve freedom from anxiety. Manilius exhorts us:[106]

> Liberate your minds, O mortals, and lift the burden of anxiety! Empty your life of so many vain complaints! Fate rules the world, everything stands firm by a fixed law, and

the long ages are marked by predestined fortunes. In our birth we begin to die, and in our beginning is our end.

Manilius then cites examples from history of human fortunes, focusing especially on reversals, much as Ovid's Pythagoras had focused on the paradoxical wonders of nature. As he says, "who can make such changes [namely, in human fortunes] without the divine power of fate?" (line 56). Reason, then, can know human destiny and reconcile the human will to it. Further, it supports virtue, for the virtuous person will be ruled by reason:[107]

> This reason does not persist in defending crime, nor does it deprive virtue of the gifts of her rewards ... So let the glory of human beings won by their virtuous actions be all the greater because they owe their reputation to the heavens.

Manilius builds his defence of astrology on the foundations of Stoic doctrine – reason, virtue, acceptance of Fate, unity of god and the human soul, divine governance of the universe. His poem has generally been underrated, largely because its subject is technical and his treatment of it falls short of the passion and power of Lucretius. Yet it has attracted the best labours of two of the greatest classical scholars, Joseph Scaliger and A. E. Housman, who saw in it, as we should too, the majesty of Stoic doctrine capable of lifting human beings above the limitations of earthly existence.

6

SENECA AND HIS
CONTEMPORARIES

With the accession of Tiberius in 14 CE the continuation of the monarchy was assured. Tiberius himself soon found that the senate, although it kept the title and forms of the Republican institution, was *de facto* powerless, and for the most part unwilling, to oppose his will in any significant matter. The schools of philosophy continued to exist in Rome, Athens and Alexandria, but the decline of free speech inevitably led to restrictions on freedom of thought. The process accelerated after 23 CE, with the ascendancy of the Praetorian Prefect, Sejanus, and especially after his fall seven years later. The fate of the historian, Cremutius Cordus, prosecuted and driven to suicide in 25, was exemplary, as Tacitus showed in his account of the trial and the burning of Cremutius' books.[1] Under Tiberius' successors, Gaius (37–41), Claudius (41–54) and Nero (54–68), free thought and free speech were increasingly dangerous. All three were constantly suspicious of claimants to the throne, and the crisis of the Pisonian conspiracy in 65 was devastating to Roman intellectuals. Both Seneca and his nephew, Lucan, were executed in its aftermath, and the Stoics Thrasea and Barea Soranus followed in the next year. The philosopher Musonius Rufus had joined the Stoic senator, Rubellius Plautus, in exile in 60 in Asia: he returned to Rome after the execution of Rubellius in 62 and was exiled to the prison island of Gyaros in 65.

The number of the Neronian Stoics (to whom we will return later) is the best evidence for the continuing study of philosophy at Rome. Nevertheless, Seneca's pessimistic summary of the state of the philosophical schools in the 60s is largely accurate.[2] The only purely Roman school, that of the Sextii, had died out with the son and successor of its founder. The Pythagoreans produced no leader at Rome of the stature of Nigidius Figulus, who is prominent in Book 1 of Lucan's *Bellum Civile*, where Lucan portrays him using his astrological knowledge to prophesy the disastrous consequences of the Civil War.[3] This, with the underground basilica near the Porta Praenestina in Rome, is evidence, however weak, for the continued interest in Pythagoreanism in the city.[4] A Pythagorean, Sotion, was Seneca's teacher.[5] He encouraged vegetarianism, since in Pythagorean doctrine the human soul might migrate to an animal body after death. Seneca practised vegetarianism for a year, but gave it up at the request of his father, who "hated philosophy". Seneca says that at this time foreign cults were being banned, and that the emperor, Tiberius, viewed refusal to eat certain animals as evidence for the practice of superstition.[6]

Two other Neopythagoreans active in the first century CE are marginal to a discussion of the Roman philosophers. Moderatus of Gades (active towards the end of the century) wrote eleven books of *Pythagorean Lectures*, focusing, it seems, particularly on Pythagorean numerology. Apollonius of Tyana (in Cappadocia, part of Asia Minor), known from the biography of Philostratus (early third century), was a Pythagorean, whose philosophy was obscured by his reputation as a wandering holy man. Neither of these colourful personages is mentioned by Seneca. Among philosophers of other schools, Philo of Alexandria (who as an old man joined in an embassy to the emperor Gaius in 40 CE), is more important for his influence on later Neoplatonism and as a prominent author of the Jewish-Greek tradition.

Also on the margins of Roman philosophy was Chaeremon of Alexandria, a scholar on Egyptian matters and a Stoic, who was summoned to Rome, probably during the years 49–51, to be tutor to Nero (born in 37).[7] (Seneca, it should be noted, was Nero's tutor in rhetoric and politics, but not in philosophy.) Michael Frede has shown that Chaeremon's Stoicism was practical, ascetic and theological, and he believes that traces of his doctrine appear in Seneca's 90th letter, in the view of Posidonius (criticized by Seneca) that philosophy contributed to improvements in human dwellings.[8] Since Seneca never mentions Chaeremon by name, we may conclude that his influence on philosophy in Rome was minimal.

Other schools of philosophy were still active in Rome, although less than in the Greek world. The Cynic Demetrius was prominent in Seneca's time and irritated Nero and Vespasian, who exiled him to an unnamed island in 71. Given the closeness of Cynic and Stoic ethical doctrines, it is not surprising that Demetrius was a friend of Seneca and of the Stoic politician and martyr, Thrasea Paetus. His name is the last word in the extant text of Tacitus' *Annals*, which break off as Thrasea commits suicide on the orders of Nero. Thrasea had been discussing "the nature of the soul and the separation of soul from body" with Demetrius when the centurion brought the order for his execution, and he withdrew to his bedroom with his son-in-law, Helvidius Priscus, and Demetrius. The nature of Stoic constancy, exhibited in the presence of the Cynic philosopher, is dramatically expressed in Thrasea's words as reported by Tacitus:[9]

> We are making a libation to Jupiter the Liberator. Watch, young man [namely, Helvidius]. And may the gods keep the omen away, but you have been born into a time when it is useful to confirm your courage by examples of constancy.

Like Seneca in the previous year, Thrasea compares his death to that of Socrates, while exemplifying the Stoic paradox that only the wise man is free, even if his freedom is obtained at the expense of his life. That the Cynic philosopher should be present at such a moment speaks for the common ground between Stoics and Cynics in their indifference to the incidents of life (including death itself) and readiness to accept willingly the decrees of Fate.

Demetrius was himself exiled later the same year (66), and was back in Rome before the end of 69. Tacitus says that at that time, before the senate, he defended the disgraced Stoic, Egnatius Celer, who in 66 had betrayed his patron and friend, the Stoic Barea Soranus.[10] Some months later Demetrius was exiled by Vespasian, who dismissed his disobedience and free speech with the words, "I do not execute a barking dog".[11]

Seneca admired Demetrius, calling him a great man and the best of men.[12] He quotes him at length in the first chapter of Book 7 of the *De Beneficiis*, a diatribe that shows how close Cynic and Stoic doctrines were. Demetrius advocates economy in thought and life: only a few philosophical maxims are needed, he says, as guides to life; unnecessary knowledge is superfluous; one should despise the chance happenings of life; death is the end of many evils and not in itself evil; the wise person consecrates his mind to Virtue; human beings are part of a community dwelling in a universe shared by human beings and gods; the wise person is free from the storms of life, standing beneath an unclouded sky and on firm ground. All these maxims are Stoic and can be found elsewhere in Seneca's writings. Seneca says:[13]

I carry Demetrius around with me; I converse with that half-naked man and I admire him – and why not? I have seen that he lacks nothing.

Demetrius represented an ideal of the simple life that Seneca tried to practise in his last years.

From the fragmentary evidence it appears that the four major schools of philosophy were still active in the first century CE but that, with the exception of the Stoics, they lacked significant leadership. The Academics and Peripatetics were in something of an eclipse, but they remained strong enough to join the Stoics and Epicureans in the next century, when professorial chairs were inaugurated at Athens by Marcus Aurelius in 176 CE for the four schools.[14] Their true revival came in the following century with the emergence of Neoplatonism. Epicureanism, likewise, seems to have been practised privately in the first century, especially in Campania, but there was no significant figure to energize its doctrines. The Epicurean doctrine of a simple life free from anxiety was congenial to the Stoics, and Seneca frequently quotes Epicurus with approval. But the Epicurean principle of living unobtrusively was inconsistent with the demands of public life, especially for senators below the age of sixty-five, for whom attendance at meetings of the senate was compulsory.

The Stoics were the only school truly to flourish at Rome in this period, in some measure because they encouraged participation in political activity, and because their doctrines provided comfort and support when participation became morally intolerable and the individual found himself at odds with those who held power. While the names of many Stoics of this period are known, that of Lucius Annaeus Seneca is uniquely important. He was born between 4 BCE and 1 CE, and he died in the aftermath of the Pisonian conspiracy, in 65 CE. His family, from the Spanish city of Corduba (modern Cordoba), was wealthy. Seneca came to Rome as a small boy, and his education focused especially on rhetoric. His father, Annaeus Seneca, was a considerable author, who wrote a History of Rome from the start of the Civil Wars, now lost, and two extant volumes of quotations from, and commentary on, declaimers whom he had heard.[15] The cumbersome title is informative: *Oratorum et Rhetorum Sententiae Divisiones Colores*, that is, examples of the epigrammatic sayings (*sententiae*), the arrangements of arguments (*divisiones*), and the way of shading those arguments (*colores*) adopted by declaimers addressing various set themes. These might have the appearance of a case at law (*Controversiae*), or they might be speeches advising a historical figure (for example, Alexander the Great or Cicero) at a decisive moment (*Suasoriae*). Although the elder Seneca compiled these works towards the end of his life, after his son's reputation as an orator was established, it shows how important for the latter's style was the epigrammatic style of the declaimers.

The elder Seneca hated philosophy, according to his son, yet the younger Seneca studied with philosophers. We have mentioned the importance of the Neopythagorean Sotion and the Cynic Demetrius. Among the most important of his teachers was Papirius Fabianus (*c.*35 BCE to 35 CE), who was a prominent declaimer and a philosopher, a follower of the Sextii. The elder Seneca says that Fabianus' philosophical writing was obscure, but that his rhetoric was flowing, epigrammatic, and especially inspired when he wished to censure contemporary morals.[16] In an extended quotation, Fabianus attacks homicide, luxury, wealth, fine buildings and artificial lakes.[17] His apostrophe to Poverty, *O paupertas, quam ignotum bonum es!* ("Oh Poverty, what an unknown good thing you are!") anticipates a frequent topic in Seneca's diatribes.[18] Fabianus was a prolific philosophical writer (he was said by Seneca to have written more works than Cicero), but his works are not extant and Seneca only once discusses them at any length (in letter 100), while he refers to a work on natural history in connection with the final flood at the end of the world.[19] Elsewhere Seneca several times mentions both the moral integrity and fluent rhetoric of Fabianus.

An equally important teacher was the Stoic, Attalus, who probably laid the foundations of Seneca's Stoicism. In the 108th letter Seneca describes how as a young man he was the first to arrive at the lectures of Attalus and the last to leave, and he implies that what Attalus taught him was of permanent value. Attalus was exiled from Rome during the domination of Sejanus (23–31 CE), presumably after Seneca had attended his lectures. The elder Seneca calls him "a most eloquent man, and the most subtle and fluent philosopher of your [the younger Seneca's] generation".[20] Attalus, like Fabianus, was both an orator and a philosopher. From Seneca's many quotations we can get a sense of his colourful style, pointed and rich in imagery, and we learn of his minimalist philosophy of life and his asceticism, principles that Seneca himself tried to imitate. In an extended quotation Seneca reports a diatribe of Attalus against wealth, illustrated by vignettes of contemporary displays of wealth.[21] These he contrasts with the life of one who is satisfied with very little ("bread and barley-cakes"). The ideal is a life pared down to the minimum: "turn your minds to true wealth: learn to be contented with a little'. Attalus' epigrams anticipate Seneca's pointed style: "Hunger puts an end to hunger" (i.e. death by starvation will be the end of need), or "that man over whom fortune has limited power is not free: he is free over whom fortune has no power at all". Seneca approves of this, commenting that "Attalus said this to us [his students]: Nature has said it to everyone." These contrasts – wealth and poverty, luxury and bare necessity, death and the tyranny of creature comforts – are very common in Seneca's teaching, and they were rooted in the teachings of Attalus.

Like Cicero, Seneca developed a new prose style for his philosophical works. Except in Renaissance Europe, readers have always been ambivalent about it. Seneca strives after brevity and "point" to present his doctrine vividly, but this very virtue palls with familiarity. Macaulay complained that reading Seneca "is like living on nothing but anchovy sauce". Seneca's words flow smoothly and inevitably: Lipsius likened Cicero's philosophical style to a pond, but Seneca was like "a fast-flowing river that carries the reader along with it". Such virtuosity invites hostile criticism. When Seneca was still quite young, the Emperor Gaius dismissed his oratory as "sand without mortar", and fifty years later Quintilian wrote a hostile critique of Seneca's style, which he believed was corrupt and corrupted the young.[22] He recognized Seneca's range of writing and excellence in rhetoric and poetry, but he found his philosophy careless, his moral criticisms tiresome, and the idiosyncrasies of his style dangerously attractive. He thought that Seneca was a narcissist and unable to practise self-criticism. This celebrated criticism has been echoed down the ages, including our own. Even after the recent modest revival of his fortunes among Latinists and philosophers, he still is little read in universities and hardly at all in schools, and his philosophy is still underrated. F. H. Sandbach dismisses Seneca as "a spare-time amateur philosopher" and states that "It is hard for the Englishman of to-day [1975] to approach Seneca with sympathy."[23] Others take refuge in psychology, and as an example of biased judgement by otherwise intelligent scholars we may take the following statement from the article (now suppressed) on Seneca in the first edition of the *Oxford Classical Dictionary* by E. P. Barker:

> In the tragedies we meet ... the primitive thought-forms ... and nightmares risen out of a tortured egoist's unconscious mind. Everywhere are traceable the erratic ability

and the limitations which are common stigmata of para-
noiac abnormality.

Much the same sort of thing has been said of Seneca's prose works,
yet in his own time his influence was palpable, and in the Renaissance
he was the Roman philosopher *par excellence*, to whom Erasmus and
Lipsius devoted some of their best work. Their editions (along with
those of Muretus and Gruter) guaranteed that Seneca was the ancient
philosopher to whom readers turned for comfort and guidance in
harsh and unpredictable times, when violence and torture could
suddenly extinguish one's possessions or even one's life.[24]

The fairest estimate of Seneca's style has been made by Anne-
Marie Guillemin in two articles whose titles are significant:
"Sénèque, directeur d'âmes" and "Sénèque, second fondateur de la
prose Latine".[25] In the mid-first century CE the Roman audience for
philosophy had changed since the time of Cicero, the founder of
Latin philosophical prose. Cicero's audience, like many of the participants in his dialogues, was homogeneous, drawn from the circle of
senatorial and equestrian intellectuals who had for the most part
been active politicians and had all grown up under the Republic.
Even though that Republic had collapsed by the time of Cicero's
greatest philosophical activity, its ideals remained alive in this circle,
whose members legitimately looked back to the idealized politics of
the second century, when (so skilfully did Cicero set his scenes)
leaders such as Scipio Aemilianus and Laelius were portrayed as
conducting their lives and their politics according to philosophical
principles. Little of this was true for Seneca and his readers, born
into a Roman world where, as Tacitus remarked, few had ever seen
the free Republic.[26] The leisurely pace of Ciceronian prose, appropriate for the exposition of unchanging moral and political
principles, was inappropriate for a world of moral and political
ambiguity. The glorious vision of the *Dream of Scipio* was refracted
into prismatic slivers of an ever-shifting political and moral scene. In
such circumstances an urgent, colourful and pointed style was needed.
As Lipsius said, Seneca's *sententiae* (pithy sayings) were pointed, lucid
and penetrating (*acres, argutae, penetrantes*), reaching their audience
with an immediacy that was all the more insightful in times when
exile and death could be inflicted by the emperor or his agents
suddenly and arbitrarily. Seneca was indeed "the second founder of
Latin prose", and it was his style, rather than the Ciceronian style of
Quintilian and Pliny, that proved to be the vehicle for the doctrines
of the Latin church fathers.

The description of Seneca as "Director of Souls" is again accurate, reflecting the ever-changing dilemmas of individuals trapped in political and moral ambiguities. Cicero had recorded the doctrines of the Greeks, which he adapted and expanded to meet the circumstances of Roman society and politics. The foundation of his philosophy was a firm belief in Roman ideals, Roman history and Roman political principles. Whatever the public rhetoric, little of this remained in the time of the emperors Claudius and Nero. Seneca's philosophy is predominantly ethical, focusing on the needs of the individual. Even the most political of his philosophical works, *De Clementia*, was addressed to the individual, Nero – a mirror in which Nero would see himself reflected.[27] Most of Seneca's prose works give moral advice to individuals, or they discuss the individual's response to moral, social or (more rarely) political situations. This is most obvious in the case of Lucilius, to whom the *Epistles* are addressed. From the very first sentence Lucilius is urged to study philosophy under Seneca's guidance: in letter 19 Seneca rejoices that he has made such moral progress, and letter 75, which begins with remarks about the nature of Seneca's letter-writing, focuses on the question of moral progress. The very last sentence of the last letter, 124, offers Lucilius a "formula" for measuring his progress towards moral perfection. Seneca, then, adopts the persona of the moral guide, "Director of Souls".

Seneca was exceptionally prolific, and I will be compelled to set some limits to the range of my survey. Although there is a great deal of Stoic doctrine in his tragedies, I will not here discuss their philosophy, beyond pointing out that Seneca's understanding of human psychology, allied to his knowledge of the workings of ambition and power, gives a uniquely powerful dramatic setting for the principles of philosophy. The conflict between private desire and public responsibility motivates the *Phaedra*. The unquenchable anger of a tyrant and a wronged brother energizes the *Thyestes*, where a world devoid of moral and religious principles is the result of emotion unrestrained by philosophy.

Seneca's philosophical treatises fall into four groups. First are the *Dialogues* (which deserve this title even less than the dialogues of Cicero), twelve books of medium length, of which nine discuss specific ethical topics. These are works on Providence, Constancy, Anger (in three books), the Happy Life, Retirement from Public Life (largely lost), Tranquillity, and Shortness of Life. The remaining three books are Consolations, two of which (those addressed to Marcia and to Helvia, Seneca's mother) are true consolations, while the third, addressed to Claudius' powerful freedman, Polybius, contains more flattery and special pleading than philosophy.

The second group of writings consists of two extended works on specific ethical topics, the *De Clementia* and the *De Beneficiis*. The former, of which only the first book and part of the second are extant, was written at the beginning of Nero's reign (54 CE), when the emperor was seventeen years old, to advise him on how to be a merciful king. The latter, in seven books, concerned a topic of great importance in Roman society, the correct relationship of giver and receiver of benefits. Seneca returned to this topic more concisely in his 81st letter.

The third – and best-known – group consists of the 124 *Epistulae Morales ad Lucilium*, divided into twenty books. These are not letters like Cicero's correspondence with Atticus, in which he expressed his state of mind from day to day and discussed his doubts, worries and hopes. They are really a course on ethics, self-contained disquisitions on specific topics, leading Lucilius from his former non-Stoic ways of thought to Stoic progress, not towards the perfection of the wise man, but as close to perfection as ordinary people may come, which is happiness based on reason and virtue.

Finally, and forming a fourth group by itself, is Seneca's sole surviving work on physics, *Quaestiones Naturales*. Although the text has been disordered, six of the eight books survive more or less complete, and two (numbered IVA and IVB in modern editions) are mutilated. While the work deals with specific natural phenomena (fire, thunder and lightning, water, the Nile, clouds, wind, earthquake, comets), it also contains moral disquisitions, like that at the end of the first book, that takes mirrors as its starting point.[28] In the following discussion, we will focus on some of the *Dialogues* and the *Epistles*.

The first two dialogues in the traditional order, *De Providentia* and *De Constantia Sapientis*, display Seneca's attitude towards the human predicament clearly and forthrightly, often with a noble simplicity, equally often with wearying dogmatism. The subtitle of each of these works is significant. That to the *De Providentia* is: "Why some bad things happen to good people, although Providence exists." The subtitle of the *De Constantia* is: "The wise man cannot be affected by insult or injury." From these sentences we can deduce the lineaments of Seneca's ethical universe. Over all human beings is Providence, which is the same as Fate or God. The etymology of *Providence*, literally "seeing in advance", indicates a power that has already foreseen human destinies, but not in such a way that human beings are its slaves or victims. On the contrary, they are free to choose whether to harmonize their individual wills with that of Fate, or whether to resist and try to change their destiny. The former choice leads to happiness and tranquillity, the latter to frustration, anger and discontent. Thus these subtitles show that the wise person will indeed be prepared for Fate to deal some harsh blows – bad things *will* happen to good people. If the wise person recognizes the overall power of Fate, which includes divine wisdom and concern for the well-being of human beings, then he (and here I use "he" and "his" inclusively) brings his will into conformity with the divine will. Thus he will understand why bad things happen, he will accept them, and endure adversity with constancy: indeed, he will be contented with it, not seeking to avoid or change the decrees of Fate. This is a challenge that requires reason and virtue – the attributes of the wise person – to be accepted successfully. Thus the wise person is pre-eminent: those who have not achieved such wisdom will allow themselves to be affected by bad things – death, disease, poverty and so forth, or insults and hostility from one's fellow human-beings. In Seneca's moral universe, then, the wise person is exceptional, and his will is in harmony with the divine will, his emotions (grief, anger, fear and frustration, for example) controlled or suppressed to the extent that he can call himself truly happy, even in the midst of suffering and adversity. The rest of humanity will strive to reach that level of wisdom, hard – indeed, impossible – as it is, and individual human beings will be found at different stages of progress towards the perfection of the wise person.

Let us see now how these austere outlines are filled out in Seneca's prose writings. In the very first sentence of the *De Providentia* Seneca says:

> You have asked me, Lucilius, why so many bad things happen to good men if providence rules the world. This could be more appropriately discussed in the context of this work if we prove that providence presides over the whole universe and that god is concerned with us.

Seneca then goes on to prove the existence of god from the order and regularity of the universe, and to assert that god is not the source of evil, rather that god loves good people. What appear to be evils, then, are not so for the good person, who recognizes that they are morally improving, like a parent's punishment of a child or medicine for the sick. And over all is the irrevocable progress of Destiny (§7):

Fate leads us on and the first hour of our birth has ordained the rest of each person's life. Cause depends on cause, the long series of things lengthens [the chain of] public and private events. Therefore we must endure everything courageously.

Elsewhere Seneca briefly doubts whether events are preordained by Fate or an all-wise god, or simply by chance.[29] His conclusion is the same in all cases: "one must be a philosopher", for philosophy will exhort us "to obey god willingly, to obey Fortune defiantly". The exhortation is not new, but Seneca's brisk and sententious style is, along with its memorable images and poetic colouring. Thus he brings philosophy to the level of the ordinary person. With Seneca it becomes the teacher and comforter for people caught in the human predicament, and from him this style of philosophical encouragement for the individual enters into the still-unfolding tradition of Roman ethics, pagan and Christian.

In a late letter Seneca returns to the theme of conforming one's will to Fate. He sees natural phenomena as a metaphor for human life:[30]

Clouds give way to clear weather; the calm sea grows rough; the winds blow from different quarters; day follows night; some stars rise while others set. Eternity exists through opposites. The human spirit must adapt itself to this law; it must follow it; it must obey it. Whatever happens we must think happens through necessity, nor may we wish to blame Nature. It is best to acquiesce when you cannot change something for the better; to follow god without complaint, for god is the origin of everything that happens. That man is a bad soldier who follows his commander with a groan.

The metaphors follow thick and fast, but it is impossible for a reader to ignore the urgency of Seneca's doctrine. Finally he addresses Jupiter himself, translating the *Hymn to Zeus* of Cleanthes:[31]

Lead me, O Father, ruler of the lofty heavens, wherever you wish: readily I will obey. Here am I, eager to follow. If I am unwilling, I shall follow groaning, and suffer myself to do with ill grace what I could have done happily. Fate leads on the willing, and drags the unwilling.

Thus Seneca associates himself with the great early Stoic master. But the doctrine is appropriate for individuals in the early Roman empire, especially under a weak and cruel ruler with arbitrary power over the lives of those who might disagree with him.

We have seen that the figure of the wise man is prominent in Seneca's philosophical universe. While Seneca admits that such a person is rare and morally far superior to ordinary human beings, he maintains that "at great intervals of the ages" such a person will exist.[32] From Roman history the younger Cato is the closest example, although Seneca is not always consistent about him.[33] He uses Cato to make the ideal "wise person" more real. At the beginning of the *De Constantia* Cato is the historical example of the dialogue's subtitle, "the wise man [who] cannot be affected by insult or injury". Seneca draws a vivid picture of Cato having his toga torn by a mob in the Forum, being violently manhandled "from the Rostra to the Arch of Fabius" (i.e. the length of the Roman Forum), being spat upon. Seneca concludes:[34]

> The immortal gods have given Cato to us as a more reliable example of the wise man than Ulysses and Hercules from earlier times, whom our Stoic philosophers have named as wise men, [heroes] unconquered by labours, who despised pleasure and were victors over every sort of terror. Cato did not wrestle with wild beasts (the opponents of hunters and farmers); he did not pursue monsters with fire and iron weapons; he did not live in times when it was possible to believe that the heavens could be carried on the shoulders of one man. Shaking off the credulity of ancient times ... he fought with corruption ... , with unlimited lust for power ... Against the vices of a state in decline and collapsing from its own weight he stood alone. He held up the republic, as far as it could be held back by one man's hand alone, until, dragged off, he shared in a collapse that he had long held off ... For Cato did not outlive Liberty, nor did Liberty outlive Cato.

This brilliant parable is a perfect example of Seneca's method. The concrete example of Cato makes the abstract notion of "the wise man" real. The labours of the great heroes of myth are contrasted with the labours of a Roman politician, less glamorous than the labours of Hercules, yet involving the disappointments and humiliations of political life. Thus the point is made: the wise man need not be a hero, for he can overcome adversity through reason and constancy. Only the wise man is free, according to the Stoic paradox: Cato, faced with the realities of an autocracy and the futilities of a dying republic, chose in life a hopeless but morally good cause and in death the way to preserve his freedom. Seneca exploits the paradox (of being free through death) by confusing the two denotations of the word "liberty". The one is moral, for the wise man does not become a slave to the emotions that motivate the autocrat's followers. The other is political, for the wise man will die rather than compromise with tyranny. In a Roman context, Cato, rather than the heroes of mythology, exemplifies the heroic status of the wise man.

Seneca admits that Cato "may be too lofty an example for us",[35] and in letters 41 and 75 he shows how ordinary human beings may admire the wise man from a distance, yet in themselves have the potential for sharing in such perfection. Since the Stoics maintained that only the wise man could be sane, virtuous, free, etc. (and the non-wise would all be imperfect, however close to or far from perfection they might be), Seneca's admission of grades of progress towards virtue was realistic. The idea, prominent in letter 41, that all human beings have the potential to share in divine perfection, seems to have much in common with the doctrines of Cicero's *Somnium Scipionis.* Yet, here again, Seneca brings a lofty ideal down from Cicero's aristocratic milieu to the level of all human beings, who are endowed with reason and capable of using reason to live according to nature. His approach was appropriate for the social and political realities of his time. In letter 41 Seneca joins two ideas – the divine nature dwelling in human beings, and the perfect example of the wise man – to show that the attributes of the wise man can be within the reach of ordinary people. He begins with the divinity immanent in human beings (§§1–2):

> We do not have to lift up our hands to heaven or get the temple-keeper to let us in to speak into the ear of the god's statue, as if that could make us more audible. God is close to you, he is with you, he is in you. Yes, Lucilius: the divine spirit has his home within us, he is our guardian and watches over us in good and bad times alike.

Then Seneca describes natural objects that inspire awe: an old tree, a vast cave, a river's source, a deep and dark lake. These he compares to a virtuous person (§§4–5):

If you see a man who is not frightened by danger, who is untouched by desires, who is happy in adversity and calm in the midst of storms, who looks at human beings from above and at the gods eye to eye – do you not feel in awe of him? Will you not say, "This is something greater and loftier than I can believe, out of all proportion to the little body in which it dwells?" A divine force has descended into that body. A divine energy drives that extraordinary spirit, which is disciplined and superior to all that it experiences, laughing at all our hopes and fears. So great a thing cannot exist without the support of the divine.

Seneca considers the nature of this spirit. It does not consist in external things – "golden reins do not make a horse better" (§6). No, what should be praised in a human being is the human nature which is peculiar to each individual (§8):

"What is this?", you ask. It is his spirit, and Reason that dwells perfected in his spirit. For a human being is a living creature endowed with Reason (*rationale animal*) ... What, then, does this Reason demand of a human being? Something very easy – to live according to his own nature.

Lipsius rightly exclaims in his commentary on this letter: "O what a beautiful and lofty letter!" The ideals are noble, the examples of human excellence inspiring; the moral advice is sensible, its goal attainable (even if we may disagree with Seneca's description of our task as "something very easy"). The link between the Stoic god and the morally perfect human being is made more immediate by the vivid examples from the familiar world of nature. Awe-inspiring objects in nature are used as metaphors for awe-inspiring virtue. Seneca easily identifies the essential attributes of such a nature, and shows that we, too, possess such attributes, if we choose to employ them. And so the familiar bases of Stoic ethics – Reason, Nature and Virtue – reappear as our means of union with the divine, and, far from being discouraged by the perfection of the wise person, we are made to feel that we, too, have the potential to realize our divine nature and, through reason, to achieve virtue.

But not many of us reach the goal, strive as we may. Here Seneca breaks with traditional Stoic severity and in letter 75 he develops the idea of stages of progress towards virtue, using the flexibility that Panaetius had introduced into orthodox Stoicism. Cicero had said that "no one should be overlooked in whom some evidence of virtue appears",[36] and from this Seneca develops the notion of the *proficiens*, the person who is progressing towards the perfection of the wise man. The letter begins in an artfully informal way, which prepares for the informal and undogmatic theory of the *proficiens*. Seneca imagines that his letters are like informal conversation between friends – "I want my letters to be like my conversation if we were sitting or walking together, easy and not artificial". So the formal distinction between the wise man and everyone else becomes blurred (§8):

> "Are there no grades below the wise man? Is there a sheer drop below wisdom?" No, in my view. For the person who is making progress is, to be sure, in the class of "fools", but already far different from them. And between those who are making progress there are great distinctions, and they can be divided into three classes, according to some people.

Seneca then defines these three classes. Highest (and close to the wise man) are those "who have not yet achieved wisdom, but stand close to it". They have abandoned the emotions and vices, yet still are diffident about their wisdom. They are cured of the diseases (*morbi*) of the mind, but still are liable to its moods (*adfectus*). Seneca defines the former as "inveterate and hardened vices, such as avarice and ambition", whereas the latter are "bad motions of the mind, sudden and swift", but not permanent. In this analysis Seneca shows his interest in human psychology, which makes him a more humane teacher than the dogmatic Stoics.[37]

Seneca's second class (§13) includes those who are free of the greatest passions and troubles of the mind, yet still may relapse. The third class (§14) consists of those who are free of many of the vices but still are liable to some. They may not be liable to avarice, but they feel anger; they may be free of lust, but they are afflicted with ambition, and so on. Seneca says that most of us will be doing well to belong to this class, and that only by exceptional effort will one reach the second class: "you will understand that we have made progress enough if we are not included with the worst people" (§15). We might object that Seneca has set too low a standard for moral progress, yet his realistic assessment of human morality gives a gentler face to Stoic austerity. The usual Stoic classification of human beings into the wise man and the rest is plainly impractical. Ordinary people need encouragement if they are to start along the road to virtue, and they need to know that progress is possible, that falling short of perfection is not total failure. The profound human dilemma between evil and unattainable good, has, of course, been basic to many religions and philosophies, and its solutions range from the heroic humanism of Sophocles to the divine saviour of Christianity. Seneca's solution is undramatic and unheroic, but it provides the majority of human beings with a practical way to escape from hopeless passivity.

The emotions are central to Seneca's moral philosophy, as they were for Chrysippus and Posidonius. He was especially concerned with anger, and *De Ira* in three books continues the debate between the Stoics, on the one hand, and the Peripatetics and Epicureans, on the other, that we have briefly discussed in connection with Virgil. It is an early work, completed possibly in 41 CE and certainly before 52. Like the *De Clementia*, which aimed to soften Nero's cruelty, *De Ira* probably had a political context, in that the disposition to anger of Claudius (emperor 41–54 CE) was well known and even admitted by the emperor himself.[38] The distinction that Seneca draws between anger (*ira*) and an angry disposition (*iracundia*) in *De Ira* 1. 4 was made by Claudius, when he promised that "his anger would be brief and harmless, his angry disposition would not lead to injustice". But the treatise is far more important as a meditation upon the emotion that Seneca perhaps feared most. It is worth noting here that anger in the Senecan tragedies is frequently the motivating and destructive emotion, reaching its climax in the character of Atreus in the late play, *Thyestes*.[39] "Anger" is the first word in European literature (*Iliad* 1. 1), and, as we have seen above, it is the crucial emotion in the *Aeneid*, the principal motivation for Juno and her human protégés, and the emotion that drives Aeneas to kill Turnus. Its importance in Roman ethics cannot be overestimated. Seneca's treatise is addressed to his older brother, Novatus (better known by his adopted name, Gallio), who had asked him to write on the means of assuaging anger, the emotion that Novatus feared above all others. In the first chapter, Seneca gives a horrifying description of human and animal anger, and the rest of Book 1 is spent largely in describing and defining anger. Seneca disagrees with one of Aristotle's definitions (that anger is the desire for revenge), and he says that the anger of animals is similar to human anger but not that emotion itself, since animals do not have human emotions, which require rational assent.[40] Therefore anger exists only where there is reason. The main doctrine of Book 1 is that anger is contrary to nature, and Seneca defends this against a number of hypothetical questions.[41] The book ends with a comparison of the meanness of anger with the sublimity of virtue.[42] The end recalls the beginning, where anger had been defined as "brief insanity", that is, a madness that deprives the angry person of reason that leads to virtue.

In the second book Seneca further examines the sources of anger and at §18 he begins to answer Novatus' basic question, "What are the remedies for anger?" In one of the most interesting passages of the work, Seneca begins his remedies with the education of children, where he shows how important are parental example and early training in controlling the emotions.[43] Here he is following Plato, and he ends the passage with an anecdote of the boy who returned home from Plato's class to see his father in a fit of anger and said, "I didn't see this at Plato's school".

The antidotes to anger are continued throughout Book 3. Here Seneca takes issue particularly with Aristotle's defence of anger as "the spur to virtue", in particular the virtue of courage.[44] Seneca's examples support the Stoic doctrine that the wise man does not feel anger, which is contrary to nature and must be suppressed by reason. In contrast, the Epicureans said that anger was natural and could be moderated by reason. The Peripatetics agreed, adding that anger could be just if so moderated. The work ends nobly with a meditation on human mortality, in which Seneca's prose rises to loftiness:[45]

> Let each person say to himself and to another, "What is the point for those born ... to eternity to make a declaration of anger and waste their short span of life? ... Why not rather put your short life in order and make it peaceful for yourself and others? ... Why do you try to crush violently the man who barks at you, a low-class, contemptible person, yet one who is bitter and hostile to his superiors? Why be angry with your slave, your master, your ruler, your client? Be patient for a little while: death, you can see, is at hand, which will make you all equal ... In the meantime, while we live, while we are among human beings, let us cultivate humanity. Let us not be a source of fear or danger for anyone. Let us despise losses, wrongs, abuse, criticism. Let us be high-minded and put up with short-lived nuisances. While we look behind us, as the proverb goes, and turn our backs, death draws near."

The *De Ira* is the most successful of Seneca's long treatises. While it draws heavily on his Stoic predecessors, it is original in its vivid examples, its realism (based on Seneca's own experience), and its understanding of human irrationality.[46] In contrast to the *De Providentia* and *De Constantia*, the work sets before us the attainable ideal of a peaceful life, marked by respect for the feelings of others (this is one of the aspects of *humanitas*), rather than the distant austerity of the wise man. And here again, Seneca's guiding principles are the fundamental Stoic attributes of virtue and reason, practised in a life lived according to nature.

The *De Ira* focuses on interpersonal relationships, another aspect of which is the relationship between giver and recipient, the subject of Seneca's longest treatise, *De Beneficiis*, in seven books, much of which is repeated in summary form in letter 81. The subject was important in Roman society, which was more contractual in its relationships than modern Western societies. The prominence of duties in the philosophy of Panaetius and Cicero is evidence enough for this, while the Roman social institution of clientship rested on the proper understanding of the giving of benefits (*beneficia*) by the patron, superior in wealth, power and social status, and of the services of the client to the patron in return. Seneca, however, does not discuss this aspect of Roman social relationships, and the exchange of benefits between social equals is his primary focus.

Ingratitude, or the failure to return a *beneficium*, is a cause of anger or mental perturbation in Seneca. It breaks the social contract, and therefore it is harmful both for the individual and for society. Therefore he begins his treatise by saying that among the worst of human errors is that "we know neither how to give nor receive benefits". In the first four books Seneca defines benefits and examines them from every aspect. In Books 5–7 he examines particular topics, the most interesting passage being his praise of Demetrius the Cynic at the beginning of Book 7.[47] He expresses his conclusions more concisely in letter 81, which begins by focusing on cases where the giver of a benefit later injures the beneficiary. Seneca expands this to affirm the Stoic paradox, that "only the wise man knows how to be grateful". For the wise man will use reason to estimate the benefit, the giver, the reason for it, and so on, and he will come to a just and dispassionate estimate of the proper extent of gratitude.[48] And in the end such a rational approach will lead to happiness and a peaceful life. Thus both the treatise and letter 81 confirm the definition of *beneficium* with which the treatise began:[49]

> It is a well-disposed action which gives joy and derives it
> from the action, when the giver is ready and willing. It is
> not the action or the gift that is important, but the inten-
> tion, because the benefit consists, not in what is done or
> given, but in the mind of the doer or giver.

Thus Seneca makes reason, not social convention or monetary value, the criterion for the giving and receiving of benefits.

Seneca also considers whether a free man can receive a benefit from a slave.[50] This had been discussed by the Stoic philosopher Hecato of Rhodes, a pupil of Panaetius, whose work on Duties was quoted by Cicero. Hecato asked whether in a shipwreck a valuable horse or a cheap slave would deserve more to be saved.[51] Like Cicero, Seneca rises above this bleak level of ethics. He says that the person who denies that a slave can give a benefit to his master is "ignorant of the rights of human beings". A slave is as human as his master: it is his body that has been enslaved, not his mind, which is free. Since it is the intention that is decisive in the giving of a benefit, the slave is just as able to give a benefit as a free person. Seneca supports his statement with a number of examples where slaves performed great benefits for their masters or mistresses, and he concludes that the free person can be just as much enslaved by his vices as the slave by his master.

Although Seneca has been vigorously criticized as being insincere in his views on slavery, letter 47 is the most humane statement about the institution from the pagan world, a striking contrast to Aristotle's view that a slave is "a living tool" and "by nature a slave".[52] Seneca does not question the institution of slavery, to be sure, but he does admit that a slave is a human being no different from his master and subject to the same fortune. He cites examples from Roman history of Roman citizens who have been enslaved (for example, after a military defeat), and he makes the point that all human beings are slaves to their vices and their desires. Slaves, then, should be treated humanely and reasonably, so that they will respect, not fear, their masters. We may rightly be disappointed that Seneca goes no further than this in his criticism of Roman slavery: we will learn more about the meaning of slavery and freedom from Epictetus, who was himself a former slave. Nevertheless, Seneca's doctrine is based on the Stoic idea that all human beings share in the same divine origin, to which they will return, and that all are endowed with reason, and thus with the potential to achieve virtue.

The doctrine of the community of human beings is extremely important for Seneca, most interestingly in the dialogues *De Otio* and *De Tranquillitate*, written probably before his retirement from Nero's court in 62 CE. Whether or not these works are closely linked to events in Seneca's life (as some scholars suppose), they address the problem of political participation, a central dilemma to the philosopher who was also a politician.[53] Important aspects of the problem are freedom and the proper course of action for the virtuous person involved in politics.

Stoic doctrine taught that the virtuous person will participate in the life of the city, that is in political activity. In Roman history this is borne out in the careers of Cato the Younger, of Seneca, and of Thrasea and Helvidius Priscus. In Zeno's ideal republic all citizens are virtuous, so that there is no need for the laws and institutions of conventional cities.[54] But in states as they actually are, the virtuous person faces an exquisite dilemma if the ruler is morally bad. Panaetius had justified the imperial mission of the senatorial class and encouraged its members to undertake heavy political responsibilities on the grounds of the community of humankind and the assurance of their place in the divinely ordered cosmos, a doctrine vindicated in Cicero's *Somnium Scipionis*. But under the Roman emperors political power flowed from the emperor, and the model of senators exercising power in competition with their peers was distorted by the concentration of military power, political influence and social patronage in the person of the emperor. The leader under the Roman republic undertook his duties in the context of service to the community of humankind, towards whom he directed his *oikeiosis*, that is, his moral affinity or orientation. Cicero, through the Academic speaker, Piso, had shown how the affinity of human beings spread from parents and family, through friends and fellow-citizens, to the whole of the human race.[55] The idea of *oikeiosis* towards all humankind, first articulated by Zeno, was extended by Chrysippus, in his work *On Nature*, to the "community of all rational beings who are citizens of the universe", including gods and humankind.[56] Thus the possibility of dual citizenship was created: one was a citizen of Rome or Athens, but also of the community of all human and divine beings.

For Seneca this was the solution to the dilemma of political participation. The *De Tranquillitate*, which is addressed to Seneca's friend Annaeus Serenus (also a high official in Nero's court, who died in or about 62 CE), begins with Serenus consulting Seneca about the malaise that he feels – he wishes to continue in public life, yet he feels the attraction of retirement (*otium*). In reply, Seneca recommends involvement in politics and he disagrees with the philosopher Athenodorus of Tarsus who advised swift and complete retreat into *otium* when public life became too corrupt for a virtuous person to participate in.[57] Seneca advises a gradual retreat "with standards uncaptured and military dignity unimpaired". Here is the virtuous man's gradual retreat:

> He may not serve in the army: let him run for political office. He must live as a private individual: let him be an orator. He is forbidden to speak: let him help his fellow-citizens by means of his private support. Even the Forum is dangerous for him to enter: in private houses, at public shows, at dinner parties, let him play the role of a good companion, a loyal friend, and a moderate fellow-guest. He has lost the duties of a citizen: let him perform those of a human being. Therefore with a generous spirit we have not shut ourselves inside the walls of one city, but we have sent ourselves to interact with the whole world. We have declared that the universe is our fatherland, so as to give ourselves a broader field for virtue.

Thus the retreat from public life is defined by broadening circles of activity, which finally include "the community of the citizens of the universe" of Chrysippus. Seneca's *otium* is active, in contrast to that of the philosophers criticized by Quintilian for shirking their duties as citizens.[58] Elsewhere, returning to the military metaphor, Seneca tells Lucilius that "to be alive is to be on campaign" and that it is shameful to be inactive while others labour. Wherever he is, the virtuous citizen will consider that he is like a soldier assigned to a post (*statio*) which he may not desert.[59]

This apparently neat theory, however, clashed with the rules for senators, who were compelled to attend the senate until the age of 65 (or 60). When Thrasea was put on trial, the charge was that he had withdrawn from the senate although he was an ex-consul, that he did not perform his duties as a priest, that he had not honoured his oath as a citizen – in brief, that he had become a traitor and an enemy of the state.[60] Some further justification was needed for withdrawal into *otium*. This Seneca provides in his *De Otio* (now incomplete) by appealing to the doctrine of the dual citizenship of the virtuous person. Denied public activity at Rome, he will still try to be actively useful to the human community:[61]

This surely is what is demanded of a human being – that he be of use to human beings, to many if that can be achieved; to few if it be less possible; to those closest to him if it be still less possible; to himself if it be less still. For whenever he makes himself useful to others he is transacting the business of the whole community.

Finally, Seneca enunciates the doctrine of the two republics:[62]

In our mind we embrace two republics. The first is large and truly "public" and includes gods and human beings. In it we do not look at this or that corner, but we limit the boundaries of our republic with the sun. The second republic is that in which the circumstances of our birth have enrolled us. This will be Athens or Carthage or some other city which belongs not to all human beings but to a definite group ... This former, greater, republic we can serve even as private individuals – indeed, perhaps better in private so that we can enquire into the nature of Virtue.

Thus Seneca adapts the doctrines of Zeno and Chrysippus to the constricting circumstances of public life under Nero. Like Cicero, he turns from the constraints of contemporary politics to the wider universe of gods and human beings, using the doctrine of dual citizenship to encourage the virtuous person still to be active on behalf of humankind, even when political activity in his own community is restricted. His theory was destined to have long-lasting influence, not least in the history of early Christianity.

Seneca recommends suicide as a way of withdrawing from public life only in the context of escaping from the cruelties of oriental tyrants.[63] He calls it in this passage "the road to liberty", and it is liberty that is the basis of his frequent discussions of suicide.[64] Thrasea had modelled his death on that of Socrates, particularly in the libation of his blood to Jupiter the Liberator, and he also had in mind Seneca's suicide the previous year (65 CE), in which Socrates was again the example and again the dying man with his last words offered a libation to Jupiter the Liberator.[65] People of high social or political rank at Rome who were condemned to death were allowed to commit suicide rather than wait for the executioner's stroke. Both Seneca and Thrasea were condemned by Nero (the former suspected of participation in the Pisonian conspiracy, the latter convicted of disloyalty for not performing his public duties), and both used their suicides both as political acts and as assertions of individual liberty. They were, then, reasoned acts, worthy of the Stoic wise man.

The basic Stoic doctrine on suicide was Zeno's:[66]

> The wise man will make a reasonable exit from life, for the sake of his country and his friends, and if he is in unyielding pain or suffers loss of his limbs or incurable disease.

Seneca was very clear that suicide was not justified by boredom with life, or lust for, or even fear of, death.[67] He says, "the brave and wise man ought not to run away from life but make his exit". He admired his friend, the historian Aufidius Bassus, for enduring the infirmities of age rather than yielding to them by committing suicide.[68] Bassus' mind was unimpaired, and therefore he used reason to continue his life, like the captain of a damaged but still seaworthy ship. Like the wise man, he contemplated death rationally, and he would meet it gladly because he was mentally prepared.

So much for reasons not to commit suicide. At the end of the *De Providentia* (§6) and in Letters 70 and 77 (along with many other incidental references) Seneca recommends it as a means to freedom, relying on Zeno's doctrine of the "reasonable exit" and the Stoic paradox that "only the wise man is free". So in the passage from the *De Providentia* he catalogues different methods of suicide as speedy ways to escape from the tyranny of intolerable evils. Death, in Stoic doctrine, belongs to the category of "indifferent" things, and therefore is not to be feared. In letter 70 he attacks philosophers who say that one must wait for a natural death (§14):

> he who says this does not see that he is closing the road to liberty: the eternal law has achieved nothing better than that it has given us one entrance into life, but many ways out.

One does not have to be a Cato to die by a noble suicide (§19), for even criminals, prisoners and gladiators have achieved this (Seneca gives a number of examples). How much more then should the person who is guided by reason, and has meditated upon death for a long time, be capable of a noble suicide! (§§27–28). What is important to Seneca is how well one dies, for dying well is to escape from living disgracefully (§6). Later, in Letter 77, Seneca describes the suicide of Tullius Marcellinus, which is especially interesting because Marcellinus is a borderline case of justifiable suicide. He was "a peaceful young man who quickly grew old", and he suffered from a chronic disease that was curable, although troublesome (§5). He took the advice of "our Stoic friend" (who is not named), that death is not to be feared and noble if one dies with honour, prudence and courage (§6). So Marcellinus fasted for three days and died (as he himself said) with a certain pleasure after being placed in a hot bath. Seneca's point here, which he makes with a series of historical examples, is that suicide is justified if it is based on reason, and that it is more virtuous to confirm one's liberty through death than to be subject to the loss of freedom. He concludes that length of life is insignificant compared with its moral quality: "what matters is not how long you live, but how well" (§20). We may deplore Seneca's morbid interest in suicide, but his own death, even if it was as histrionic as Tacitus describes it, exemplified his principles.[69]

In letter 89. 9 Seneca accepts the traditional Stoic division of philosophy into three parts, which he names in this order: moral (ethics), natural (physics, including theology), and rational (logic, which he defines as requiring accuracy in vocabulary, structure and argument). Like the Epicureans (§11), who, he says, got rid of the "rational" category, Seneca appears to have very little interest in logic and epistemology.[70] He does discuss these matters in several letters: for example, in the 65th letter he discusses causes and material, including the Aristotelian "form" (*eidos*) and the Platonic "ideas" (§§4–11), but he quickly dismisses them as "including either too little or too much" (§11), and he hurries to give his own definition of the original cause, which he says is "reason, that is, god" (§12). In letter 58. 26 he dismisses Plato's "ideas" by asking, "How can Plato's "ideas" make me [morally] better?" While he can on occasion use Stoic logic (for example, the series of syllogisms in letter 87), his primary concern is with ethics. The letters constitute a programme of moral improvement, and the focus on Reason and Virtue is exclusively moral. Even the discussion of philosophical categories in letter 89 ends with a diatribe against luxury and greed, in keeping with Seneca's earlier remark (89. 8), that "Philosophy is the study of virtue."

Yet his attitude to logic is not simply hostile. As Jonathan Barnes has shown, he is hostile to the wrong uses of logic, for example, for intellectual showing-off or for raising logical problems that have no ulterior purpose. His warnings to Lucilius about logic indicate concern that Lucilius was too much involved in its study, for it is worthless unless it is subordinated to the goal of moral improvement.[71] To him, then, logic is an instrument for leading a better life or for the study of physics, if such study will lead us to a better life.

Seneca was deeply interested in natural philosophy: he wrote a work (now lost) on earthquakes, and the *Naturales Quaestiones* is an extended exposition of Stoic natural philosophy – the most complete that survives.[72] Towards the end of letter 65, after the discussion of causes, he imagines Lucilius criticizing him for wasting time in such enquiries (§15) because they have no moral effect. "But", replies Seneca, "you cannot forbid me to study the nature of things (*rerum natura*, perhaps an intentional reminiscence of Lucretius), or the origin of the universe and its creator, the secrets of cosmology and the origin of light and fire, or the home of the soul after the death of the body. These are lofty subjects worthy of the human mind, for they lift it above its prison in the body to contemplation of the universe and of god" (§§19–24).

Seneca believed that philosophy is the supreme activity of the human mind and that it alone will lead to the virtuous and happy life. Perhaps the most well-known of his letters is Letter 88, in which he attacks "liberal studies" for being at best introductory to the study of wisdom and generally morally inferior. He examines the conventional stages of Roman education and asks (§3), "Which of these builds the road to virtue?" He looks at the subjects which later became the mediaeval *quadrivium* – geometry, arithmetic, astronomy (to which he adds astrology, §14), and music – and finds that none of them teach virtue (§20). Even literature fails in this: Homer was not a philosopher (§§5–8) – does the *Odyssey* teach "how I may love my country, my wife, my father, or how I may travel over the seas to reach these good things even if shipwrecked?" Posidonius is attacked for his fourfold division of "the arts" (in Greek, *technai*: §§21–23). The inferior categories, which concern the practical details of life or the increase of pleasure or the elementary training of children, are easily dismissed; the highest Posidonian category, *artes liberales*, Seneca will admit only if the liberal arts are truly "free" (*liberae*: he plays on the words *libera* and *liberalis*), for only the wise person is free, and in education freedom belongs only to the study of virtue. At the end of the letter Seneca dismisses Greek epistemology, reserving his greatest scorn for the Sceptics, including the new Academy (§§43–46):

for they have introduced a new kind of knowledge, knowing nothing ... [The earlier philosophers] do not shine a light to direct my sight towards the truth, while these [the Academic Sceptics] gouge out my eyes.

Seneca returns to the attack in Letter 90, where he criticizes Posidonius for claiming for philosophy the invention of buildings and architectural improvements (§§7–10, 32). He denies the possibility of philosophy in the early stages of human development, and – perhaps answering Book 5 of Lucretius – he sees the progress of human civilization as accompanied by vice. The primitive golden age was morally innocent because of ignorance, and virtues such as prudence, temperance and courage did not exist, for they occur only "in a mind that is educated and trained and brought to the heights [of virtue] by constant practice" (§46).

Finally, in letter 108, Seneca recalls his early enthusiasm for philosophy under his teachers, Attalus and Sotion. He contrasts philosophers like them with pedants who miss the philosophical importance of the words that they read in their search for answers to trivial questions. And so, says Seneca (§23), "What had been philosophy became philology". In this same letter (§1) Seneca refers to his intention of "setting out in order the whole of moral philosophy", as if ethics were all that concerned him in philosophy. In reality, as we have seen, physics and logic had their part in leading the student to reason and virtue.

Thus in the *Naturales Quaestiones* the moral dimension is as important to Seneca as the physical. In the opening chapter he contrasts ethics and physics: the former "teach what is to be done on earth, the other what is being done in the heavens", for an enquiry into the natural world concerns the gods and shows how far different their perspective is from that of human beings. In the Preface to Book 3 (§18) he says that study of "the nature of things" raises the mind above low things (*sordida*) and liberates it from the body. Here again Seneca is debating Lucretius, who expounded the nature of things in order to prove that the gods do not concern themselves with human affairs and that human beings will be liberated from fear by knowledge of the material composition of the universe and of the human soul.

Seneca has always been a controversial figure. As a politician he had learned to compromise, if only to survive. His passivity in Nero's more egregious crimes cannot be reconciled with his ethical doctrines.[73] His insistence on the "indifference" of money is inconsistent with his own wealth, and he does defend himself on this charge in the *De Vita Beata* 17–22, quoting his critics at some length. "You speak one way and live another", they said (§18). His defence is summarized in §21.4:

> For the wise man does not think himself unworthy of chance gifts. He does not love wealth, but he prefers it. He admits it not into his mind, but into his house. He does not reject the wealth that he has, but he knows its limits, and he wishes to make his greater means the servants of his virtue.

Finally, Seneca says (§22. 4): "If my wealth disappeared, it would take away nothing except itself."

We must form our own opinions on the efficacy of this defence. Certainly it did not impress Seneca's contemporaries (as Tacitus reports in narrating the attack on Seneca by Suillius in 58 CE), or the third-century historian, Cassius Dio.[74] The charge of hypocrisy was expressed pithily by Milton: "Seneca, in his books a philosopher." Yet it his books that are important. In his language he created a new vehicle for Roman philosophy, and he expressed truths about the human condition and human aspirations that have been an inspiration to countless readers in times of perplexity. Macaulay sneers at the impracticality of Seneca's Stoic categories, for bereavement, grief, anger and loss are all too real to their sufferers. Is it helpful, he asks, to call these things "indifferent"? Contrasting the Stoicism of Seneca and Epictetus with the "common-sense" practicality of Bacon, Macaulay says:[75]

> They (a Stoic and a Baconian) come to a village where the smallpox has just begun to rage ... .The Stoic assures the dismayed population that there is nothing bad in the smallpox, and that to a wise man disease, deformity, death, the loss of friends, are not evils. The Baconian takes out a lancet and begins to vaccinate.

To Macaulay, Seneca's philosophy is "a philosophy of thorns ... a philosophy of words". Against the charge of barrenness and hypocrisy we can and must set the very real achievement of Seneca in setting forth in a new Latin prose style a way of looking at the world that has brought comfort and inspiration to people through the ages in times of trouble. For Seneca understood the shortcomings, and especially the emotions, of human beings as they are, and he sought to heal them by setting before them an ideal to which every person might aspire, however distant the goal. Let us end, then, by setting against the satire of Macaulay the judgement of Justus Lipsius:[76]

> And so I boldly cast my vote for you, Seneca. In philosophy, and especially in moral philosophy, you are the best.

7

STOICISM UNDER NERO
AND THE FLAVIANS

Unshaken by the deaths of Seneca, Thrasea and Barea, the Stoics continued to be the most vigorous philosophical sect in the Roman world, although Platonists and Epicureans remained active. In this chapter, which covers the period from the accession of Nero (54 CE) to the end of the reign of Domitian (96 CE), almost all the philosophers whom we shall discuss were Stoics. We shall need first to review the social and political context of Stoicism in this period.

The death of Nero in 68 CE brought to an end the Julio-Claudian dynasty, rulers who were descended either from Augustus (adopted son of Julius Caesar) or Tiberius Claudius Nero (d. 33 BCE), first husband of Livia, the wife of Augustus, and father of the Emperor Tiberius. Nero was descended from both, and with his suicide the field was open for claimants to the throne, for no one seriously expected the Republic to be restored. For over a year civil wars were fought by four claimants, each of whom became emperor in succession, until the fourth, Flavius Vespasianus, emerged to reign for a decade (69–79 CE) and found a new dynasty. These events affected the development of Roman philosophy in several ways.

First, there was the weakening of the central position of Rome in politics, patronage and culture. Tacitus remarked that in 68–69 CE "a secret of empire had been revealed – that an emperor could be made elsewhere than at Rome".[1] In 68–69 the armies in Gaul, Germany and Syria chose, and fought amongst themselves for, Nero's successors, and thereafter the central authority of the emperor and senate depended on the armies in the provinces. Ambitious men from the provinces rose in the Roman hierarchy in greater numbers, and the first non-Italian emperor, Trajan (from Spain), succeeded in 98 CE. Other centres competed with Rome for intellectual and cultural leadership, and the importance of centres in the provinces was increased by the foreign wars of the emperors or their tours of inspection (true especially of Hadrian). Increasingly, the Roman philosophers did not have to teach at Rome, and neither did they necessarily depend on the patronage of aristocratic Romans, among whom the emperor was the dominant patron.[2]

Second, Greek recovered its near-monopoly as the language of philosophy, even for Roman audiences. Cornutus (perhaps a native of Lepcis, in Libya), Musonius (a Roman knight of Etruscan descent), and Epictetus (from Phrygia in Asia Minor) all lectured in Greek. Plutarch spent nearly all his time in his home town of Chaeronea, visiting Rome twice, probably around 80 and 90 CE. He wrote exclusively in Greek and admits that he did not learn Latin thoroughly:[3]

> I live in a small city ... When I was in Rome and staying in other areas of Italy, I did not have the leisure to exercise myself in the Roman dialect because of my political duties and the numbers of people who came to hear me lecture on philosophy.

Even the Emperor Marcus Aurelius wrote in Greek. Of the philosophers whom we shall consider in this chapter and the next, only Apuleius wrote in Latin. The dissipation of political and military power in the century between Nero and Marcus Aurelius was accompanied by intellectual decentralization, which benefited the Greeks. Greek intellectual hegemony was recognized and symbolized by the establishment of the four chairs of philosophy at Athens by Marcus Aurelius in 176 CE.

Nevertheless, philosophy was less prominent in the Greek world than rhetoric, and the period between the reign of Nero and that of Alexander Severus (d. 235 CE) is that of the Second Sophistic, a term coined by the third-century writer, Philostratus (*fl. c.* 230 CE), author of the biography of Apollonius of Tyana.[4] In this period Greek declaimers flourished, who, Philostratus believed, were the intellectual heirs of the early Greek Sophists. He wrote about 40 "biographies", which, with few exceptions, are no more than short sketches. Of the longer ones, that on Herodes Atticus (2. 1) is exceptionally full and appears to be the central feature of the whole work. Philostratus includes about ten of the early sophists (for example, Gorgias and Protagoras) and orators, ending with the fourth-century BCE orator and opponent of Demosthenes, Aeschines (1. 18), whom he credits with the founding of the second sophistic, although Aeschines died in about 322 BCE. Rather surprisingly,

Carneades is included with the sophists (1. 4), because of the force of his oratory. After Aeschines, Philostratus names an orator of Nero's time, Nicetes of Smyrna (1. 19), who, he says, revived the art of oratory in the Greco-Roman world, and so, we are led to assume, was really the initiator of the Second Sophistic. The sophists after Nicetes, whose oratory brought them wealth and prestige, were prominent in the cultural and intellectual life of the Greek world in the second century. The emperors Antoninus Pius (138–61 CE) and Marcus Aurelius (161–80 CE) had much to do with these flamboyant polymaths, whose arrogance and egoism amused and irritated them. The rhetorical fireworks of the sophists contrast with the focused intensity of Epictetus and Marcus Aurelius, who pointedly thanks his tutor in philosophy, Rusticus (Quintus Junius Rusticus, consul in 133 and 162 CE), for preventing him from "being diverted to sophistic exhibitionism".[5] Some sophists did claim to be philosophers, but Rutherford is right to say of their philosophy that "in general they peddled second-hand ideas and richly wrought trivialities".[6] There were exceptions, such as the Academic Favorinus (c.85–165 CE) and Galen (c.129–200 CE), the great doctor, medical writer, and author of works in logic and psychology and commentaries on earlier philosophers. Favorinus came from Arelate (Arles) in southern Gaul, and Galen from Pergamum in Asia Minor, and both wrote in Greek for Greek and Roman audiences.[7] But they were exceptions: for the most part the serious philosophers pursued their studies apart from the sophists.

In the aftermath of the Pisonian conspiracy of 65 CE, several Stoic politicians perished. Seneca, Thrasea, Barea and Lucan (Seneca's nephew), were executed, and Thrasea's son-in-law, Helvidius Priscus, was "relegated", that is, expelled from Italy but not exiled to a particular place. These people were convicted on political grounds, although Stoicism influenced their political decisions. Nevertheless, many scholars have believed that there was a "Stoic opposition" to the monarchy. This is unlikely: men like Barea, Rubellius and Thrasea opposed Nero or were thought to threaten his position for other reasons than Stoic ideology, while Seneca was condemned, not for being a Stoic, but because he was believed to have been involved in the Pisonian conspiracy. On the other hand, the Stoic veneration of the younger Cato would make any ruler nervous, for Cato was the paragon of liberty, defined in this context as the refusal to accept the rule of a tyrant. As the trial and death of Thrasea showed, the line between a morally acceptable monarch and a tyrant was easily crossed. Thus the Stoic emphasis on liberty – political and intellectual – could and did lead to refusal to cooperate with a ruler and thus to a charge of treason. Philosophers, as opposed to philosophical politicians, were not executed,[8] but they were exiled, as was the fate of the two most prominent Stoic philosophers of Nero's reign. Cornutus was exiled, ostensibly for insulting comments on Nero's plans for an epic poem.[9] More probably his exile was connected with that of Musonius, who was exiled after the Pisonian conspiracy, recalled by Galba, and exiled again by Vespasian.

Of the senators, Helvidius Priscus returned from his relegation and became praetor under Vespasian in 70 CE. He attacked Thrasea's accuser, Eprius Marcellus, in the senate, and addressed Vespasian as his peer, not as his inferior. Eventually his freedom of speech drove Vespasian to relegate him a second time, and shortly after he was executed, almost certainly without the approval of Vespasian. Helvidius was relegated on political, not philosophical, grounds: it was his freedom of speech, not his philosophy, that destroyed him.[10] Nevertheless, his words and actions made it easy for his enemies to confuse his Stoicism with Cynic outspokenness and thus to accuse him of behaviour inappropriate for a senator.[11] Vespasian did expel philosophers from Italy in or about 74 CE, with the exception of Musonius, no doubt because of their freedom of speech.[12]

Vespasian's younger son, Domitian (reigned 81–96 CE), was hostile to philosophers as a group and again expelled them from Italy in 93 CE, the fourth such expulsion in Roman history.[13] Suetonius connects the expulsion with the executions of the Stoic politicians, the younger Helvidius Priscus (son of Thrasea's Helvidius), and Junius Arulenus Rusticus, both of whom had held the consulship. To these Tacitus and Pliny add the names of the senators Herennius Senecio, who was executed, and Junius Mauricus, brother of Rusticus, who was relegated.[14] Pliny recalled that seven of his friends were executed or relegated in 93 CE (including the four named above), and Tacitus regretted his part as a senator in the condemnation of these men. Evidently Domitian linked the philosophers to the speech and actions of the Stoic politicians. Pliny, in praising Thrasea's widow, Arria, and her daughter, Fannia, showed that the independent spirit of Thrasea was still a threat to Domitian nearly thirty years after his death.[15]

At the time of the Pisonian conspiracy the most prominent professional philosophers in Rome were Cornutus and Musonius.

Lucius Annaeus Cornutus was born in Lepcis, the chief city of Tripolitania, part of the Roman province of Africa. He lived and taught in Rome, and his name, Annaeus, may be evidence for the patronage of Seneca's family – for example, in helping him obtain Roman citizenship – but certainly not for his being a freedman of the Annaei. Very little is known of his life after his exile (there is a single literary reference that dates to 84 CE), and for us his importance lies in his relations with the two greatest poets of the Neronian age, Persius and Lucan, and in the survival of a single work written in Greek, the *Epidrome* or "Summary" (the full title is "Summary of the Traditions of Greek Theology"). Lost are works on Aristotle, while a few fragments exist of commentaries on Virgil and works on language and rhetoric. The *Epidrome* is a short prose work (about seventy-five small printed pages) addressed to a young student. It reviews Greek mythology, using etymology and allegory to explain the names and myths of the Greek gods.[16] Zeus, for example (chapter 2), is so called because he is the cause of life (in Greek, *zen*); destiny, Aisa, is so called because it is the unseen (*aistos*) cause of events (chapter 13); Atlas is named because "without tiring" (*atalaiporos*) "he represents the events in the myths about him and in this way [i.e. without tiring] he holds up the heavens" (chapter 26). This kind of etymological interpretation has a long history in Greek and Latin literature, going back at least to the fifth-century sophist, Gorgias, to whom Plato refers when he makes Socrates say that "I have heard a clever man say that our body is our tomb" (*soma*, body, and *sema*, tomb).[17] The theory that the resemblance in the sounds of two words corresponds to a factual relationship is analogous to the idea that the attributes of a mythical figure may be allegories for human circumstances or attributes. At the beginning of Cornutus' *Epidrome* we learn that "the heaven encircles the earth and the sea and all that is upon the earth and in the sea" (1. 1). All these entities constitute the cosmos, whose nature is fiery, while the gods are responsible for "the changes in the air and the security of the whole". Then Cornutus compares the order of the cosmos, whose existence is parallel to that of human beings, to the order of human nature (2. 1):

> just as we are governed by the soul, thus the cosmos has soul which holds it together, and this is called Zeus ... and he is said to rule over the whole just as in us our soul and nature are said to rule.

As A. D. Nock and Malcolm Lapidge have shown, Cornutus is expounding existing Stoic doctrine rather than developing new views, both in his cosmology and in the other topics of the *Epidrome*.[18] The work is in fact a student textbook (unique in surviving classical literature), whose apparently naïve use of traditional mythology rests on Stoic orthodoxy, much of which goes back to Chrysippus. In this way it throws light on several places that the largely ethical Stoicism of Seneca had left in the dark.

The teaching of Cornutus appears much more vividly in the poetry of his student and friend, the satirist Aules [*sic*] Persius Flaccus (34–62 CE). Persius was Etruscan in origin, a Roman of high social standing and connected with prominent Romans, including Thrasea, whose close friend he was for ten years. According to an ancient biography he was 16 years old when he began his friendship with Cornutus "in such a way that he never left his company", and, according to the biographer, "he made some progress in philosophy". The *Life* further says that Cornutus was both his financial and literary executor, and its evidence is probably reliable for both the life of Persius and the teaching of Cornutus.

The six satires of Persius (amounting to about 640 lines in all) are in the tradition of Horace, but their philosophy is clearly Stoic.[19] In the fifth satire, Persius begins by showing how Cornutus criticized and disciplined his style, teaching him to use Latin vocabulary (*verba togae*) with striking collocation of words (*iunctura callidus acri*: line 14). Cornutus is "a great part of Persius' soul" (lines 22–23) and as a result Persius' poetry is sincere, the true representation of his inmost heart (lines 24–29). This is as much a philosophical theme as a literary one, for Seneca's 114th letter is on the theme of the similarity between a person's speech and character as shown in his way of life.[20] This is also the main theme of Persius' first satire – a corrupt style, he says, is the expression of a corrupt character, and the debased literary taste of the Romans is evidence for the moral debasement of Roman society. The importance of vocabulary and style for philosophy had been shown by Cicero, Horace, Lucretius and Seneca, but Persius sees it more as a criterion of morality.

Next, in the fifth satire, Persius describes the close relationship that he began with Cornutus in his "tender years", when a youth on the threshold of adulthood can make many wrong choices (lines 30–51). Cornutus received Persius in his "Socratic bosom" and became, like Seneca, a "director of souls", whose moral guidance was exercised night and day in friendship and shared living. Indeed, Persius concludes, their horoscopes and the influence of the stars at their births brought them together, an idea consistent with the astrological doctrines of the Stoic Manilius.

Other prominent themes of the fifth satire are freedom and slavery, familiar from the Stoic paradox that only the wise man is free. So Persius describes the many pursuits which enslave a human being – in contrast to the "harvest of Cleanthes" (i.e. Stoic doctrine: line 64) from seed planted by Cornutus. He continues with many striking images and vivid examples, ending with a contrast between the philosophy of Cornutus and his poetry on the one hand, and the values of the common man on the other (lines 189–91).

In the third satire Persius focuses on the paradox that only the wise man is sane and healthy. In this poem the student (perhaps Persius himself) reluctantly rises to study, and again his poetry is valued at nothing by the common man, here a "hairy centurion" and "muscular youths" (lines 77–87). But the critics do not know how morally sick they are: they do not think they are ill, but show them a pretty girl or money and they behave like madmen (lines 88–119).

Persius and Cornutus looked back to Socrates as the fountainhead of philosophy, and based their lives on Stoic freedom from the *pathe* and use of reason. In the second satire Persius addresses the theme of prayer (a reminder of the focus on theology in Cornutus' *Epidrome*), and in the fourth the necessity for self-knowledge and morality if one aspires to public office – perhaps the most Socratic of Persius' themes. As a critic of contemporary morals, Persius is less subtle than Horace and less abrasive than Juvenal. While Horace is personally Epicurean and Juvenal expressly refuses any philosophical allegiance, he is explicitly Stoic.[21] Seneca and Cornutus are directors of souls, but Persius is the critic of society, and his unique style is the vehicle for Stoic doctrine that criticizes and at the same time heals and liberates his contemporaries.

The epic poet, Lucan (Marcus Annaeus Lucanus (39–65 CE), studied under Cornutus with Persius. Since he was seven years younger than Persius, their relationship would not have been one of equals, for when Lucan joined Cornutus (probably in 55 CE) Persius already had made progress in philosophy (as the *Life* tells us) and poetry. Lucan admired Persius, whose poems, he said, "were true poems, while mine are child's play (*ludos*)". Lucan was not a modest man, and this remark must have been made before he composed his epic poem and while he was still engaged with the study of philosophy. Unlike Persius, Lucan entered on an ambitious political career, helped by the fact that he was the nephew of Seneca. He was an official "friend" of Nero (two years his senior), a status which admitted him to the emperor's inner circle, and Nero advanced him to the quaestorship and membership of the senate. He and Nero certainly shared cultural and literary interests, but by 63 CE the friendship had soured, perhaps out of personal rivalry, but more likely for political reasons connected with the weakening of Seneca's position after 62. Lucan was deeply involved in the Pisonian conspiracy and was forced to commit suicide in April of 65, evidently after the death of Seneca. His father and his other uncle (Seneca's brothers) perished in the aftermath of the conspiracy, while his mother, Acilia, although implicated, was neither charged nor acquitted.

Lucan's epic in ten books, *De Bello Civili* (also known as *Pharsalia*), was unfinished. It is the only Latin epic worthy to stand beside those of Virgil and Lucretius. It emulates Virgil in its epic themes of war and political and moral disintegration (as opposed to Virgil's narrative of war and political and moral renewal), and it emulates Lucretius in its contrasting view of the cosmos, in which the destruction of Roman liberty is bound up with the fate of the cosmos. Its narrative focuses on the first two years of the civil war between Caesar and Pompey, with its climax at the battle of Pharsalus and the subsequent murder of Pompey in Egypt. These events occur in Books 7 and 8 of the poem, which extends its narrative to a wide range of political and philosophical speculation. René Pichon's catalogue of Lucan's Stoic passages is still valuable, but his conclusion, that Lucan is "a sincere disciple of Seneca", cannot be maintained.[22] There are many similarities, but Lucan's attitude towards the gods and fate – to give but one example – is quite different from that of Seneca.

The account of the Nile given by the Egyptian priest, Acoreus, has much in common with Seneca's.[23] Lucan dismisses earlier explanations of the Nile's annual flood, preferring to affirm the laws of Nature (10. 238) and the existence of underground springs created by the world's intelligent creator (10. 262–67). Here he adapts a theory of the fifth-century pre-Socratic philosopher, Diogenes of Apollonia, who believed that the sun was responsible for the underground stores of water. Seneca quotes Diogenes only to criticize him, and Lucan seems to answer the criticism by supposing that the divine creator was responsible.[24]

There are many other passages in which Lucan shows his interest in physics, cosmology, astronomy and astrology. They are aspects of Lucan's conviction that the macrocosm of the universe and microcosm of Rome are involved with each other. We have seen that Cornutus used allegory as a principal mode of interpretation of the myths of the gods, and this is the principle on which Lucan's interpretation of human events rests. He sees the civil war not only in political terms – the loss of liberty with the collapse of the Roman republic – but as a cosmic disaster. In the introduction to Book 1 he explicitly makes the comparison, first listing the causes of the collapse:[25]

> [The causes were] the envious progress of Fate, the denial of a long period of stability to the greatest [states], the collapse under their own weight of those that are too heavy – and Rome that could not bear its own weight. So when the world's frame is loosened and the final hour gathers in so many ages of the universe and original chaos returns, the fiery stars will join the sea, the earth will be unwilling to extend its level shores and will shake off the waters of the ocean, the moon will travel contrary to her brother [the sun]; refusing to drive her chariot across the arch of heaven, she will demand daylight for herself, and the whole discordant structure of the shattered universe will throw its laws into confusion.

In this remarkable sentence, Lucan uses the Stoic doctrine of cyclical creation and destruction of the cosmos to describe a world where the destruction of the laws of the Roman republic involves the destruction of the laws of nature. Again, Lucan invokes the Stoic *ekpyrosis* after a vivid passage in which Caesar surveys the battlefield of Pharsalus the day after his victory, and denies the customary cremation to the corpses of the Pompeian soldiers. Lucan addresses Caesar:[26]

> You achieve nothing by this anger of yours. It makes no difference whether corpses perish through decay or the pyre. Nature takes everything to her peaceful bosom, and corpses owe their end to themselves. If, Caesar, fire will not burn these peoples now, it will burn them with the earth, with the ocean's waters. The common pyre of the universe remains, which will mix the stars with [human] bones.

The Roman civil war is a cosmic event, and the destruction wrought by Caesar's anger anticipates the destruction of the final *ekpyrosis*.

Lucan's Stoic view of fate is orthodox, but his attitude to it is different from that of Seneca, and it is further complicated by his ambiguous views on the gods. In 1. 70–80 (quoted above) Lucan refers to "the envious progress of Fate" (*invida fatorum series*), where the word *series* denotes an inexorably linked chain of events through which fate is unfolded. But the word *invida* reveals pessimism towards fate, for it is jealous of human happiness, and in return Lucan refuses to accept its dictates cheerfully. This is contrary to Seneca's doctrine in the *De Providentia* and the 107th letter (discussed in the previous chapter). Indeed, Lucan is driven by frustration and anger against fate. He is, as Otto Steen Due has remarked, "a Stoic who has lost his faith".[27]

Lucan speculates on foreknowledge, wondering if the intelligent creator, at the start of the present cycle of the history of the cosmos, has fixed immutable destiny and set the inexorable course of future ages.[28] If this is so (and Lucan seems to accept it), while the chain of events cannot be changed, it can be revealed by divination or other methods of prediction. Therefore Lucan devotes many lines to revelations of the future, which arouse fear and foreboding in the actors in the poem, and helplessness, anger and frustration in the poet and his readers.[29] Lucan himself says of his narrative:[30]

> When also future generations and our grandchildren's descendants read of these wars – whether their own fame brings them to future ages, or whether my labours can help great names survive – then they [namely, these wars] will rouse hope and fear and vain prayers, and all [my readers] will be stunned as they read of destiny as if it were in the future, not in the past.

Even the most powerful of Lucan's agents of prophecy, the witch and necromancer Erichtho, confesses that she has no power to change fate:[31]

> Once the chain of events descends from the beginning of the universe, and if all fate will be disrupted should you wish to change anything, and if the whole human race stands subject to one powerful stroke, then we, the Thessalian band [of witches], confess that Fortune is more powerful.

There are two exceptions to Lucan's pessimism, the poor man and the wise man. The former is represented by the fisherman, Amyclas, who is the "captain of his boat" and "safe enjoying the life of a poor man".[32] For Lucan and his readers this is ironical, for the world of

Amyclas is as far distant from the facts of Lucan's life as the Stoic indifference to wealth was from the life of Seneca. As for the wise man, Lucan admits that he can respond to the dictates of fate as Seneca would have prescribed. Lucan portrays Cato as an ideal leader in episodes in which historical facts are elaborated so as to show Cato's wisdom and virtue in splendid isolation and superiority.[33] In the first two (2. 234–391) Cato advises Brutus on the correct attitude to civil war and then takes back his former wife, Marcia (now the widow of Hortensius), exhibiting a moral perfection that pitilessly focuses on the gulf between himself and ordinary human beings.[34] After Pompey's death, Cato assumes the leadership of Pompey's forces, and then sets out across the Libyan desert in perhaps the most colourful episode of the whole poem.[35] Its crucial passage is Cato's arrival at the oracle of Jupiter Ammon, where (as Lucan's readers well knew), Alexander the Great had been saluted as the Son of Zeus.[36] Labienus encourages Cato to consult the oracle and learn the future. Here is Cato's reply:

> Cato, full of the god whom he carried in his calm mind, uttered words from his heart that were worthy of the oracle. "What question do you suggest, Labienus? Should I ask if I should wish to die in battle a free man, rather than witness tyranny? Whether it makes any difference if our life is long or short? Whether any violence can harm the good man? Whether Fortune can lose her terrors when faced with virtue? ... I know, and Ammon will not plant knowledge any deeper in my heart. We all are one with the powers above, and though the oracle be silent, we do nothing without the will of god. The divine power needs no [oracular] utterances, and our creator has told us at our birth whatever we may know. Has he chosen desert sands to chant his oracles to a few [enquirers]? Has he buried the truth in this dust? Is the god's home anywhere except in earth and sea and air and heaven – and virtue? Why look for the gods any further? Jupiter is whatever you see, whatever you do."

The wise man needs no external assurance, no divination or prophecy. The god is within him, and he proceeds through life unmoved by fear and other emotions, knowing one fact about the future – that he must die.[37] This is the obvious significance of the passage. Cato, however, also sees that divine power is immanent in the four "elements" of the universe ("heaven" standing for the fiery upper air of Stoic cosmology) and in virtue, meaning the virtue of all wise men rather than of a particular individual. Lucan, then, follows Seneca in seeing the divine everywhere in the universe and the wise man as being himself divine.[38] Thus it comes as no surprise when Lucan ends his eulogy of Cato by equating him with the gods:[39]

> See, then, the true father of his country, most worthy, Rome, of your altars! Never will you be ashamed to take your oaths by him, for if ever you stand free from the yoke of slavery, him will you make – now, in the future – a god.

Lucan's portrait of Cato as the *sapiens*, for all its bizarre features and exaggerations, is based on philosophical principle.

For Lucan, Fortune is the dynamic and universal power, replacing Jupiter and the Olympians. He dispenses with the gods of Homeric and Virgilian epic, except for Hercules, whose struggle with Antaeus is narrated more as a parable of Roman success in Africa than as an affirmation of the reality of the Olympian gods.[40] Nevertheless, the Stoic god pervades the poem. Among mortals, only Cato is worthy of divine status and the deified Caesar and other emperors are worthy only of scorn.[41] In passionate despair Lucan consoles himself for the victory of Caesar with the hollowness of his divinity:[42]

> Still, we have this consolation for the disaster, as much as it is right for the divine power to give to mortals: the civil wars will create gods equal to the gods above. Rome will equip dead mortals with thunderbolts and radiate crowns and stars, and in temples of the gods she will swear her oaths by dead ghosts.

These words follow the surprising cry:

> Indeed we have no gods: since the ages are hurried along by blind chance, we lie when we say that Jupiter is king.

A few lines later Lucan says "mortal affairs are of no interest to god". Is he then being inconsistent with Stoic doctrine? I think not. Repeatedly he appeals to the "chain of fate", and emphasizes that fate is unkind to mortals – most particularly those who supported the republican cause against Caesar and their sympathizers in later ages. The inconsistency lies, not so much in the nihilism evident in these lines, but in Lucan's refusal to accept the dictates of fate. If fate has dealt mortals such a terrible hand, then how can one accept it willingly? The only answer must be nihilism, he says. And this is consistent, for, as we have seen, Lucan shows that the only person secure against such despair is the wise man – Cato – who is in a different category from other human beings. For the rest of us the divine power – whether of the Olympian gods or the Stoic divinity – is irrelevant, for our world is disintegrating.

Lucan links Roman and cosmic disaster in another dynamic feature of the poem, Caesar's anger. The governing principle in the great storm of Book 5 is the interaction of Caesar's madness (*furor*) with the raging of the elements – and madness, as Seneca had taught, is part of anger.[43] At the climax of the storm, the universe itself collapses:

> then the vault of heaven trembles and the axis [of the world] thunders and the poles begin to collapse, their structure shaken. Nature fears chaos: the elements seem to have broken the restraints that held them in harmony and night seems to return, to confuse the spirits of the dead with the gods.

We see here once more Cornutus' principle of allegory – the raging of the individual, Caesar, involves the raging of nature, and the destruction to be wrought by Caesar finds its parallel in cosmic disruption.

Lucan is a Stoic with a difference, a Stoic who cannot accept the injustice of the Roman republic destroyed and liberty removed, except by seeing in these disasters the dismantling of the ordered cosmos. His wise man, Cato, points out the difference between the Stoic ideal (which Seneca taught was possibly attainable) and the cruel reality of the world of the *Bellum Civile*.

Lucan's attitude to the divine power, to fate and to the cosmos, is one of two essential aspects of his philosophy. The second is his attitude towards Roman history and its great disaster, the loss of republican liberty with the victory of Caesar at Pharsalus. Repeatedly he hammers at the theme of lost liberty. Caesar and Liberty are like a pair of gladiators; after Caesar's victory "Liberty retreated beyond the Tigris and the Rhine", never to return to the Roman world.[44] Faced with tyranny, how should the individual react? We have seen in Cato, the wise man, the ideal answer, but ordinary mortals, Lucan seems to say, give way to their emotions.

Occasionally there are exceptions: Cotta dissuades Metellus from opposing Caesar's efforts to plunder the Roman treasury by saying that "the people's liberty, when suppressed by a tyrant, perishes through liberty", that is, the person who tries to speak freely under a tyranny discovers how much freedom he has lost.[45] The corollary is silence and a withdrawal into the freedom of the mind, as the Roman people do, suppressing their grief at the loss of liberty even while outwardly celebrating the tyrant's triumphs.[46] Equally pointedly, Caesar's entourage openly rejoice at the sight of Pompey's head, while Caesar appears to grieve. "This", says the poet, "is good Liberty – to dare to be happy while Caesar weeps". Liberty, then, is the victim of the civil war: as the Egyptian vizier, Pothinus, says to the young Ptolemy:[47]

> Let the man who wants to be morally good (*pius*) leave the court. Virtue and supreme power cannot coexist.

Withdrawal into *otium*, Seneca's solution for maintaining freedom under a tyranny, is not an option for Lucan. He does, however, consider Seneca's extreme solution, suicide. He seems to have been fascinated by death and modes of death, and his most elaborate portrayal of suicide in the cause of liberty is the episode of Vulteius and his men.[48] They are trapped on a raft, surrounded by the enemy, and Vulteius urges them to die through mutual suicide rather than let the Pompeians kill them (lines 476–520). The first word of his speech is "Free" (*libera*), and his theme is that to assert one's freedom through death is to die happy (line 520). Yet Vulteius is hardly a rational man, for he is driven by "madness, the goads of death" (line 517), and, in a final irony, he is a Caesarian. Lucan reflects on his death:

> Yet even after these examples future generations will not see how virtue is not difficult to attain, if one escapes slavery by one's own hand. Yet tyrants are feared and peoples do not know that swords are given so that no one need be a slave.

The last line (*ignorantque datos, ne quisquam serviat, enses*) has long been admired by patriots. While the sentiment may be disturbing, the expression epitomizes the noblest aspirations of Lucan's philosophy.

One death, however, stands apart, the murder of Pompey.[49]

Pompey has been at best a morally ambiguous figure throughout the poem, but here Lucan portrays him as facing death with Stoic courage. "I am", he says, "happy, O gods ... Death cannot make a man unhappy" (lines 630–32). At the beginning of Book 9 Pompey's soul rejoins the divine fire dwelling among the stars, where "the half-divine dead spirits dwell, those whom fiery virtue has allowed to endure without guilt the life below" (lines 7–8). But Lucan diverges from the pattern of Cicero's *Dream of Scipio*, for he imagines the soul returning to earth to exact vengeance on Caesar by taking up its residence in the "pure heart of Brutus" and "the unconquered mind of Cato" (lines 17–18). While this seems to be a kind of Pythagorean transmigration of the soul, it should be interpreted rather as an expression of Lucan's unwillingness to leave the disembodied Pompey to enjoy the rewards of virtue when the victory over the tyrant (Caesar) is still to be won.

Like Virgil, Lucan is an epic poet whose philosophy is integral to his poetry. It is basically Stoic, but his despair sets him apart from other Stoics, and his tempestuous commitment to the ideal of republican liberty opens a gulf between his view of life and the *ataraxia* of the Stoics. He is closest to Seneca in his speculations on the cosmos and the physical world, and to Cornutus in his allegorical interpretation of events in human history. Whatever our judgement of his philosophical views (and there is huge disagreement among his readers), they are expressed with a vigour unique in classical literature. Samuel Johnson's view is closest to the truth:[50]

> Lucan is distinguished by a kind of dictatorial or philosophic dignity ... ; full of ambitious morality and pointed sentences, comprised in vigorous and animated lines.

The most distinguished Roman philosopher of the later part of the first century was Gaius Musonius Rufus (*c.*30–101).[51] Like Persius, he was Etruscan by descent and of equestrian rank (that is, he belonged to the upper socio-economic class of Roman society but was not a senator). He joined the exiled Rubellius Plautus in Asia and returned to Rome after the execution of Rubellius in 62. He was exiled to the island of Gyaros in 65, and while there he discovered a spring of water which became an object of pilgrimage for the students who came to Gyaros to hear him lecture. Musonius himself reflects on his exile in his 9th Discourse. Clearly he endured it with courage and equanimity, for he practised the Stoic belief that exile did not "deprive a man of things that are truly good", such as courage, justice, moderation or reason. He was recalled after the death of Nero, and Tacitus reports that when the army of Vespasian's general, Antonius Primus, was poised to capture Rome in December of 69 CE, the emperor Vitellius included Musonius in a mission sent out to attempt to find a peaceful solution to the war. His efforts to show the soldiers that peace was preferable to war were met with derision and violence – philosophy and soldiers thirsting for battle do not mix.[52]

After the death of Vitellius and the establishment of Vespasian's supporters in Rome, the senate began to settle old scores.[53] Musonius, although not a senator, addressed the senate as prosecutor of the Stoic, Egnatius Celer, who had gained the conviction and execution of his teacher, Barea Soranus, in 66. Although Egnatius was defended by the Cynic philosopher, Demetrius, he was condemned and executed. About four years later Musonius was again exiled, although he had at first been exempted from Vespasian's order expelling philosophers. On this occasion he seems to have travelled to Syria (for he lectured to "a Syrian king" in Discourse 8), and to have met Pliny's close friend, the philosopher Artemidorus, who became his son-in-law.[54] Musonius was recalled, perhaps in 81 (the year of Pliny's military service in Syria), and seems to have spent the remaining twenty years of his life in Rome studying and lecturing.

Among Musonius' students were Epictetus, Dio Cocceianus of Prusa (Dio Chrysostom), and the Stoic philosopher Euphrates, whom Pliny met in Syria and greatly admired.[55] Pliny says that Euphrates taught that "the most beautiful part of philosophy is to transact public business ... and to make practical use of the philosophers' doctrines". Epictetus quotes a lecture of Euphrates defending his refusal to flaunt his philosophy openly, preferring to practise it privately ("everything for myself and God") and to live publicly like other people.[56]

Musonius taught in Greek, and in his time Roman intellectual life was becoming more catholic, socially and geographically, as the following examples show. Musonius himself spoke Greek and Latin, and Artemidorus, his son-in-law, was very probably a Greek citizen. Euphrates and Artemidorus conversed easily with Pliny in Syria and at Rome. When Epictetus was driven from Rome he set up his school at Nicopolis in western Greece, where many young Romans came to hear him lecture in Greek. Dio Chrysostom, expelled from Italy by Domitian, travelled all over the Mediterranean world before returning to his original home at Prusa in Bithynia.

Musonius seems to have left no written works. Twenty-one of his discourses (short lectures addressed to non-specialist audiences) were recorded by his student Lucius, perhaps not long after his death, and there are thirty-two shorter fragments, of which six are quoted by Epictetus. The discourses and nineteen of the fragments were preserved by the fifth-century scholar, John of Stobi (Stobaeus). Some scholars optimistically refer to Musonius as "the Roman Socrates" because of his high moral character (on which all ancient sources are unanimous) and because he committed nothing to writing, as far as can be known.

The twenty-one discourses fall into three groups: the first eleven deal with general philosophical questions; numbers 12–17 with social questions; and numbers 18–21 with questions concerning the minutiae of daily life. Like Seneca and Epictetus, Musonius was not greatly concerned with logic, although Epictetus quotes an episode in which Musonius criticized him for not understanding a syllogism.[57] Unlike Seneca, he discouraged giving many examples to support a philosophical point. The first discourse is on the subject "that there is no need for many proofs in dealing with one problem", a statement he supports with analogies from medicine – the doctor who can cure you is better than the one who prescribes many medicines. The medical analogy is more than decorative, for underlying it is Musonius' belief that philosophy must lead to practical results in one's daily life. In Discourse 5 he argues that ethical behaviour in accordance with theory is the goal of the student of philosophy, and that therefore it is more important than theory because it is practical. In Discourse 6 he says:[58]

> Virtue consists not only in theoretical knowledge but also in practical [living], like medicine and music. Just as the doctor and the musician must learn not only the theories of each one's art but also train themselves to act in accordance with theory, so the man who will be morally good must not only learn the lessons that lead to virtue but must also train himself in them with enthusiasm and hard work.

This doctrine is not entirely new: for example, Seneca said that "virtue only touches a mind that is thoroughly educated and taught and has reached the highest point through constant practice". Socrates frequently used analogies from the practical arts (carpentry, shoe-making and so on) to illustrate the process of acquiring virtue, but the professional sophists who came after him went beyond analogy and claimed that they could teach virtue as if it were a *techne* (that is, an art or skill). Musonius' focus is the moral excellence of the individual, who can study it theoretically but acquire it and maintain it only through constant practice.

In Musonius' moral scheme, the first stage is reason (*logos*), the second is virtuous action (*ethos*), and the key to virtuous behaviour is practice (*askesis*, perhaps better translated as "training"). The sixth discourse (the beginning of which is quoted above) is devoted to *askesis*, which seems to have been Musonius' particular contribution to Roman ethics.[59] He says:

> One kind of training rightly concerns the soul alone; the other is common to the soul and the body. The kind common to both will occur if we accustom ourselves to cold, heat, thirst, hunger, limited food, hard beds, abstinence from pleasure and endurance of hard labour.

Musonius says that this kind of training will harden the body and direct the soul to courage and self-control. The training for the soul alone prepares the student to distinguish between good and evil, to know what things are truly good or evil (as opposed to seeming to be so), and so to avoid the one and pursue the other. The focus on training the body as part of philosophy appears in Cicero, as does the doctrine that specific virtues (for example, courage) will follow from training the mind.[60] Seneca and Epictetus are more concerned with the mind, and for the former, especially, virtuous behaviour will follow from the right exercise of reason.

Musonius discusses the education of women and the proper relations between husband and wife. In Discourse 3 he says that women should study philosophy, for they are endowed with reason no less than men, and they have the same disposition (*orexis*) towards and natural affinity (*oikeiosis*) for virtue as men. Seneca, it is true, had said that nature had been as generous with virtues to women as to men, and he gives examples of virtuous women from Roman history.[61] But Musonius is more precise and works out the details of a woman's virtuous activity in daily life. He concludes:

> Hence it is reasonable to expect that such a woman will be industrious and able to endure evil, a woman who will nurse her own children at her breast and minister to her husband with her own hands. Activities that some people think are appropriate for slaves she will do without

shrinking. Is not such a woman a help to her husband, an ornament to her family, and a good example for those who know her?

While this picture of the woman who has studied philosophy is more or less one of the ideal Roman matron, it is based on Musonius' doctrine that right reason will be followed by right action, which will be maintained through continuous practice. As part of his doctrine that the individual must take responsibility for the moral quality of her life, he particularly takes issue with the custom among Roman upper-class mothers of giving their babies to wet-nurse slaves and relying on slaves to perform all domestic chores. We may deplore Musonius' assumptions about the comparative roles of men and women in domestic activities, but we should at least give him credit for some practical advice on the proper role of slaves in the economy of a house, as opposed to the generalizations of Seneca's 47th letter. And we should applaud his pleas for the equal education of women, which he repeats in the 4th discourse on "whether daughters should have equal education with sons". He points out that "all human tasks are perhaps common to men and women", while education in virtue is equally appropriate for both sexes.[62] He concludes that since philosophy is training for noble character, it cannot be limited just to boys and men.

Musonius discusses sexual behaviour more than most Roman philosophers. He believes that extramarital sexual relations are wrong, and that within marriage their purpose should be the procreation of children, not pleasure. Husband and wife should provide mutual companionship and share all things and offer mutual love, respect and support.[63] Neither should marriage hinder the study of philosophy, for the result of such study is right action.[64] Musonius seems to be answering the bleak picture of Stoic marriage given by Lucan in Cato's remarriage to Marcia, for, in place of the unbending priggishness of Cato, he recommends mutual support and love, with as much being given by the husband as by the wife.[65]

The Dutch scholar, A. C. van Geytenbeek, says that "If one judges Musonius as a philosopher, the judgement will have to be damning if one applies modern standards."[66] He is troubled by the gulf between the high reputation of Musonius in his own time and the lack of philosophical originality or depth in the discourses. It is true that the discourses that deal with traditional Stoic topics (for example, luxury) are unoriginal, and van Geytenbeek rightly judges Musonius' treatment of equality of education for women and of sexual activity (along with other topics such as the exposure of infants and obedience of children to their parents) to be superior. Musonius is important for his position in Roman society as a teacher who successfully related Stoic doctrine to the problems of daily life, that is, one who preferred applied ethics to theory. In this he is an interesting foil to Seneca, who constantly seeks to apply Stoic doctrine to daily life, yet leaves the impression that there is a gulf between what he writes and how he lives his life. Thus Seneca's readers, in his own time and ever since, have had conflicting views about him. About Musonius, who was less ambitious as a stylist and philosopher, there seems to have been unanimity. Even Tacitus, so ironic in recording the tragicomedy of his mission to the soldiers of Antonius Primus, says of him (in a passage written perhaps two decades after his death), that he was exiled in 65 CE "because of his distinguished reputation ... as a teacher of the young in the precepts of wisdom".[67]

8

FROM EPICTETUS TO
MARCUS AURELIUS

Epictetus was the most famous pupil of Musonius. He was a
Phrygian from the town of Hierapolis (one of several with this
name), situated in the southern part of central Turkey. He was born
in about 50 CE and probably lived into the reign of Hadrian
(117–38 CE). He was a slave of Nero's freedman, Epaphroditus, but
we do not know how he became a slave, or when was freed.[1]
Epaphroditus himself was one of Nero's most trusted ministers and
was present at his suicide, in which he is reported to have assisted.
He survived for nearly thirty years after this, but was executed by
Domitian in 95, perhaps because of his part in Nero's death.
Epictetus studied under Musonius while he was still a slave, and by
93 he was well enough established as a freedman at Rome to be
expelled along with the other philosophers that year. He went to the
city of Nicopolis (on the western mainland of Greece, close to the
site of the battle of Actium) and there established his school, where
many students came to hear him. He described his school as a
"hospital" (*iatreion*), and he exhorted his students to leave it "in pain,
not with feelings of pleasure", because their souls were sick in the
way that one's body might have a dislocated shoulder or a headache.[2]

Epictetus focused largely on practical ethics, while allowing that
logic was essential in the training of the philosopher. In *Disc.* 1. 7,
his most important discussion of logic, he argues that it has a direct
effect on morality and behaviour.[3] Right behaviour is the result of
reason, and logic is essential in training for the proper use of reason.
Therefore logical errors lead to ethical errors, a point that Epictetus
supports with an anecdote from his own training in logic under
Musonius.[4]

Among the students of Epictetus was the historian Arrian of
Nicomedia (in Bithynia), consul in 129 CE, whose name is attached
to the four extant books (out of eight originally published) of the

discourses of Epictetus, together with a digest with the title *Encheiridion* ("Handbook").[5] Arrian says in his preface that he did not compose the discourses, and neither did he "bring them out to the public", and that they were circulating without his knowledge before he published his edition. Further, he says that he transcribed them word for word as he heard Epictetus deliver them. Thus the actual authorship of the *Discourses* and *Handbook* is uncertain, although there is no doubt that they reproduce the views of Epictetus himself. It is possible – but far from certain – that they were actually composed by Epictetus (for example, their language is the *koine*, not Attic Greek, which Arrian used in his own writings), and circulated, as Arrian indicates, before Arrian issued them in a definitive form. They were popular in antiquity, and the *Handbook* has been amongst the most widely admired of all philosophical books in any language.[6]

The most important of Epictetus' doctrines concerns the freedom of the will, the subject of the first chapter of the *Discourses* and the first chapter of the *Handbook*, quoted here:[7]

> Of things that exist some are in our control, and some are not in our control. In our control are thought, impulse (towards an end), desire, rejection (of desire) – in a word, everything that is *our* doing. Not in our control are our body, property, reputation, political power – in a word, everything that is not our doing. And the things that are in our control are by nature free, without hindrance, without impediment, but the things that are not in our control are weak, slavish, subject to hindrance, in the control of others. Remember, then, that if you think that the things that are by nature slavish are free, and that what is in another's control is yours, you will be frustrated, you will be unhappy, you will be disturbed, and you will find fault with gods and men. But if you think that only what is under your control is yours (and that what belongs to another is another's), no one can compel you, no one will prevent you, you will not blame anyone, you will not accuse anyone. You will not do one single thing against your will, you will not have enemies, no one will harm you, for you cannot suffer harm.

Epictetus focuses on the concept of "what is in our control" repeatedly. It is closely linked to his doctrine of moral choice (*prohairesis*).[8] The chief component of the Greek word is "choice", and it was used in this sense by Aristotle, but extended by Aristotle's contemporary, Demosthenes, to mean "purpose". Epictetus combines the two connotations, so that *prohairesis* means "moral choice leading to a practical end", in other words, moral purpose. Obviously, the category of "things that are in our control" implies "things about which we can make a choice", which Epictetus divides into two categories, things to be chosen (*prohaireta*) or rejected (*apoprohaireta*). He thinks that the physical body is unimportant compared to the human capacity for making moral choices: "you are not flesh or hair, but moral choice".[9] He teaches, further, that it is our impressions (*phantasiai*) about which choices have to be made.[10]

> First you must make your governing principle (*hegemonikon*) pure and make this your attitude: "Thought is my material, just as wood is the carpenter's material ... My task is the right use of impressions. My little body is nothing to me ... Death? Let it come when it wishes."

Epictetus' moral scheme, then, requires the use of reason to evaluate impressions, refusing to be affected by impressions of things that are not in our control. For those that are in our control, we must use reason to decide which are to be rejected and which accepted, and these decisions are our moral choices.

Perhaps *Disc.* 3. 24 is Epictetus' most detailed exposition of the practical effects of this doctrine. Its subject is "That we should not suffer by anticipating things that are not in our control". Epictetus shows that emotions such as grief or sorrow (for our own misfortunes or those of others) do us no good, for these misfortunes are not in our control. "To long for something that is impossible is slavish, foolish, the desire of a stranger who fights against God" (§21). The mention of God introduces a new part of Epictetus' scheme, for, as Cleanthes and Seneca had taught, the wise person will make his will conform to the will of God, who controls all things. Epictetus uses the military metaphor, familiar to us from Seneca and Sextius, as in §§31–32:

> Do you not know that the matter [i.e. of right living] is a campaign? One man must be on guard duty, another on reconnaissance patrol, another fighting in battle. All soldiers cannot be in the same place ... But you fail to carry out the general's orders, and you complain when you are given a hard task.

Epictetus draws another analogy from a ship's crew, and he continues (§34):

Life is a long and varied campaign for each individual. You must observe the duties of a soldier and perform each task as the general orders.

The parable here involves a double analogy, for "the general" is the Stoic divine being, and the individual is a citizen of "no mean city", a reference to the universal Stoic community of gods and human beings. So in *Handbook* 7 he says:

Likewise on a voyage, if the ship is at anchor and you leave it to find water, and on the way you find a sea-shell or an edible bulb, you must be attentive to the ship and continually turn round, lest the captain call. If he does, you must drop them immediately, so as to avoid being trussed up like sheep and thrown on board. So in life, if instead of a shell and a bulb, you are given a little wife and a little child, well and good. But if the captain calls, give them up and run to the ship ... And if you are old, do not go too far from the ship, in case you are absent when he calls.

So Epictetus' doctrine of moral choice includes the disciplined life of one who is obedient to the commands of God and whose will conforms to the will of fate. In *Handbook* 31, he says that one must have right opinions about the gods, obey them and follow them willingly. And this one can only do by placing what is good and evil in the category of things under one's control. Again and again, Epictetus emphasizes obedience to the divine will. Here, for example, he combines the metaphor of military discipline with obedience to the divine will:[11]

The good and fine individual will remember who he is, from where he came, and by whom he was created. He will focus on this one thing, how he will fill his own [assigned] place in proper order, obedient to the god.

More systematically than Seneca, Epictetus analyses the process of moral choice, and, like Musonius, he teaches that training (*askesis*) is essential for the person who will be disposed to make the right choices. He describes the philosopher's *askesis* vividly with the analogy of an athlete training for the Olympic Games.[12] Elsewhere he is less austere:[13]

> Training should not be by means of activities contrary to nature ... : not every difficult and dangerous thing is necessary for training ... And what is the goal of our labours? To live one's life without obstacles to our desire (*orexis*) and aversion (*ekklisis*). And what is this? Not to fail in achieving what we desire and not to experience that to which we are averse. This is the goal of our training.

Epictetus next analyses the attributes of each stage of moral choice, basing himself on the three "areas" (*topoi*) of training for the student which he had discussed earlier:[14]

> There are three areas in which the future good and fine person must be trained. First, concerning desire and aversion ... Second, concerning impulse (*horme*) and refusal (*aphorme*) – in a word, concerning duty, that he may act with order and reason ... Third, concerning avoidance of delusions and rashness – in a word, concerning assent (*synkatathesis*).

The first *topos* concerns the emotions (*pathe*), and the second the desires and aversion. Epictetus extends the latter to include duty, but he takes a different line from Cicero's *De Officiis*, for he focuses on the student as an individual rather than on Cicero's citizen as a member of society. Nevertheless, he keeps Cicero's theory of the expanding circles of the objects of duty. A person who has mastered the emotions through practice in the first *topos* will use reason to act appropriately, that is, he will know what his duty is. But such a person must still be a human being, linked to other human and divine beings to whom he owes his duty:[15]

> I do not have to be unfeeling like a statue, but I must keep up my attitudes (*hexeis*) both towards those who are physically related to me and to those with whom I have come to have a relationship, in so far as I am pious, a son, a brother, a father, a citizen.

The third *topos* concerns the training of the intellect through logic. It is for the person who has made some progress in philosophy, so that they will not be not liable to false judgements or rash actions. Their assent is based on reason, and thus they are assured of making the right moral choices, even if they are impaired by wine or sadness or are acting unconsciously, as in a dream.[16] Here again Epictetus agrees with Seneca in allowing for the notion of stages of progress towards wisdom, something that he has previously discussed.[17] He says, moreover, that the philosophers of his time have devoted themselves to the third *topos*, to the exclusion of the first two, whereas the good student of philosophy must study all three *topoi*, for logic is a necessary instrument for success in studying the first two. Epictetus, then, is attacking the fashionable and exclusive focus on logic among his contemporaries, but he also finds a place for it in his system.[18]

To return now to *Disc.* 3. 12, the discussion of *askesis* expands on the doctrine of *topoi* set forth in 3. 2. To achieve the right choices between desire and aversion one must train to counteract that which is wrong, one must "go to the opposite side of the rolling ship".[19] Here, too, Epictetus is more understanding of human weakness than most Stoics. Like Persius he warns the young student against temptation:[20]

> A young beginning student in philosophy has an unequal battle against a smart girl. As the proverb goes, "the pot and the stone do not match".

He shows that the second *topos*, that of duty, is governed by reason, which will lead the philosopher to choose actions that are appropriate for the time, place and context. In commenting on the third *topos*, that of assent, Epictetus appeals to Socrates, who said that "the unexamined life is not worth living".[21] So the philosopher must be sceptical of his impressions: like the sentry who asks for the password, he must ask each impression, "Do you have Nature's password?"

Epictetus' doctrine of freedom of the will and its related topics is the most coherent exposition of the process of moral choice in Roman philosophy. Equally distinguished is his second principal doctrine, that of liberty. Here he speaks from unique experience, for alone of Roman philosophers he had been a slave. The longest of his *Discourses* (4. 1) is also his most important discussion of liberty. Here is its opening:

> Free is the man who lives as he wishes. It is not possible to
> compel him or prevent him or force him. His impulses are
> not hindered, what he aims at he achieves, and what he
> tries to avoid he misses. Who then wishes to live in error?
> "No one." Who wishes to live being deceived, being hasty
> in his judgements, unjust, undisciplined, cantankerous,
> ignoble? "No one." So no one who is bad lives as he wishes,
> and no bad person is free. And who wishes to live being
> subject to grief, fear, envy, pity, aiming for things and
> missing, trying to avoid things and meeting with them?
> "No one at all." Can we point to any bad person who is free
> from grief and fear, from meeting what he wishes to avoid,
> from failure to achieve his goal? "No one." Then we cannot
> point to any bad person who is free.

This splendid passage brings to life the dry Stoic paradox, "Only
the wise man is free". As we read further in the discourse, we find
familiar doctrines, themselves liberated from the ethical imperatives
of the discussions of *prohairesis* and *askesis*, to become part of a life
truly free from moral slavery. The analogy with physical slavery is
especially forceful in the light of Epictetus' experience. Yet he
shows that human slaves or caged animals are subject to other forms
of slavery on their release (§§24–40). The problems of life as a free
man still enslave the freedman, even if he rises to the highest posts
of political power. Their solution lies in the Socratic principle of
scepticism, asking "What each thing that exists *is*" (§41). And the
result of such enquiry will be to know the distinction between what
is in our control and what is not (§§62–75). Then comes the hard
part, which is to let go of things that are dear to us but whose fate
we cannot control – one's body, one's wife, one's children: since the
body is like a donkey and the other things are accoutrements for the
donkey, let them go! (§80). This, then, is the first way to freedom,
summarized in a single, cumulative, sentence (§81):

> If you have prepared yourself with this preparation and
> have trained yourself with this training – to distinguish
> between what is your own from what is another's, what is
> subject to hindrance from what is not, to think that the
> former is your concern and the latter is not, to make your
> desire continually for the former and your aversion from the
> latter, well, will you have anyone to fear?

Yet there still remains a higher power to which the free person must submit (§89):

> I have subordinated my impulse (*horme*) to God ... He wants me to desire something – I want to desire it.

The things we count most dear are but gifts from God, to whom we must return them willingly, if he so wills (§§107–10). Like Seneca, Epictetus quotes Cleanthes' *Hymn to Zeus* (§131) to prove that true freedom consists in conforming one's will to that of the divine power. Unlike Seneca, however, he admits that this is difficult: the Cynic, Diogenes, and Socrates himself succeeded, but what of ordinary people? "Make the effort", is his reply, "and you will know from experience that the philosophers speak the truth, even if it is contrary to generally accepted opinion" (§§173–74). He concludes (§§175–77):

> Freedom is achieved not by fulfilling one's desires, but by suppressing them. And so that you may know that this is true, just as you laboured to fulfil those things [i.e. your desires], so transfer your labour to these. Endure sleeplessness to master a doctrine that will make you free: pay court to a philosopher, not to a rich old man ... Try it! You need not be ashamed of trying.

In *Handbook* 14 the basic principle concerning "things that are under our control" is once more stated forcefully, a final reminder of its essential part in the doctrine of liberty:

> So whoever wishes to be free, let him not wish for anything nor avoid anything that is in the control of others. Otherwise he must inevitably be a slave.

A prominent feature of the *Discourses* is Epictetus' use of the Socratic dialogue, the subject of *Discourse* 2. 12. Socrates, he says (§5), "compelled his interlocutor to be his witness". Although relentless in his discovery of the truth, Socrates was never angry with his interlocutors. As Epictetus points out, this was a lot easier in democratic Athens than in the Rome of his time (§17), where Socratic interrogation of a social superior (for example, an ex-consul) might end (and evidently did for Epictetus) in a beating (§§24–26). In his own school Epictetus must have been a lively and demanding teacher, for there was constant give and take with his students, who would have needed to concentrate hard to catch the stream of analogies and questions with which he enlivened his presentations. Arrian has left us a unique portrait of a philosophical teacher, for Seneca and Cicero both had constructed artificial situations for dialogue or lecture, and Lucretius and Marcus Aurelius were writing in very different circumstances from those of the classroom. Persius, however, does lift the curtain on the teaching of Cornutus, and it is likely that Musonius was also a forceful teacher.[22] Aulus Gellius, quoting Favorinus, reveals the integrity and passion of Epictetus' teaching.[23] Like the satirists (for example, Juvenal in his second satire) Epictetus could not endure a "philosopher" whose squalid life belied his fine words – this was, he said, like pouring a pure liquid into a dirty jar, where it turns into "urine or something worse". In a second anecdote, Favorinus reported that Epictetus was upset by two vices in particular – inability to be patient when others harm us and lack of self-control when we are tempted by pleasure. The former calls for patience, the latter for restraint. Hence, says Gellius, Epictetus' famous maxim, "Bear and forbear" (*anechou kai apechou*).

Epicurus shares with the Cynics a focus on training, endurance and consistency in one's way of life and one's philosophy. As our brief discussion in Chapter 1 has shown, Stoic ethics had much in common with Cynicism, but the unconventional behaviour of individual Cynics was offensive to most Romans. Epictetus attempted to resolve the conflict between the good and unattractive aspects of Cynicism, and in so doing he has left us the most comprehensive discussions of the Cynics by a Stoic philosopher.

Twice, Diogenes, the paragon of the Cynics, is described as a "scout" (*kataskopos*), that is, a soldier sent to find out the facts about the enemy and to report the truth to those who sent him.[24] The military metaphor, as we have seen, was used by the Sextii and by Seneca for the disciplined life of the philosopher, for the most dangerous of military assignments was that of the scout.[25] Epictetus had sent one of his students from Nicopolis to Rome as a scout, to report on affairs there.[26] In the same way, Diogenes had been sent into the world to report to us, ordinary people and his hearers, the truth about the dangers among which a person trying to live a good life must live. Thus Epictetus meets the dangers of life in his Roman world with the timeless answers of Diogenes: death is not an evil; what men say about us is not worth our notice; the body needs only minimal clothing and comfort to be satisfied. Diogenes could truly say that he was at peace, that he had attained tranquillity and freedom.

In this parable Epictetus summarizes the fundamental principles of the Cynics – control of the emotions (especially fear of death), disregard of physical comforts, contempt for reputation in the eyes of the community, and the assurance that the person who lives according to these principles will be tranquil and free. In *Disc.* 3. 22 and 4. 8 he develops these themes in such a way as to soften the features of Cynicism that the Romans found offensive, and to focus on those that were consistent with Stoic ethics.

Discourse 3. 22 begins with a warning – the student who is inclined to Cynicism must know how great a challenge the Cynic's calling presents. Unconventional clothing and an ascetic life mean nothing unless they involve a conversion (§§13–15):

> First, in everything that concerns you your behaviour must not appear to be like your present way of life in any respect. You must not blame God nor human beings. You must eradicate desire and change aversion towards only those things that concern moral purpose (*prohairetika*). You must not show anger or fury or envy or pity. No little boy or girl may seem attractive to you, no bit of glory, no sweet little piece of cake. You must know that other men protect themselves with walls and houses and darkness when they act in this way ... But the Cynic's duty is to protect himself with the wall of integrity (*aidos*), otherwise he will be behaving disgracefully [even if] he is scantily clad and homeless.

In this way Epictetus answers the commonest criticism against the Cynics. The person who lives and acts unconventionally is a hypocrite unless his clothing and behaviour are the outward signs of an inner moral certainty, which can be achieved only through conviction that the divine being has called him to a life based on absolute moral and physical discipline. Again, in *Disc.* 4.8, Epictetus distinguishes between the true Cynic philosopher and the person who merely looks like one. You do not become a musician, he says, just because you carry a musical instrument; no more are you a philosopher just because you have a long beard and coarse clothing (§§15–16). Socrates, he says, was the example of the true philosopher, even if people failed to recognize him as one from his outward appearance, for he knew how solid his principles were

(§§22–23). Thus the true Cynic philosopher will say to his listeners (§§30–31):

> Look at me, my [fellow] human beings, so that you can see that you are searching for happiness and tranquillity not where they are, but where they are not. I am your example, sent by the god. I have neither possessions nor home nor wife nor children, not even a mat or a garment or a cooking-pot. Yet see how healthy I am. Test me, and if you find that I am free from disturbance, let me tell you the medicines that healed me.

Like the Stoics, the Cynic exploits the medical metaphor, consistent with the Stoic paradox that "only the wise man is healthy". The picture given here of the sincere Cynic is at variance with the skin-deep would-be Cynic, with his beard, his coarse clothing, and his uncouth manners – all unsupported by the long training of the true philosopher (§34–35). Such "cardboard" philosophers are all show and no substance. The true path to happiness is inner certainty and outward anonymity: "know yourself" and do not attempt the Cynic way without the help of God.[27] And, as a corollary, "take care not to have your real character be known: spend a little time being a philosopher to yourself".[28]

So the true Cynic is assured of his philosophical calling and principles, and he alone has a just pretext for unconventional behaviour. Epictetus, however, does not favour the shamelessness (*anaideia*) of the typical Cynic and prefers a more conventional appearance that will not disgust those who meet him: "even his squalor should be pure".[29]

Epictetus again and again emphasizes the preparation (*paraskeue*) necessary for the true Cynic, for this will allow him to show his superiority to kings and other powerful leaders.[30] He may marry, but he should not be distracted by the time-consuming chores of being a husband and a parent.[31] The Cynic philosopher contributes more to society than the citizen who begets many children, and he cares for the community like a father (§§81–82):

> All men are his children; he has [all] men for his sons, women for his daughters. This is his approach to all, this is how he cares for all. Or do you think that he carelessly castigates those whom he meets? He does it as a father, as a brother, as the servant of Zeus, his father and the father of his hearers.

Another difficulty for a Roman Cynic is non-participation in politics, which puts him at odds, too, with Stoic principle. Epictetus has already contrasted the Cynic with political and military leaders, in the dialogue with Agamemnon (§§30–44). Now he shows that the Cynic's activity on behalf of his fellow human beings is more noble than political activity in a particular city working for particular short-term goals (§§84–85). Discussing the finances of Athens or Corinth is nothing compared to the philosopher's discussions of universal human issues:

> [his discussion is] about happiness and unhappiness, about good and bad fortune, about slavery and freedom. How can you ask if a man who is involved in this sort of activity for the commonwealth will take part in politics? You can ask me further if he will be elected to office. What a stupid question! What greater office is there than that which he holds?

Epictetus is playing on the word *politeia* and its cognates: it means both "politics" and "republic" and he refers both to the "republic" of a particular city and to the Stoic "commonwealth" shared by gods and all humankind. The English translation lacks the economy of the Greek, but the point is clear enough – the philosopher is a citizen of a wider community than any one city or state, and his activity has infinitely wider scope than that of any politician or statesman. As Epictetus says later, "when he [the Cynic philosopher] oversees the affairs of human beings, he oversees his own".[32]

In his discussions Epictetus has done much more than "idealize" the Cynics.[33] He has made an extended argument for including them in the Roman state and for reconciling their philosophy with Stoicism. He has sought to explain in what way their unconventional manners can be assimilated to conventional society, and he has justified their marginal status by reference to the universality of their concerns. He has shown where they march in step with the Stoics: his picture of the self-sufficient Cynic realizes the ideal wise man of the Stoic paradoxes, who alone is free, happy, a king. So Epictetus, far from sanitizing the uncomfortable figure of the Cynic, shows how such a philosopher fits into even such a conventional society as that of Rome, while he reminds his hearers of the roots of Stoic ethics in the philosophy of Zeno's master, Crates the Cynic. He quotes the Stoic *Hymn* of Cleanthes in support of the Cynic's unity with the divine will.[34] His picture of the Cynic's patience in the face of injustice and physical hardship is consistent with Stoic constancy.[35] In this way Epictetus bridges the gap between the Stoic ideal and reality that is so disturbing to critics of Seneca's lifestyle. His Cynic, in the context of real life, is an example, therefore, as much for Stoics as for would-be Cynics.

It would be easy to quote Epictetus for pages on end, so lucid and attractive are his doctrines. Let us leave him, however, with his own moving self-portrait, which ends his discussion of divine providence. It is consistent with all that we have seen of his teaching:[36]

> We must sing the greatest and most pious hymn [to God], that he has given us the power to follow these things [i.e. the gifts of God] and to use his path [i.e. the path of reason]. What then? Since the majority of you have blinded yourselves, should not one person fill the gap and on behalf of all sing the hymn to the god? I am a lame old man: what else do I have the power to do other than sing the hymn to the god? To be sure, if I were a nightingale I would sing like a nightingale, and if I were a swan I would sing like a swan. But as it is I am endowed with reason: I am compelled to sing the hymn to the god. This is my task: I perform it and I will not leave this post that has been assigned to me, so long as it has been given to me. And I summon you to sing this same song with me.

Epictetus probably lived into the reign of Hadrian (117–138 CE). An almost exact contemporary was Plutarch, whose dates are usually given as *c.*45–120. We have mentioned (at the beginning of the previous chapter) that he chose to spend the greater part of his life in his birthplace, Chaeronea, a strategically placed town in north-west Boeotia, the site of Philip of Macedon's victory over the league of southern Greek states in 338 BCE and of Sulla's victory over Mithradates in 86 BCE. The town was about 30 km east of Delphi, where for the last part of his life Plutarch was a priest and honorary citizen. Many people deny that Plutarch is a philosopher (he is not listed, for example, in the *Oxford Companion to Philosophy*), still less that he is a *Roman* philosopher, for he made but two visits to Italy and himself admitted that he was not expert in Latin. Certainly he was not a professional philosopher like Musonius or Epictetus, and his intense local loyalty limited his impact on Roman thought. Nevertheless, he was trained in philosophy and many of his essays are on philosophical subjects. He had many influential friends at Rome, including his patron L. Mestrius Florus (consul before 82 CE), whose name he took when he became a Roman citizen as L. Mestrius Plutarchus, and Q. Sosius Senecio, consul in 99 and 107 CE, to whom he dedicated several of the *Lives*, the essay on *Moral Progress*, and the *Quaestiones Convivales* ("Table Talk"). Further, he probably was given significant honorary titles by Trajan and Hadrian.

His vast output makes it impossible to deal with him at any length in this chapter. The ancient catalogue (under the name of Lamprias) of his works lists 227 titles: surviving are forty-eight *Lives* and about seventy-eight essays and dialogues, collectively called "ethical works" or *Moralia*. His claim to be a philosopher rests on many of the works in the latter group. Significant also is the fact that his *Lives*, along with Livy's history *Ab Urbe Condita*, have been the most important ancient prose works by which Renaissance and modern readers have formed their ideas of Roman moral character.

Plutarch was an Academic, a follower of Plato, and in this respect good evidence for the survival of Platonism in the early second century, anticipating its reinvigoration later in the century and its triumph in the third century.[37] We have seen that he was consistently critical of Epicureanism,[38] while his views on Stoicism were somewhat more complex, if on the whole hostile.[39] He wrote nine works against the Stoics, only two of which survive, along with a prospectus for a third. Three other works criticizing the Stoics should be mentioned here before we examine the three openly anti-Stoic works. These are the essays on *Moral Virtue* (*De virtute morali*), on *Moral Progress* (*Quomodo quis suos in virtute sentiat profectus*), and *Gryllus* (*Bruta animalia ratione uti*).

Plutarch approaches these subjects as a common-sense enquirer. Much like Cicero in his satirical attack on Cato, he focuses on the rigid definitions of Stoic ethics and their corollary paradoxes, which contradict the experience of ordinary people, especially warm-hearted empiricists like himself.[40] In both *Moral Virtue* and *Moral Progress* he is especially critical of the Stoic paradox that all moral delicts are equal and its corollary, that all emotions (*pathe*) are equally bad.[41] The essay on *Moral Progress*, dedicated to Sosius Senecio, is especially lively, dealing with the topic of the person who makes progress in virtue, which was the subject of Seneca's 75th letter and of several of the discourses of Epictetus. Plutarch asks, "How can a person suddenly become wise without perceiving that he has been making progress?" For the Stoics say that the wise man is one who "does not yet perceive that he has become wise", that is, that he is unaware of his progress. This, says Plutarch, is "to fit the line to the stone", rather than "to fit the stone to the line", a proverb meaning that one's doctrine should fit the facts, not the other way around.[42] As an example of distorting the evidence of experience, Plutarch attacks a second Stoic doctrine, that all moral delicts are equally bad.[43] If this is so, then how is moral progress possible? Having set up these targets of his criticism, Plutarch then shows that there *are* degrees of vice, so that moral progress is possible. For the rest of the essay he produces examples of signs of moral progress, enlivened by literary references, quotations and analogies, all resting on the foundation of common-sense experience as opposed to the rigid and unreal dogmas of the Stoics. In fact, Plutarch does not do justice to the Stoic positions, for the Stoics did allow for moral progress, as Seneca and Epictetus showed, even though all delicts, even the most innocuous, fell short of virtue. This essay is a good example of Plutarch's philosophical method: focus on practical ethics, accurate (but incomplete) quotation of Stoic sources, and persuasive use of a vast array of literary allusions and rhetorical devices.

The essay on the intelligence of animals, *Bruta animalia*, also known by the name of its principal character, *Gryllus*, shows a different technique in attacking the Stoic doctrine that animals lack reason and exist for the use of human beings.[44] The essay is in the form of a dialogue between Odysseus and one of his men who has been turned into a pig by Circe. The pig, Gryllus (a common Greek name, but also a noun meaning "Porker"), eloquently declines the opportunity offered him by Odysseus and Circe of returning to human form: life in the pigsty is preferable to life on Ithaca, and a pig's intelligence is more pure and moral than that of human beings, as Gryllus observes in his opening argument (986F):

> I must begin with the virtues, in which I see you take great pride. [You say that] you differ greatly from the animals in justice and reason, and in courage and the other virtues ... [987B] Well, you agree already that the soul of animals is more suitably formed for the birth of virtue and more perfect. For without orders and without instruction ... it brings forth and increases in accordance with nature the virtue that is suitable for each animal.

Odysseus, most intelligent of human beings, is defeated in argument by a pig! Here Plutarch accurately sets up Chrysippus' doctrine of human superiority, to demolish it by brilliant literary and rhetorical methods, of which George Orwell would have been proud. The topic itself – the proper attitude towards animals – had had a long history in Greek philosophy, going back at least to Plato.[45] It was a matter of special importance to the Pythagoreans, although influences other than Pythagorean doctrine seem to have led to Plutarch's vegetarianism, to judge from his dialogue *On the Intelligence of Animals* and the two fragmentary speeches *On Eating Flesh (De Esu Carnium).*[46]

Plutarch's three extant anti-Stoic works are *On Stoic Self-Contradictions (De Stoicorum Repugnantiis)*, *The Stoics Talk More Paradoxically than the Poets* (no more than a summary with the Latin title, *Compendium argumenti Stoicos absurdiora poetis dicere*), and *On Common Conceptions (De Communibus Notitiis)*. The treatise on self-contradictions is the most substantial of the three.[47] In it Plutarch takes well-known Stoic doctrines, for example, that all delicts are equally bad, to show that they are self-contradictory, or that they are at variance with the Stoics' actual lives. This is a long and intricate essay, which has been carefully analysed by Harold Cherniss: here it will be enough to say that once again Plutarch shows his knowledge of Stoic sources, even as he argues against them with the weapons of the skilled controversialist. He criticizes primarily the early Stoics, above all Chrysippus. In other works of the *Moralia* and in the *Lives* he occasionally mentions Posidonius and Panaetius, but it is hard to know how far he had read them. He never refers to current Stoic debates and never names Seneca, Musonius or Epictetus. Probably this is not out of ignorance, but rather it is a way of arguing *a fortiori* – if Chrysippus can be proved wrong, then there is no need to criticize later Stoics.

The treatise on *Common Conceptions* is ostensibly a dialogue, but in fact a speech by an Academic philosopher, Diadoumenos, against the Stoics, with an introductory dialogue and a few interruptions by an unnamed interlocutor.[48] Its basic topic is the Stoic doctrine best set forth by Diogenes Laertius:[49]

> [Chrysippus says that] virtue is a consistent disposition and one to be chosen for itself, not because of some fear or hope or anything external. Happiness consists in virtue, since virtue is a soul that has become consistent with regard to life as a whole. But a rational being is perverted [from virtue], sometimes because of a wrong belief in

external matters, sometimes because of the influence of other people. For nature gives starting-points that cannot be perverted.

Diadoumenos begins his speech by showing that the Stoic doctrines − that common conceptions agree with nature and that virtue consists of living in agreement with nature, and that living happily consists in living virtuously − contradict common experience and contain self-contradictions, for the Stoics sometimes reject the conceptions of ordinary people, and sometimes appeal to them for support.[50] As in the treatise *On Stoic Self-Contradictions*, Plutarch exploits both these weaknesses, ranging over the whole field of Stoic logic, physics (including theology) and ethics. Diadoumenos divides his speech at chapter 29 (1073D), where he turns to criticism of Stoic physics. Here, as for Epictetus, the three areas of philosophical enquiry are seen to be interdependent, so that ethics is inseparable from logic and physics.[51]

Plutarch was not consistently hostile to the Stoics.[52] While there are passages in several treatises which appear to be based on Stoic doctrine, his approval of Stoic ethics is undeniable in several of the *Lives*, for example, those of Phocion, Cato the Younger and Otho. The deaths of Cato and Otho are made to be consistent with Stoic doctrine, and Plutarch's narrative is approving.[53] Phocion, the just man unjustly executed, is an example of Stoic virtue. His *Life* begins with a comparison with that of Cato, who "was involved in the great struggle with Fortune".[54] Plutarch continues:

> The virtues of these men ... exhibit one character and form, and their moral behaviour was dyed with the same colour, mixed, as it were, with a common measure with regard to their austere love of humanity, their unshaken courage, their care for others and their lack of fear for themselves, their avoidance of shameful acts, and the tension [of their souls] in harmony with justice.

These are Stoic virtues, and the terminology of "tension" or being "in tune with" virtue is Chrysippean.[55]

When Phocion and his colleagues were led off to execution, the onlookers "wondered at his control of his emotions (*apatheia*) and his noble spirit (*megalopsychia*)" − again Stoic virtues. The last sentence of the *Life of Phocion* (38. 5) expressly compares him with Socrates:

But what was done to Phocion reminded the Greeks of what had been done to Socrates, for the injustice done to him was very similar to the case of Socrates, as was the misfortune that it brought to the city.

Plutarch, then, also recognized the excellence of Stoic virtue in the context of public life and political leadership.

About the time of Plutarch's death, a very different Platonist, Apuleius, was born at Madaurus in the Roman province of Africa, about 230 km south-west of Carthage.[56] He received his basic education at Carthage and lived there for the last decades of his life, dying some time after 170 CE. He went to Athens for his higher education and there studied philosophy. Before returning to Africa he spent some time in Rome. He spoke three languages – Latin (his principal language), Greek and Punic – and his surviving works are all in Latin. Like Plutarch, he combined philosophy and rhetoric, and he covered a wide range of subjects.[57] While he was known as *philosophus Platonicus*, his rhetoric is at least as important as his philosophy, for his Latin prose is rich and colourful, often as magical as the stories that he tells. The hero of the *Metamorphoses*, Lucius, is called a descendant of Plutarch, and in the prologue Lucius says that he was first educated in Greek at Athens, Corinth and Sparta, and that later he learned Latin, self-taught, at Rome. While it is impossible to know how far Lucius represents Apuleius himself, Lucius' knowledge of Greek and Latin literature, rhetoric and philosophy is similar to that of Apuleius. He is the Latin equivalent of a sophist of the Greek Second Sophistic, flamboyant and colourful in presentation, catholic in intellectual range, a serious but unoriginal philosopher.[58]

In no. 7 of *Florida* (23 extracts from his speeches and lectures) Apuleius describes how Alexander the Great insisted on idealism and conformity in his statues, and he laments that philosophers have not done the same.[59] Many so-called philosophers, he says, have, by their sordid speech and way of life, degraded philosophy, "a royal discipline invented as much for good speech as for morally good living". In a later extract he elaborates on the breadth of his philosophical education:[60]

The more you drink of the cup of the Muses and the stronger its wine becomes, the closer you get to health of mind. The first cup, that of the primary teacher, awakens the students with basic education; the second, that of the

secondary school-teacher, instils disciplined learning; the
third, that of the *rhetor*, arms the student with eloquence.
These cups are drunk by most people. But *I* also drank
other cups at Athens: the elegant cup of poetry, the clear
cup of geometry, the sweet cup of music, the austere cup of
dialectic, and finally the cup of universal philosophy that
can never be filled. For Empedocles sings in poetry, Plato in
dialogues, Socrates in hymns, Epicharmus in verse, Xenophon
in histories, Crates in satire – your Apuleius cultivates all
these and the nine Muses with equal enthusiasm.

Apuleius ends this tribute with praise of Carthage, "where the
citizens are all most completely educated ... , and the children
study every intellectual discipline", a city that is the "divine Muse
of Africa, the Muse of [Africa's] Roman inhabitants".[61]

Apuleius the philosopher inhabits a very different world from
Plutarch. As with Seneca, rhetorical style is all-important to his
discourse: his medium is his message. His range is impressive.
Extant are treatises *On the God of Socrates* (*De Deo Socratis*), *On Plato
and his Doctrine* (*De Platone et eius Dogmate*), *On the Universe* (*De
Mundo*), and *On Interpretation* (*Peri Hermeneias*). The last of these may
not be by Apuleius and is written in Latin, despite its Greek title.
The other three works are authentic, while an *Asclepius* (a Latin
translation of a Greek "hermetic" work, that is, one associated with
the Egyptian cult of Hermes Trimegistus) is not by Apuleius.[62]

The *De Deo Socratis* is especially interesting for its doctrine about
daimones, intermediaries between the world of the gods and that of
human beings:[63]

There exist certain divine powers, intermediate between
the highest upper air (*aether*) and the lowest earth, situated
in the space of the air (*aer*). By their means our desires and
our deserts are made known to the gods. These the Greeks
call *daimones*.

Apuleius is building on a passage from Plato's *Symposium*, where
Diotima says, in reply to Socrates' question:[64]

Love (*Eros*) is intermediate between mortal and immortal.
He is a great *daimon*, for all that concerns the *daimones*
exists between god and mortal. [His power is] to be
messenger and interpreter for human beings to the gods,

and from the gods to human beings: for the prayers and sacrifices of mortals, and for the commands of the gods and their rewards for sacrifices.

Towards the end (§167) Apuleius urges his hearers to "follow the example of Socrates" and study philosophy, and he concludes with the example of Odysseus, whose constant companion was wisdom, through whom he was able to overcome all difficulties and temptations.

The treatise *De Platone et eius Dogmate*, in two books, is comparatively restrained in style, as befits a summary of Platonic physics, ethics and political doctrines. It is in fact closely related to an earlier "Handbook of Plato's Teaching" or *Didaskalikos* by Alcinous (which until recently was ascribed to Albinus).[65] Not all the doctrines in the *De Platone* are Platonic, for some come from later Academics, some even from Stoics. The topic of Plato's logic, missing from the *De Platone*, is dealt with in *Peri Hermeneias*, which is one of the few sustained Latin treatments of logic, focusing on the syllogism, for which the author uses the Latin term *propositio*.

Finally, the work on cosmology, *De Mundo*, is an adaptation of a work (still extant) spuriously ascribed to Aristotle but in fact dating from around 1 BCE.[66] This work deals first with cosmology (§§1–23) and then with theology (§§24–38), mostly concerning God as creator and ruler (*rector* or *gubernator*) of the universe. Apuleius says that "although he is one, he is addressed by many names", including the Roman *Jupiter* and the Greek *Zeus* (§37), whose all-embracing functions are quoted from an Orphic hymn. The work ends with Fate or Necessity, but the connection between Fate and the divine being is not worked out.

The one god who "is addressed by many names" is important in Apuleius' masterpiece, *Metamorphoses* (also known as *The Golden Ass*).[67] It is a novel in which the curiosity of the hero, Lucius, leads to his metamorphosis into a donkey as the result of a magic ritual that goes wrong. After many adventures, he is saved from an act of public copulation at Corinth by the goddess, Isis. She appears to him and tells him how he may recover his human form the next day at Cenchreae (the port of Corinth). He does this, and he becomes an initiate and devotee of Isis.[68] There is great disagreement as to how far the final scene is autobiographical – is the final metamorphosis that from Lucius into Apuleius? – and as to the significance of the central episode of the novel, the story of Cupid and Psyche, which on one level, at least, is an allegory of Love and the Soul, related in some way to the final conversion. We can be quite sure, however, that theology is essential to Apuleius' philosophy. We have seen how in the *De Mundo* the one god has many names, a sign of the syncretism of second-century religious beliefs.[69] Lucius prays for help to Isis as "Queen of Heaven", uncertain whether to address her as Ceres or Venus or Diana or Proserpine (11. 2). Here is how Isis speaks at her epiphany (11. 5):

> Behold, Lucius, I am here, moved by your prayers. I am the mother of nature, the mistress of all the elements, the first child of the ages, the highest of the gods, the queen of the dead, the first of the gods of heaven, the unchanging epiphany of the gods and goddesses. By my power I dispense the shining lights of the highest heavens, the health-giving winds of the sea, the mourning silences of the underworld. The whole world worships my divine power, for it is one, yet with many aspects, many rituals, and many titles. [Isis then recites the names by which different peoples address her, finishing with the Egyptians], who ... call me by my true name – Queen Isis.

Lucius describes his conversion in mystical terms (11. 23):

> I approached the confines of death; I entered the realm of Proserpine; I was carried through all the elements, and I returned. At midnight I saw the sun shining with brilliant light; I approached the gods below and the gods above, face to face, and I worshipped them in their presence. Behold, I have told you all, and yet ... you cannot know it.

How far we have come from the *Dream of Scipio*! The philosopher is also the religious devotee, but his experience is ecstatic, leading to a better individual life and better hope for the life after death, not to a moral imperative to improve the lot of human beings by duty and service. In his enthusiasm Lucius anticipates third-century Neoplatonism with its focus upon union with the One.

The last of the Roman philosophers in our survey is Marcus Annius Verus, known to us as Marcus Aurelius (121–80 CE, emperor 161–80 CE), a contemporary of Apuleius. His family came from Spain and, like the Spanish Annaei in the time of Claudius and Nero, climbed to the top of the political ladder in Rome. Marcus was favoured by the emperor Hadrian, and was adopted, shortly before

Hadrian's death in 138, by his successor, Antoninus Pius (emperor 138–61 CE), with the names Marcus Aelius Aurelius Verus.[70] His reign was marked by pressure on the northern and eastern frontiers of the empire. Marcus himself campaigned against the Germanic tribes on and beyond the Danube frontier in 170–74 and 178–80, and he died on campaign in the Roman province of Pannonia, either at Vindobona (modern Vienna in Austria) or at Sirmium (modern Sremska Mitrovica in Serbia). His colleagues also campaigned against the Parthians beyond the eastern borders of the empire in 162–66 (bringing the plague back with them to Italy), and Marcus himself was in the east in 175–76. His brother and colleague as emperor, Lucius Verus, died in 169, and his wife, Faustina, died in Cappadocia in 176, the same year that he made his son, Commodus, his colleague in place of Verus. His German campaigns are recorded on the Antonine Column (Column of Marcus Aurelius), which still stands in Rome.

All this is necessary background for an understanding of both the context and tone of Marcus' philosophy, recorded in his private diary addressed to himself: its proper title is *To Himself* (Greek, *Eis Heauton*), although it is usually referred to as *Meditations*.[71] The work is in twelve books, written in Greek, but the divisions into books and chapters were not made by Marcus. How it was preserved and copied we do not know. It was known in Byzantine times (the earliest reference to it dates from the later fourth century, but the next is not until the tenth century), and it was first published in Zürich in 1559 by Andreas Gesner, with a Latin translation by Xylander (Wilhelm Holtzmann). The manuscript used by Xylander is lost. At the beginning of Books 2 and 3 (or possibly the end of Books 1 and 2) are notes saying "[written] amongst the Quadi" (Book 2) and "[written] at Carnuntum" (Book 3), indications that Marcus was writing on campaign against the Germanic tribes (one of which was the Quadi) or at the Roman military base at Carnuntum, a few kilometres below Vienna on the Danube, to the north of which was the territory of the Quadi. It seems, then, that the *Meditations* were written during the campaigns of the 170s, and that they were a personal record (Peter Brunt calls them "a spiritual diary"), addressed solely to Marcus himself. Books 2–12 contain the *Meditations* proper, while Book 1 is a catalogue of those to whom Marcus was indebted for moral instruction and example. The overall tone is one of moral earnestness and pessimism. These are the meditations of a lonely ruler under the stress of heavy responsibilities, one who is concerned to be a morally good ruler, fulfilling his duties towards the Romans and their empire and towards the gods, or rather, the Stoic god. His concerns, then, are first his place as a ruler in the world of his time, and second as a human being in the universal community of gods and human beings.

Among the instructors to whom Marcus expresses his gratitude in Book 1 are six philosophers and a seventh, Severus, whom he calls "my brother", since his son married Marcus Aurelius' daughter.[72] Five of these men were Stoics, one was a Platonist and one, Severus, a Peripatetic, although Marcus credits him with introducing him to the Stoic heroes Thrasea, Helvidius and Cato. The most influential was Q. Junius Rusticus, the son (or grandson) of Domitian's victim, Arulenus Rusticus, and consul in 133 and 162 CE. As city prefect (*praefectus urbi*) he condemned the Christian, Justin the Martyr, to death in 166 CE. Marcus thanks him for practical advice towards becoming a philosopher whose life matched his doctrine in its discipline and virtuous behaviour. He says that Rusticus "gave me a copy from his own home of the discourses of Epictetus".[73] Of all earlier philosophers, Epictetus was the most important influence on Marcus, for from him he learned the importance of developing a character in keeping with one's philosophy. Like Epictetus, he gave high priority to the relationship between the human and the divine, that is, to the proper place of human beings in the universe of gods and mortals.

Marcus' teacher in rhetoric was M. Cornelius Fronto (*c.*95–167; consul in 143 CE), with whom he corresponded in Latin until 166.[74] Marcus valued philosophy more than rhetoric (not that the *Meditations* are devoid of rhetorical elements), and in his brief tribute to Fronto he thanks him, not for his rhetorical teaching, but for teaching him to be wary of the dissimulation that pervades life at court. It is worth noting, also, that he thanks Rusticus for saving him from being "diverted to sophistic exhibitionism" and for teaching him "to stand apart from rhetoric".[75]

The longest tributes in Book 1 are those to his [adoptive] father, Antoninus Pius, whose virtues were those of the ideal Roman leader – including a sense of duty, thoroughness, constancy, clemency and integrity.[76] The portrait of such a leader recalls Cicero's *Dream of Scipio* and Virgil's Aeneas, but in this tribute we have a unique statement from a Roman ruler of the ideals that he saw in his predecessor and wished himself to follow. This is quite different in quality and credibility from public policy statements or political documents such as the *Res Gestae* of Augustus. For example, Marcus specifies:[77]

> Always to watch over the needs of the empire, to admin-
> ister its finances, and to be patient with critics. Not to be
> superstitious as regards the gods, nor to curry favour with
> the people, nor to seek popularity or to become the favourite
> of the masses, but to be sober in everything and steadfast.

Later he exhorts himself "to do everything as a pupil of Antoninus".[78]

In the last chapter of Book 1 (1. 17) Marcus thanks the gods for things belonging to Epictetus' categories of things under his control and out of it. From the latter category he was thankful for the fact that he had good parents, brother, wife and children (§§1, 4, 7); that he was strong enough to live as long as he had (§6); that he had friends like Rusticus and models to emulate like Antoninus Pius (§§3, 4). Marcus adds a "mixed" category between the two cate-gories of Epictetus, in cases where his will (under his control) was helped by something not under his control. Thus his will to control his emotions (especially in sexual matters) was helped by the removal of his grandfather's concubine (§2); his impulse to study philosophy was helped because "I did not fall under the control of a sophist ... nor did I resolve syllogisms or become an expert in celes-tial matters (*meteorologika*)" (§8). In the category of things under his control was his decision to be chaste (§2); to live simply without detracting from the dignity of his position as the heir apparent to Antoninus (§3); to have clear perceptions of the meaning of "living according to nature" and not to be hindered in that (§5); to be generous to those in need (§7). In the last sentence of Book 1 (17. 8) he says that "all these things need the help of the gods and fortune", a significant difference from the doctrine of Epictetus, who taught that one's will was sufficient for making right moral choices.

These two chapters (1. 16 and 17) outline the structure of Marcus' system of philosophy, for he did have a system, even if the *Meditations* are unstructured, informally written, sometimes ungrammatical and hard to follow. What else would one expect from a genuinely personal diary, written without thought of publi-cation? Yet Marcus' "preoccupations" (Brunt's term) are clear – to be a virtuous ruler, to be a virtuous human being, and to understand the proper place of the good man in the divinely ordered universe. The two chapters focus first on Antoninus as the good ruler, which he could not have been without the virtues of the good man; second, they focus on the gods. Both categories reappear throughout the *Meditations*, so that here we will necessarily have to base our review on many discrete passages. Marcus was almost exclusively concerned with ethics and very little with logic or physics (except in so far as theology was a part of physics): an exception is 8. 13, where he exhorts himself to test his impressions against the "reasoning of physics, ethics and logic". His philosophy is Stoic, in spite of the many non-Stoic philosophers whom he quotes with approval.[79] Of these, the Platonists are the most important, with Socrates at their head. Socrates, however, was revered by the Stoics, and there is nothing in Marcus' references to him (more than to any other philosopher) that is inconsistent with Stoicism. Of the Stoics, he is closest to Epictetus. He quotes him frequently, for example at 6. 41, where he reminds himself that, "if we judge good and evil by what is under our control and what is not", then we have no cause to blame the gods or other human beings for our misfortunes. At 5. 33 he quotes "bear and forbear" – the virtues of patience and self-control – the rule for a life unaffected by the injustice of human beings and the attractions of pleasure.

As Marcus meditates on his moral duty as a ruler he often expresses distaste for the people with whom he must deal:[80]

> Say to yourself in the morning: "I shall meet people who are officious, ungracious, arrogant, deceitful, malicious and self-centred. They have all become like that because they are ignorant of good and evil. But I have seen the nature of the good, that it is beautiful, and the nature of the evil, that it is ugly ... and I cannot be hurt by any of these people ... I cannot be angry with my fellow human being and I cannot be his enemy. For we have come into existence in order to work together.

Like Antoninus, he will be "sober and steadfast" as a ruler. For example:[81]

> Every hour be strong and think, as a Roman and a man should, how you can do your job meticulously and with genuine dignity and charity and independence and justice.

He is concerned to be a human being among human beings while maintaining the dignity proper to his position:[82]

> See that you do not become "Caesarized" or dyed [in royal colours]. For it does happen. Watch yourself: see that you

are sincere, good, straightforward, dignified, modest, a lover of justice, reverent towards the gods, approachable, sympathetic, and strong in bearing your responsibilities. Strive to maintain the character that Philosophy intended for you. Revere the gods, protect human beings. Life is short. There is one fruit of life on earth – a pure character and deeds for the good of the community.

The "community" to which Marcus refers extends beyond Rome to the universe (6. 44):[83]

My city and my fatherland is Rome, in so far as I am Antoninus. In so far as I am a human being, the universe is my city and my fatherland.

Neither does he look for a return for his good deeds; his view of *beneficia* is less complex than that of Seneca:[84]

One man, when he does a good deed for another, is ready to credit it to his account, that he is owed a debt of gratitude. Another ... thinks privately about the debt and knows what he has done. But another does not know ... : he is like a vine which bears grapes and does not want anything else after it has once borne its proper fruit ... The man who has done good does not make an issue of it, but he turns to another task, just as the vine turns back again in due season to produce grapes.

Marcus returns to this theme at 9. 42, where he says that it is his own fault if he misreads the character of a man whom he has benefited and who is ungrateful (§5):

What more do you want if you do a good deed for someone? Is it not enough that you have acted in accordance with your nature, but you still seek some reward for this?

Marcus was especially worried by anger, which he discusses in his longest and most systematic chapter.[85] We have seen how he tried not to be irritated by people he had to deal with every day. Here he considers nine headings ("like gifts of the Muses", §10) under which he should analyse his feelings and control them. He must consider the character of those who irritate him, realizing that it is *their* failure of reason that has caused them to act badly, and *his* failure of perception if he lets their actions cause him to be angry (§§2–3, 7). He must expect other people to be morally bad (this, he says, is "a tenth gift from the leader of the Muses [Apollo]", §11). Only a tyrant would allow their bad actions to harm others, without trying to correct them by humane admonition given "not as if by a schoolmaster" (§9). As for his own emotions, it is more manly to be gentle and mild, in this becoming closer to achieving Stoic *apatheia*, freedom from the passions (§10). While many of these details are traditional to Stoic discussions of anger, Marcus is original in his focus on the moral condition of the person causing anger, for a morally bad person harms himself and the community. His own anger must be controlled by looking at his attitude (Greek, *schesis*) towards all human beings (§1), for, as a ruler and a human being, he exists for the sake of other human beings. This *schesis* protects him from being resentful if he is slighted by others, an attitude which Plutarch, following Aristotle, had said was the chief cause of anger.[86] While Marcus does not mention this source of anger, he does follow Aristotle in trying to achieve that mildness which Aristotle had defined as the "calming of anger".

Marcus' ethics are best expressed in the famous chapter where he sets his own emotions in the context of the divine nature of the human soul:[87]

> If you find something in human life that is better than justice or truth or self-control or courage or, in a word, self-sufficiency in your mind ... – if, as I say, you find something better than these, then turn to it with all your soul ... But if there seems to be nothing better than the divine spirit that has been placed within you ... , and if you find everything else smaller and more insignificant, then allow no room for anything else ... Simply and freely choose that which is better and hold on to it.

The sense of the community of the human soul with the divine is the basis of the second principal category in Marcus' philosophical system, the place of human beings in the divinely ordered cosmos.[88] In 1. 3 he thanks the gods that his mother had taught him to be god-fearing, and in 1. 16. 3 that Antoninus had been an example to him of freedom from superstition. Like many Stoics he believes that the gods do communicate with human beings, especially through dreams (1. 17. 6, 9) and in answer to prayer (9. 40), but their help is predicated upon his own self-sufficiency. Thus his prayers should be for support in overcoming the *pathe* of fear or lust (9. 40), not for the fulfilling of some particular desire. As a rational being he must willingly acquiesce in what happens to him (10. 28), for human beings alone are endowed with reason that allows them to follow willingly the necessity of fate. Elsewhere he says:[89]

> What the gods bring about is full of Providence. What Fate brings about is not separate from Nature nor from the closely-woven works of Providence.

This belief in the texture of the universe, which cannot be unravelled by the desires or fears of an individual human being, is the foundation of Marcus' religious views, as it is of his ethics:[90]

> Everything is woven together with everything else, and the binding together is sacred, and virtually nothing is alien to anything else. For all things have been arranged together and make up the order of one universe. For the universe is one, made up of all things, and god is one, existing in all things, and substance is one, and law is one, and reason is common to all intelligent beings, and truth is one. *If* indeed there is one goal of perfection (*teleiotes*) for beings that have the same origin and share in the same reason.

Despite the doubt expressed in the final sentence, this is the dynamic source of Marcus' striving for virtuous character and action, so powerful that it does not need the precise definitions of a theologian. This is a sufficient explanation of the ambiguities in his views of the survival of the soul after death. In 12. 5 he asks why good men should perish at their death, and he answers that *if* this is so, then it has been so ordained justly by the gods. In 4. 21 he ponders how there can be sufficient space in air and on earth for the souls of the dead "*if* they continue after death". He does not pursue this question and, as Rutherford has said, "he maintains a firm agnosticism".[91]

Marcus therefore falls back on the unity of the cosmos as an answer to the question of 4. 21. He confesses:[92]

> Everything is in harmony with me, O Cosmos, that is in harmony with you! Nothing is too early or too late for me

that is at the right time for you. Everything is fruit for me,
O Nature, that your seasons bring. From you comes everything, in you is everything, to you everything [will return].
One man says, "I love the city of Cecrops [Athens]", but
will you [Marcus] not say, "I love the city of Zeus"?

Marcus' sense of citizenship in the universe energized his principles as a ruler, and it allows him to contemplate death more
positively:[93]

It makes no difference where you live, if one lives everywhere as if the universe were his city. Let others see, let
them observe closely, a man who is truly living according
to nature.

In the first chapter of Book 12 he exhorts himself "to let go of
the past and leave the future to Providence, and for the present keep
to the straight path of purity and justice". Thus, he continues, he
will be ready for death:

If, when it is time for you to go, you leave everything else
and honour your guiding spirit (*hegemonikon*) and the divine
element in you, and you are not afraid of ceasing to live ...,
you will be a human being worthy of the universe that
created you and no longer will you be a stranger in your
own country.

Finally, in the last chapter of the *Meditations* (12. 36), he takes
his leave of a life well lived:

O human being, you have been a citizen in this great city
[i.e. the world]. What difference does it make if you have
been one for five years or for one hundred? For all are equal
under the law. Why should you be fearful, then, if he who
sends you away is not a tyrant nor an unjust judge, but
Nature, which brought you there? You are like an actor
whom the presiding judge dismisses from the stage: "But I
have not finished five acts, but only three!" Right! But in
life three acts make up the whole play. For he who was the
cause of the composition of your body is now the cause of
its dissolution: he it is who sets the limit of your completed

life. You are not responsible for either. Depart, then, graciously, for he who dismisses you is gracious.

Marcus Aurelius is an appropriate terminus for our survey of the Roman philosophers, even if we may rightly say, "We have finished only three acts!" Philosophy continued to flourish in the Roman empire for centuries after his death, and the four schools of philosophy at Athens, for whom he had endowed professorial chairs in 176 CE, continued to exist until they were formally closed by Justinian in 529 CE.

Two of Marcus' contemporaries, both doctor–philosophers, should still be mentioned, although discussion of their doctrines is beyond the limits of this book. The Asiatic Greek, Galen of Pergamum (c.129–199), who was physician to Marcus, believed that the physician must also be a philosopher, as he showed in his vast output in Greek prose, covering both medicine and philosophy.[94] The short treatise *On My Own Books* (supplemented by the brief *On the Arrangement of My Own Books*) not only gives the titles of many of his works, but also has valuable details about Galen's life, his relations with Marcus Aurelius, and the effects of the plague in Rome. The title of another short work, *That the Best Doctor is also a Philosopher*, is self-explanatory. Galen's interest in philosophical topics other than ethics appears in the *Introduction to Logic*. His most important extant philosophical work is *On the Doctrines of Hippocrates and Plato* (in nine books), a valuable source for the doctrines of earlier philosophers (for example, Posidonius) whose works are no longer extant, with much perceptive criticism.[95]

Probably contemporary with Galen was another doctor–philosopher, Sextus Empiricus, about whose life nothing is known. Of his extant works, *Against the Professors* (*Adversus Mathematicos*, in eleven books) and *Outlines of Pyrrhonism* are our most prolific ancient source for the sceptical doctrines of Pyrrhonism and criticism of Stoic logic.[96]

The obsessive concern of second-century Roman philosophers with philosophy as a practical guide for daily life comes to an end effectively with Marcus Aurelius, for philosophy in the next century is marked by other trends. Doxographers such as Diogenes Laertius recorded and excerpted the doctrines of earlier philosophers, while the principal concerns of philosophy turned from daily life to efforts to apprehend the divine, to understand the relationship between the universal intelligence of God and human beings. While this quest had practical effects on how people chose to live their lives, its primary goal was not so much happiness (*eudaimonia*), as personal fulfillment in union with the divine. In their focus on the divine being, Epictetus, Apuleius and Marcus to some extent anticipate the doctrines of Neoplatonism that flourished from the third century onwards. Much of Stoic ethics was subsumed into Christian doctrine, which grew in the third century and triumphed in the fourth. The Church Fathers both needed and criticized Stoicism, a tension that makes an early appearance in Clement of Alexandria (*c.*150–215). Even fourteen centuries later it reappears with the Neostoic Justus Lipsius (1547–1606), whose popular dialogue *De Constantia* (first published in 1584) and later dogmatic works on Stoicism (published in 1604) tried to reconcile Stoicism and Christianity.

As a measure of the vitality of Roman philosophy we can look ahead from Marcus Aurelius for more than three centuries, to a Roman ex-consul waiting in prison at Ticinum (modern Pavia) for unjust execution on the orders of the Gothic King Theoderic. The *Consolation of Philosophy* of Boethius (*c.*480–524) justifies divine providence by relying largely on Stoic and Neoplatonist doctrine, and it ends with Philosophy exhorting Boethius:[97]

> Turn away from vice, cultivate virtue, raise your mind to upright hopes, offer your humble prayers to the highest heavens. Great is the necessity for virtuous living that has been imposed on you, if you are honest with yourself, when you put before your eyes the judge who sees all.

Cicero, Seneca, Epictetus and Marcus Aurelius would have agreed! In the lonely voice of Theoderic's victim we can recognize the vitality of the Roman philosophers and perceive their continuity over a period of six centuries.

BIBLIOGRAPHICAL NOTE

The bibliography on Hellenistic and Roman philosophy is enormous and grows exponentially every year. Good bibliographies for the Roman philosophers are to be found in Griffin and Barnes (1989) and Long and Sedley (1987) (abbreviated as "LS" in the text of this book). The list of references that follows mentions all works to which reference has been made in the notes, where their relative usefulness has usually been indicated. A few works will be exceptionally useful for readers of this volume: first, Long and Sedley (1987), who have collected and translated a large selection of texts on Hellenistic philosophy, many of them by Roman authors. The editors have added helpful commentary as well as the bibliography mentioned above. Second, Long (1986) is a lucid introduction to Hellenistic philosophy, the basis of Roman philosophy. To this should be added Sharples (1996), whose book is arranged thematically. The essays in the pioneering first volume of Griffin and Barnes, *Philosophia Togata* (1989), form a good introduction to the Roman philosophers under the Republic.

Of the making of dictionaries and encyclopedias there is no end. Of one-volume works, the *Oxford Companion to Philosophy* (1995) is refreshing and fair to Roman philosophers. The Oxford and Cambridge University Presses have published a number of other Companions and Dictionaries of Philosophy (Oxford, 1994, edited by S. Blackburn; Cambridge, 1995, edited by R. Audi). The third edition of the *Oxford Classical Dictionary* (1996, edited by S. Hornblower and A. Spawforth) is a vast improvement on its predecessors. Its entries on philosophers are generally informative and free of the prejudices that devalued entries in earlier editions: some, such as the article on Lucretius by P. and D. Fowler, are distinguished and more useful than many journal articles and books. Of multi-volume works Routledge's *Encyclopedia of Philosophy* (10 vols,

1998, edited by E. Craig) has many entries useful to students of the Roman philosophers. The venerable German *Paulys Realencyclopädie* is still indispensable for its articles on individual philosophers, such as the one on Cicero. Its successor, *Der Neue Pauly* (Stuttgart: Metzler, 1996–), is easier on the eyes and generally more concise. It is still in progress, and (at the time of this writing) has not reached the volume that will include M. Tullius Cicero.

The most exhaustive resource for the Roman philosophers is the massive and ongoing *Aufstieg und Niedergang der römischen Welt*, edited by H. Temporini and W. Haase. The articles in volumes II. 36. 1–6 are especially relevant, as the following list of references makes clear. Too many of these are prolix, but the surveys of particular subjects and authors, with their bibliographies, are often valuable.

Texts and translations of the major authors are generally available in the Loeb series, although many of these are in need of modernizing. There are good English translations in the Cambridge series of translations (those by Griffin and Atkins and by Zetzel are listed below), and in the series of texts and translations published by Aris and Phillips. Many of the major works are available in translation in the Penguin series. Less well-known or fragmentary authors have been well served in extracts printed by Long and Sedley (1987), but some are available only in Greek or Latin Teubner texts or in the collections of fragments edited by Usener (*Epicurea*, 1887) and Von Arnim (*Stoicorum Veterum Fragmenta*, 1905), from which a few translations have been provided in this book.

NOTES

1 *PHILOSOPHIA TOGATA*

1 Griffin and Barnes (1989); Barnes and Griffin (1996).
2 This is the basic argument of the astringent work of Barnes (1997), largely devoted to Epictetus.
3 Maurach (1997), 7–14.
4 Buechner (1982), p. 6, frag. 1.
5 Cic., *T.D.* 4. 1–7.
6 Virgil, *Aen.* 8. 9; 11. 225–30.
7 *Aen.* 8. 51–54, 333–36.
8 Livy, 1. 18; Cicero, *T. D.* 4. 3. Both authors point out the chronological impossibility of the story. The Romans adopted the Greek concept of Numa as the "Philosopher King", as is explained by Ogilvie (1965), 89.
9 Livy, 3. 31. 7–8; Ogilvie (1965), 449–50.
10 Greece was reorganized into two provinces, Macedonia and Achaea, in 27 BCE.
11 See Pelling, "Plutarch: Roman Heroes and Greek Culture", in Griffin and Barnes (1997), 199–232.
12 Plutarch, *Sulla* 12–14.
13 Plutarch, *Sulla* 26; cf. Strabo, 13. 1. 54 (608–09).
14 Barnes, J., "Roman Aristotle", in Barnes and Griffin (1997), 1–69; 64–66 for a summary and demolition of the standard picture.
15 It is not mentioned in Cicero's tour of philosophical sites set in Athens in 79 BCE (*De Finibus* 5. 1–2). For its remains see Travlos (1971), 345–47, s.v. "Lykeion", and 169, map of Athens, no. 202. Recent excavations for the new Athens subway have revealed its site.
16 Cic., *De Fin.* 5. 7.
17 See Gottschalk (1989): 1083–97 for Andronicus.
18 For Cynicism, especially useful is Branham and Goulet-Cazé (1996). For Cynicism in the Roman world, note Branham's introduction (1–27), and Griffin, M., "Cynicism and the Romans: Attraction and Repulsion", 190–204. Still useful is Dudley (1937).
19 They are linked, for example, by Epictetus, *Disc.* 2. 13. 24 and 16. 35. Many people in antiquity believed that the first Cynic was Antisthenes of Athens (*c.*445–365 BCE), a follower of Socrates, who was present at his death, according to Plato, *Phaedo* 59B.

242

20 Diogenes Laertius, 6. 54.
21 For Zeno's *Politeia* see Schofield (1991).
22 Augustine, *Civ. Dei* 19. 1–3.
23 The key statement is at *De Off.* 1. 128: "we must not listen to the Cynics or those Stoics who have been almost Cynics". For Cicero's discomfort with plain speaking see Griffin (above, note 18), 191–92.
24 Horace, *Ep.* 2. 2. 60: *sermones Bionei.* Horace called his own satires *Sermones.*
25 Branham and Goulet-Cazé (1996), 25. For the Cynics in the imperial age see Goulet-Cazé (1990).
26 Epictetus, *Disc.* 1. 24. 6–10, and 3. 22, discussed in Chapter 8. Goulet-Cazé (1990), 2773–74, warns against accepting Epictetus' picture of Cynicism uncritically. She is also sceptical of the Cynic credentials of Dio Chrysostom (*Ibid.*, 2810–12).
27 See Griffin (1996), 196–200.
28 Much of Cynic lack of decorum concerned the human body and its functions: see Krueger (1996).
29 Sen., *N.Q.* 7. 32. 1–2, quoted in Chapter 5, p. 133.
30 Juvenal, *Sat.* 13. 120–25. For analysis of philosophical influences in *Sat.* 10, the most philosophical of the satires, see Courtney (1980), 448–54, whose conclusion, that this is not "poetry of the top class", is wide of the mark.
31 The apparent praise of Hadrian in *Sat.* 7. 1–21 is tempered by irony and indirection.
32 For Favorinus see Holford-Strevens (1997); Barigazzi (1993); Michel (1993).
33 Cic., *De Off.* 1. 58, 160. For Hierocles see Parente (1989).
34 Harrison (2000) gives proper consideration to Apuleius' philosophical credentials, especially in chapters 3–5.
35 Books 6 for the Cynics, 7 for the Stoics (wrongly given as Book 8 in *OCD*[3], 475) and 10 for the Epicureans. Analysis and discussion by Goulet-Cazé (1992); Hahm (1992); Gigante (1992).

2 THE ARRIVAL OF THE GREEK PHILOSOPHERS IN ROME

1 For the facts see Astin (1978), 174–75.
2 Cicero, *De Oratore* 2. 155. Many other ancient references are given by Astin (1978), 175.
3 Cicero, *De Off.* 3. 114; Livy, *Per.* 53.
4 See Astin (1978), 164, for Cato's withering remarks about Albinus, reported by Polybius, 39. 1. 1.
5 Gellius, *N.A.* 6. 14. 9.
6 Cicero, *De Oratore* 2. 157–61.
7 Cic., *Top.* 6 (= LS 31F).
8 Sources for Diogenes are collected in *SVF* 3. 210–43. New evidence for his importance is being found in the Herculaneum papyri, for which see Chapter 4, pp. 100–01.
9 For sources for and fragments of Carneades, see Mette (1985), 39–148 (53–141 for Carneades).

10 Gellius, *N.A.* 6. 14. 10, quoting Polybius (*Hist.* 33. 2, the Greek text of which is not extant) and Rutilius Rufus (frag. 3). Polybius may have heard Carneades in Rome, and Rutilius (b. *c.*160 BCE) was a pupil of Panaetius.

11 Cic., *Rep.* 3. 9–31 for Philus' version of Carneades' speech against justice; 33–41 for Laelius' defence (which is not explicitly said to be a reproduction of Carneades' first speech). Lactantius, *Inst.* 5. 14–18 (= frag. 11b1 Mette) and *Epit.* 50–52 (= frag. 11b2 Mette), rebuts Carneades. Augustine summarizes parts of the speeches of Philus and Laelius in *Civ. Dei* 19. 21 and 22. 6 (= frag. 11b3 Mette). For Philus' speech see Hahm (1999), 167–83.

12 Livy, 39. 6. 7 – 7. 5; Polybius 31. 25. 6–7.

13 Pol., 31. 23–24. For Scipio see Astin, A. E., *Scipio Aemilianus*, Oxford: Clarendon Press, 1967.

14 Pol., 31. 25. 2–9.

15 Polybius' description of a Roman nobleman's funeral (6. 53–54) is the *locus classicus* for Roman ancestral tradition.

16 Cicero, *Brutus* 77; Livy, 45. 8. 6.

17 Plutarch, *Aemilius* 6. 8–9; Astin (1967), 15–16.

18 Livy, 44. 44; Plutarch, *Aem.* 22. 3–9; Polybius, 31. 29. 1–7.

19 Plutarch, *Aem.* 28. 11. E. Rawson speculates about the contents of the library in *CAH²* 8. 464.

20 Astin (1978), chapter 8 (pp. 157–81), with complete references for ancient sources.

21 Quoted by the elder Pliny, *N.H.* 29. 13–14.

22 Astin (1978), 339, who discusses the *Ad Filium* in Appendix 8, 332–42.

23 Plutarch, *Cato Mai.* 8. 18.

24 *HRR* frag. 6, 56, 50.

25 Plutarch, *Cato Mai.* 23. 1.

26 *mera mortualia* (Gell. *N.A.* 18. 7. 3).

27 Gellius, *N.A.* 15. 11. 1; Suetonius, *Gramm.* 25; *MRR* 1. 444. The other expulsions were in 92 BCE and 89 or 92 CE.

28 Athenaeus, 12. 547a.

29 *Cato Mai.* 23. 3.

30 Suetonius, *Nero* 52.

31 Cicero, *Ac.* 1. 19. Diogenes Laertius (3. 56) more accurately says that physics was the original and sole philosophical subject, to which Socrates added ethics, and Plato dialectics. See Barnes (1997a), especially 140–46, analysing problems in translating Cicero's terminology.

32 Cic., *Ac.* 1. 30.

33 Diogenes Laertius 7. 41–44 (= LS 31A).

34 D. L., 7. 83 (= *SVF* 2. 130 and LS 31C). Plato establishes dialectic as the "coping-stone" of education in *Rep.* 8. 534b–e.

35 Aristotle, *Rhet.* 1. 2 (1355b 25).

36 *vir bonus, dicendi peritus*, quoted by Quintilian, *Inst.* 12. 1. 1, in support of his argument that the orator must be morally good. But Astin (1978), 147 and 154, points out the ambiguities in Cato's phrase.

37 Lactantius, *Inst.* 5. 14. 5 (= LS 68M), discussed by Long (1986), 104–06.

38 Long (1986), 104.

39 Cic., *De Rep.* 3. 33.
40 Lucilius, frag. 200–07W, quoted by Cicero, *De Fin.* 2. 24.
41 Cic., *T.D.* 4. 5.
42 Cic., *Pro Murena* 66; *De Fin.* 2. 24, 4. 23.
43 Cicero, *Acad. Pr.* 2. 5 (= Panaetius, frag. 23V); Astin (1967), 296–99. Panaetius' fragments are quoted from Van Straaten (1962).
44 Astin (1967), 17 and 302–06.
45 Cic., *Pro Murena* 61–63.
46 Long (1986), 211.
47 Cic., *De Off.* 1. 46. A corollary of including those who show "some evidence of virtue" is the idea of progress towards virtue (as opposed to the sharp distinction between the virtuous person and all others), discussed by Seneca in *Ep.* 75, for which see Chapter 6, pp. 174–6.
48 Cic., *De Fin.* 4. 79 (= Panaetius, frag. 55V). Xenocrates was a disciple of Plato, Theophrastus and Dicaearchus were followers of Aristotle.
49 *De Off.* 2. 35 (= Panaetius, frag. 62V); *De Leg.* 3. 14 (= frag. 61V).
50 As can be seen from the names listed in Panaetius, frag. 137–63V.
51 Seneca, *Ep.* 116. 5 (= Panaetius, frag. 114V).
52 Frag. 55V, quoted above.
53 Frag. 64–69V.
54 Frag. 70–74V.
55 LS 54I–Q; 55A, E, J–M; 62A–C, K.
56 Cic., *De Off.* 1. 101 (= frag. 87V); cf. *De Off.* 1. 132, 2. 18 (= frag. 88–89V).
57 Aristotle, *N.E.* 1102a27–28.
58 LS 53R (= *SVF* 3. 175).
59 Tertullian, *De Anima* 14. 2 (= frag. 85V), ascribes to Panaetius a six-part division of the soul.
60 Cic., *De Rep.* 1. 34 (= frag. 119V).
61 Cic., *De Rep.* 1. 35–36.
62 Cic., *De Off.* 1. 124 (= frag. 121V). The phrase "define its rights" translates the reading *describere*: the alternative reading, *discribere*, gives the sense "to distribute rights [namely, to citizens]".
63 Polybius 6. 53–54.
64 Long (1986), 216.
65 Cic., *Ad Att.* 2. 1. 8.
66 *De Fin.* 1. 6 (cf. *N.D.* 1. 123 and 2. 88); *T.D.* 2. 61.
67 Cic., *Ad Att.* 2. 1. 12.
68 Frag. 255 EK; Plutarch, *Marius* 45.
69 The leader of this school was Karl Reinhardt, especially in his book (1926).
70 Edelstein and Kidd (1972 and 1989); Kidd (1988 and 1999).
71 Frag. 91 EK; cf. Panaetius, frag. 63V.
72 Kidd, s.v. "Posidonius", in *OCD*^{3}, 1232.
73 Posidonius, frag. 88 EK (= *SVF* 2. 38).
74 The same objection applied to the simile of the egg.
75 Posidonius, frag. 99a EK: cf. frag. 97a EK.
76 Nock (1959), p. 15 quoted.
77 Strabo 2. 3. 8 (= Posidonius, frag. T85 EK).
78 *SVF* 2. 973.
79 Frag. 164 EK, esp. §5.

80 They constitute most of frag. 150a–87 EK: see Kidd (1988) for commentary, along with Kidd (1971).
81 Galen, *De Plac.*, 5. 469 (= Posidonius, frag. 30 EK).
82 Greek *pleonazousa horme* (*SVF* 3. 377).
83 Frag. 152 and 157 EK (= Galen, *De Plac.* 5. 429–30). Frag. 157 is also quoted in frag. 34 EK.
84 The tripartite nature of the soul, and its analogy to the tripartite city, is a central argument in Plato's *Republic*, set forth in *Rep.* 4. 434e–444e. Plato's terms for the irrational parts of the soul are *thymoeides* ("spirited") and *epithymetikon* ("desiring").
85 *SVF* 1. 179, quoted by Posidonius in frag. 187B EK (= Galen, *De Plac.* 5. 469–76), line 35.
86 Frag. 186 EK (= Clement, *Strom.*, 2. 21. 129).
87 See Hahm (1989) and the commentary on frag. 252–84 in Kidd (1988), 861–971.
88 Frag. 255 EK.
89 Frag. 253 EK (= Athenaeus 5. 211D–215B).
90 Frag. 67–69, 274–76 EK.
91 Frag. 284 EK (= Seneca, *Ep.* 90. 5–13, 20–25, 30–32), with Kidd (1988), 961–71.
92 Frag. 60 EK (= Athenaeus 6. 263c–d).

3 CICERO AND HIS CONTEMPORARIES

1 Powell (1995). The quotation is from Long (1995), p. 50.
2 Cato, frag. 14 Jordan, quoted by Quintilian, *Inst.* 12. 1. 1. See p. 22 above.
3 See Powell (1995), 12.
4 Diodotus died in 59 BCE: see *Ad Att.* 2. 20. 6.
5 *N.D.* 1. 6.
6 For example, at the end of the *De Natura Deorum* (3. 95) he admits that he prefers the views of the Stoic Balbus to those of the Epicurean Velleius and the Academic Cotta.
7 See p. 59 for Cicero's ambivalence towards the Stoic doctrine that virtue alone is sufficient for the good life.
8 Cicero, *Ad Fam.* 13. 1. 2. Memmius was the patron of Lucretius. Phaedrus became head of the Epicurean school at Athens and was succeeded by Patron in 70 BCE.
9 *Brutus* 316.
10 The fragments and testimonia for Philo and Antiochus are printed in Mette (1986–87), 9–24 for Philo, 25–63 for Antiochus; frag. 9 Mette (= Cicero, *T. D.* 2. 9) for Philo's teaching. For Philo's life and philosophy see Brittain (2001), who, 173–91, is critical of Cicero's evidence.
11 See Frede (1999), p. 280 for the end of the Academic school.
12 Long (1986), 231.
13 Cic., *Ac.* 1. 45.
14 See Sharples (1996), 9–10 and 27–32.
15 For Aristotle's criticism of the Platonic theory of ideas, see, for example, *N.E.* 1096a–1097a.

16 "Cognitive impression" approximates to the Greek *kataleptike phantasia*. Cicero translates *katalepsis* ("cognition") as *comprehensio* and uses various terms such as *percipere* and *impressio* and *visum* for "impression".

17 Greek, *eulogon*. LS 69B (= Sext. Emp., *Adv. Math.* 7. 158).

18 Cicero translates the Greek *pithanon* as *probabile* (*Luc.* 103). He quotes Clitomachus, Carneades' successor as head of the Academy *c.*128–110 BCE, for this theory (*Luc.* 103–04 = LS 69I,J). Carneades' theory is set forth at greater length by Sextus Empiricus (LS 69D,E = Sext. Emp., *Adv. Math.* 7. 166–84).

19 Cicero, *Luc.* 11–12.

20 Cicero, *Ac.* 1. 40–42 (excerpts in LS 40B and 41B); *Luc.*, 16–39. Cic., *De Fin.* 5. 7, for Aristotle's authority.

21 For differences between the ethics of Antiochus and the Stoics, see Cicero, *De Fin.* 4. 37–41, 78. For Antiochus' physics, see *Ac.* 1. 24–29, where the reference to Aristotle's fifth element is non-Stoic.

22 Cicero, *N.D.* 1. 16, where Balbus criticizes Antiochus.

23 *Luc.* 132.

24 LS 71C, §§9–11: see Barnes (1989), 93–94, Appendix C. For Aenesidemus see the commentary on LS 71, vol. 1, 470–73. The quarrel was still between Academics: see Striker (1997).

25 Barnes (1989), 90.

26 Cic., *N.D.* 1. 6.

27 Cic., *Luc.* 29.

28 Long (1986), 229.

29 Plato, *Rep.* 621b–d.

30 Barnes (1989), 90.

31 The Introduction and Commentary of Reid (1881) are still valuable. The text edited by O. Plasberg (Leipzig: Teubner, 1908) includes the texts of Cicero's letters that chart the course of the work's creation. Inwood and Mansfeld (1997) contains ten essays on the *Academica*, with bibliographies. For Antiochus, basic is Barnes (1989). For Philo see Brittain (2001), especially 38–72 ("Philo's Life"), with extensive bibliography.

32 The relevant passages are printed in Plasberg (1908), 28–32, and in appendix A to Griffin (1997a), which is the best discussion of the subject. For most readers the brief and lucid summary in Powell (1995), xiv–xvi, will be sufficiently informative.

33 Cicero, *Brutus*, 307. Cicero admired the elder Catulus and made him a participant in Books 2 and 3 of *De Oratore*. He could not make him a participant in the *Catulus*, the dramatic date of which was twenty-five years after his death.

34 *Ad Att.* 13. 16, written on 26 June, 45 (T14 in Appendix A of Griffin, 1997a). Griffin discusses this version on pp. 20–27.

35 Matters are further confused by the convention of referring to the extant book of the first version (*Lucullus*) as *Academica Priora* (although it is actually the second book) and the final version as *Academica Posteriora* (although the extant book is actually the first book and is printed before the *Lucullus*). For illumination see Powell (1995), xv, and Griffin (1997a), appendix B, pp. 33–34.

36 *De Fin.* 5. 9–75 (Piso) and 76–95 (Cicero).
37 Augustine, *C.D.* 19, 1–3, for the *De Philosophia.*
38 *Ad Fam.* 9. 6. 4.
39 *Ad Att.* 13. 16. 1.
40 *Ad Att.* 13. 12–19, 21–25, 33a, 35.
41 *Ad Att.* 13. 25. 3.
42 This was the *De Lingua Latina,* published probably in 43 in twenty-five books, of which Books 5–25 were dedicated to Cicero.
43 *Ad Fam.* 9. 8.
44 *Ad Att.* 13. 44. 2 (T20 in Griffin, 1997a, b).
45 *Ad Att.* 13. 13. 1 (T12 in Griffin, 1997a, b).
46 *Ad Att.* 13. 12–25.
47 Clarke (1981), chapter 1, has useful sections on Brutus as an intellectual (pp. 22–33) and on his death and his attitude to suicide (pp. 67–72). Clarke accepts the narrative of Plutarch rather than that of Dio.
48 Plutarch, *Brutus* 40. 7–8.
49 Plutarch, *Brutus* 52.
50 Plutarch, *Brutus* 56. 11 (= *Comparison with Dion* 3. 11).
51 Cicero, *Ad Brut.* 1. 9.
52 *Brutus* 311–12, 330.
53 Quintilian, *Inst.* 10. 1. 123.
54 *Brutus* 10.
55 Tacitus, *Dial.* 18. 4.
56 *De Fin.* 1. 1–12.
57 *De Fin.* 3. 6.
58 *Paradox. Stoic.*, *Preface* 1.
59 Plutarch, *Cato Min.* 4. 4.
60 *Cato Min.* 4. 2–3.
61 *Cato Min.* 10; Strabo 14. 674.
62 Suetonius, *Divus Julius* 19. 1: "not even Cato denied that this bribery was in the interests of the Republic." See Syme (1939), 34, 100.
63 As recorded in their letters: Cicero, *Ad Fam.* 15. 3–6.
64 *Ad Att.* 7. 2. 7.
65 Cicero, *Pro Murena* 83; Lucan, *B.C.* 2. 383.
66 *Cato Min.* 70.
67 *Cato Min.* 65. 11, 67. 2.
68 Cicero discusses Cato's example at *T.D.* 1. 74.
69 Plutarch, *Cato Min.* 72. 2.
70 Sallust, *Cat.* 51–53.
71 References are to Mueller's Teubner edition, 1890.
72 See Lesky (1966), 553–55 for the *Protrepticus.* For Cicero's philosophical works see Süss (1966), 136–37 for the *Hortensius*; Philippson (1939). There is no comparable survey in English: McKendrick (1989) is written for a different readership.
73 Augustine, *Confessions* 3. 7 (= *Hortensius*, frag. 10M).
74 Aug., *De Trinitate* 14. 9 (= frag. 50M).
75 Aug., *De Trin.* 14. 19 (= frag. 97M).
76 Süss (1966), 53.
77 *T.D.* 4. 82.
78 *De Fin.* 3. 5.
79 *De Fin.* 3. 15.

80 *De Fin.* 3. 35.

81 *De Fin.* 3. 40.

82 Catullus 61. It is doubtful that Torquatus is the Allius of Catullus 68.

83 *De Fin.* 1. 29.

84 *De Fin.* 1. 16, 2. 119.

85 Philippson (1939), 1136–37.

86 For example, the argument of 2. 31 is the same as the Antiochean argument of *De Fin.* 5. 45.

87 *De Fin.* 2. 17.

88 *De Fin.* 5. 22; *T.D.* 5. 32.

89 As Cato says (3. 14): "I will set forth the whole of the doctrine of Zeno and the Stoics."

90 Greek *adiaphora*: 3. 53 for explanation of the Latin translation.

91 *De Fin.* 3. 31 (= LS 64A).

92 The definitions of Diogenes and Antipater are given in LS 58K (= Stobaeus 2. 76. 9–15) and discussed in LS I, pp. 398–401. Chrysippus said that the end was "living in accordance with nature" (LS 64C [= D.L. 7. 87–89]); Diogenes that it was "to use reason rightly in choosing and not-choosing things in accordance with nature"; Antipater that it was "to live choosing things in accordance with nature and not-choosing things contrary to nature".

93 3. 75. "Revere" is used to translate *colendum*, which in Latin denotes both "worship" and "study".

94 *T.D.* 5. 32.

95 5. 1–8.

96 See Travlos (1971), 233–41, 578–79.

97 See the bird's-eye view in LS I, p. 4.

98 See Pohlenz's Teubner text (1967), iv–v, for their survival in late antiquity and revival in the Carolingian age, when the principal manuscripts were copied.

99 *T.D.* 1. 7 (*seniles declamationes*).

100 *De Div.* 2. 2.

101 Summarily expressed in 3. 14–15 and developed in 3. 16–84.

102 He had used the plural of *inventrix* a decade earlier in *De Oratore* 1. 13.

103 Philippson (1939), 1149.

104 *Ad Att.* 12. 14. 3.

105 Frag. 7M: quotations are from Mueller's Teubner edition, 1890.

106 See Dudley (1937), 114–15.

107 *Ad Att.* 12. 14. 3.

108 *T.D.* 1. 65–66.

109 Frag. 11M (= Lactantius, *Inst.* 1. 15–16).

110 *Ad Fam.* 4. 5.

111 *De Div.* 2. 3.

112 Süss (1966), 93.

113 *N.D.* 1. 123 (= Posidonius, frag. 22a EK), quoted also by Lactantius, *De Ira Dei* 4. 7 (= frag. 22b EK).

114 *N.D.* 2. 3, repeated by Cotta at 3. 6. Balbus' four sections are respectively 2. 4–44, 45–72, 73–153, 154–67.

115 2. 154.

116 3. 29–37 (= Carneades, frag. 8a Mette).

117 3. 5–6.

118 3. 93.
119 *N.D.* 2. 104–14.
120 *N.D.* 2. 104.
121 *De Div.* 1. 13–15. Quintus also quotes thirteen lines from Cicero's *Marius* at *De Div.* 1. 106, and seventy-eight lines from his poem *De Consulatu Suo* at *De Div.* 1. 17–22.
122 See Courtney (1993), 235–46.
123 1. 1–7.
124 2. 8.
125 For the "intellectual and cultural context" of *De Divinatione* see Beard (1986).
126 *De Div.* 1. 3–4.
127 Rawson (1985), 304–06; Seneca, *N.Q.*, 2. 39–49.
128 Cicero, *Ad Fam.* 6. 5–9; Rawson (1978, reprinted in Rawson 1991, 289–323).
129 *De Div*, 1. 34, 82–83, 117–18 (= LS 42C-E). Cf., *De Div.* 2. 9–10, and *De Fato* 26–33 (= LS 70 F,G).
130 *De Div*, 1. 7; 1. 6 for Panaetius' doubts.
131 Schofield (1986), p. 63 quoted, with a summary of the work's structure on p. 64.
132 As Cicero points out at 2. 8.
133 *De Div.* 2. 70.
134 2. 148.
135 2. 150.
136 Schofield (1986), 50.
137 See LS 20,55,62, 70G.
138 Criticized by Cicero at *De Fato* 5–7 (= Posidonius, frag. 104 EK).
139 See Sharples (1995).
140 *De Fato* 28–30 (= LS 55S), with Carneades' argument quoted at §31. The "lazy argument" (Greek, *argos logos*; Latin, *ignava ratio*) says that action is useless because what will happen is fated to happen.
141 *De Fato* 46–48, the final sections of the extant text.
142 Cicero, *Ad Fam.* 9. 4. See Griffin (1995), 339–41.
143 *De Div.* 2. 7.
144 Macrobius was Prefect of Italy in 430 CE: see Cameron (1966). There are 230 manuscripts of the *Commentary* and 276 of the *Somnium*: see Reynolds (1983), 222–32.
145 For Zeno's *Politeia* see Schofield (1991), especially chapter 2.
146 Cicero, *De Div.* 2. 3.
147 *De Rep.* 1. 2.
148 See Sharples (1986).
149 Cicero discusses this in a letter to his brother written about the end of October, 54 (*Ad Q. F.* 3. 5. 1).
150 *De Rep.* 1. 14. 3 for political instability in 129.
151 As he recalls at 6. 9. 1.
152 For valuable introductions to *De Republica* see Zetzel (1995) and (1999). The most comprehensive survey of scholarship on the *De Republica* is still Schmidt (1973).
153 1. 15.
154 1. 30–33: 1. 33 quoted.
155 *Ad Q. F.* 3. 5. 1: *de optimo statu civitatis et de optimo cive.*

156 Ennius, frag. 156 Sk: *moribus antiquis res stat Romana virisque.*
157 1. 36: *unum e togatis.*
158 1. 39: *est igitur res publica res populi.* The epigram depends for its effect on a double play on words, reflecting the traditional Roman distinction between public affairs (*res publica*, which can mean "politics" as well as "republic") and private property (*res privata*).
159 1. 45 for the mixed constitution; 1 54 and 69 for Scipio's preference for monarchy.
160 Powell (1994), who (p. 22) refers to "a class of persons designated as *rectores* and helmsmen of the state" and connects Cicero's *rector* with Plato's statesman (*politikos*), "the good man skilled in government" (pp. 24–25).
161 Zetzel (1995), 20.
162 *De Rep.* 2. 1–2.
163 See Astin (1978), 225–26.
164 *De Rep.* 3. 8–31. See pp. 22–3.
165 *De Rep.* 3. 32–41, §33 quoted (= Lactantius, *Inst.* 6. 8. 6–9, and LS 67S).
166 See LS 67, esp. A, K–L: 67S is this passage.
167 See Powell (1994), and cf. note 160 above.
168 For a tactful selection of names see Zetzel (1995), 27.
169 Zetzel (1995), 224.
170 The *Somnium*, however, does have its detractors, for example Kenney (1977), 9: "The elaborate Pythagorean cosmology of the *Somnium Scipionis* is no more than a technicolor backdrop to his [Cicero's] Sunset Home for Retired Statesmen."
171 For an introduction to *De Legibus* see Zetzel (1999), xx–xxiv, with bibliography on xxxv.
172 Text, 2. 19–23; commentary, 2. 24–69.
173 Text, 3. 6–11; commentary, 3. 18–47. The beginning of the commentary is lost, and the work breaks off after 3. 49.
174 *De Leg.* 2. 17.
175 Respectively *Brutus* 306–16 (see pp. 35–7 of this book) and 118–21.
176 *Or.* 8–16: see pp. 34–5.
177 *De Or.* 1. 5.
178 *De Inv.* 2. 8.
179 *De Inv.* 1. 1–5.
180 1. 213.
181 Scaevola was related by marriage to Crassus, Laelius and Marius. Cicero – who compares him, Crassus and Antonius as orators in *Brutus* 139–55 – studied law under him (*Brutus* 306). He is the narrator of Cicero's dialogue *On Friendship.*
182 *De Or.* 3. 9–10.
183 *De Or.* 1. 29.
184 1. 31–34.
185 1. 45–47.
186 1. 211.
187 1. 212.
188 1. 223.
189 1. 224.

190 3. 54–143.
191 3. 142.
192 *Ad Att.* 15. 27. 2; 16. 2. 6 and 6. 4; *De Off.* 2. 31.
193 Val. Max. 8. 14.
194 *De Sen.* 3. Ariston of Ceos was head of the Peripatetic school *c.* 225
　　 BCE. The principal speaker in his dialogue on old age was the ever-
　　 aging Tithonus, loved by Eos (Aurora).
195 Shown in *De Agri Cultura* 2. 56–69 (attitude towards slaves); 2. 143
　　 (attitude towards the female housekeeper).
196 *De Sen.* 56: see Livy 3. 26–29.
197 *De Sen.* 82–84 (§82 quoted).
198 *Ad Fam.* 11. 27, 28. See Griffin (1997b).
199 D. L., 7. 124 (= LS 67P).
200 *De Fin.* 1. 65–70 (Torquatus: = LS 22 O); 2. 82–85 (Cicero: cf. *De
　　 Amic.* 27). For Epicurus' sayings on friendship see D. L. 10. 148 (*K.D.*
　　 27, 28: = LS 22E), and 10. 120; LS 22F. See Rist (1972), 127–39.
201 For Atticus see Rawson (1985), 100–01. She believes that Atticus
　　 "was not a serious Epicurean".
202 *Top.* 1–5.
203 See Barnes, in Barnes and Griffin (1997), 54–57.
204 *Top.* 6.
205 See Sharples (1995).
206 See Stump (1988).
207 *Ad Fam.* 4. 13.
208 *Ad Fam.* 4. 13. 3, 7.
209 *Ad Att.* 15. 13. 6; 16. 11. 4.
210 Horace, *Carm.* 3. 3; Cicero, *De Off.* 3. 99–115.
211 *De Off.* 3. 121.
212 See Astin (1978), 332–40.
213 *Ad Att.* 15. 13. 6.
214 *De Off.* 3. 121.
215 For commentary see Dyck (1996). For translation see Griffin and
　　 Atkins (1991).
216 D. L. 7. 108: "*kathekonta* are the things that reason tells us to do".
217 *Ad Att.* 16. 14. 4; cf. 16. 11. 4.
218 Dyck (1996), 3–8.
219 *Ad Att.* 16. 11. 4.
220 *De Off.* 2. 60.
221 *De Off.* 3. 99–115.
222 *De Off.* 3. 7–8; *Ad Att.* 16. 11. 4; 16. 14. 4.
223 *De Off.* 3. 34.
224 *De Off.* 1. 7, reading *conformari*.
225 *De Off.* 1. 9–10.
226 1. 12–14.
227 1. 18–19 (wisdom); 1. 21–60 (justice).
228 *De Off.* 2. 69–71.
229 *De Off.* 1. 61–92; 1. 78 for Cicero's career.
230 *De Off.* 1. 93–151.
231 *De Off.* 1. 152–60; 1. 153 for the definition of wisdom.
232 *De Off.* 1. 60; cf. 1. 58.
233 *De Off.* 2. 1.

234 *De Off.* 1. 6; 2. 7–8 (cf. 3. 20).
235 *De Off.* 2. 9–10.
236 2. 11–22.
237 2. 23–38.
238 2. 39–51.
239 3. 43–46.
240 2. 52–64.
241 Griffin and Atkins (1991), 91.
242 For example, Horace, *Sat.* 2. 8 and *Ep.* 1. 17 and 18; Seneca, *De Ben.* 6. 33–34; Juvenal, *Sat.* 1, 3, 5.
243 2. 72–85; §85 quoted.
244 2. 88–89.
245 The story of Gyges, 3. 38–39, taken from Plato (*Rep.* 359d–60e), is an exception.
246 3. 1–3.
247 3. 79–85.
248 3. 20–28.
249 Dyck (1996), 492.
250 3. 99–115 (Regulus); 3. 97–98 (Ulysses); 3. 25 (Hercules).
251 3. 100.
252 3. 116–20.
253 See Reynolds (1983), 130–31.
254 Süss (1966), 143; Montaigne, *Essais*, 2. 10.
255 See Douglas (1968), 5. See Mommsen (1856), 3. 619–21 (Dickson, 1883, 4. 724–30). See Drumann (1929), 6. 574–96, for the attack on Cicero, who is the subject of this volume and much of vol. 5. The editor of the second edition, P. Groebe, quotes (p. vii) E. Meyer's estimate that this attack is "a master-example of partisan treatment" and "das bizarrste Produkt deutscher Gelehrsamkeit".
256 In the OCT series, *De Officiis*, ed. M. Winterbottom, 1994; *De Finibus*, ed. L. D. Reynolds, 1998.
257 Wilkinson, L. P., in *CHCL*, 1983, 2. 92.
258 S.v. "Cicero", in *OCPhil.*, 135.
259 See Douglas (1964), especially 157–66.

4 LUCRETIUS AND THE EPICUREANS

1 *Q.F.* 2. 9. 4. For the punctuation of this passage see Sedley (1998), 1 and 203.
2 Cicero, *Ac.* 1. 5–6; *T.D.* 4. 6–7.
3 For Epicurean political participation see Griffin and Barnes (1989); Fowler (1989); Sedley (1997). For Epicureans and the murder of Julius Caesar, see Momigliano (1941), together with Griffin and Barnes (1989), 28–31.
4 Cicero, *De Fin.* 1. 37.
5 Cicero, *Ad Fam.* 15. 15, 16, and 19; see Sedley (1997), 41, and Griffin (1989), 28–31.
6 *Ad Fam.* 15. 16. 1 (which also mentions the death of Catius); 15. 19. 1–2, where Cassius calls Amafinius and Catius "bad translators" (*mali verborum interpretes*).

7 For Philodemus see Philippson (1938); Dorandi (1990); Asmis (1990); Auvray-Assayas and Delattre (2001).

8 See Griffin (2001), who discusses Piso's Epicureanism in the context of his political career.

9 For their story see Sedley (1998), 65–68 and 94–99. For the texts of the papyri see the bibliography in Griffin and Barnes (1989), 259–60.

10 Cicero, *T.D.* 3. 38.

11 Asmis (1990), 2392; see Kuiper, (1925).

12 Col. 12–14 for death in old age (cf. Epicurus *Vatican Sayings* 17); 25. 2 for the bereaved; 25. 37–26. 7 for death in a foreign country (cf. Cic., *T.D.* 5. 107, with the examples of Panaetius and Posidonius).

13 Cols 28. 5 and 37. 27–29; cf. LS 24B (= *Vatican Sayings* 31); Usener, *Epicurea*, fr. 339, ascribes the original saying both to Metrodorus and Epicurus.

14 Nor Philodemus by Lucretius: see Sedley (1998), 65–68.

15 See Sedley (1998), 67–85.

16 Sedley (1998), 91–93.

17 Sedley (1998), 94–165; still useful is Steckel (1968), 601–11 for *De Natura*.

18 D.L. 10. 35–83; cf. Sedley (1998), chart 1, p. 133.

19 D.L. 10. 39–44, 54–62.

20 D.L. 10. 46–53.

21 D.L. 10. 63–67.

22 D.L. 10. 68–71.

23 D.L. 10. 73b–74; Lucr., *DRN* 2. 1048–174.

24 *DRN* 5. 771–1457; D.L. 10. 75–76a.

25 D.L. 10. 76b–82.

26 See the chart in Bailey (1947), 1. 23.

27 Sedley (1998), 138–44.

28 D.L. 10. 84–116.

29 D.L. 10. 91; Lucr., *DRN* 5. 564–613; Cicero, *De Fin.* 1. 20 and *Ac.* 2. 123. See Bailey (1947), 3. 1406–10.

30 D.L. 10. 85–86, 116.

31 D.L. 10. 121–35; §122 quoted (= LS 25A).

32 D.L. 10. 123–24a; Lucr. *DRN* 6. 50–91, with Bailey (1947), 3. 1560; Cicero, *N.D.*, 1. 49 (= LS 23E, with explanation at LS 1. 145); Sedley (1998), 122–23.

33 D.L. 10. 124b–127a (= LS 24A); Lucr., *DRN* 3. 830–1094 (830–31 quoted).

34 D.L. 10. 127b–132 (= LS 21B): 129 quoted.

35 D.L. 10. 133–35 (135 quoted).

36 D.L. 10. 139–54; cf. Cicero, *De Fin.* 2. 20.

37 *Against the Sophists* 4. 9–14; LS 25J; Usener, *Epicurea*, p. 69; cf. Cicero, *De Fin.* 1. 40–41.

38 Cf. Sedley (1998), 163.

39 *KD* 5 (cf. 17).

40 *KD* 33 (31–38 expand on this).

41 *KD* 14 (cf. 39).

42 *KD* 27–28 (cf. 7 and 40); LS 22F (quoting various *Vatican Sayings*).

43 *DRN* 5. 1120–30.

44 *DRN* 2. 1–19.

45 See Schofield (1991), chapter 2.
46 *KD* 27–28.
47 See Sedley (1997), 41 and 46–47; cf. notes 3 and 5 above.
48 See Griffin (2001), especially 88–92.
49 *N.E.* 1155a22.
50 *KD* 10–11.
51 *KD* 12–13.
52 *KD* 18–30; cf. LS 21E–H.
53 In Greek, respectively, *katastematike* and *kinetike*, which has no equivalent in English beyond the Graecism "kinetic".
54 D.L. 10. 127.
55 Plato, *Gorgias* 493a.
56 *DRN* 3. 1007–10. The Danaids were condemned in the Underworld to draw water in jars full of holes.
57 *DRN* 6. 20–21, 25.
58 *DRN* 5. 1117–19.
59 Thuc. 2. 47–54.
60 Lucretius says that he is "speeding towards the finishing-line" (6. 92–93).
61 *DRN* 6. 1–41.
62 Keeping the manuscript reading *cortice* in 4. 43.
63 *DRN* 1. 54–61.
64 *DRN* 1. 136–39.
65 *DRN* 4. 1–9.
66 See Sharples (1996), 12–16.
67 *DRN* 4. 499. See LS 16A (= *DRN* 4. 469–521) and B (= D.L. 10. 31–32).
68 *DRN* 4. 524–614.
69 *OCD*³ 890.
70 Sedley (1998), 58–59.
71 *DRN* 1. 473–77.
72 *DRN* 5. 1036.
73 *DRN* 3. 6–8.
74 *DRN* 1. 55–56.
75 *DRN* 1. 62–135.
76 Sedley (1998), 22, part of an extended discussion, with references to other theories, 1–34.
77 *DRN* 1. 716–62.
78 For example, Spenser, *F.Q.* 4. 10. 44–47.
79 *DRN* 1. 62–79.
80 *DRN* 6. 58–79.
81 *DRN* 1. 84–101.
82 *DRN* 1. 146–48.
83 *DRN* 1. 117–26.
84 *DRN* 1. 150, 215–16, 419–20.
85 *DRN* 2. 62–66 (formation and dissolution); 80–332 (motion); 333–729 (shapes and compounds); 730–990 (secondary qualities); 216–93 (*clinamen*).
86 *DRN* 2. 990–1174; 2. 1048–51 for the limitless void; 1173–74 for the farmer's death.
87 *DRN* 2. 991–98.

88 *DRN* 3. 1–93; 1–30 for praise of Epicurus, 13–30 quoted. Lines 6–8 are quoted on p. 113.
89 *DRN* 3. 94–416.
90 *DRN* 3. 323–69, 417–829.
91 *DRN* 3. 830–1094.
92 *DRN* 3. 830–42; Epicurus, *KD* 2.
93 *DRN* 3. 894–99.
94 D.L. 10. 120. *DRN* 3. 1042 for Epicurus' death.
95 *DRN* 4. 1–25, partially quoted on p. 111.
96 *DRN* 4. 26–44 (29–30 quoted), replacing 4. 45–53.
97 *DRN* 4. 1–822.
98 *DRN* 4. 739–43 for Centaurs; 788–99 for dreams ("latent image" at 796).
99 D.L. 10. 127b–32; *KD* 18–30.
100 *DRN* 5. 117–19; 6. 25.
101 *DRN* 5. 1–54 (7–12 quoted).
102 Bailey (1947), 3. 1393; Sedley (1998), 152–54 (154 quoted).
103 *DRN* 5. 771–924.
104 *DRN* 5. 925–1457; Kenney (1977), 20.
105 *DRN* 5. 1120–35.
106 *DRN* 5. 1194–1203.
107 *DRN* 5. 990–98.
108 *DRN* 6. 1–42.
109 *DRN* 6. 43–534, 535–1137.
110 *DRN* 6. 83–89.
111 *DRN* 6. 379–422, with repetition of 6. 87–89.
112 Cicero, *De Div.* 2. 42–43.
113 *DRN* 6. 379–82.
114 *DRN* 6. 1090–1137; Sedley (1998), 123.
115 Bailey (1947), 3. 1719. It is unlikely that the treatise *On Epidemics* (which does not mention the plague at Athens) was a source.
116 *DRN* 6. 1093–97.
117 *DRN* 6. 1138–1286; Thuc., 2. 47–54.
118 Another Epicurean survivor in public life was L. Calpurnius Piso. For the problem of Cassius' Epicureanism see Sedley (1997) and Momigliano (1941).
119 Virgil, *Geo.* 2. 490–93.
120 Virgil, *Aen.* 1. 742–46.
121 Statius, *Silvae* 2. 7. 76; Quintilian, *Inst.* 10. 1. 87. See Ferguson (1990).
122 Persius, *Sat.* 3. 77–84; Lucretius, *DRN* 1. 150, 248.
123 Seneca, *Ep.* 95. 11, quoting *DRN* 1. 54–57.
124 Seneca, *Ep.* 106. 8, quoting *DRN* 1. 304; 106. 11, 12.
125 Seneca, *Ep.* 110. 6, quoting *DRN* 2. 55–56.
126 Seneca, *De Tranquillitate* 2. 14, quoting *DRN* 3. 1068 (inaccurately). See Kenney (1971), 241, for the view that the use of this idea by later authors places Lucretius "near the source of the Roman tradition of diatribe satire".
127 Gellius, *N.A.* 10. 26. 9, quoting *DRN* 4. 528.
128 See Hershbell (1992 a, b).
129 *An Recte Dictum* 6.
130 See Ferguson (1990), 2326–27.

131 See Mejer (1992: 3586–90 for Epicurus); Gigante (1986) (partly excerpted and translated into German in Gigante, 1992).

132 See Clay (1990): Chilton (1971). For M. Smith's publications see Clay (1990), 2554–56 and 2558, and add Smith (1993).

133 See Clay (1990), 2481–90.

134 *Non Posse* 1094E–1095B.

135 Clay (1990), 2526–48.

136 Clay (1990), 2529, for the Greek text (= frag. 49 Koerte and *Vatican Sayings* 47).

5 PHILOSOPHERS AND POETS IN THE AUGUSTAN AGE

1 Augustus' words in *Res Gestae* 34 are: *rem publicam ex mea potestate in senatus populique Romani arbitrium transtuli*: "I transferred the republic from my power into the disposal of the senate and people of Rome." This implies transference of the government, since the Republic (so Augustus implies) had continued to exist throughout the period of the second triumvirate and the years that followed the collapse of the triumvirate.

2 Tacitus, *Ann.* 1. 3. 7: *eadem magistratuum vocabula*.

3 Tacitus, *Dialogus* 38. 2.

4 Tacitus wrote his history of the period 69–96 CE first, with the title *Historiae*, followed by the *Annales*, the history of the period 14–68 CE (the terminal date is not definite, since the extant work breaks off in 66).

5 See Griffin (1976), 38–40.

6 Seneca, *N.Q.* 7. 32. 1–2.

7 Seneca, *Ep.* 59. 7–8, 64. 2.

8 Seneca, *Ep.* 64. 3.

9 Griffin (1976), 38, note 8; Seneca, *Ep.* 107. 17–22; Sorabji (1993), 125.

10 Seneca, *Ep.* 100. 9.

11 Quintilian, *Inst.* 10. 1. 124.

12 See Mansfeld (1990), especially 3179–83.

13 See Hahm (1990), especially 3035–47 and 3234–43.

14 Hahm (1990), 2939.

15 For the Stoic doxography see Pomeroy (1999).

16 Plutarch, *Ant.* 80–81; Suetonius, *Aug.* 89. 1; further references in Hahm (1990), 3035.

17 Dio, 51. 16. 4; Seneca, *Cons. ad Marc.*, 4. 2; Marcus Aurelius, *Med.* 8. 31.

18 Seneca, *Cons. ad Marc.* 4–5, §5. 5 quoted.

19 Long (1986), 75–76; LS 71–72.

20 As Horace himself says, *Sat.* 1. 6. 76–78.

21 *Ep.* 2. 2. 42–45, written in about 19 BCE.

22 The *Epodes* were published as a whole in 30 BCE; Book 1 of the *Satires* was finished perhaps in 35 BCE, and Book 2 in 30 BCE.

23 Fraenkel (1957), vii.

24 *Ep.* 1. 4: *Epicuri de grege porcum* is at line 16.

25 *Ep.* 1. 1, lines 10–14 quoted.

26 D.L. 2. 77.

27 Xenophon, *Mem.* 2. 21–34 (cf. Cicero, *De Off.* 1. 118); Seneca, *De Vita Beata* 17–23.

28 *Ep.* 1. 1. 41, 106–08.
29 *Ep.* 1. 2. 3. Chrysippus (d. 207 BCE) was head of the Stoic school, and Crantor (d. 275 BCE) was a member of the early Academy.
30 *Ep.* 1. 18 (lines 96–112 quoted).
31 Fraenkel (1957), 309.
32 *Sat.* 1. 5. 105–31; cf. *Sat.* 1. 6. 81–84. Quoted are *Sat.* 1. 4. 116–17, where the speaker is Horace's father.
33 *Sat.* 1. 3. 96–98, further developed in lines 113–42.
34 D.L. 10. 135.
35 *Ep.* 2. 2. 60. Diogenes Laertius, 4. 46–58, includes Bion with the Academics, but he says (4. 51) that he became a Cynic. His style of lecturing was certainly Cynic.
36 The word "diatribe" is controversial: see the lucid article by Moles, J. L., in *OCD³* 463–64, s.v. "diatribe". Diogenes Laertius, 2. 77, calls Bion's lectures "Diatribes".
37 *Ridentem dicere verum*, *Sat.* 1. 1. 24; *de te fabula narratur*, *Sat.* 1. 1. 69–70.
38 See *Sat.* 2. 2. 55–66, for criticism of the "dog" Avidienus, and cf. Griffin (1996), 196. Kiessling-Heinze, however, in their commentary on 2. 55, deny any connection between Avidienus' epithet, *canis*, and Cynicism.
39 Fifteen friends are named in *Sat.* 1. 10. 81–86.
40 See Lebek (1981).
41 *Essay on Criticism* 653–56.
42 V. P., 2. 88. 2.
43 While the notion of having poverty as one's wife is similar to Cynic doctrine, the metaphor of being clothed in virtue was used by Plato, *Rep.* 5. 457a: "the guardians' wives will be clothed in virtue". *Virtus* in Horace, however, has the added connotation of *Roman* manliness.
44 *DRN* 6. 400–01.
45 D.L. 10. 133–34.
46 *DRN* 3. 912–17.
47 The mention of Ancus Martius (third king of Rome) in line 15 alludes to Lucretius, *DRN* 3. 1025.
48 Ferguson (1990), 2269.
49 For example, Bacchus, source of poetic inspiration, in *Odes* 2. 19 and 3. 25.
50 *Aurea mediocritas*, *Odes* 2. 10. 5. Cf. Aristotle, *N.E.* 1106a26–29.
51 *Ep.* 1. 1. 14.
52 *Catalepton* 5. 8–10, 8. 1–5; *Vita Donati* 35.
53 *Arg.* 1. 496–511.
54 *Aen.* 1. 740–46.
55 *Geo.* 2. 475–94, 477–82 quoted.
56 *Geo.* 2. 483–89.
57 *Geo.* 2. 490–94. Cf. Aristotle, *Post. An.* 2. 645a5, for "those who are able to know causes".
58 *Geo.* 2. 495–522: cf. *DRN* 2. 1–19.
59 *Geo.* 2. 523–40.
60 *Geo.* 3. 1–48.
61 *Geo.* 4. 219–27; 210–18 for the bees' social coherence.

62 *Geo.* 4. 559–66, 563–64 quoted.

63 *Aen.* 6. 703–51.

64 *Aen.* 6. 756–853.

65 For Juno's centrality see Johnson (1976), esp. 114–34.

66 *Aen.* 1. 277–78.

67 *Aen.* 10. 112.

68 *Menin, Iliad* 1. 1.

69 *Aen.* 12. 946–47. Virgil had used the phrase "set on fire by furies" of Dido (4. 376) and of Amata and the Latin matrons (7. 392).

70 The standard-bearer of this school is Putnam (1986: 1st edn, 1965), 151–201. For a summary of the present state of opinion and bibliography see Hardie (1998), especially 99–101.

71 Galinsky (1988) and (1994).

72 LS 65A, E, G; Arius Didymus in Stobaeus 2. 10a–c (= Pomeroy [1999] 56–60).

73 The principal source for Epicurean doctrine on anger is Philodemus, *On Anger*: see the analysis by Asmis (1990), 2395–99. Note also Lucretius, *DRN* 3. 319–22.

74 Aristotle, *N.E.* 1126a–b.

75 Aristotle, *Rhet.* 1178a30.

76 Cf. Cicero, *T.D.* 4. 43–50.

77 Horace, *Ep.* 1. 2. 62: *ira furor brevis est.*

78 Hardie (1998), 100. Martindale (1993, 51) aptly calls Virgil's ambiguities "energizing contradictions".

79 *Tristia* 4. 10, lines 103–04 quoted.

80 *Tristia* 4. 10. 35–40 (*otium*); 103–04 (exile).

81 See Myers (1994).

82 *Met.* 6. 687–701.

83 Compare Lucretius, *DRN* 6. 96–159 (thunder); 160–322 (lightning); 557–84 (earthquakes), and Seneca, *N.Q.* 2. 12–59 (thunder and lightning); 6. 20 (earthquakes, quoting Democritus and Epicurus).

84 *Met.* 15. 75–478. The traditional dates for Numa's reign are 715–673 BCE, while Pythagoras came to Croton *c.*530. The impossibility of the meeting is pointed out by Cicero, *De Rep.* 2. 28–29, and Livy, 1. 18. 2. For the speech see Myers (1994), 133–65.

85 *Met.* 15. 6: *quae sit rerum natura requirit.*

86 *Met.* 15. 60, *vir Samius; DRN* 1. 66, *Graius homo.*

87 *Met.* 15. 62–64.

88 *Met.* 15. 66–72.

89 *Met.* 15. 75–142, 456–78. Sorabji (1993) has many references to Pythagoras: note 130–33 and 172–75.

90 *Met.* 15. 143–455; 143–51 for inspiration and authority (contrast *DRN* 1. 102–03).

91 *Met.* 15. 153–57.

92 *Met.* 15. 262–72 (flood: cf. *Met.* 1. 262–347); 273–417 (natural wonders); 420–52 (cities and peoples).

93 *Met.* 15. 147–52.

94 Myers (1994), 158.

95 *Met.* 15. 871–79.

96 1. 7–10; 4. 764.

97 1. 113–14. There were earlier astrological works: the names of Nechepso and Petosiris are attached to an influential Greek treatise on astrology of *c.*150 BCE (of which only fragments are extant). They may be among the "priests" mentioned by Manilius in 1. 47 as founders of the discipline of astrology. See Barton (1994), 26–29.

98 1. 483–92.

99 Cicero, *De Div.* 1. 91.

100 *De Div.* 2. 87–99; 2. 9 (Carneades); 2. 88 (Panaetius).

101 Manilius, 1. 66–112 (96–98 quoted); Lucretius, 5. 925–1497.

102 4. 866–935 (885 and 886–97 quoted).

103 4. 932: *ratio omnia vincit.*

104 1. 250: *vis animae divina regit.*

105 2. 115–16: *quis caelum posset nisi caeli munere nosse,/et reperire deum, nisi qui pars ipse deorum est?*

106 4. 12–16. In Latin line 16 reads: *nascentes morimur, finisque ab origine pendet.*

107 4. 108–09, 114–15.

6 SENECA AND HIS CONTEMPORARIES

1 Tac., *Ann.* 4. 34–35.

2 Sen., *N.Q.* 7. 32. 1–2. André (1987, 35), however, believes that philosophy still "occupied an important place in social and cultural life".

3 Lucan, *B.C.* 1. 639–72.

4 See Richardson (1992), 57, s.v. "Basilica Subterranea".

5 Seneca, *Ep.* 49. 2, 108. 17–21.

6 Sen., *Ep.* 108. 22, evidently referring to the suppression of Egyptian and Jewish rites in 19 CE (Tac., *Ann.* 2. 85. 4), for these sects forbade the eating of pork. In 16 CE, by decrees of the senate, astrologers and magicians (*mathematici magique*) were expelled from Italy, and two were executed (Tac., *Ann.* 2. 32. 3).

7 For Chaeremon see Frede (1989).

8 Sen., *Ep.* 90. 7–10.

9 *Ann.* 16. 35. 1.

10 Tac., *Hist.* 4. 40. 3; *Ann.* 16. 32.

11 Dio 66. 13. Vespasian was punning on the Greek word *kynikos*, "dog-like".

12 *Ben.* 7. 1; *Ep.* 62. 3.

13 *Ep.* 62 3.

14 See Rutherford (1989), 81–82; André (1987), 53.

15 See *PIR²* A616. His first name is not known. He was born before 43 BCE and died between 37 and 41 CE.

16 Sen. Rhet. *Contr.* 2, *Praef.* 2.

17 *Contr.* 2. 10–13.

18 Cf. Seneca, *Ep.* 87, especially 39–41.

19 *N.Q.* 3. 27. 3.

20 *Suas.* 2. 12.

21 *Ep.* 110. 13–20.

22 *Inst.* 10. 1. 125–31.

23 Sandbach (1975), 149, 161. For a review of *iudicia super Senecam* see Boyle (1983), 1–5.

24 The editions of Seneca mentioned were published as follows: Erasmus, Basel: Froben, 1515, 2nd edn, 1529; Lipsius, Antwerp: Moretus, 1605, 2nd edn 1615; Muretus, Rome: Grassi and Zannetti, 1585–86; Gruter, Heidelberg: Commelin, 1592, and Paris: Sonnius, 1599.

25 Guillemin (1952–54 and 1957).

26 *Ann.* 1. 3. 7.

27 *De Clem.* 1. 1.

28 *N.Q.* 1. 16–17.

29 *Ep.* 16. 5.

30 *Ep.* 107. 8–10.

31 *Ep.* 107. 11. This fragment of Cleanthes' *Hymn to Zeus* is known only in this quotation.

32 *De Const.* 7. 1.

33 See Griffin (1968).

34 *De Const.* 2. 1–2.

35 *De Const.* 7. 1.

36 *De Off.* 1. 46, possibly adapting Panaetius.

37 Cf. LS 59I (= *SVF* 3. 510), where Chrysippus says that the person who has progressed to the furthest point is still not truly happy, because his actions lack "firmness and stability".

38 Suetonius, *Claud.* 38.

39 See Braden (1985), 28–62.

40 *De Ira* 1. 3. 3–8. Sorabji (1993), 60–61, finds Seneca's discussion of anger in animals "entirely implausible".

41 The doctrine is stated in *De Ira* 1. 5.

42 *De Ira* 1. 21. 4.

43 *De Ira* 2. 19–21. Plato is concerned, for example, with the effect of music and wine on children's emotions in *Laws* 2. 664b–666c (cf. *De Ira* 2. 20. 2).

44 *De Ira* 3. 3. 1 (cf. 1. 9. 2, 1. 17. 1); Aristotle, *NE* 1116b23–31.

45 *De Ira* 3. 42. 2–43. 5 (42. 2 and 43. 1 and 5 quoted).

46 See Fillion-Lahille (1989).

47 *De Ben.* 7. 1. 3–7. Examples of specific topics are "Should one be outdone in giving benefits?" (5. 2–6) and "Should one ask for the repayment of a benefit?" (5. 20. 6–25).

48 *Ep.* 81. 3 (the injured beneficiary); 10–13 (the *sapiens*).

49 *De Ben.* 1. 6. 1.

50 *De Ben.* 3. 18–28.

51 Cicero, *De Off.* 3. 63, 89.

52 Aristotle, *Pol.* 1253b32–1254a15. For Seneca see Griffin (1976), 256–85; Manning (1989), especially 1525–31.

53 See Griffin (1976), 315–66 (chapter 10, "The Philosopher on Political Participation").

54 See Schofield (1991), chapter 2.

55 Cicero, *De Fin.* 5. 65.

56 Schofield (1991), 102.

57 *De Tranq.* 3–4 (4. 3–4 quoted). There were two philosophers from Tarsus with the name of Athenodorus: this one was probably son of Sandon and was a friend of Cicero and Augustus.

58 *Inst.* 11. 1. 35; cf. Sen., *Ep.* 55. 4.

59 *Ep.* 96. 5; 120. 18.

60 Tacitus, *Ann.* 16. 28. 2.
61 *De Otio* 3. 5.
62 *De Otio* 4. 1–2.
63 *De Ira* 3. 15. 4.
64 See Griffin (1976), 367–88; Grisé (1982), chapter 7.
65 Tacitus, *Ann.* 15. 64. 4; Plato, *Phaedo* 118a, where Socrates instructs his friends to offer a cock to Asclepius as a thank-offering for liberation from the disease of life.
66 D.L. 7. 130.
67 *Ep.* 24. 22–25, quoting and agreeing with Epicurus.
68 *Ep.* 30. 1–3, 12.
69 Tacitus, *Ann.* 15. 62–64.
70 See Barnes (1997), 12–23, whose arguments are followed here; Griffin (1976), 175, accepts the traditional view that Seneca "had nothing but contempt" for rhetoric and dialectic.
71 See Barnes (1997), 12–13, for a selection of warnings to Lucilius against the trivialities of logic, e.g. *Ep.* 113. 26.
72 See Barnes (1997), 21–23; Griffin (1976), 175, "Seneca's interest in physics was intense".
73 He was Nero's speech-writer (Tac., *Ann.* 13. 3. 1); he was impotent to prevent Britannicus' murder (13. 14. 3) and probably rewarded for his silence after the murder (13. 18. 1, which does not mention him by name); he did nothing to prevent the murder of Agrippina (14. 7. 3–4).
74 Tac., *Ann.* 13. 42. 4; Dio 61. 10,
75 Macaulay (1900), 14. 114.
76 Lipsius (1615), xi.

7 STOICISM UNDER NERO AND THE FLAVIANS

1 *Hist.* 1. 4. 2.
2 Examples are Epictetus and Plutarch (in Greece), Apuleius (in Africa), Favorinus (in Gaul and Greece, settling later in Rome).
3 *Demosthenes* 2.
4 See Anderson (1989): Bowersock (1969), despite the criticisms of Brunt (1994). Brunt (37) rightly says that the "efflorescence of Greek oratory ... was an illusion" (an idea credited to Wilamowitz) and denies that the second-century sophists "absorbed or dominated the literary and intellectual life of the second century AD". His statement (46), that "Plutarch's ... curiosity and a capacity for rational argument ... sets him on an intellectual level far above that of Epictetus", is bizarre.
5 *Med.* 1. 7.
6 Rutherford (1989), 81, part of his discussion, 80–89.
7 For Favorinus see Holford-Strevens (1997); for Galen and the sophists, Brunt (1994), 43–46, demolishing Bowersock (1969), chapter 5.
8 Justin Martyr, executed in 165 CE, seems to be a rare example. He was condemned, however, for his Christian beliefs.
9 Dio 62. 2.
10 *PIR*^{2} H59; Tac., *Hist.* 4. 5–9; Suet., *Vesp.* 15.
11 See Griffin (1997b), 194–97.
12 Dio 65. 13.

13 Gellius 15. 11. 1, omitting the expulsion of 74; Suetonius, *Dom.* 10. 3.

14 Tacitus, *Agricola* 45 (published in 98); Pliny, *Ep.* 3. 11. 3, written shortly after 100. Arulenus had published a eulogy of Thrasea, and Herennius one of Helvidius (Tac., *Agr.* 2). Pliny also says that Titinius Capito was publishing [accounts of] "the deaths of distinguished men, including some who were very dear to me" (*Ep.* 8. 12. 4, written after 100).

15 Pliny, *Ep.* 7. 19: Fannia's spirit was "most worthy of her husband Helvidius and her father Thrasea".

16 See Most (1989). The standard text for Cornutus is Lang (1881).

17 Plato, *Gorgias* 493a.

18 Nock (1931): Lapidge (1989), esp. 1402–05.

19 See Saccone (1985) for bibliography. Few scholars have discussed Persius' philosophy: still the best is Casaubon (1605).

20 Seneca, *Ep.* 114. 1: *talis hominibus fuit oratio qualis vita.*

21 Juvenal, *Sat.* 13. 120–23. Persius' phrase "harvest of Cleanthes" (5. 64) is explicitly Stoic, for example.

22 Pichon (1912), 165–216, 216 quoted.

23 *B.C.* 10. 194–331; Seneca *N.Q.* 4. 1–2. Cf. Lucretius, *DRN* 6. 712–37.

24 Kirk and Raven (1957), 439–40, no. 613; Seneca, *N.Q.* 4. 1. 28–30.

25 *B.C.* 1. 70–80.

26 *B.C.* 7. 809–15.

27 Due (1970), 214 quoted.

28 *B.C.* 2. 7–11. Cf. Lapidge (1989), 1386–90, 1407.

29 The most important are *B.C.* 1. 583–696 (series of prophecies concerning the coming war); 5. 67–236 (Delphic oracle); 6. 413–830 (Erictho's necromancy); 7. 151–205 (omens and signs presaging battle). See Le Bonniec (1970), especially 182–91; Morford (1967), 59–74.

30 *B.C.* 7. 207–13.

31 *B.C.* 6. 611–17.

32 *B.C.* 5. 515–31.

33 This has led Johnson to portray Lucan's Cato in a witty but misguided chapter ("Cato: the Delusions of Virtue") as a caricature, inhuman, a bore, and "funny": Johnson (1987), 35–66.

34 *B.C.* 2. 234–391; Cf. Plutarch, *Cato Min.* 25 and 52, and see the measured remarks of Fantham (1992), 138–39.

35 *B.C.* 9. 186–293 (assumption of leadership), 294–949 (desert march).

36 *B.C.* 9. 511–86 (564–80 quoted).

37 *B.C.* 9. 581–84.

38 Cf. Seneca, *N.Q.* 1, *Praef.* 13; *Ep.* 41. 1–2, 4–5.

39 *B.C.* 9. 601–04.

40 *B.C.* 4. 593–653.

41 The praise of Nero, *B.C.* 1. 33–66, cannot be taken as a serious expression of theological or philosophical views.

42 *B.C.* 9. 455–59 and 445–47.

43 *B.C.* 5. 504–677, 632–36 quoted: see Morford (1967), 20–58.

44 *B.C.* 7. 695, 433.

45 *B.C.* 3. 145–46.

46 *B.C.* 7. 43.

47 *B.C.* 8. 493–95.

48 *B.C.* 4. 404–581, 575–79 quoted.
49 *B.C.* 8. 610–36.
50 *Life of Rowe*, in Johnson (1973), 398.
51 For biographical details see *PIR*² M753 (1987, the fullest); Von Fritz (1935). For the philosophy of Musonius see Laurenti (1989).
52 Tac., *Hist.* 3. 81.
53 Tac., *Hist.* 4. 10, 40.
54 Pliny, *Ep.* 3. 11. 5–7: see Sherwin-White (1966), 240–44, who says that Musonius "was the first to apply philosophy to senatorial politics", certainly an exaggeration.
55 Pliny, *Ep.* 10. 1 (§10 quoted).
56 Epictetus, *Disc.* 4. 8. 17–20.
57 Epictetus, *Disc.* 1. 7. 30–33 = Musonius, frag. 44.
58 *Discourse* 6 (p. 22, Hense, 1990): cf. Seneca, *Ep.* 90. 46 (quoted).
59 See Laurenti (1989), 2113–20; cf. Hijmans (1959).
60 Cicero, *De Off.* 1. 79, 67.
61 Seneca, *Cons. ad Marciam*, 16. 1–4.
62 *Disc.* 4. 17, lines 12–13 and 21–22, Hense.
63 *Disc.* 13a, pp. 69–70, Hense.
64 *Disc.* 13b.
65 Lucan himself was an attentive husband, and his wife continued to love and honour his memory long after his death, as Statius tells us in *Silvae* 2. 7.
66 Van Geytenbeek (1962), 159.
67 Tac., *Ann.* 15. 71. 4.

8 FROM EPICTETUS TO MARCUS AURELIUS

1 The known facts of Epictetus' life are discussed by Dobbin (1998), xi–xiv. Epictetus refers to his experience as a slave at 1. 9. 29 and 1. 19. 20–21.
2 *Disc.* 3. 23. 30.
3 Barnes (1997) devotes chapter 3 (pp. 24–125) to Epictetus; in *Appendix*, 129–45, he adds text, translation and commentary on *Disc.* 1. 7. See also Dobbin (1998), 113–18, for excellent commentary.
4 *Disc.* 1. 7. 30–33.
5 The authorship of the *Discourses* is discussed by Dobbin, 1998, xx–xxiii, supporting the view that Epictetus was the author.
6 As late as the sixth century CE the Neoplatonist Simplicius wrote a vast commentary on the *Handbook*.
7 See the discussion by Dobbin (1998), 65–78, who sketches the background of the topic in Aristotle and Chrysippus. He notes that by using the second-person address ("You ...") Epictetus reinforces the impression of the individual's freedom of choice.
8 See Hershbell (1989), especially 2159–60; Dobbin (1998), 76–77.
9 *Disc.* 3. 1. 40: cf. 4. 5. 12.
10 *Disc.* 3. 22. 20. Cf. Musonius, fr. 38 (= Epictetus, fr. 4).
11 *Disc.* 3. 24. 95.
12 *Disc.* 3. 22. 52.
13 *Disc.* 3. 12. 1–4.
14 *Disc.* 3. 2 (§§1–2 quoted).

15 *Disc.* 3. 2. 4.
16 *Disc.* 3. 2. 5.
17 In *Disc.* 1. 4, for which see Dobbin (1998), 88–98.
18 See Barnes (1997), chapter 3 *passim*, especially 33–42.
19 *Disc.* 3. 12. 7.
20 *Disc.* 3. 12. 12: cf. Persius, *Sat.* 3. 109–11.
21 Plato, *Apology* 38A.
22 As Epictetus himself reports at *Disc.* 1. 7. 32.
23 Aulus Gellius, *N.A.* 17. 19 (= Epictetus, fr. 10).
24 *Disc.* 1. 24. 6–10; 3. 22. 24–25.
25 Seneca, *De Prov.* 4. 7–8.
26 *Disc.* 1. 24. 3–5. Since Domitian had banished philosophers from Rome the "scout's" mission was dangerous.
27 *Disc.* 3. 22. 53. "Know yourself" refers to the long-revered Greek principle inscribed on the temple of Apollo at Delphi.
28 *Disc.* 4. 8. 35.
29 *Disc.* 3. 22. 86–92. For Epictetus' more extended views on the subject of cleanliness, see *Disc.* 4. 11.
30 In 3. 22. 30–44 the Cynic shows Agamemnon how inferior his quality of life is to that of the philosopher.
31 3. 22. 62–76. Epictetus admits that the marriage of Crates and Hipparchia was a special case.
32 *Disc.* 3. 22. 97. The theme is an old one in Roman literature. In the second century BCE Terence wrote: "I am a human being: nothing that is human is irrelevant to me" (*Heaut.* 77).
33 As the Loeb translator, W. A. Oldfather, among others, has said of *Disc.* 3. 22. Even Barnes (1997), who is generally sympathetic to Epictetus, says (25): "he offered to the world a pin-striped cynicism, Diogenes without the barrel", hardly a fair comment on *Disc.* 3. 22 and 4. 11.
34 *Disc.* 3. 22. 94, following a portrait of the Cynic as having a guiding principle (*hegemonikon*) "purer than the sun", and a pure conscience that is a more powerful defence than the military guards that protect kings. Epictetus quotes the same line from the *Hymn to Zeus* at *Disc.* 2. 23. 42 and 4. 1. 131.
35 *Disc.* 3. 22. 100–06.
36 *Disc.* 1. 16. 17–21.
37 See Swain (1997), especially 177–81, for the change in the second century from *Academicus* to *Platonikos*.
38 See pp. 127–28. See Hershbell (1992a).
39 See Hershbell (1992b).
40 Cf. Cicero, *Pro Murena* 60–66; see p. 24.
41 LS 61I (= D. L. 7. 127); cf. LS 61T, U (= Plutarch, *On Common Conceptions* 1063a–b and 1062b).
42 *Moral Progress* 75d–f.
43 *SVF* 3. 527 (= D. L. 7. 120, quoting Chrysippus; 3. 529 (= LS 59 O).
44 *SVF* 2. 1152–54. The problem of animal intelligence is discussed by Sorabji (1993), 160–61 for *Gryllus* and 178–79 for Plutarch.
45 Sorabji (1993), 9, takes the debate back to Alcmaeon of Croton (*c.*500 BCE), who said that human beings have understanding, while animals

have perception. The crucial stage was Aristotle's denial of reason and belief in animals (Sorabji, 1993, 12–16).

46 Cf. Seneca, *Ep.* 121; Epictetus, *Disc.* 2. 8. See Tsekourakis (1987).

47 See Cherniss (1976), 369–411.

48 See Cherniss (1976), 622–59.

49 D.L. 7. 89 (= *SVF* 3. 39, 228).

50 *De Comm. Not.* 1060B–D. The Greek word for "common conceptions" is *ennoiai*, as in *SVF* 2. 104.

51 For the unity of the categories of Stoic philosophy see Long (1986), 118–21.

52 See Hershbell (1992), 3344–45.

53 Plutarch, *Cato* 67–70; *Otho* 16–17. Plutarch notes, however, that Cato was reading "Plato's dialogue about the soul" (i.e. *Phaedo*) before his suicide. In Plutarch, *Brutus* 40 (quoted above, p. 45), Brutus distinguishes between Academic and Stoic attitudes to suicide. Cf. p. 49 for Cato's suicide.

54 *Phocion.* 3. 4; the next quotation is from 3. 9.

55 See Plutarch, *De Comm. Not.* 1085C–D (= *SVF* 2. 444 and LS 47G).

56 See Harrison (2000), 1–10, for details of his life. Sandy (1997) discusses his education (chapter 1) and his relationship to the second sophistic (especially chapters 2–3).

57 See Harrison (2000) for discussion of Apuleius' works; also Hijmans, B. L., "Apuleius Philosophus Platonicus", in *ANRW* 2. 36. 1 (1987), 395–475; Sandy (1997), chapters 4–5.

58 Note the subtitle of Harrison (2000): *Apuleius: A Latin Sophist.*

59 *Florida* is discussed by Harrison (2000), chapter 3, 89–135 (103–04 for §7; 126–27 for §20). Quotations are from the Teubner text edited by R. Helm, Leipzig, 1910.

60 *Florida* 20. 97–98, probably from a speech in praise of Carthage.

61 *Camena togatorum, Camena* being the Latin equivalent of the Greek *Mousa.*

62 See Harrison (2000), chapter 4 (136–73) for *De Deo Socratis*; chapter 5 (174–209) for *De Mundo* and *De Platone.* Harrison (11–12) is sceptical about the authenticity of *Peri Hermeneias*, which is accepted by Hijmans (1987) and Sandy (1997), who discusses all these works in chapter 5. For introduction, text, translation (French) and commentary on the three authentic works see Beaujeu (1973), who (vii–viii) does not think that the *Peri Hermeneias* is authentic.

63 *De Deo Soc.* 132–33.

64 *Symp.* 202d–e.

65 See Harrison (2000), 195–209, especially 196–203 for a comparison of the two works; cf. Beaujeu (1973), 49–59.

66 See Harrison (2000), 174–95, with useful summary on 181–82. Cf. Beaujeu (1973), 111–19 and commentary on 309–37.

67 See Harrison (2000), chapter 6, 210–59.

68 *Met.* Book 11: §§5 and 23 quoted. See Harrison 235–38 for interpretations of Book 11, together with the enormous bibliography on Book 11. He inclines "towards an interpretation of a largely parodic and satirical kind" (p. 238), seeing the purpose of the novel as "pleasure and not enlightenment" (p. 259). It is hard to see how the passionate conversion of Book 11 is in any way "parodic and satirical".

69 See Rives (1995), for religious structure and practice in Africa under the Roman empire. His discussion is relevant to Apuleius, even though the setting for *Met.* 11 is in Greece. See Rives (1995), 190–91, for *Met.* 11. 5, seeing this text and others like it as "an expression of the tendency towards monotheism"; 262–63 for the initiation of Lucius, seen more as a genuine religious document, in particular as a "type of religious authority, based on control of secret yet essential religious knowledge".

70 He is no. A697 in *PIR2* (pp. 119–24; 121 for his adoptive names), s.v. M. Annius Verus.

71 See Brunt (1974); Asmis (1989); Rutherford (1989).

72 *Med.* 1. 14. *PIR2* C1022 is the philosopher Claudius Severus, identified with C1027, the consul of 146 CE; C1023 is the son-in-law of Marcus, consul in 173 CE.

73 *Med.* 1. 7. See Rutherford (1989), 225–50.

74 *Med.* 1. 11. See Champlin (1974).

75 *Med.* 1. 7.

76 *Med.* 1. 16; cf. 6. 30.

77 *Med.* 1. 16. 3.

78 *Med.* 6. 30. 2.

79 See Asmis (1989), 2337–45.

80 *Med.* 2. 1.

81 *Med.* 2. 5.

82 *Med.* 6. 30.

83 *Med.* 6. 44.

84 *Med.* 5. 6.

85 *Med.* 11. 18. See Brunt (1974), 4–5, 11–12.

86 Plutarch, *De Ira* 460D; Aristotle, *Rhet.* 1380a9.

87 *Med.* 3. 6.

88 See Rutherford (1989), 178–220.

89 *Med.* 2. 3.

90 *Med.* 7. 9.

91 Rutherford (1989), 213.

92 *Med.* 4. 23.

93 *Med.* 10. 15.

94 See Bowersock (1969), 59–75, criticized by Brunt (1994), 43–46, who denies any connection between Galen and the sophists.

95 The standard edition of Galen's works is Kühn (1821–33; reprinted 1964). *Quod Optimus Medicus* is in Vol. 1; *De Placitis Hippocratis et Platonis* in Vol. 5; *De Libris Propriis* and *De Ordine* in Vol. 19. The texts of *Quod Optimus*, *De Libris*, and *De Ordine* are in Mueller 1891 (repr. 1967), Vol. 2. The text of *Institutio Logica* (first published in 1844) is edited by Kalbfleisch (1896); introduction, translation and commentary by Kieffer (1964). See also Donini (1992); Hankinson (1992); Hülser (1992).

96 See Barnes (1990); Allen (1990).

97 *Cons.* 5. 6.

REFERENCES

BOOKS

Astin, A. E., *Scipio Aemilianus*, Oxford: Clarendon Press, 1967.

—— *Cato the Censor*, Oxford: Clarendon Press, 1978.

Auvray-Assayas, C. and Delattre, D., *Cicéron et Philodème: la Polémique en Philosophie (Études de Littérature Ancienne 12)*, Paris: École Normale Supérieure, 2001.

Bailey, C., *T. Lucreti Cari De Rerum Natura Libri Sex*, 3 vols, Oxford: Clarendon Press, 1947.

Barnes, J., *Logic and the Imperial Stoa (Philosophia Antiqua 75)*, Leiden: Brill, 1997.

Barnes, J. and Griffin, M., *Philosophia Togata II: Plato and Aristotle at Rome*, Oxford: Clarendon Press, 1997.

Barton, T., *Ancient Astrology*, London: Routledge, 1994.

Beaujeu, J., *Apulée: Opuscules Philosophiques et Fragments*, Paris: Les Belles Lettres (Éditions Budé), 1973.

Bowersock, G. W., *Greek Sophists in the Roman Empire*, Oxford: Clarendon Press, 1969.

Boyle, A. J., *Seneca Tragicus*, Berwick, Victoria, Australia: Aureal Press, 1983.

Braden, G., *Renaissance Tragedy and the Senecan Tradition: Anger's Privilege*, New Haven: Yale University Press, 1985.

Branham, R. Bracht and Goulet-Cazé, M.-O., *The Cynics*, Berkeley: University of California Press, 1996.

Brittain, C., *Philo of Larissa*, Oxford: Oxford University Press, 2001.

Buechner, C., *Fragmenta Poetarum Latinorum*, Leipzig: Teubner, 1982.

Casaubon, I. (ed.), *Auli Persi Flacci Satirarum Liber*, Paris: Drouart, 1605.

Cherniss, H. (ed. and trans.), *Plutarch: Moralia XIII.2* (Loeb Classical Library 470), Cambridge, Mass.: Harvard University Press, 1976.

Chilton, C. W., *Diogenes of Oenoanda: the Fragments*, Oxford: Clarendon Press, 1971.

Clarke, M. L., *The Noblest Roman: Marcus Brutus and his Reputation*, London: Thames and Hudson, 1981.

Courtney, E., *A Commentary on the Satires of Juvenal*, London: Athlone Press, 1980.

—— *The Fragmentary Latin Poets*, Oxford: Clarendon Press, 1993.

Dobbin, R., *Epictetus: Discourses, Book I*, Oxford: Clarendon Press, 1998.

Dorey, T. A., *Cicero*, London: Routledge, 1964.

Douglas, A. E., *Cicero (Greece and Rome, New Surveys in the Classics* 2), Oxford: Clarendon Press, 1968.

Drumann, W., *Geschichte Roms*, 2nd edn, 1929 (reprinted Hildesheim: Olms, 1964: first edn, 1844).

Dudley, D. R., *A History of Cynicism from Diogenes to the Sixth Century A.D.*, London: Methuen, 1937.

Durry, M., *Lucain (Entretiens sur l'Antiquité Classique 15)*, Geneva: Vandoeuvres, 1970.

Dyck, A. R., *A Commentary on Cicero, De Officiis*, Ann Arbor, MI: University of Michigan Press, 1996.

Edelstein, L. and Kidd, I. G., *Posidonius, Vol. I: The Fragments*, Cambridge: Cambridge University Press, 1972.

Fantham, E. (ed.), *Lucan, De Bello Civili II*, Cambridge: Cambridge University Press, 1992.

Fraenkel, E., *Horace*, Oxford: Clarendon Press, 1957.

Furley, D. J., *From Aristotle to Augustine* (Routledge History of Philosophy, Vol. II), London: Routledge, 1999.

Griffin, M., *Seneca: a Philosopher in Politics*, Oxford: Clarendon Press, 1976 (2nd edn, 1992).

Griffin, M. and Atkins, E. M., *Cicero: On Duties*, Cambridge: Cambridge University Press, 1991.

Griffin, M. and Barnes, J. (eds), *Philosophia Togata I: Essays on Philosophy and Roman Society*, Oxford: Clarendon Press, 1989 (corrected edition, 1997).

Grisé, Y., *Le Suicide dans la Rome Antique*, Montreal: Bellarmin and Paris: Les Belles Lettres, 1982.

Hardie, P., *Virgil (Greece and Rome New Studies in the Classics 28)*, Oxford: Clarendon Press, 1998.

Harrison, S. J., *Apuleius: A Latin Sophist*, Oxford: Oxford University Press, 2000.

Hense, O. (ed.), *Musonii Rufi Reliquiae*, Leipzig: Teubner, 1905 (reprinted 1990).

Hijmans, B. L., *ASKESIS: Notes on Epictetus' Educational System (Wijsgerige Teksten en Studies 2)*, Assen: van Gorcum, 1959.

Inwood, B. and Mansfeld, J., *Assent and Argument: Studies in Cicero's Academic Books (Philosophia Antiqua 76)*, Leiden: Brill, 1997.

Johnson, S., *Lives of the Poets*, Oxford: Clarendon Press, 1973 (1st edn, 1789–91).

Johnson, W. R., *Darkness Visible*, Berkeley: University of California Press, 1976.

Kalbfleisch, K., *Galenus: Institutio Logica*, Leipzig: Teubner, 1896.

Kenney, E. J., *Lucretius De Rerum Natura, Book III*, Cambridge: Cambridge University Press, 1971.

—— *Lucretius (Greece and Rome New Surveys in the Classics*, 11), Oxford: Clarendon Press, 1977.

Kidd, I. G., *Posidonius, Vol. II: The Commentary*, Cambridge: Cambridge University Press, 1988.

—— *Posidonius, Vol III: The Translation of the Fragments*, Cambridge: Cambridge University Press, 1999.

Kieffer, J. S., *Galen's Institutio Logica*, Baltimore: Johns Hopkins Press, 1964.

Kirk, G. S. and Raven, J. E., *The Presocratic Philosophers*, Cambridge: Cambridge University Press, 1957.

Kühn, C. G. (ed.), *Galeni Opera Omnia*, 20 vols, Leipzig, 1821–33 (repr. Hildesheim: Olms, 1964).

Kuiper, T., *Philodemus over den Dood*, Amsterdam: H. J. Paris, 1925.

Lang, C. (ed.), *Cornuti Theologiae Graecae Compendium*, Leipzig: Teubner, 1881.

Lesky A., *A History of Greek Literature* (trans. J. Willis and C. de Heer), London: Methuen, 1966.

Lipsius, J. (ed.), *Opera Omnia L. Annaei Senecae*, 2nd edn, Antwerp: Moretus, 1615.

Long, A. A., *Problems in Stoicism*, London: Athlone Press, 1971.

—— *Hellenistic Philosophy*, 2nd edn, Berkeley: University of California Press, 1986.

Macaulay, T. B., *Complete Works*, Boston: Houghton Mifflin, 1900.

McKendrick, P., *The Philosophical Books of Cicero*, London: Routledge, 1989.

Martindale, C., *Redeeming the Text*, Cambridge: Cambridge University Press, 1993.

Maurach, G., *Geschichte der Römischen Philosophie*, 2nd edn, Darmstadt: Wissenschaftliche Buchgesellschaft, 1997.

Mommsen, T., *Römische Geschichte*, Berlin, 1856 (trans. Dickson, W. G., *History of Rome*, New York: Scribner, 1883).

Morford, M., *The Poet Lucan*, Oxford: Blackwell, 1967.

Mueller, I. (ed.), *Galenus: Scripta Minora*, Leipzig: Teubner, 1891 (reprinted Stuttgart, 1967).

Myers, K. S., *Ovid's Causes: Cosmogony and Aetiology in the Metamorphoses*, Ann Arbor: University of Michigan Press, 1994.

Ogilvie, R. M., *A Commentary on Livy, Books 1–5*, Oxford: Clarendon Press, 1965.

Pichon, R., *Les Sources de Lucain*, Paris: Leroux, 1912.

Plasberg, O., *M. Tullii Ciceronis Paradoxa Stoicorum, Academicorum Reliquiae cum Lucullo, etc.*, Leipzig: Teubner, 1908.

Pomeroy, A., *Epitome of Stoic Ethics: Arius Didymus*, Atlanta: Society of Biblical Studies (Texts and Translations, Graeco-Roman Series, 14), 1999.

Powell, J. G. F., *Cicero the Philosopher*, Oxford: Clarendon Press, 1995.

Putnam, M., *Poetry in the Aeneid*, 2nd edn, Ithaca: Cornell University Press, 1986 (1st edn, 1965).

Rawson, E., *Intellectual Life in the Late Roman Republic*, Baltimore: Johns Hopkins Press, 1985.

—— *Roman Culture and Society*, Oxford: Clarendon Press, 1991.

Reid, J. S., *Cicero: Academica*, London: Macmillan, 1881.

Reinhardt, K., *Kosmos und Sympathie: Neue Untersuchungen über Poseidonios*, Munich: Beck, 1926.

Reynolds, L. D., *Texts and Transmission*, Oxford: Clarendon Press, 1983.

Richardson, L., *A New Topographical Dictionary of Ancient Rome*, Baltimore: Johns Hopkins Press, 1992.

Rist, J. M., *Epicurus: an Introduction*, Cambridge: Cambridge University Press, 1972.

Rives, J. B., *Religion and Authority in Roman Carthage from Augustus to Constantine*, Oxford: Clarendon Press, 1995.

Rutherford, R. B., *The Meditations of Marcus Aurelius*, Oxford: Oxford University Press, 1989.

Sandbach, F. H., *The Stoics*, London: Chatto and Windus, 1975.

Sandy, G. N., *The Greek World of Apuleius: Apuleius and the Second Sophistic* (*Mnemosyne*, Supplement 174), Leiden: Brill, 1997.

Schofield, M., *The Stoic Idea of the City*, Cambridge: Cambridge University Press, 1991.

Sedley, D., *Lucretius and the Transformation of Greek Wisdom*, Cambridge: Cambridge University Press, 1998.

Sharples, R. W., *Stoics, Epicureans and Sceptics*, London: Routledge, 1996.

Sherwin-White, A. N., *The Letters of Pliny: a Historical and Social Commentary*, Oxford: Clarendon Press, 1966.

Smith, M. F., *The Epicurean Inscription of Diogenes of Oenoanda*, Naples: Bibliopolis, 1993.

Sorabji, R., *Animal Minds and Human Morals*, Ithaca: Cornell University Press, 1993.

Stephens, W. O., *The Ethics of the Stoic Epictetus: an English Translation*, New York: Lang, 1996 (translation of Bonhoeffer, A. F., *Die Ethik des Stoikers Epictet*, Stuttgart: Enke, 1894).

Stump, E., *Boethius's In Ciceronis Topica*, Ithaca: Cornell University Press, 1988.

Süss, W., *Cicero: Eine Einführung in seine Philosophische Schriften*, Wiesbaden: Verlag der Akad. der Wiss. und Lit. in Mainz, 1966.

Syme, R., *The Roman Revolution*, Oxford: Clarendon Press, 1939.

Tarrant, H., *Scepticism or Platonism?*, Cambridge: Cambridge University Press, 1985.

Travlos, J., *Pictorial Dictionary of Ancient Athens*, New York: Praeger, 1971.

Usener, H., *Epicurea*, Leipzig: Teubner, 1887.

Van Geytenbeek, A. C., *Musonius Rufus and Greek Diatribe (Wijsgerige Teksten en Studies 8)*, Assen: van Gorcum, 1962 (original Dutch edition, Amsterdam: H. J. Paris, 1948).

Van Straaten, M., *Panaetii Rhodii Fragmenta*, 3rd edn, Leiden: Brill, 1962 (1st edn, *Panétius, sa Vie, ses Écrits et sa Doctrine*, Amsterdam, 1946).

Zetzel, J. E. G., *Cicero: De Re Publica*, Cambridge: Cambridge University Press, 1995.

—— *Cicero: On the Commonwealth and On the Laws*, Cambridge: Cambridge University Press, 1999.

ARTICLES AND BOOK CHAPTERS

Allen, J., "The Skepticism of Sextus Empiricus", *ANRW* II. 36. 4 (1990), 2582–607.

Anderson, G., "Sophists and their outlook", *ANRW* II. 33. 1 (1989), 80–208.

André, J.-M., "Les écoles philosophiques aux deux premiers siècles de l'Empire", *ANRW* II. 36. 1 (1987), 5–77.

Asmis, E., "The Stoicism of Marcus Aurelius", *ANRW* II. 36. 3 (1989), 2228–52.

—— "Philodemus' Epicureanism", *ANRW* II. 36. 4 (1990), 2369–406.

Barigazzi, A., "Favorino di Arelate", *ANRW* II. 34. 1 (1993), 556–81.

Barnes, J., "Antiochus of Ascalon", in Griffin, M. and Barnes, J. (eds), *Philosophia Togata I: Essays on Philosophy and Roman Society*, Oxford: Clarendon Press, 1989 (corrected edition, 1997), pp. 51–86.

—— "Pyrrhonism, belief and causation. Observations on the Scepticism of Sextus Empiricus", *ANRW* II. 36. 4 (1990), 2608–95.

—— "Logic in the *Academica* and the *Lucullus*", in Inwood, B. and Mansfeld, J. (eds), *Assent and Argument: Studies in Cicero's Academic Books (Philosophia Antiqua 76)*, Leiden: Brill, 1997a, pp. 140–60.

—— "Roman Aristotle", in Barnes, J. and Griffin, M., *Philosophia Togata II: Plato and Aristotle at Rome*, Oxford: Clarendon Press, 1997b, pp. 1–69.

Beard, M., "Cicero and divination: the formation of a Latin discourse", *JRS* 76 (1986), 33–46.

Brunt, P. A., "Marcus Aurelius in his *Meditations*, *JRS* 64 (1974), 1–20.

—— "The bubble of the Second Sophistic", *BICS* 39 (1994), 25–52.

Cameron, A., "The date and identity of Macrobius", *JRS* 56 (1966), 25–38.

Champlin, E., "The chronology of Fronto", *JRS* 64 (1974), 136–59.

Clay, D., "The philosophical inscription of Diogenes of Oenoanda: new discoveries 1969–1983", *ANRW* II. 36. 4 (1990), 2446–559, 3231–32.

Donini, P., "Galeno e la Filosofia", *ANRW* II. 36. 5 (1992), 3484–504.

Dorandi, T., "Filodemo: gli orientamenti della ricerca attuale", *ANRW* II. 36. 4 (1990), 2328–68.

Douglas, A. E., "Cicero the Philosopher", in Dorey, T. A., *Cicero*, London: Routledge, 1964, pp. 135–70.

Due, O. S., "Lucain et la Philosophie", in Durry, M., *Lucain (Entretiens sur l'Antiquité Classique 15)*, Geneva: Vandoeuvres, 1970, pp. 201–24.

Ferguson, J., "Epicureanism under the Roman empire", *ANRW* II. 36. 4 (1990), 2257–327 (revised by J. Hershbell).

Fillion-Lahille, J., "La production littéraire de Sénèque sous les règnes de Caligula et de Claude, sens philosophique et portée politique: les "Consolationes" et le "De Ira", *ANRW* II. 36. 3 (1989), 1606–38.

Fowler, D., "Lucretius and politics", in Griffin, M. and Barnes, J. (eds), *Philosophia Togata I: Essays on Philosophy and Roman Society*, Oxford: Clarendon Press, 1989 (corrected edition, 1997), pp. 120–50.

Fowler, P. and Fowler, D., "Lucretius", *OCD³* (1989), 888–90

Frede, M., "Chaeremon", *ANRW* II. 36. 3 (1989), 2067–103.

—— "The Skeptics", in Furley, D. J., *From Aristotle to Augustine* (Routledge History of Philosophy, Vol. II), London: Routledge, 1999, pp. 253–86.

Galinsky, G. K., "The anger of Aeneas", *AJP* 109 (1988), 321–48.

—— "How to be philosophical about the end of the *Aeneid*", *Illinois Classical Studies* 19 (1994), 191–201.

Gigante, M., "Biografia e Dossografia in Diogene Laerzio", *Elenchos* 7 (1986), 7–102.

—— "Das Zehnte Buch des Diogenes Laertius: Epikur und der Epikureismus", *ANRW* II. 36. 6 (1992), 4302–07.

Gottschalk, H. B., "Aristotelian philosophy in the Roman world from the time of Cicero to the end of the second century A.D.", *ANRW* II. 36. 2 (1989), 1079–174.

Goulet-Cazé, M.-O., "Le Cynisme à l'Époque Impériale", *ANRW* II. 36. 4 (1990), 2720–2833.

Goulet-Cazé, M.-O., "Le Livre Vi de Diogène Laerce: étude de sa structure et réflexions méthodologiques", *ANRW* II. 36. 6 (1992), 3880–4048.

Griffin, M., "Seneca on Cato's politics: *Epistle* 14. 12–13", *CQ* 18 (1968), 373–75.

Griffin, M., "Philosophy, politics and politicians", in Griffin, M. and Barnes, J. (eds), *Philosophia Togata I: Essays on Philosophy and Roman Society*, Oxford: Clarendon Press, 1989 (corrected edition, 1997), pp. 1–37.

—— "Philosophical badinage in Cicero's letters to his friends", in Powell, J. G. F., *Cicero the Philosopher*, Oxford: Clarendon Press, 1995, pp. 325–46.

—— "Cynicism and the Romans: attraction and repulsion", in Branham, R. Bracht and Goulet-Cazé, M-O., *The Cynics*, Berkeley: University of California Press, 1996, pp. 190–204.

—— "The composition of the *Academica*: motives and versions", in Inwood, B. and Mansfeld, J., *Assent and Argument: Studies in Cicero's Academic Books (Philosophia Antiqua 76)*, Leiden: Brill, 1997 (1997a), pp. 1–35.

—— "From Aristotle to Atticus: Cicero and Matius on friendship", in Barnes, J. and Griffin, M., *Philosophia Togata II: Plato and Aristotle at Rome*, Oxford: Clarendon Press, 1997, pp. 86–109.

—— "Piso, Cicero and their audience", in Auvray-Assayas, C. and Delattre, D., *Cicéron et Philodème: la Polémique en Philosophie (Études de*

Littérature Ancienne 12), Paris: École Normale Supérieure, 2001, pp. 85–99.

Guillemin, A.-M., "Sénèque, Directeur d'Âmes", *REL* 30 (1952), 202–19; 31 (1953), 215–34; 32 (1954), 250–74.

—— "Sénèque, Second Fondateur de la Prose Latine", *REL* 35 (1957), 265–84.

Hahm, D. E., "Posidonius's theory of historical causation", *ANRW* II. 36. 3 (1989), 1325–63.

—— "The ethical doxography of Arius Didymus", *ANRW* II. 36. 4 (1990), 2935–3055.

—— "Diogenes Laertius VII: on the Stoics", *ANRW* II. 36. 6 (1992), 4076–182, 4404–11.

—— "Plato, Carneades, and Cicero's Philus (Cicero, *Rep.* 3. 8–31)", *CQ* 49 (1999), 167–83.

Hankinson, R. J., "Galen's philosophical eclecticism", *ANRW* II. 36. 5 (1992), 3505–22.

Hershbell, J., "The Stoicism of Epictetus", *ANRW* II. 36. 3 (1989), 2148–63.

—— "Plutarch and Epicureanism", *ANRW* II. 36. 5 (1992a), 3353–83.

—— "Plutarch and Stoicism", *ANRW* II. 36. 5 (1992b), 3336–52.

Hijmans, B. L., "Apuleius Philosophus Platonicus", *ANRW* II. 36. 1 (1987), 395–475.

Holford-Strevens, L., "Favorinus: the man of paradoxes", in Barnes, J. and Griffin, M., *Philosophia Togata II: Plato and Aristotle at Rome*, Oxford: Clarendon Press, 1997, pp. 188–217.

Hülser, K., "Galen und die Logik", *ANRW* II. 36. 5 (1992), 3523–54.

Kidd, I. G., "Posidonius on Emotions", in Long, A. A., *Problems in Stoicism*, London: Athlone Press, 1971, pp. 200–15.

Krueger, D., "The bawdy and society: the shamelessness of Diogenes in Roman imperial culture", in Branham, R. Bracht and Goulet-Cazé, M.-O., *The Cynics*, Berkeley: University of California Press, 1996, pp. 222–39.

Lapidge, M., "Stoic cosmology and Roman literature, first to third centuries A.D.", *ANRW* II. 36. 3 (1989), 1379–429.

Laurenti, R., "Musonio, Maestro di Epitteto", *ANRW* II. 36. 3 (1989), 2105–46.

Lebek, W. D., "Horaz und die Philosophie: die *Oden*", *ANRW* II. 31. 3 (1981), 2031–92.

Le Bonniec, H., "Lucain et la Religion", in Durry, M., *Lucain (Entretiens sur l'Antiquité Classique 15)*, Geneva: Vandoeuvres, 1970, pp. 159–95.

Long, A. A., "Cicero's Plato and Aristotle", in Powell, J. G. F., *Cicero the Philosopher*, Oxford: Clarendon Press, 1995, pp. 37–61.

Manning, C. E., "Stoicism and slavery in the Roman empire", *ANRW* II. 36. 3 (1989), 1518–43.

Mansfeld, J., "Doxography and dialectic. The *Sitz im Leben* of the *Placita*", *ANRW* II. 36. 4 (1990), 3026–229.

Mejer, J., "Diogenes Laertius and the transmission of Greek philosophy", *ANRW* II. 36. 5 (1992), 3556–603.

Mette, H. J., "Weitere Akademiker heute: von Lakydes bis zu Kleitomachos", *Lustrum* 27 (1985), 39–148.

—— "Philon von Larisa und Antiochos von Askalon", *Lustrum* 28–29 (1986–87), 9–63.

Michel, A., "Rhétorique et Philosophie au second siècle après J-C", *ANRW* II. 34. 1 (1993), 3–78.

Moles, J. L., "Diatribe", *OCD*³, 463–64.

Momigliano, A., Review of B. Farrington, *Science and Politics in the Ancient World*, *JRS* 31 (1941), 149–57 (repr. in *Secondo Contributo alla Storia degli Studi Classici*, Rome, 1960).

Most, G. W., "Cornutus and Stoic allegoresis: a preliminary report", *ANRW* II. 36. 3 (1989), 2014–65.

Nisbet, R., "Persius", in Sullivan, J. P. (ed.), *Critical Essays on Roman Literature: Satire*, Bloomington: Indiana University Press, 1968, pp. 39–71.

Nock, A. D., "Kornutos", *RE*, Suppl. 5 (1931), 995–1005.

—— "Posidonius", *JRS* 49 (1959), 1–15.

Parente, M. Isnardi, "Ierocle Stoico. Oikeiosis e doveri sociali", *ANRW* II. 36. 3 (1989), 2201–26.

Pelling, C. B., "Plutarch: Roman heroes and Greek culture", in Griffin, M. and Barnes, J. (eds), *Philosophia Togata I: Essays on Philosophy and Roman Society*, Oxford: Clarendon Press, 1989 (corrected edition, 1997), 199–232.

—— "Marcus Tullius Cicero: die philosophischen Schriften", *RE* VII A1 (1939), 1104–92.

Philippson, R., "Philodemos", *RE* XIX (1938), 2444–82.

Powell, J. G. F., "The *rector rei publicae* of Cicero's *De Republica*", *Scripta Classica Israelica* 13 (1994), 19–29.

Rawson, E., "Caesar, Etruria and the *Disciplina Etrusca*", *JRS* 68 (1978), 132–52 (reprinted in Rawson, E., *Roman Culture and Society*, Oxford: Clarendon Press, 1991, pp. 289–323).

Reckford, K. J., "Studies in Persius", *Hermes* 90 (1962), 476–504.

Rist, J. M., "The problem of friendship", in Rist, J. M., *Epicurus: an Introduction*, Cambridge: Cambridge University Press, 1972, pp. 127–39.

Saccone, M. S., "La Poesia di Persio (1964–83)", *ANRW* II. 33. 3 (1985), 1781–812.

Schmidt, P. L., "Cicero *De Re Publica*: die Forschung der letzten fünf Dezennien", *ANRW* I. 4 (1973), 262–333.

Schofield, M., "Cicero for and against divination", *JRS* 76 (1986), 47–65.

Sedley, D., "The ethics of Brutus and Cassius", *JRS* 87 (1997), 41–53.

Sharples, R. W., "Cicero's *Republic* and Greek political theory", *Polis* 5 (1986), 30–50.

—— "Causes and necessary conditions in the *Topica* and the *De Fato*", in Powell, J. G. F., *Cicero the Philosopher*, Oxford: Clarendon Press, 1995, pp. 247–71.

Steckel, H., "Epikuros", *RE*, Suppl. 11 (1968), 579–652.

Striker, G., "Academics fighting academics", in Inwood, B. and Mansfeld, J., *Assent and Argument: Studies in Cicero's Academic Books (Philosophia Antiqua 76)*, Leiden: Brill, 1997, pp. 257–76.

Swain, S., "Plutarch, Plato, Athens, and Rome", in Barnes, J. and Griffin, M., *Philosophia Togata II: Plato and Aristotle at Rome*, Oxford: Clarendon Press, 1997, pp. 165–87.

Tsekourakis, D., "Pythagoreanism or Platonism and ancient medicine? The reasons for vegetarianism in Plutarch's *Moralia*", *ANRW* II. 36. 1 (1987), 366–93.

Von Fritz, K., "Musonius", *RE* XVI (1935), 893–97.

PHILOSOPHERS NAMED IN
THE TEXT

[All dates are BCE unless indicated by CE]

AENESIDEMUS 1st. cent., former Academic and founder of Pyrrhonist revival at Rome.

ANAXAGORAS early 5th. cent., pre-Socratic enquirer into the origin and nature of the cosmos.

ANDRONICUS mid-first cent., Peripatetic; editor of Aristotle's works.

ANTIOCHUS OF ASKALON early 1st. cent., Academic who reverted to Plato's dogmatism.

ANTIPATER OF TYRE 1st. cent., Stoic; teacher of Cato Uticensis.

APOLLONIDES mid-1st. cent., Stoic; adviser of Cato Uticensis.

APOLLONIUS OF TYANA 1st. cent. CE, Neopythagorean; a wandering guru and subject of a biography by Philostratus.

APULEIUS OF MADAURUS ca.125–180 CE, orator and Platonic philosopher, author of *Metamorphoses*.

ARCESILAUS mid-3rd.cent., Academic sceptic, head of the New Academy.

ARISTIPPUS OF CYRENE late-5th. cent., member of Socrates' circle.

ARISTON OF CEOS 3rd. cent., Peripatetic and head of the Lyceum.

ARISTOTLE 384–322, founder of the Peripatetic school.

ARISTUS early 1st. cent., head of the Academy and teacher of Brutus.

ARIUS DIDYMUS 1st. cent., philosopher and doxographer, adviser to Augustus.

ARTEMIDORUS 1st. cent. CE, perhaps a Stoic; friend of Pliny the Younger and son-in-law of Musonius.

ATHENODORUS KORDYLION of Tarsus, mid-1st. cent., Stoic and adviser to Cato Uticensis, in whose house he lived.

ATHENODORUS SANDON of Tarsus, mid-first cent., Stoic and friend of Cicero.

ATTALUS 1st. cent. CE, Stoic; teacher of Seneca.

AUGUSTINE 354–430 CE, Bishop of Hippo; orator, Neoplatonist philosopher and one of the Fathers of the Christian church.

BION OF BORYSTHENES ca. 335–245, Cynic philosopher (for the most part) and popular teacher.

BOETHIUS ca. 480–524 CE, philosopher and politician, with Stoic and Neoplatonist views; author of the *Consolation of Philosophy*.

CARNEADES mid-2nd. cent., head of the New Academy; sceptic and star of the Athenian embassy to Rome in 155.

CHAEREMON OF ALEXANDRIA mid-1st. cent., CE, Stoic; tutor to Nero.

CHRYSIPPUS ca. 280–206, head of the Stoic school from 232 and one of its most influential early figures.

CICERO, M. TULLIUS 106–43, orator, statesman and leading transmitter of Hellenistic philosophy to Rome and Renaissance Europe. Follower of the New Academy and pupil of Philo of Larissa.

CLEANTHES 331–232, Zeno's successor as head of the Stoic school from 262 and, with Zeno and Chrysippus, one of the most important figures in early Stoicism.

CLITOMACHUS late-2nd. cent., Sceptic and pupil of Carneades; head of the New Academy from 127.

CORNUTUS OF LEPCIS 1st. cent. CE, Stoic; teacher and friend of Persius and Lucan.

CRANTOR ca. 335–275, Academic, the first commentator on Plato, and an influential writer on grief.

CRATES OF THEBES ca.365–285, Cynic, follower of Diogenes of Sinope and teacher of Zeno of Citium.

CRATIPPUS mid-1st. cent., Peripatetic; friend of Cicero and Nigidius and teacher at Athens of Cicero's son.

CRITOLAUS first half of 2nd. cent., head of the Peripatetic school and member of the Athenian embassy to Rome in 155.

DEMETRIUS THE CYNIC 1st. cent. CE, friend of Seneca.

DEMETRIUS THE PERIPATETIC mid-1st.cent., adviser of Cato Uticensis.

DEMOCRITUS OF ABDERA second half of 5th. cent., pre-Socratic philosopher and founder of atomism.

DICHAEARCHUS OF MESSANA late 4th. cent., Peripatetic, pupil of Aristotle and prolific author.

DIODOTUS first of 1st.cent., Stoic, teacher and friend of Cicero, in whose house he lived.

DIOGENES LAERTIUS first half of 3rd. cent. CE, doxographer and author of *Lives of the Philosophers*.

DIOGENES OF APOLLONIA second half of 5th. cent., pre-Socratic philosopher and enquirer into the natural world; a source for Seneca's *Naturales Quaestiones*.

DIOGENES OF BABYLON mid-2nd. cent., head of the Stoic school and member of the Athenian embassy to Rome in 155; teacher of Panaetius.

DIOGENES OF OENOANDA late 2nd. cent. CE, Epicurean and part-author of the inscription on the stoa which he caused to be set up in Oenoanda.

DIOGENES OF SINOPE mid-4th.cent., founder of Cynicism.

EPICTETUS OF HIERAPOLIS (in Phrygia) ca. 50–120 CE, Stoic, pupil of Musonius, an ex-slave and head of his own school at Nicopolis.

EPICURUS 341–271, founder of Epicureanism and principal source for Lucretius' poem.

EUPHRATES late-1st. cent. CE, Stoic; student of Musonius and friend of Pliny the Younger.

FAVORINUS OF ARELATE (Arles), ca. 85–155 CE, philosopher of the Second Sophistic, friend of Plutarch and teacher of Fronto.

GALEN OF PERGAMUM late-second cent. CE, physician to Marcus Aurelius, medical writer and Platonist philosopher.

HECATO OF RHODES early 1st. cent., Stoic, pupil of Panaetius and member of circle of Posidonius.

HERMARCHUS OF MYTILENE first half of 3rd. cent., pupil of Epicurus and his successor as head of the Epicurean school from 271; with Epicurus, Metrodorus and Polyaenus, one of "The Four Men", founders of the Epicurean school.

HIEROCLES early 2nd. cent. CE, Stoic philosopher and writer on ethics.

LAELIUS, GAIUS ca. 190–125, consul in 140; friend of Scipio Aemilianus and Panaetius and called by Cicero the first Roman philosopher.

LEUCIPPUS second half of 5th. cent., co-founder with Democritus of atomism.

LUCRETIUS first half of 1st. cent., Epicurean poet, author of *De Rerum Natura*.

MANILIUS, MARCUS late-1st. cent. BCE and early-1st. cent CE, Stoic author of poem on astrology, *Astronomica*.

MARCUS AURELIUS (M. Annius Verus), 121–180 CE, Roman emperor (161–180) and Stoic, author of *To Himself*, a private diary known also as *Meditations*.

MENIPPUS OF GADARA first half of 3rd. cent., Cynic and satirical author in prose and verse on philosophical subjects.

METRODORUS OF LAMPSACUS ca. 331–278, friend of Epicurus and one "The Four Men", founders of Epicureanism.

MODERATUS OF GADES second half of 1st. cent. CE, Neopythagorean philosopher and numerologist.

MUSONIUS RUFUS second half of 1st. cent. CE, Roman of Etruscan descent, Stoic; teacher of Epictetus.

NIGIDIUS FIGULUS 1st. cent., Neopythagorean scholar and expert on astrology.

PANAETIUS OF RHODES ca. 185–109, Stoic, head of the Stoic school from 129; influential at Rome, friend of Scipio Aemilianus and major source for Cicero's *De Officiis*.

PARMENIDES OF ELEA first half of 5th. cent., pre-Socratic philosopher and poet, pioneer enquirer into the nature of "what is".

PATRON first half of 1st. cent., friend of Cicero and successor of Phaedrus as head of the Epicurean school.

PHAEDRUS ca. 140–70, Epicurean philosopher admired by Cicero; head of the Epicurean school in the last years of his life.

PHILO OF ALEXANDRIA first half of 1st. cent. CE, Jewish philosopher, sympathetic to Stoic ethics and influential in the later development of Neoplatonism.

PHILO OF LARISSA ca.159–84, head of the New Academy, 110–88; the most influential of Cicero's teachers.

PHILODEMUS OF GADARA ca. 110–40, Epicurean philosopher; protegé of Piso Caesoninus and an influence on Virgil and Horace; many of his fragmentary writings are preserved in the Herculaneum papyri.

PLATO ca. 429–347, founder of the Academy and disciple and interpreter of Socrates.

PLOTINUS 205–270 CE, Neoplatonist philosopher, perhaps an Egyptian but resident in Rome and Campania. The most important of 3rd. century CE philosophers and architect of the revival of Neoplatonism.

PLUTARCH OF CHAERONEA (L. Mestrius Plutarchus) ca. 50–120 CE, Platonist philosopher, biographer and polymath.

POLEMO died 270, Platonist and head of the Academy from 314.

POLYAENUS OF LAMPSACUS died before 271, friend of Epicurus and one of "The Four Men", founders of Epicureanism.

POSIDONIUS OF APAMEA ca. 135–50, Stoic philosopher and historian, student of Panaetius and head of his own school in Rhodes, where Cicero heard him. The dominant figure in middle Stoicism, whose works encompassed the whole range of intellectual enquiry.

PYRRHO OF ELIS ca. 365–270, the founder of Scepticism, whose doctrines were revived at Rome by Aenesidemus.

PYTHAGORAS OF SAMOS 6th. cent., founder of Pythagoreanism and head of a community at Croton in S. Italy; he emphasized the importance of number and proportion, and his doctrines included vegetarianism and the transmigration of souls. He influenced Plato and his philosophy was revived at Rome by Nigidius Figulus and the Sextii.

RUSTICUS, JUNIUS consul in 133 and 162 CE, Stoic; friend and teacher of Marcus Aurelius.

SENECA, LUCIUS ANNAEUS, 4 BCE-65 CE, Stoic philosopher and politician; tutor, adviser and victim of Nero; prolific author of tragedies and philosophical treatises, including *Dialogi* and *Epistulae Morales*.

SEVERUS, CLAUDIUS consul in 146 CE, Stoic friend and teacher of Marcus Aurelius, whose son married his daughter.

SEXTIUS, QUINTUS mid-1st. cent., Neopythagorean, founder of the only genuinely Roman school of philosophy; admired by Seneca for his disciplined Roman ethos.

SEXTUS EMPIRICUS late-2nd. cent. CE, Sceptic, author of philosophical and medical works and critic of Stoicism; principal source for Pyrrhonism.

SIRO 1st. cent., Epicurean, teacher in Campania of Virgil.

SOCRATES 469–399, iconic Athenian philosopher and one of the most influential figures in Greek philosophy; he wrote nothing but is the central figure in Plato's dialogues; admired by non-Academics, including the Stoic Marcus Aurelius nearly six hundred years after his death.

SOTION 1st. cent. CE, Neopythagorean, teacher of Seneca.

SPEUSIPPUS ca. 407–339, Plato's successor as head of the Academy.

TELES OF MEGARA second half of 3rd. cent., Cynic, author of diatribes on ethical subjects.

THEOPHRASTUS 372–287, Peripatetic, successor to Aristotle as head of the Lyceum from 322.

VARRO, MARCUS TERENTIUS 116–27, Academic, Roman polymath, author of works on language, agriculture, history and philosophy, as well as satires, and principal speaker in the later version of Cicero's *Academica*.

XENOCRATES OF CHALCEDON died 314, head of the Academy from 339.

ZENO OF CITIUM 335–263, founder of Stoicism; originally a follower of the Cynic Crates, he taught at Athens in the Stoa Poikile, which gave its name to his school.

ZENO OF SIDON ca. 155–75, head of the Epicurean school at Athens, where he taught Philodemus and was heard by Cicero.

PASSAGES DISCUSSED

GENERAL INDEX

Porcia 45–46
Posidonius 4, 11, 12–13, **28–33**, 34,
  38–39, 63, 65, 67, 89, 122, 162,
  185, 224, 238; *History* 32–33; *On
  the Emotions* 31; *On Ocean* 29; *Peri
  Kathekontos* 89
Pothinus 202
principate, *princeps* 6, 131–32, 136
Prodicus 138
proficiens 174–76
prohairesis 210–11, 215, 218
Prometheus 147, 154
prose style: 34, 99; of Apuleius 226; of
  Cicero 5, 37, 44, 59, 77, 96; of
  Seneca 8–9, 167, 187
Protagoras 190
providence 26, 67–68, 169–71,
  236–37, 239
Prusa 204
Pydna 3, 15–18, 20
Pyrrho, Pyrrhonism 11–12, 39–41,
  133, 136, 238
Pythagoras, Pythagoreanism 2, 56, 87,
  133–34, 149–50, **155–57**, 160,
  161–62

Quintilian 46, 126, 166–67, 181

Rabirius 98
ratio (*phronesis*, reason) 11, 26, 31, 37,
  58, 104, 108–09, 158–60, 174,
  176–78, 184, 195, 206, 209, 214
rector reipublicae 72, 74–75
Regulus 88–89, 93–94, 144
Religion, in Lucretius 113–15, 122–23
rhetoric 14–15, 20–22, 34–36, 38, 56,
  79–82, 164–66, 190–91, 226–27,
  231
Rhodes 4, 28, 38–39
Romulus 63, 65
Rubellius Plautus 161, 191, 203
Rusticus, Q. Junius 191, 231–32
Rutilius Rufus 29, 71

Sallust 49–50, 95
Sallustius 98
sapiens, wise man 21–22, 23, 25, 37,
  55, 58, 82, 85, 133, 139, 141, 159,
  163, 169–70, **172–76**, 178, 183,
  198–201, 211, 222–23
Scaevola, P. Mucius 63; Q. Mucius 80,
  84, 251n.181
sceptics, scepticism 11–12, 37, 39–42,
  64–65, 101, 136, 185, 215
schesis 235
Scipio Aemilianus, 1, 2, 3, 4, 9, 16–17,

19, 23–27, 29, 56, **69–78**, 81,
  83–84, 167
Scipio Africanus (Maior), 16, 75–77;
  (Minor) 16
Scipio, Nasica (cos. 162 BCE) 63
Second Sophistic 10, 190–91, 226
Sejanus 161
Seneca, Annaeus (the elder) 164–65
Seneca, L. Annaeus, 1, 8–10, 20, 29,
  33, 34, 49, 62, 67, 92, 96, 126–27,
  132–36, 138, **161–88**, 189, 191,
  193–99, 201–03, 205, 208,
  211–12, 214, 216–17, 221, 223,
  224, 239; prose style 8–9, 34, 166,
  227; *Consolationes* 168–69; *De
  Beneficiis* 169, **178–79**; *De Clementia*
  168–69, 176; *De Constantia* 169,
  172–73; *De Ira* **176–78**; *De Otio* 62,
  180–81; *De Providentia* 67–68,
  169–71, 183, 198; *De Tranquillitate*
  62, 127, **180–81**; *De Vita Beata*
  186–87; *Dialogi* 168–69; *Epistulae
  Morales* 25, 33, 60, 126–27,
  168–69, 178–79, 183–86, 194,
  198, 207, 222; *Naturales Quaestiones*
  9, 65, 169, 185–86; *Phaedra* 168;
  Thyestes 168, 176
Senecio, Q. Sosius 222
sense-perception 111–12, **119–21**
Serenus, Annaeus 180–81
Sestius, L. Quirinus (cos. 23 BCE) 143
Severus 231
Sextius, Sextii 8, 133–34, 156, 161,
  165, 211, 217
Sextus Empiricus 11–12, 136, 238;
  Against the Professors 238; *Outlines of
  Pyrrhonism* 238
sexual behaviour 207, 232
Sibylline Books 65
Sicily 2, 3, 114
simulacra 103, 109, 120–21
Siro 54, 100, 147
slave, slavery 137, 141, **179**, 194–95,
  207, 214–16
Smyrna 29, 71
Socrates 7, 12–13, 19, 21, 39–42, 71,
  96, 163, 193, 195, 214, 216,
  225–28, 233; Socratic method
  39–40, 65, 108, 138, 182, 216–17
Solon 2
song of Iopas 147; of Orpheus 147; of
  Silenus 147–48
sophists 190–91, 206, 226, 231–32
Sophocles 176
Sotion 134, 162, 165, 186
soul 11, 26, 31–32, 57, 60, 63, 75–77,
  84, 102, 109, 118, 134, 149–50,

Printed in Great Britain
by Amazon